AN AMERICAN TALE

The Real Moskovitch Family Journey From Russia to America 1850–1950 and Beyond

Howard I. Schwartz, PhD

standing on the shoulders of research by

David Chapin and memories of other descendants

JewishGen

מרכז עולמי לגנאלוגיה יהודית

The Global Home for Jewish Genealogy

A Publication of JewishGen
Edmond J. Safra Plaza, 36 Battery Place, New York, NY 10280
646.494.2972 | info@JewishGen.org | www.jewishgen.org

MUSEUM OF JEWISH HERITAGE
A LIVING MEMORIAL TO THE HOLOCAUST

An American Tale
The Real Moskovitch Family Journey From Russia to America 1850–1950 and Beyond

Copyright © 2024 by Howard Schwartz, PhD All rights reserved.
First Printing: July 2024, Tammuz, 5784
Cover Design: Rachel Kolokoff Hopper
Layout: Howard Schwartz

JewishGen Press is not responsible for inaccuracies or omissions in the original work.

Library of Congress Control Number (LCCN): 2024940492

ISBN: 978-1-962054-02-7 (hard cover: 206 pages, alk. paper)

About JewishGen.org

JewishGen, is a Genealogical Research Division of the Museum of Jewish Heritage - A Living Memorial to the Holocaust, serves as the global home for Jewish genealogy.

Featuring unparalleled access to 30+ million records, it offers unique search tools, along with opportunities for researchers to connect with others who share similar interests. Award winning resources such as the Family Finder, Discussion Groups, and ViewMate, are relied upon by thousands each day.

In addition, JewishGen's extensive informational, educational and historical offerings, such as the Jewish Communities Database, Yizkor Book translations, InfoFiles, Family Tree of the Jewish People, and KehilaLinks, provide critical insights, first-hand accounts, and context about Jewish communal and familial life throughout the world.

Offered as a free resource, JewishGen.org has facilitated thousands of family connections and success stories, and is currently engaged in an intensive expansion effort that will bring many more records, tools, and resources to its collections.

Please visit https://www.jewishgen.org/ to learn more.

Vice President for JewishGen: Avraham Groll

About JewishGen Press

JewishGen Press (formerly the Yizkor Books-in-Print Project) is the publishing division of JewishGen.org, and provides a venue for the publication of non-fiction books pertaining to Jewish genealogy, history, culture, and heritage.

In addition to the Yizkor Book category, publications in the Other Non-Fiction category include Shoah memoirs and research, genealogical research, collections of genealogical and historical materials, biographies, diaries and letters, studies of Jewish experience and cultural life in the past, academic theses, and other books of interest to the Jewish community.

Please visit https://www.jewishgen.org/Yizkor/ybip.html to learn more.

Director of JewishGen Press: Joel Alpert
Managing Editor - Jessica Feinstein
Publications Manager - Susan Rosin

Cover Photo Credits

Cover Design by: Rachel Kolokoff Hopper

Front and Back cover background, texture and color: Rachel Kolokoff Hopper

Front Cover:

Family of Itsig Moskovitch and Risia (Dovida) in Kishinev, circa 1911, Courtesy of Howard Schwartz, page 144

Back Cover:

Upper Left: *Baltimore Moshkevich Families circa 1919,* Courtesy of David Chapin, page 14,
Upper Right: *Samuel Moskovitch with his violin back in Russia,* Courtesy of Sharon Moss, page 8
Lower Left: *Gertrude Schabb, 1907–1908,* Courtesy of Oscar Schabb, page 79
Lower Right: *Sam Moskevich in shoe store, date unknown,* Courtesy of Linda Rose, page 100

AN AMERICAN TALE

THE REAL MOSKOVITCH FAMILY JOURNEY
FROM RUSSIA TO AMERICA
1850–1950 and Beyond

by

Howard I. Schwartz, PhD
standing on the shoulders of research by
David Chapin and memories of other descendants

From Bessarabia to America

To the memory of my grandmother
Mariam (Moskovitch) Schinker/ Drezner
and the other Moskovitch ancestors
who made the journey

From Bessarabia to America

TABLE OF CONTENTS

LIST OF PHOTOS

LIST OF FIGURES

***

ACKNOWLEDGEMENTS

This narrative builds on the earlier family history and genealogy efforts by other Moskovitch descendants and relatives, notably the efforts of David Chapin, who began asking questions about the family history fifty years ago at Moss family events in Baltimore. David is a great-grandson of Aaron Moshkevich and Sophie (Nausecha). David developed the Moss Family tree that has been circulating in the family and to which I refer in this narrative. David also read this narrative on multiple occasions and offered helpful additions and suggestions. In addition, Richard Jaeger,[1] who married into the Detroit branch of the family, researched and documented that branch of the family.

This narrative draws as well on photos and stories shared with me by several other descendants who were kind enough to share their knowledge and photos with me. I am grateful to Reva (Moss) Greenspan (daughter of Leon Moss), Marie (Schabb) Schwartz, daughter of Max Schabb, Linda Rose, daughter of Gertrude (Haberer) Rose, Sharon Moss, daughter of Solomon ("Sol") Moskovitch in the Detroit line, Howard Green, son of Charlotte (Kahn) Green, Debra Goldschmitt (and her husband Norman), daughter of Edith (Goldberg) Kahn, David Greenspan, son of Reva (Moss) Greenspan, Steve Moss and Gabrielle Manske, children of Stuart Moss. Some of the records and photos related to the Moss/Moskovitch journey are available online.[2]

I also wish to thank the volunteer staff of JewishGen who work tirelessly to publish family histories, memoirs, and Memorial books, to help recover so much of our lost collective histories. They are engaged in a sacred calling. I am grateful especially to Rachel Kolokoff Hopper, who spent days leveraging her graphics and photographic editing skills to improve the old worn-out photos and records that appear in these pages. Rachel went above and beyond in offering me help. I also wish to thank the editor of this series Jessica Feinstein, and the publishing team, Susan Rosin, Jonathan Wind, and Helene Held, who put up with my demanding expectations about publishing in times past and will do so again with this volume. I am grateful to all of them for their efforts and generosity with their time and patience.

Finally, I wish to thank my wife, Carroll, for her patience and tolerance as I spent hours researching my maternal family, and my daughter, Penina, for always finding the results of my efforts interesting.

---

[1] Richard married Caryn Brodie, a granddaughter of Isaac Moskovitch, the son of Hyman Moskovitch, who came to Canada and Detroit.

[2] See the collection of Howard Schwartz, https://www.forever.com/app/users/howard-schwartz/albums/moss-moskevitch-historical-family-photos/6iimt62mh95i1dw2jvexq1ngw

***

INTRODUCTION

The 1986 animated musical adventure film called "An American Tail" recounts the story of a seven-year-old mouse, Fievel Mousekewitz, whose family leaves Russia and migrates to the United States. They do so with the conviction that "there are no cats in America." Back in Russia, Fievel's family lived in the home of a Russian Jewish family called Moskowitz.

When I first watched this delightful, animated film with my three-year-old daughter in 1989, I had only the vaguest of recollections that the surname of my maternal grandmother was "Moskovitch." I knew almost nothing about my Moskovitch family, in part because my mother's family fell apart soon after arriving here in America in 1937. Because of that fracture in her family, my mother didn't talk about her family history and perhaps didn't know much about it.

This book unearths the story of my real Moskovitch family, which I like to imagine now as the one in whose home Fievel Mousekewitz lived (though the film identifies him from a shtetl elsewhere in Russia). My Moskovitch family surfaces for the first time in about 1870 in Bessarabia, the area that the Russian Empire annexed in 1812 after six years of fighting against the Ottoman Empire. The patriarch and matriarch of the family, Mordechai and Gitel Moskovitch, were living in the city of Kishinev (now Chişinău, Moldova) when their eldest child was born.

The Moskovitch family appears to have been peripatetic, moving around Southern Russia as the next six children were born. They were born in two towns which were about 460 miles east of Kishinev and situated along the Dnieper River (now called the Dnipro River). Three of their children were born in the city of Ekaterinoslav, the city named for empress Catherine the Great and now called Dnipro. The other three were born in Kremenchuk, a town 100 miles northwest of Ekaterinoslav and also along the Dnieper River (see map in Figure 3 on page 6). The available records suggest the Moskovitch family moved back and forth a few times between Kremenchuk and Ekaterinoslav in the period their six children were born (1862–1880).

The Moskovitch family migration to the US began in about 1902. One of the seven Moskovitch siblings (hereafter called the "Moskovitch Seven"), headed to England before settling with his family in Canada around 1904 in a town then known as "Berlin." A decade later, on the eve of WWI, this Moskovitch family migrated to Detroit, pulled there by the explosion in the auto industry. The other Moskovitch siblings who left Russia settled in Baltimore, arriving between 1904 and 1940. Most migrated via the northern European port of Bremen, though one of the grandchildren migrated with her family in 1937 after settling in Paris and another migrated with his family in 1940 after a long stay in China. What follows is the story of their journey.

***

The patriarch and matriarch of this Moskovitch family are remembered in family trees as Mordechai and Gertrude (probably Gitel) Moskovitch, and several descendants appear to be named for them. There were, in fact, three Gertrudes in the immigrant generation, creating some confusion as to which Gertrude is which.[1]

The English spelling of the surname "Moskovitch" was fluid for some time in the US and Canadian records and appears in several variations until the name is eventually gets shortened to Moss in several of the family lines.

The surname appears in records as "Moshkovich," "Moshkovitch," "Moskowitz," "Muskovitch," "Moskowitch," "Moschkevich," "Moshkevich," "Muscowitz," and "Moslikevich," among other variations. Sometimes different spellings even appear in the same document.[2] The Detroit branch of the family tended to spell their surname with an "o" and "t" (e.g., variations of Moskovitch) while the Baltimore branch tended to spell the surname without the "t" but with an "h" and "e" (e.g. variations of Moshkevich). These were not hard and fast rules, by any means, and there are many variations in the records of both branches of the family. In this narrative, I use "Moskovitch" when referring to the period of Russian origins and to the Canadian branch and "Moshkevich" to refer to the Baltimore branches. When referring to specific records, I use the actual spelling as it appears, to the extent it can be deciphered.

The Moshkevich family historian and descendant, David Chapin,[3] reminded me in an email exchange that Russia forced Jews to adopt surnames en masse in the early part of the 19th century as part of an effort to manage the empire's ethnic populations. Following the enactment of the "Regulations on the Organization of Jews," on Dec. 9, 1804, surnames were assigned by special officials who had discretion to assign names that reflected a person's character, occupation, or geographical origin among other influences. Sometimes surnames were based on the name of a father, a mother, or some other ancestor (what anthropologists call "patronymic" or "matronymic" naming conventions).[4] Since the name was never written originally in English characters, the family probably did not feel initially very loyal to any particular English rendering, though the spelling tends to stabilize a few years after the family's arrival.

The surname Moskovitch and its variations probably indicates that Mordechai's father or another male ancestor in the family was named Moshe, perhaps from the years 1820–1840, the surname being formed by adding the Russian "ovitch" (son of) to the Yiddish "Moshk" (Moshe). On the back of one old photo postcard found in my family collection, the surname appears spelled in Yiddish as מושקעוויש.[5] In Russian records, the name is consistently spelled Мошкович.

Russian censuses (called "Revision lists") from Bessarabia reveal two possible candidates for the family ancestor: The first is "Mosko" who was 25 in 1859. His father was "El" and his mother was Krensia, from Kishinev. The second was a man named Moshka from Orgeev, Bessarabia who was 36 in 1854. This Moshka

---

[1] Gertrude Schabb, the daughter of Anna (Moskevitch) Schabb, was born in 1898 and married Alexander Cohn. Gertrude Goldberg, daughter of Sarah (Moskevitch) Goldberg, was also born in 1898 and married Samuel Kauff. Gertrude Haberer, daughter of Sarah (Moshkevich) Haberer was born in 1909 and later married Charlie Rose. It seems likely that their namesake, Gitel wife of Mordechai, died in 1898 or shortly before then, given the Jewish custom of naming a baby after a recently deceased ancestor.

[2] In Hyman Moskovitch's 1914 passenger manifest, his surname is spelled twice: once as *Moskowitz* and once as *Moskovitch*. In a 1911 newspaper article about the wedding of Hyman's son Benjamin Moskovitch, his brother Samuel's name is spelled *Muskovitch* ("Wedded on Christmas Day," Dec. 28, 1911, *The Berlin News Record*). The 1910 census of Samuel spells his name as "Moschkevich" and in his 1912 Petition it is spelled "Moshkevich."

[3] As discussed below, David documented the Moskovitch/Moss Family tree over the years and my effort is only possible because of his earlier efforts. David is a great-grandson of Aaron and Sophie Moshkevich, the first to arrive in Baltimore.

[4] See "Russian Jewish surnames" by Alina Borisov-Rebel, https://www.myheritage.com/wiki/Russian_Jewish_surnames. Accessed 12/16/2023. See also the entry "Moskowitz" in Wikipedia, https://en.wikipedia.org/wiki/Moskowitz.

[5] This spelling of Moskovitch in Yiddish appears on the back of a 1929 photo postcard of Risia Moskovitch, wife of Itsig (Isaac) Moskovitch, digitized in the collection of Howard Schwartz. https://www.forever.com/app/users/howard-schwartz/albums/moss-moskevitch-historical-family-photos

was son of Ioyn (Jonah). It appears that his younger brother, Mordka (Mordechai) took his surname from his brother who was head of household (hence Mordechai Moshkevitch). It is conceivable this is the Mordechai who married Gitel of this Bessarabian family.[6] This Mordka was 24 in the 1854 Revision List. If he's the right person, then he was born in 1830.

The oldest son named for Mordechai in the immigrant generation was Itsig's son, Mordechai (Mark Moss), who was born in 1891. Since he was probably named for his grandfather, we can surmise that the patriarch Mordechai Moskovitch died not long before 1891.

There is no family oral tradition concerning Gitel's surname at birth. One record from Baltimore lists her birth surname as "Schwartz," but this record was filled out by a son-in-law in 1923 and the information has not been verified.[7] Since two daughters in the next generation were named Gitel in 1898 after their grandmother, we can assume the matriarch passed away not long before that date.

Background

I am a great grandson of Itsig (also called Isko and Isaac) Moskovitch (1862–1925), the eldest or second eldest of the seven Moskovitch siblings.[8] One of Itsig's daughters, Mania Moskovitch (married names Mariam Schinker and Mariam Drezner), was my grandmother. She was born in 1900 in Kishinev, Russia (now Chişinău, Moldova) like her siblings and some of her first cousins.

In 1926, Mariam married my maternal grandfather, Odessa-born Solomon ("Sam") Schinker. They left for France soon thereafter so Solomon could attend an agricultural school. My mother, Jeanne (Joan Schinker, married name Joan Schwartz) was born in Paris in 1932. Her family arrived in the US in 1937 when she was five years old. They were almost, but not quite, the last of the Moskovitch families to arrive in the US. One more family arrived in 1940, as we shall see.

Photo 1 Itsig Moskovitch and wife Risia circa 1926
My maternal great-grandparents

---

[6] This information is based on the research by David Chapin.

[7] As discussed later, Gitel's surname at birth is listed in the death certificate of her daughter Mariesa (Moshkevitch) Goldfield from 1923 (see p. 143).

[8] As discussed below, the family tree developed by David Chapin lists Chaim (Hyman) as the eldest sibling and Isko (Isaac) second. However, Hyman's records indicate he was born in 1863 and Isko records suggest he was born in 1862.

My great-grandfather, Itsig (Isaac) Moskovitch, arrived in the US many years before his daughter. He immigrated to America with his son Boris in August 1920, following WWI. On Aug. 7, 1920, they departed from Yokahama, Japan on the SS Empress of Asia arriving in Victoria, Canada on Aug. 16, 1920. By then Itsig's sons (Gersh), and several of Itsig's siblings and their children, were already settled in North America.

As narrated in detail below, most settled in Baltimore starting in 1904, while one family began to settle around the same time or slightly earlier in Ontario, Canada, in a town called Berlin. In the wake of rising anti-German sentiment during WWI, the town name Berlin was renamed "Kitchener." According to oral traditions, my great-grandfather, Itsig, apparently didn't like it in America and he left the US and returned to his family in Russia, leaving no further records in the US.[9]

***

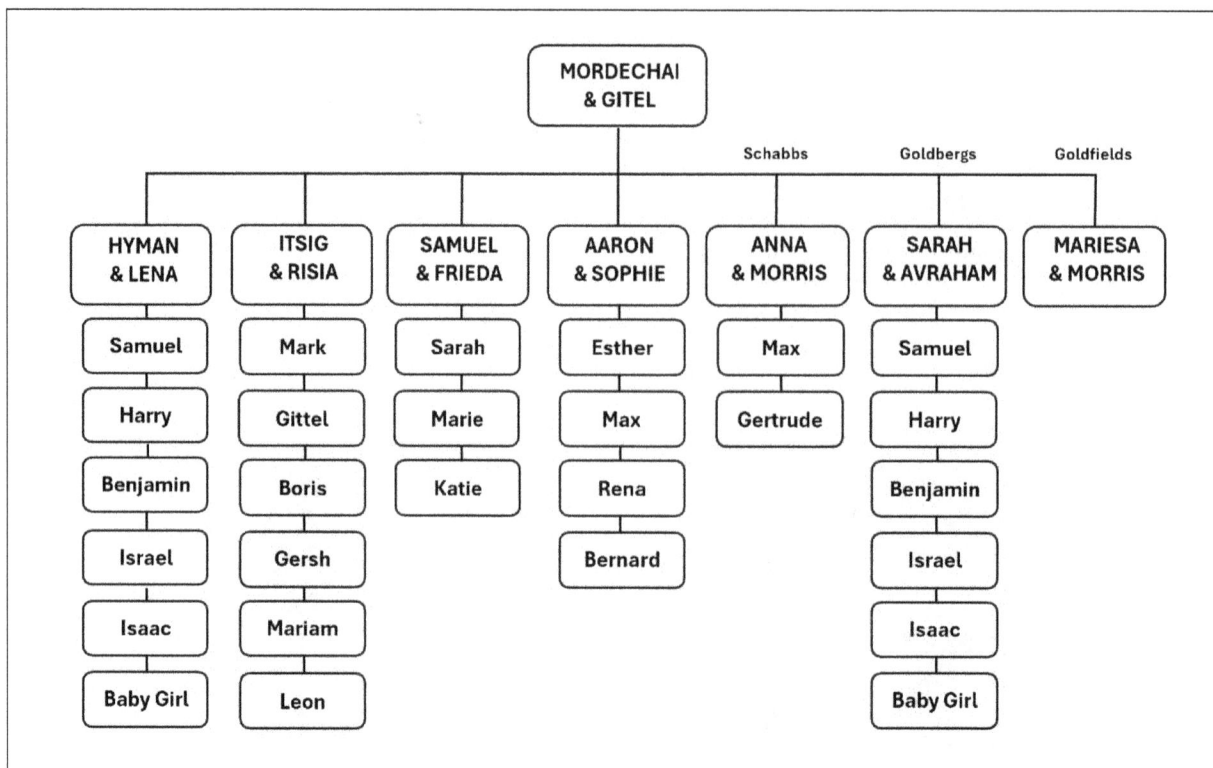

Figure 1 Moskovitch Family Tree

---

[9] I was told this by Isko's granddaughter, Reva (Moss) Greenspan.

***

1.

THE MOSKOVITCH FAMILY FROM RUSSIA

The patriarch and matriarch, Mordechai and Gertrude (Gitel) Moskovitch, were probably born in the 1830s or early 1840s judging from the birth years of their seven children (referred to as the "**Moskovitch Seven**"): **Hyman (Chaim) Moskovitch** (born between 1855-1865[1]), **Itsig (Isaac) Moshkovitch** (born 1862), **Shlomo (Samuel) Moshkovitch** (born 1868), **Aaron Moshkovitch** (born 1870), **Henie (Anna/Annie) Moshkovitch** (married name Anna Schabb) (born 1872), **Sore Moskovitch** (married name Sarah Goldberg) (born between 1873-76), and **Mariasha Moskovitch** (married name Mary/Marie Goldfield) (born 1878).

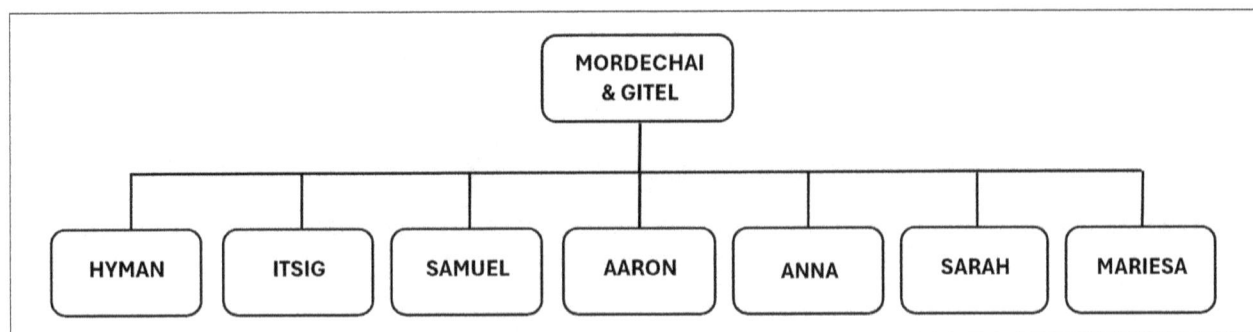

Figure 2 Mordechai and Gitel's Children

When the seven Moskovitch children were born, the family was apparently migrating among several cities in the Bessarabia Governorate of Russia. "Bessarabia" was the name given to the territory annexed by Russia following the Turkish-Russian War (1806–1812). In 1918, the area became part of Romania as part of the Treaty of Paris. For this reason, some of the later Moskovitch records list Romania as a birthplace which earlier would have been identified as Bessarabia, Russia. A special connection to Bessarabia led one the Moshkevich immigrants (Leon Moss) to organize a Bessarabian society in Baltimore for charitable and social purposes, as discussed later. This society was an example of a "Landsmanshaften" organization, social clubs and mutual aid societies organized by Jews who came from the same villages or geographical areas.

Almost nothing is known, as far as I know, about Mordechai and Gitel Moskovitch before they began having children in the late 1850s and early 1860s. We do know Mordechai was a "cohen," a descendant of the priestly family, as evident from tombstones of his male descendants. We can guess too that Mordechai

---

[1] Hyman Moskovitch's passenger manifest from Canada into the US dated Oct. 1914 indicates he was 49 and thus born around 1865. His 1911 Census in Canada lists his birth year as 1864. His 1920 census suggests his birth year was 1865.

and Gitel may have been among families that migrated to Bessarabia when it was included in the Russian Pale of Settlement, following its annexation.

The initial autonomy of Bessarabia in Russia gave Jews more freedoms than they had elsewhere in the Pale, one of the reasons Jews began migrating to this area in Russia. The Jewish population, mainly concentrated in Kishinev and its district (now Chişinău, the capital of Moldova), grew from 43,062 in 1836 to 94,045 in 1867, and to 228,620 by 1897 (11.8% of the total). Of these, 109,703 (48%) lived in towns, 60,701 (26.5%) in small towns, and 58,216 (25.5%) in villages. They formed 37.4% of town populations, 55.7% of the population of the small towns, and 3.8% of the village population.

Though we don't know anything about Mordechai and Gitel, six of their seven children and most of their grandchildren made their way to the US leaving behind records that, though not entirely consistent, point to their birthyears and birthplaces and hint at the Moskovitch family migration within Southern Russia at the time they were born. The family tree developed by David Chapin and circulated in the family is mostly consistent with the available records (with a few exceptions noted below) and fills in some of the gaps in the record, based on oral traditions in the family.

Figure 3 A contemporary map showing birth locations of Moskovitch children
Kishinev (now Chişinău Moldova), Kremenchuk, and Ekaterinoslav (now Dnipro)

From the available records and the family tree, it appears the Moskovitch family was moving among two and possibly three cities in Southern Russia during the period when Mordechai and Gitel's children were born. They may have been in Kishinev, Bessarabia when Chaim (Hyman) was born in 1863 (according to his passenger manifest into Detroit in 1915 and his death certificate), though the circulating family tree lists him as the eldest of the siblings born in 1855 in the generic region of Bessarabia.[2] Several children of the

---

[2] Hyman Moskovitch's 1914 manifest from Canada to Detroit appears to say "Kishn" as his birthplace, suggesting the family was there in 1863–1865 based on his birthdates. His death certificate filled out by his son Benjamin also appears to identify "Chisinau" (Kishinev) as his birthplace. Aaron's Naturalization Petition from 1911 indicates he was born in Ekaterinoslav (today the city of Dnipro). Itsko (Isaac's) manifest in 1920 is difficult to read but it appears his birthplace is a version of Kremenchu[k]. Samuel/Solomon's Petition from 1912 indicates he was born in Kremenchuk as well.

"Moskovitch Seven" who migrated to America were also born in Kishinev or in Kalarash near Kishinev, as we shall see.

The records of the siblings, Itsig/Isaac (born 1862), Samuel (born 1868) and Anna (born 1871/1872) indicate they were all born in Kremenchuk, Russia, a port on the Dnieper River (now the Dnipro River). The family's continuity in Kremenchuk appears to have been broken during the birth of Aaron. Born in 1870 between his siblings Samuel and Anna, Aaron's records list his birthplace as Ykaterinaslav (also spelled variously as Ekaterinoslav, Ecoterinslav, and Katerynoslav). Ykaterinaslav was named originally for Tsarina Catherine the Great and means "Catherine's town." The name of Ekaterinoslav was changed in 1926 to Dniepropetrovsk (after most of the Moskevitches were already in the US), and then in 2016 was shortened to Dnipro as part of a decommunization effort.[3]

The Moskovitch sibling named Sarah (married named Goldberg) died before her children and her husband migrated to Baltimore.[4] There are no records to confirm Sarah's birthplace or birthdate. In the Moss family tree, she is listed as second youngest and born in Ekaterinoslav.[5]

Though the youngest Moskovitch sister, Mariasha (married name Mary Goldfeld/Goldfield), came to the US, she died as a young adult and the records she and her husband left behind do not list her birthplace. The family tree lists Ekaterinoslav as her birthplace, based on oral traditions in the family. Old photos in the family also show her as a teenager in Ektaterinoslav with her elder brother Aaron and his family.

Based on available knowledge from records it thus appears that the Moskovitch family was migrating among several towns in Southern Russia from Kishinev in Bessarabia, to Kremenchuk, to Ekaterinoslav, back to Kremenchuk, and then back to Ekaterinoslav as illustrated in the table below.

Table 1 Movement of family in Bessarabia based on records and the Moss family tree

YEARS	BIRTHPLACES	WHO
1855 or 1862/63	Kishinev	Hyman
1862–1868	Kremenchuk	Itsig and Samuel
1870	Ekaterinoslav	Aaron
1871/1872	Kremenchuk	Anna
1873–1878	Ekaterinoslav	Sarah and Mary

In the late 19th century, the Jewish population of **Kremenchuk** increased rapidly as a result of emigration from the northwestern provinces of Russia to the southeastern ones. In 1847 there were 3,475 Jews registered in the community; by the 1897 census there was a large Jewish population of 29,869 persons (47% of the total population). The Jews played an important role in the economic development of the town, especially in the grain and timber trades and the manufacture of tobacco.[6]

Ekaterinoslav underwent a similar expansion in this period. As of 1850, Jews comprised close to nineteen percent of the population as the city began to industrialize, drawing workers, financiers, and traders, all customary occupations of Jews. The soil in the region was fertile and the area yielded large grain crops. In addition, iron and anthracite mines were discovered near the town. As the railroad was built, connecting Ekaterinoslav with other Russian cities and with the iron and coal mines, some of the largest factories in the

---

Annie (Moshkowitch) Schabb is also listed as born in Kremenchuk in the Petition of her husband, Morris Shabb dated 1911.

[3] See "Dnipro." https://www.britannica.com/place/Dnipropetrovsk-Ukraine

[4] As we shall see, a US record of Sarah's husband, Abraham, indicates he was widowed before he arrived.

[5] Sarah never came to the US so there are no US records to indicate her birthplace.

[6] See https://www.jewishvirtuallibrary.org/kremenchug and https://en.wikipedia.org/wiki/Kremenchuk

country were built in this town. Commerce in lumber and grains flourished, the town developed, and the population grew. As of 1897, Jews comprised 40,971 persons or 37% percent of the population.[7] It was during this period of growth that the "Moskovitch Seven" were born and grew up.

***

Overview of the Canadian Migration

Hyman married a woman named Leah Wolpinsky (also called Lena in some records). They had five sons according to Canadian and US records, though the Moss family tree lists the birth of a daughter who died in Bessarabia before the family arrived in North America. According to the family tree, Hyman was born in 1855 and was the eldest son in the family. Records, however, suggest he was born in 1863 or 1865 and may have been the second eldest child after Itsig.[8]

Photo 2 Samuel Moskovitch with his violin back in Russia
Courtesy of Sharon Moss

Hyman, his wife, and five sons arrived in Canada in the first decade of the 20th century, probably between 1902–1907 though the records are fragmentary and inconsistent in specifying where and when each arrived, as we shall see. After living for about 10 years in Berlin, a town in Ontario, Canada, they migrated to Detroit starting in 1914, taking advantage of the migration opportunity and economic possibilities spurred by the growth of the auto industry.

The family's migration from Canada to Detroit is amply documented in the records and we can follow Hyman, his wife and each of their sons—two of whom are married by this time—as they make their way into Detroit at the heyday of the auto industry. Their migration began just before growing tension exploded among residents in Berlin, Ontario during WWI over loyalty to Germany. The town was initially called "Berlin" after the Prussian capital. In a book called *The Battle for Berlin Ontario* about this growing tension in the Canadian town, the author W.R. Chadwick writes:

---

[7] https://www.jewishgen.org/yizkor/ekaterinoslav/eka021.html

[8] The 1911 census in Berlin, Ontario indicates he was born in June 1863. His passenger manifest from Canada to Detroit in Oct. 1914 indicates he was 49 [implied birth year 1865] and his January 1920 census indicates he was 55, again with an implied birth year of 1865.

In August 1914, Berlin, Ontario, settled largely by people of German origin, was a thriving, peaceful city. By the spring of 1915 it was a city torn apart by the tensions of war. By September 1916, Berlin had become Kitchener. It began with the need to raise a battalion of 1,100 men to support the British war effort.

Meeting with resistance from a peace-loving community and spurred on by the jingoistic nationalism that demanded troops to fight the hated "Hun," frustrated soldiers began assaulting citizens in the streets and, on one infamous occasion, a Lutheran clergyman in his parsonage. Out of this turmoil arose a movement to rid the city of its German name, and this campaign, together with the recruiting efforts, made 1916 the most turbulent year in Kitchener's history.

The 1911 census for Hyman's family in Berlin, Ontario is the earliest unambiguous record of the family found in Canada at the time of this writing. It provides immigration dates indicating that Hyman and Lena arrived in 1907 and the boys came in 1906. However, this record is not consistent with the more detailed later records from their migration out of Canada into Detroit. The later records include clues about their births and their original migration into Canada, though the records are far from consistent. Still, it appears that the family arrived in North America between 1902 and 1906, though one record seems to suggest that Hyman's son, Ben, arrived in 1899, as discussed in detail below.

Photo 3 Hyman Moskovitch and Lena (Wolpinski) with sons, circa 1905 in Berlin, Ontario
(standing l to r) Ben, Isaac, Samuel, (seated center l to r), Isaac (Frank) and Harry
Courtesy of Sharon Moss

Several records indicate that the sons, Isaac, Sam, and Harry, and Hyman's wife Lena, landed first in Portland, Maine in 1904 and 1905 and from there made their way to Canada. One of Hyman's records suggests he came via ferry to Quebec in Aug. 1904. According to an oral tradition reported by Hyman's great-granddaughter Sharon Moss,[9] the sons went first to England to earn money and came to Canada from the UK. This memory may be validated by the naturalization records of at least two of Hyman's sons who

[9] Sharon is the granddaughter of Samuel Moskovitch, who was son of Hyman and Lena Moskovitch.

renounce their UK citizenship in the process of becoming US citizens.[10] A summary of these and other records follows the story of Hyman's family and will be discussed in detail when recounting their migration to Detroit.

Table 2 Immigration dates into Canada of Hyman and Family

NAME	SEAPORT / DATE OF LANDING	SOURCE OF INFO
Hyman	Aug. 1904 Quebec	Oct. 24, 1914, List of Passengers entering Detroit
Lena	Jan. 1904 Portland Maine	Oct. 26, 1914, Primary Inspection Memorandum and Nov. 24, 1914, Border Crossing list
Isaac (Frank Moss)	1904 Portland Maine	Oct. 26, 1914, Primary Inspection Memorandum
	1899 Quebec, Steamship Canada	Nov. 23, 1914, Primary Inspection Memorandum
	1905 in transit from Portland, Me	March 29, 1915, Border Crossing list
Harry	1905 in transit from Portland, Me	March 29, 1915, Border Crossing list
Benjamin (Ben/ Beryl)	Quebec, April 24, 1899, on SS Canada	Mar. 23, 1914, Primary Inspection Memorandum
	Quebec Aug 24, 1902, on SS Canada	Mar. 23, 1916, Border Crossing Record
	Quebec 1901 on SS Canada	Nov. 16, 1916, Border Crossing Record
Israel	December 1906 in Halifax Nova Scotia.	Jan. 12, 1916, Border Crossing List
Samuel	April 14, 1905, on SS Canada in Quebec	Feb. 24, 1916, Border Crossing List

Even with this information, it is difficult to conclusively identify the manifests belonging to Hyman's family from their migration to Maine and Canada because the documents in this period have little identifying information.

One possible record (see below), identified by descendant Sharon Moss, is a viable candidate but also illustrates how hard it is to identify their records with certainty. This snippet comes from the manifest of the SS Canada leaving England for Quebec in May 1906. The manifest lists "Barnet Moscovitch" line 3 and Samuel [Moscovitch] in line 4. Is this Benjamin and Samuel Moskovitch, sons of Hyman? Probably.

You can see how little information is provided to confirm their identity. Barnet could be a variation on "Bernhars" which is the spelling of Benjamin's name in the 1911 Canadian census we explore below, or "Bernard" which is a variation of his name that appears in his daughter's birth record. In this passenger manifest, Barnet is listed as 20 years old, putting his birth year around 1886. The 1911 census puts Bernharst's birth year in December 1887 but that's close enough, especially as he may have had a reason to make himself appear older than he was when he was migrating. Samuel is listed in the record as age 21, which would make him older than Benjamin and born in about 1885 which matches at least one of his later records.

---

[10] Israel's US Naturalization Petition, Benjamin's Declaration and Samuel's Declaration indicate they previously had British citizenship. As noted below, Canada was part of the British Empire during this period and might be the source of this status as British citizenship.

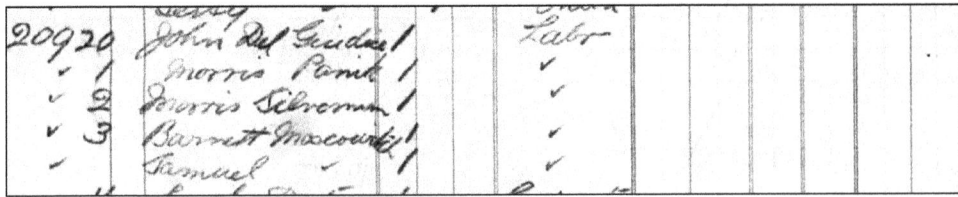

Figure 4 A possible manifest of Benjamin and Samuel in 1906

The best evidence that this record belongs to the two brothers, however, is the presence two lines above Benjamin of a man named Morris Panik. We shall see that a man named Morris Panick plays a key role in the Moskovitch migration to Detroit. The Panick and Moskovitch migrations were doubly entwined.

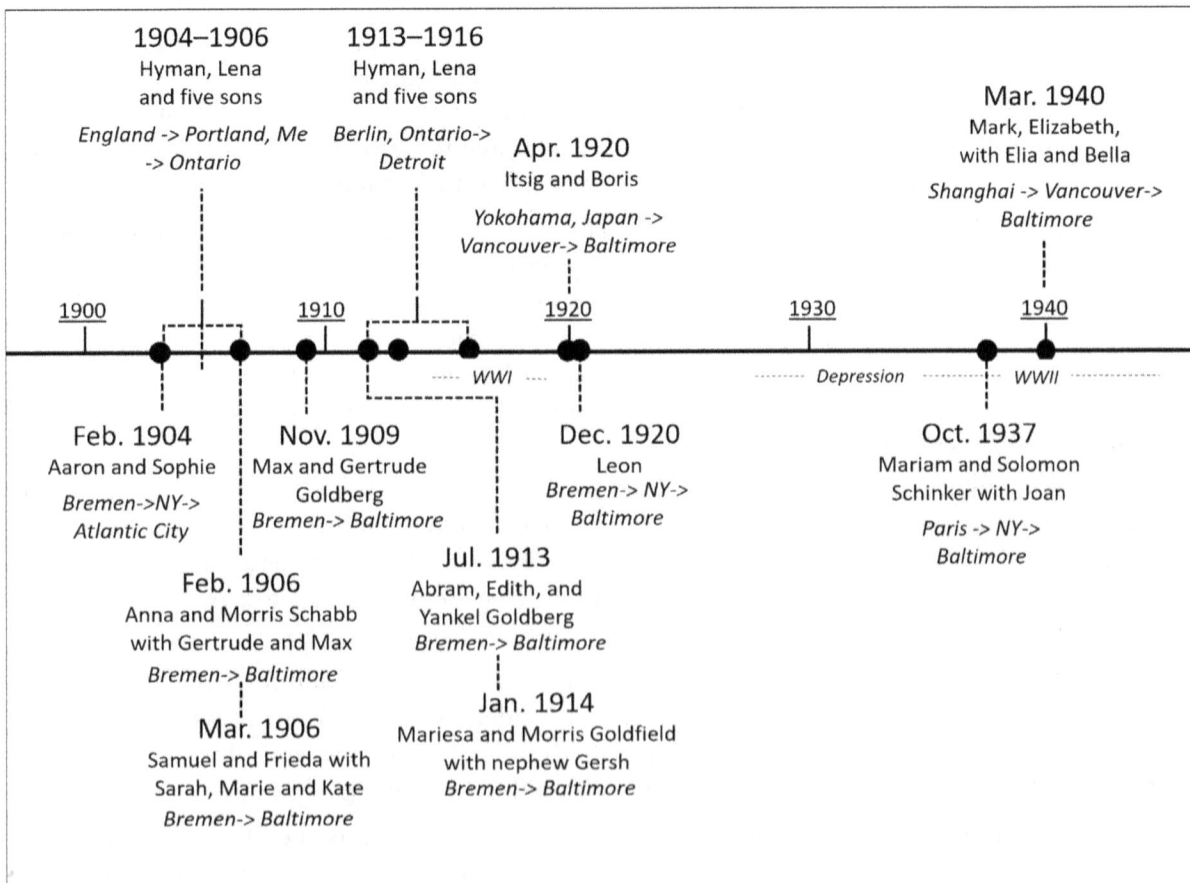

Figure 5 Visual Timeline of Moskovitch Family Migration

***

Overview of the Baltimore Migration

Around the same time that the family of Hyman Moskovitch headed to Canada, his younger brother, Aaron (called Harry in some records), was the first to arrive in Baltimore in 1904. Aaron was fourth in the birth order of the "Moskovitch Seven." It is not clear why the two brothers went in different directions, though Aaron and his wife Sophie were headed to a cousin in Atlantic City, as discussed in detail below.

Aaron and Sophie were soon followed by other siblings and children to Baltimore. Perhaps the other siblings followed Aaron because they knew him better since they too lived in Ekaterinoslav, while their older brother Hyman lived in Kishinev. They may also have preferred to get into the US where Aaron settled rather than in Canada which is where Hyman and his family initially resided.

The families of Aaron's sister, Anna (Moshkevich) Schabb, and his brother Solomon Moshkevich (soon to be Samuel), both arrived in early 1906. Three years later, in November 1909, Aaron's teenage nephew (Motel) and niece (Gitel) arrived. They were children of his sister Sarah (Moshkevich) Goldberg. In America they soon became Max and Gertrude Goldberg (later married name Gertrude Kauff).

Motel and Gitel were followed to Baltimore in 1913 by their father, Abraham Goldberg and their two siblings, Yankel and Ides Goldberg (married name Edith Kahn). Abraham's manifest indicates he was a widower and that his wife Sarah (Moshkovitch), passed away before his arrival. What became of Abraham and his son Yankel in America is not known. They have not been identified in subsequent records, nor is there an oral tradition about them in the family. One descendant has a vague memory that Abraham may have gone back to Russia. But no one seems sure.

In 1914, the youngest Moshkevich sister, Mariesa (called Mary in America), arrived with her husband Moshe (Morris) Goldfeld/Goldfield. They were traveling with her nephew, Gersh Moshkevich (son of Mariesa's brother Itsig/Isaac). Gersh was the first of Itsig's children to arrive. It seems probable that others in Itsig's family would have followed Gersh soon thereafter had WWI not intervened.

In April 1920, after the War ended, Gersh's father, Itsig, and his brother Boruch (Boris) landed in the US. To avoid the Russian Civil War, they traveled eastward rather than west and north to the ports of Bremen and Rotterdam. They probably made their way on the Siberian railroad to Vladivostok which, from 1918–1922 was occupied by Japan, and then across the Sea of Japan to Japan proper. From there they sailed via Manilla, Philippines to Victoria and Vancouver, Canada before entering the US and heading to Baltimore to join Itsig's son Gersh who arrived in 1914. From their manifest, it is clear that Itsig's wife Risia was back in Ekaterinoslav when they left.

Itsig's son Leib [Leon Moss] followed his father and brother Boris to Baltimore soon thereafter. Instead of coming via Japan, he made his way to Rotterdam, Holland and then sailed on the SS Nieuw Amsterdam arriving in New York on December 20, 1920. He was 19 years old according to the manifest. According to a family oral tradition, Leib and his then girlfriend Betty were agitators possibly with socialist leanings and had to go underground when a price was put on their heads.[11]

Itsig's daughter (and my grandmother) Mania (also called Mariam) did not arrive in the US until 1937. As we shall see in detail later, in 1926 she married a debonair man from Odessa named Solomon Schinker and they made their way to Paris in the late 1920s. In 1932, they had a daughter Jeanne (Joan), my mother. They remained in Paris until 1937 and then migrated to Baltimore.

Itsig's oldest son, Mordechai (Mark), and his family arrived three years later. In a remarkable journey detailed later, Mark made his way into China near the end of WWI, possibly seeking economic opportunities or escaping military conscription and/or the Russian civil war. There he married a girl from Lutsk by the name of Elizabeth (known as Liza in the family). They had a daughter, Elia (pronounced "eel-ya") who was born in Harbin, China in 1919, and a second daughter, Bella, who was born in Tsientsin, China in 1928. They eventually migrated to the US in 1940.

An overview of the Moshkevich arrivals in Baltimore is provided below with the details and discussion developed in the narrative that follows. As we shall see, the information about ages and birthplaces needs to be taken with a grain of salt.

---

[11] Related to me by David Chapin, though Leon and Betty's grandson never heard this story.

Table 3 Summary of Moskevitch Migration to Baltimore

ARRIVAL DATES	SUMMARY OF MANIFESTS
Feb. 14 1904	**Aaron** ("Aron Moschkewitch") age 34 and wife **Sophie** ("Sore") leave Bremen on Jan. 30 on SS Main and arrive in NY on Feb. 14, 1904. They are headed to Sophie's cousin, Katherine Goldstein in Atlantic City. Sophie is pregnant with their son Max who is born in Baltimore in 1904.
Feb. 1 1906	**Anna Schabb** ("Henie Sabosowitz"), age 34 and her husband **Morris Schabb** ("Mathes Sabosowitz) age 33, and two children Mottl [Max], age 9 and Gitel [married name Gertrude Cohn] age 8 depart Bremen on Jan. 19, 1906 on the SS Frankfort and arrive in Baltimore on Feb. 1, 1906. Their destination is the home of Samuel's brother, "Aron Moschkewitz" at 316 S. High St.
Mar. 3 1906	**Samuel Moshkevich** ("Shloma Moskewitz"), age 43, and wife Fanny (Frieda/Freda), age 38, and three children, **Sarah** (married name Sarah Haberer) age 17, **Maria** (married name Marie Cooper) age 15, **Gitel** (married name Kate Shpetner) age 4, depart Bremen on Feb. 15, 1906 on the SS Roland and arrive in Baltimore on March 3, 1906. They are headed to Sam's brother, Aaron at 316 E. High Street.
Nov. 5 1909	Two children of Sarah (Moshkevich) Goldberg arrive in Baltimore. **Motel (Max) Goldberg**, age 17, clerk and **Gitel Goldberg** (married name Gertrude Kauff), age 16, sail from Bremen on SS Chemnitz on Oct. 21, 1909 and arrive in Baltimore on Nov. 5. They are headed to the home of their uncle "Sam Moskowitz" at 316 S. High St.
July 26 1913	Arrival of **Abram Goldberg** [husband of Sarah Moshkevich], age 44, with [daughter] **Ides** [married name Edith Kahn] age 15, and [son] **Jankel** age 6. Departing Bremen on SS Breslau on July 5, 1913, arriving in Baltimore July 26.
Jan. 26 1914	Arrival in Baltimore of **Marie Goldfeld** (Mariasha Moshkevich) age 38 and husband along with her 17-year-old nephew **Gersh Moskwiz** [son of Marie's brother Itsig Moskewitz]. They sailed from Bremen on Jan. 10, 1914 on the SS Neckar. Their last residence was "Kisineff". Their destination was Marie's brother/uncle Samuel Moskewich at 923 E. Baltimore.
Apr. 7 1920	**Isko** (Itsig/Isaac Moshkevich), age 58, with [son] Boris age 24. Departing Yokohama, Japan on SS Empress of Asia Aug 7th, 1920 arriving at port of Victoria / Vancouver Aug. 16, 1920 in transit to the US. Their closest relative is Isaac's wife "Risia" in Ekaterinoslav; destination is Isaac's son/brother "G. [Gersh] Moshkevich at 2432 Greenmount Ave in Baltimore. Isko's birthplace is listed as Kremenchu [Kremenchuk] and Boris's birthplace is Chishinew [Kishinev]
Dec. 27 1920	**Leib Moskowitch** [Leon Moss] sailed from Rotterdam Holland on Dec. 10, 1920 on the SS Niuew Amsterdam and arrived in New York, Dec. 20. He was 19 years old. His last residence was "Kichineff Rumenian" and his mother Risia was listed as his closest relative still there. His destination was his brother "G. I. Moskewitsch" [Gersh] at 2432 Greenmount Ave, the home also of his aunt Mariasha [Marie Goldfield].
Oct. 5 1937	Arrival of Itsig's daughter, **Mariam (Mania Moshkevich) Schinker** with husband and daughter. Sailed on the SS Ile De France from Le Havre, France on September 29, 1937 and arrived in New York, Oct 5, 1937. Mariam is listed as 37, her daughter Jeanne (Joan) age 5. Their last residence

	Boulogne France, Mariam. Mariam birthplace is listed as Tichinoff Rumenia [Kishinev]. They are headed to Mariam's brother "Mr. Moss"
Mar. 16 1940	"**Morduhai Moshkevich**" [Mark Moss, son of Itsig] arrives with family. They left from Shanghai, China on Mar. 1, 1940 and arrived in Victoria, Vancouver, Canada. Morduhai is 48, his wife **Elizabeth** ("Liza") is 41, their daughter **Gita Rachel** ("Elia") was 20, and their daughter **Bella** was 10.

Photo 4 Photo of Baltimore Moshkevich Families circa 1919

1. Aaron "Harry" Moshkevich
2. (Aaron's wife) Sophie (Nausecha)
3. Moshe (Morris) Goldfield
4. Mariasha (Moshkevich) Goldfield
5. Morris Schabb
6. Anna (Moshkevich) Schabb
7. Edith (Goldberg) Kahn with baby Morton (Edith is daughter of deceased Sarah (Moshkevich) Goldberg)
8. Hyman Kahn (Edith's husband)
9. Sarah (Moshkevich) Haberer (daughter of Samuel and Frieda, her husband B. B. Haberer passed away in 1918)
10. Gersh I. Moss (son of Itsig)

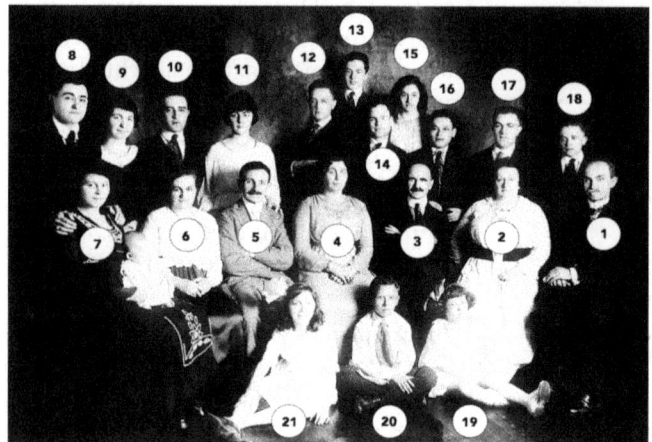

11. Gertrude (Schabb) Cohn (daughter of Morris and Anna #5 and #6)
12. Saul Sheptner
13. Max "Mack" Moshkevich (son of Aaron and Sophie #1 and #2)
14. Nephew of Moshe Goldfield (#3)
15. Rena Moshkevich, daughter of Aaron and Sophie #1 and #2)
16. Another nephew of Moshe Goldfield (#3)
17. Max Schabb (son of Morris and Anna #5 and #6)
18. unknown
19. Clair Haberer, daughter of Sarah (Moshkevich) Haberer (#9) and Berthold B. B. Haberer
20. Bernard Moshkevich, son of Aaron and Sophie
21. Gertrude Haberer daughter of Sarah (Moshkevich) Haberer #9 and Berthold Haberer

***

Which Gertrude is Which?

Since several children of the "Moskovitch Seven" siblings were named for their grandparents, Mordechai and Gitel Moshkevitch, it is sometimes difficult to follow the who's who in the family. There were three Gertrudes (Gitel's) in the next generation. The first two were born in 1898 suggesting that their grandmother, Gitel, probably passed away about that time, since it was Jewish practice to honor a close, recently deceased relative with a namesake. The following table helps to keep track of the various Gertrudes.

Table 4 Disambiguating Gertrudes

BIRTH NAME	MARRIED NAME	BIRTH YEAR AND LOCATION	PARENTS	HUSBAND
Gertrude Schabb	Gertrude Cohn	1898 Ekaterinoslav, Russia	Anna (Moshkevitch) and Morris Schabb	Alexander Cohn
Gertrude Goldberg	Gertrude Kauff	1898 Kalarash, Russia	Sarah (Moshkevitch) and Abraham Goldberg	Samuel Kauff
Gertrude Haberer	Gertrude Rose	1909 District of Columbia	Sarah (Moshkevich) [i.e., daughter of Samuel Moshkevich] and B.B. Haberer	Charlie Rose

***

2.

FAMILY OF HYMAN MOSKOVITCH AND LENA (WOLPINSKY)

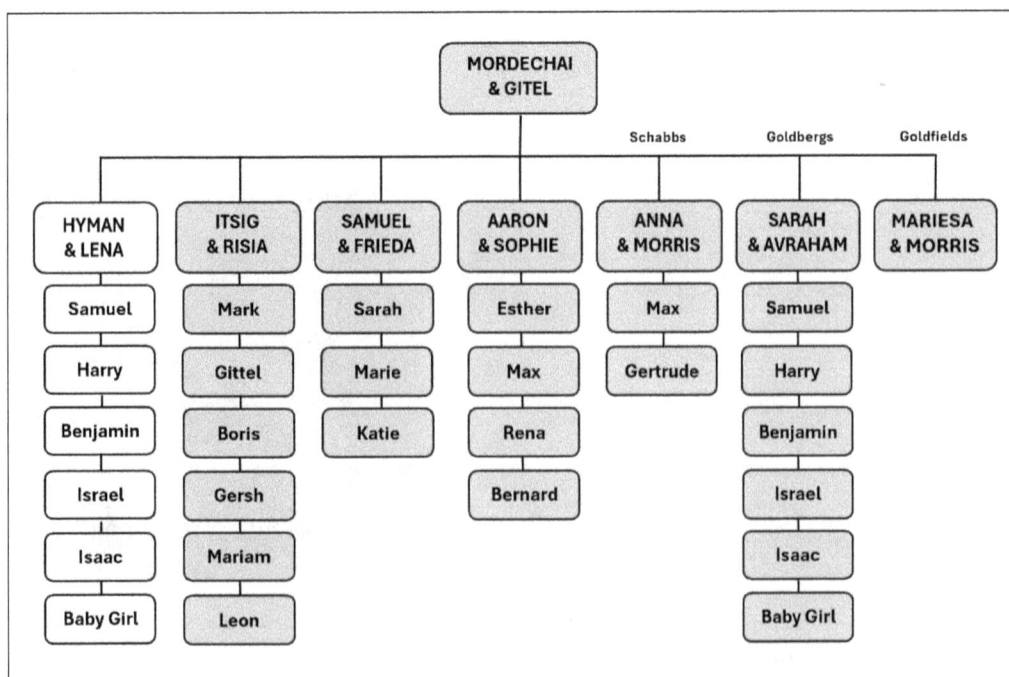

Figure 6 Family of Hyman Moskovitch and Lena (Wolpinsky)

***

The Canadian Period (˜1902–1914)

The 1911 census in Canada is the first unambiguous record of the Moskovitch family presence in Berlin, Ontario and a good place to start a deeper dive. They were living at 30 Stahl Street. "Himan Moskovitch" is head of the family. His birth year is given as June 1863 (which differs from 1855 in the family tree). He is 47 years old and his year of arrival in Canada is listed as 1907.

Himan's year of naturalization (second column from the right below) appears to be 1800 but is obviously impossible and is probably intended to be 1910, like that of his sons. Himan's wife Lena (called Leah in other records) is 48 years old which would make her birthyear 1863–64 though the census appears to list it as 1865. Her arrival in Canada is also listed as 1907. She too is "Na" [naturalized].

The five sons of Hyman and Lena are **Sam**, age 24-born Aug 1886, **Israel**, age 20-born Dec 1890, **Harry,** age 15-born in Aug 1895, **Isaac,** age 14-born in Jun 1896, and **"Bernhurst"** listed last but second oldest, at age 23–born Dec 1887. Bernhurst appears in other records as Beryl, Benjamin, and even on one occasion as Bernard.[1] The record indicates all the boys arrived in 1906, though later records do not have them coming all together and the boys' arrival in those records is earlier than indicated here.

28	17D 17	Moshkovitch	Simon	30 Stall	–	M	Head	M		June	186347	Russia	1907	19...	Russia
29		"	Lena		–	7	wife	M		July	186546	Russia	1907		Russia
30		"	Sam	6		M	Son	S		Aug	188624	Russia	14.6	1901	Russia
31		"	Hyman		–	M	Son	S		Dec	189020	Russia	1908	1111	Russia
32		"	Harry		–	M	Son	S		Aug	189515	Russia	1900		Russia
33		"	Josse		–	M	Son	S		June	189617	Russia	1906		Russia
34		"	Bernhurst		–	M	Son			Dec	1887	Russia	1906	1910	Russian

Figure 7 The 1911 census of Himan and Lena Moshkovitch and sons in Berlin, Ontario

The ages and birthdates in this record, as in others, must be taken with a grain of salt. Later records are inconsistent, making it impossible to know exactly when and where each of the sons was born and when he arrived in Canada.

Photo 5 Samuel Moskovitch (seated)
with first cousin, Jack Leibow
Courtesy of Sharon Moss

This fluidity in birthdates is typical of the first generation of immigrants, due in part to the shift from the Julian calendar in use in Russia, to the Gregorian one used in the States and Canada. Birthdates were not that important to the Jewish communities in Russia and were not tracked, though the Russian government increasingly tried to collect such records from the community over time.[2] Sometimes birthdates were guesses by new immigrants who later forgot the dates they proposed in earlier records. Immigrants sometimes had motivations to say they were older or younger than they were to ease their way through customs and/or to avoid conscription before they left. For all these reasons, birthdates and even birth years are not consistent in the records for the immigrants—especially the older generation.

More surprising, perhaps, is the inconsistency in birthplaces found in the records for the same person. Sometimes immigrants simplified answers on passenger lists to pass through customs. In records I

---

[1] An oral tradition recalled by a Baltimore descendant recalls that people in the Baltimore family knew Benjamin later as "Barnie Moss." David Chapin tells the story that in 1968 his father Jerry Chapin was in Detroit on business and wanted to look up Benjamin in the phone book but couldn't find his name listed under Benjamin Moskevitch or Moss. He found another Moss at random and called him. It turned out he knew Benjamin but was not related. Jerry got together with "Barnie," only to later find out that his own mother, Rena, knew his cousin was called Barnie because she had a long pen pal relationship with his eldest daughter Esther.

[2] See Eugene M. Avrutin, *Jews and the Imperial State: Identification Politics in Tsarist Russia*. Ithaca: Cornell, 2010.

have found in earlier family history efforts, family members listed their birthplaces based on the locations where they last lived, where their children were born, or the larger nearby towns that were more familiar to English speaking officials. For all these reasons, the specific birthdates and birth locations of the Moskovitch immigrants are inconsistent (as documented in the summary of records to follow the narrative of each family line). Still a general picture emerges of Hyman and Lena's family.

It appears the Hyman and Lena's sons were born in Kishinev and/or the nearby town of Kalarash (now Călăraşi Moldova). Kalarash is today 54 km (33 m) northeast of Kishinev (see map on page 6 above). Kishinev may have been used as a more familiar substitute for Kalarash which was nearby and appears on some of the later records. This may partially explain the inconsistency we find in the records of the sons. It is also possible that one or two of the sons were born in Odessa.

- **Samuel** (~1885–1950) (not to be confused with his Baltimore uncle by the same name) was the eldest of Hyman and Lena's sons and was born between 1884–1886. The family tree says only that he was born in Bessarabia, though his Naturalization Petition indicates he was born in Kalarash (now Călăraşi Moldova).

- **Benjamin** (1888–1971) appears to have been born in 1887 and the family tree lists Kishinev as his birthplace. His passenger manifest from 1914 into Detroit also lists "Kischineff" as his birthplace. However, his 1920 Declaration of Intention lists his birthplace as "Kalarash." It is possible that Benjamin was born in Kalarash, like his older brother Samuel, but that Kishinev was given as an alternative because it was close and better known.

- **Harry** (1895–1934) is listed as born in Aug 1895 in the 1911 census and several immigration records in 1915 seem to confirm his birth in 1895/96. Two of those records, however, indicate he was born in Odessa. As we shall see, Harry had a disability reflected in the records which made it difficult for him to enter the US and hold an occupation. He apparently never married, was still living with his parents in 1920 in Detroit and with his brother Samuel in 1930. He died prematurely in 1934.

- **Isaac** (aka Frank Moss) (1897–1983) was born in Kishinev in 1897 according to the family tree. Records also indicate a birth date between 1895 and 1897. Isaac's 1915 border crossing records, when he accompanied and assisted his brother Harry into the US, identify Odessa as his birthplace. It is possible he made his birthplace consistent with his brother Harry, who had a disability, in order to simplify and ease his brother's entrance into the US.

- **Israel** (~1898–1978) was probably born between 1897–98 based on most of the records, though the 1911 census indicates his birthdate in Dec. 1890. The family tree lists his birthplace as Kishinev in Dec. 1897 and one of his immigration records in 1916 also implies Kishinev was his birthplace. Other records are inconsistent. His 1915 immigration card lists Odessa as his birthplace and his 1929 Naturalization Petition lists "Catarashi, Rumania" [i.e., called Kalarash Russia when he was born].

***

Life in Berlin, Ontario

On Christmas day, not long after the 1911 Canadian census, the local newspaper, *The Berlin News Record*, covered the wedding of Benjamin Moskovitch and Nellie Debow of Toronto. The article provides an interesting glimpse into the life of the Moskovitch family at this time in Canada.

The wedding was quite substantial and included three hundred guests. Even the mayor of Berlin attended. The article notes the observance of traditional Jewish wedding rituals and the fact that the bride's veil caught fire from the candles. The newlyweds planned to take up their new lives at the Moskovitch home at 30 Stahl Ave. Hyman is referred to in this article and other records as "Herman" Moskovitch. The Moskovitch surname appears in other spelling variations in the same article.

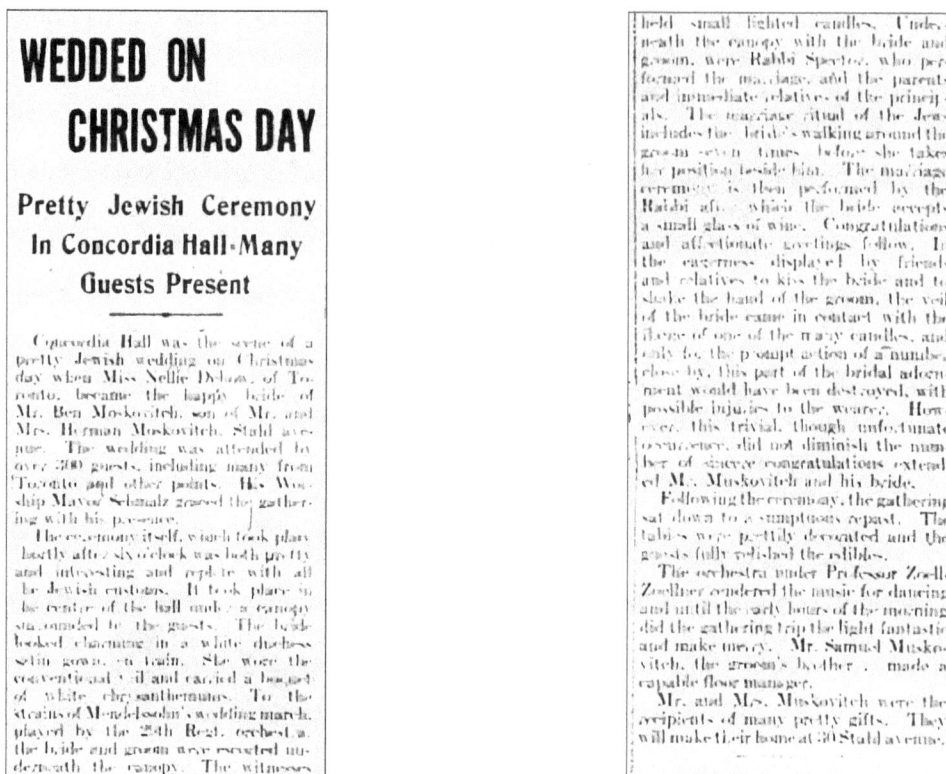

Figure 8 The Berlin News Record, Thur. Dec. 28, 1911

Transcription: The Berlin News Record, Thur. Dec. 28, 1911

Pretty Jewish Ceremony in Concordia Hall- Many Guests Present

Concordia Hall was the scene of a pretty Jewish wedding on Christmas day when Miss Nellie Debow of Toronto, became the happy bride of Mr. Ben Moskovitch, son of Mr. and Mrs. Herman Moskovitch, Stahl avenue. The wedding was attended by over 300 guests including many from Toronto and other points. His Worship Mayor Schmalz graced the gathering with his presence.

The ceremony itself, which took place shortly after six o'clock was both pretty and interesting and replete with all the Jewish customs. It took place in the center of the hall under a canopy surrounded by the guests. The bride looked charming in a white duchess satin gown, en train. She wore the conventional veil and carried a bouquet of white chrysanthemums. To the strains of Mendelssohn's wedding march played by the 29th Regt. orchestra, the bride and groom were escorted underneath the canopy.

The witnesses held small lighted candles. Underneath the canopy with the bride and groom were Rabbi Spector, who performed the marriage, and the parents and immediate relatives of the principals. The marriage ritual of the Jews includes the bride's walking around the groom seven times *before* she takes her position beside him. The marriage ceremony is then performed by the Rabbi after which the bride accepts a small glass of wine. Congratulations and affectionate greetings follow. In the eagerness displayed by friends and relatives to kiss the bride and to shake the hand of the groom, the veil of the bride came in contact with the flame of one of the many candles, and only for the prompt action of a number close by, this part of the bridal adornment would have been destroyed, with possible injuries to the wearer. However, this trivial, though unfortunate occurrence, did not diminish the number of sincere congratulations extended Mr. Muskovitch and his bride.

Following the ceremony, the gathering sat down to a sumptuous repast. The tables were prettily decorated and the guests fully relished the edibles.

The orchestra under Professor Zoell-Zoellner rendered the music for dancing and until the early hours of the morning did the gathering trip the light fantastic and make merry. Mr. Samuel Muskovitch, the groom's brother, made a capable floor manager.

Mr. and Mrs. Muskovitch were the recipients of many pretty gifts. They will make their home at 30 Stahl avenue.

Not long after Ben and Nellie's wedding, Ben's older brother Samuel also married, and the wedding was again covered in the local paper. The article appeared Aug. 18, 1913, on page one. *The Berlin News Record* reported that "Victoria Hall was the scene of a pretty Jewish wedding on Saturday afternoon when Miss Dora Levitin, daughter of Mrs. M. Levitin became the wife of Mr. Samuel Moskovitch, son of Mr. and Mrs. Herman Mokovitch, 30 Stahl avenue." The ceremony took place under a canvas canopy (chupah) and was conducted by Rabbi Andrewson with all the Jewish customs.

JEWISH WEDDING AT VICTORIA HALL

Victoria Hall was the scene of a pretty Jewish wedding on Saturday afternoon when Miss Dora Levitin, daughter of Mrs. M. Levitin became the wife of Mr. Samuel Moskovitch, son of Mr. and Mrs. Herman Moskovitch, 30 Stahl avenue. The ceremony took place at 9.30 o'clock and was conducted by Rabbi Andrewson with all the Jewish customs.

The bride looked pretty in a white silk gown, with silver trimmings, and carried white and pink carnations. The attendants were Mr. and Mrs. B. Moskovitch and Mr. and Mrs. N. Chernikow. The ceremony took place under a canvas canopy. Relatives of the principals held lighted candles.

During the ceremony, according to Jewish ritual the bride walked around the groom a number of times. The Rabbi pronounced the words that make them man and wife. A glass of wine is presented to the bride and groom, and an empty glass is crushed beneath the groom's foot. All this is a significant part of the Hebrew ceremony.

The wedding over, congratulations and confetti were showered upon the bride and groom and then commenced merry-making. Supper was served in the hall and the guests numbered about 200 including several from Toronto, Woodstock, New York and other points.

Messages of congratulation were received by telegram from Mr. and Mrs. Harry Wolpinski, Brooklyn, Messrs. Harry and Soloman Moskovtich of Baltimore and others.

The guests enjoyed themselves in dancing until a late hour.

Figure 9 Wedding of Samuel Moskovitch

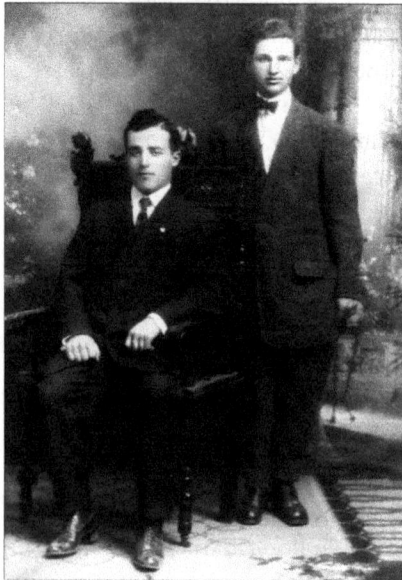

Photo 6 Two of the Moskevitch Brothers

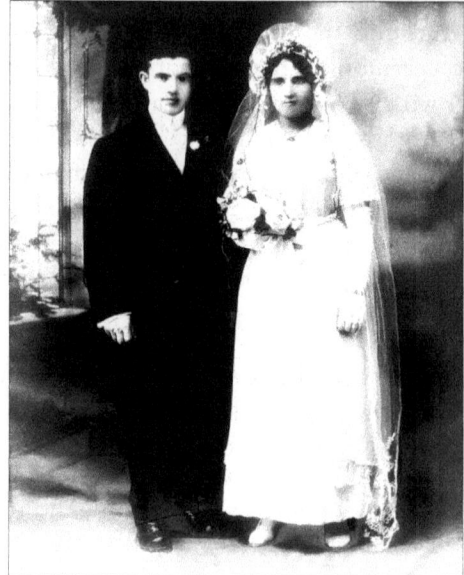

Photo 7 Samuel and Vita on wedding day

Courtesy of Sharon Moss

Benjamin and Nellie had two children before their move to Detroit. Their first daughter Esther Golda Moskovitch was born on Nov. 16, 1912. On her birth record, her father "Bernard" is listed as a finisher. Her mother Nellie's surname is here spelled Debof. Two years later, "Ben" and Nellie had a second child, Morris David Moskovitch (called just David later) on April 15, 1914. Their address on David's birth certificate is 122 King St. E., where Ben's parents were also living.

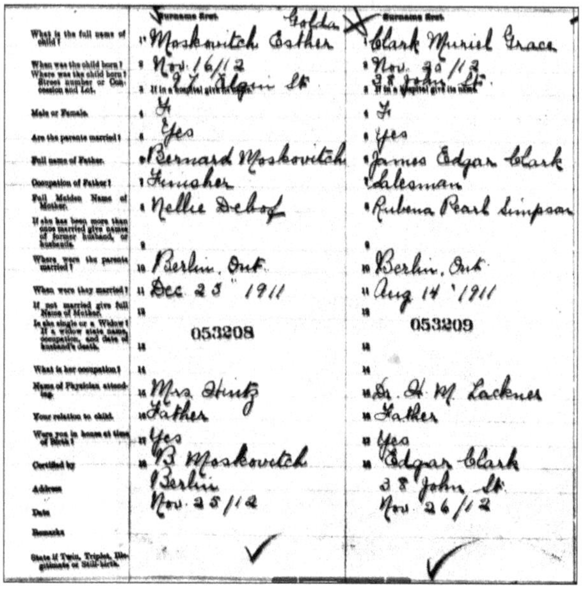

What is the full name of child?	Moskovitch Esther Golda	Clark Muriel Grace
When was the child born? Where was the child born?	Nov. 16/12, 27 Elgin St	Nov. 20/12, 38 John St
Male or Female	F	F
Are the parents married?	Yes	Yes
Full name of Father	Bernard Moskovitch	James Edgar Clark
Occupation of Father	Finisher	Salesman
Full Maiden Name of Mother	Nellie Debof	Rubena Pearl Simpson
Where were the parents married?	Berlin, Ont	Berlin, Ont
When were they married?	Dec 25 1911	Aug 14 1911
	053208	053209
Name of Physician attending	Mrs Hintz	Dr. H. M. Lackner
Your relation to child	Father	Father
Were you in house at time of birth?	Yes	Yes
Certified by	B Moskovitch	Edgar Clark
Address	Berlin	38 John St
Date	Nov. 25/12	Nov 26/12

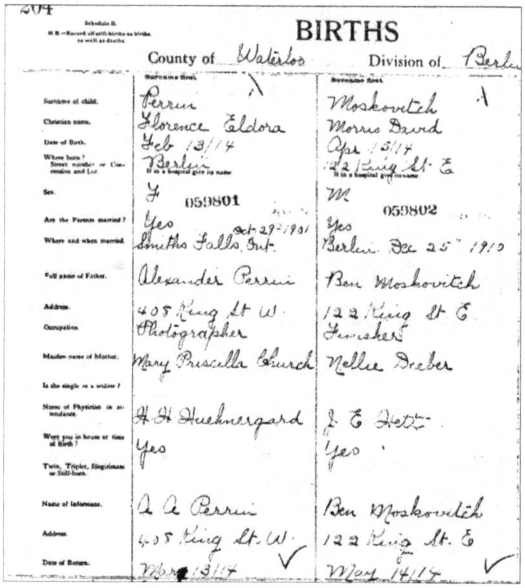

BIRTHS

County of Waterloo Division of Berlin

Surname of child	Perrin	Moskovitch
Christian name	Florence Eldora	Morris David
Date of Birth	Feb 13/14	Apr 15/14
Where born?	Berlin	122 King St. E
Sex	F	M
	059801	059802
Are the Parents married?	Yes	Yes
Where and when married	Smiths Falls, Ont. Oct 29 1901	Berlin Dec 25 1910
Full name of Father	Alexander Perrin	Ben Moskovitch
Address	405 King St W.	122 King St E
Occupation	Photographer	Finisher
Maiden name of Mother	Mary Priscilla Church	Nellie Dreber
Name of Physician in attendance	H. H. Huehnergard	J. E. Hett
Were you in house at time of birth?	Yes	Yes
Name of Informant	A. A. Perrin	Ben Moskovitch
Address	405 King St. W.	122 King St. E
Date of Return	Mar 13/14	May 14/14

Figure 10 Birth Certificates of Benjamin and Nellie's children

Ben's brother, Samuel, and his wife Vita (also called Dora) had their first child a few months after Ben and Nellie had their second child and not long before their migration to Detroit. Their son, Joseph Moskovitch, was born on June 9, 1914. They were living next door at 124 King St. E.

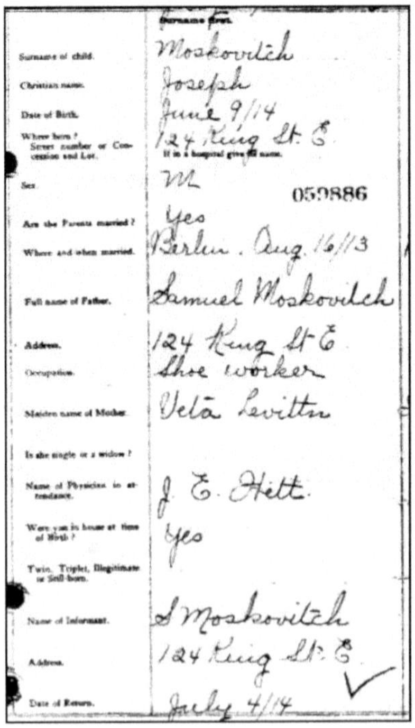
Surname first.

Surname of child.	Moskovitch
Christian name.	Joseph
Date of Birth.	June 9/14
Where born? Street number or Concession and Lot.	124 King St. E. (If in a hospital give full name.)
Sex.	M
Are the Parents married?	Yes
Where and when married.	Berlin. Aug. 16/13
Full name of Father.	Samuel Moskovitch
Address.	124 King St E
Occupation.	Shoe worker
Maiden name of Mother.	Veta Levitten
Is she single or a widow?	
Name of Physician in attendance.	J. E. Hett.
Were you in house at time of Birth?	Yes
Twin, Triplet, Illegitimate or Still-born.	
Name of Informant.	S Moskovitch
Address.	124 King St. E.
Date of Return.	July 4/14

059886

Figure 11 Canadian Birth record of Joseph Moskovitch Samuel and Vita's son

***

The Detroit Migration

By 1914, the Moskovitch family began their migration to Detroit, just as immigration was becoming more difficult into the US due to the outbreak of WWII. As we shall see, relatives of theirs from Berlin, Ontario made the move to Detroit first and provided a soft landing as the Moskovitch family began their migration.

Detroit, of course, was a magnet during this time; the explosion in the auto industry was transforming the city and was attracting workers from various backgrounds and regions. In 1908, just six years before the Moskovitch migration began, the fledgling Ford company introduced the Model T, a car whose standardized production would revolutionize the industry.

In 1911, Chevrolet opened its first factory in Detroit, a significant event in the birth of Detroit as the center of the American automobile industry.[3] In 1914, the year the Moskovitch migration began, Ford announced the five-dollar day, leading to a dramatic increase in pay for industrial workers. Word of Ford's high wages—along with Ford's international recruiting efforts—turned the Motor City into one of the most racially and ethnically diverse places in America with a prosperous population of about 465,000.[4] The Moskovitches were in the process of joining too.

---

[3] See "Timeline of Detroit," https://en.wikipedia.org/wiki/Timeline_of_Detroit

[4] "Motor City: The Story of Detroit." AP US History Study Guide, The Gilder Lehrman Institute of American History. https://ap.gilderlehrman.org/history-by-era/politics-reform/essays/motor-city-story-detroit. Accessed Dec. 2023.

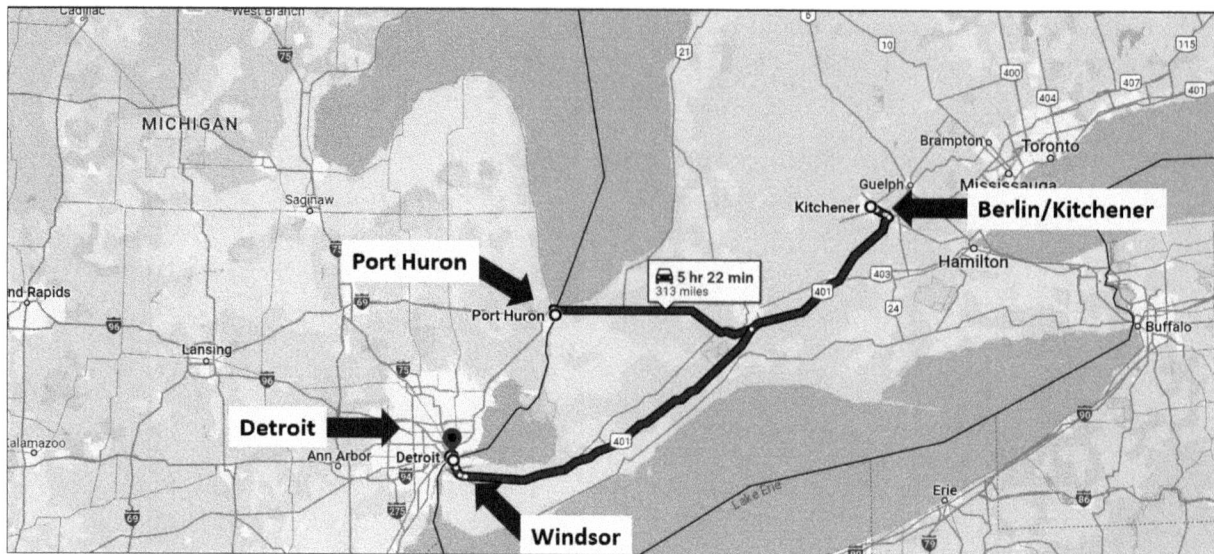

Figure 12 Map of Berlin, Ontario [now Kitchener], Port Huron and Detroit, Michigan

***

Hyman Leaves for Detroit

Hyman Moskovitch left for Detroit just two weeks after the birth of his third grandchild, Joseph. A passenger manifest shows he crossed into the US at Detroit on Oct. 24, 1914. WWI had already begun. The official spelled Hyman's surname two different ways (Moskowitz and Moskovitz) perhaps at Hyman's own advice. The official also wrote LPC (likely public charge) above Hyman's name indicating there was some concern about him being a burden to society. Hyman was admitted anyway, perhaps because he said he was headed to "a daughter" who was living there already. She was, as it turns out, not his daughter at all.

In the record, Hyman is age 49 placing his birth year in about 1865/64. As noted earlier, his 1911 census indicated he was born in June 1863. Both of these dates are later than the 1855 listed in the Moss family tree making it unclear if Hyman was the eldest or second eldest among his siblings. The right-hand columns of the manifest show his last residence was Oberlin [Ontario] and his closest relative there his wife Leah Moskowitz at 122 King Street E.

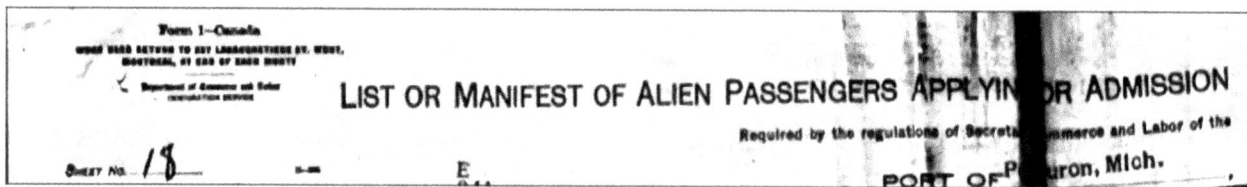

Figure 13 Manifest of Hyman Moskowitz/Moskovitch entering Detroit, Oct. 24, 1914

Hyman Moskowitz/Moskovitch age 49, merchant, last residence Berlin

Right-hand columns showing Hyman's last residence in Berlin [Ontario] and closest relative his wife Leah Moskowitz

The second page of Hyman's manifest (below) has several important details. The first is his birthplace: Russia is the country and "Kishev" for city /town. I suspect that "Kishev" is a shortened form of Kishinev. This is one of two records I have found that suggests Kishinev as the birthplace of Hyman. As discussed earlier, the family tree circulating in the family lists only the region "Bessarabia" for Hyman without specifying a town. Hyman is the only one of his siblings who has a birthplace listed as Kishinev in the available records.

It is possible that Hyman was born in Kishinev and that his parents migrated to the town of Kremenchuk where his siblings, Itsig and Samuel, were born (see Table 1 on page 7). However, we can't rule out the possibility that Hyman was simplifying his background by aligning his birthplace with that of his children who would soon follow him from Canada into Detroit.

Page 2, right-hand columns showing Hyman's birthplace and his earlier arrival

Of great interest too is the information Hyman gave for his original arrival in the US. Column headings in the record include "Seaport of Landing," "Date of Landing" and "Name of SS." The official wrote "D&W" [Detroit and Windsor] above Quebec for seaport, and Aug. 1904 as the date of landing. The name of the vessel is "unknown."

This record thus suggests that Hyman landed in Canada three years before the arrival indicated on the 1911 Oberlin census. "D&W" and "Quebec" are written on different horizontal rows and probably refer to two different landings. D&W probably refers to the Detroit/Windsor Ferry and explains how he entered Detroit. Quebec is probably his port of landing in Canada in 1904.

Page 2, left-hand columns indicating destination: "Daughter Mrs. M. Panick 283 Rowena St"

Of even greater surprise on page 2 of the manifest is Hyman's destination. He was headed to his "daughter Mrs. M. Panish at 283 Rowena St" in Detroit. His daughter?

According to the family tree, Hyman and Lena had only five sons who grew to adulthood. The only girl listed in the family tree as "baby girl Moskovitch" was born and died in Bessarabia before their migration to Canada. Was the family tree wrong? Was Mrs. M. Panish a daughter who grew up, married and came to Detroit? Other Moskovitch migration records revealed other clues about the identity of Mrs. M. Panish, as we shall see.

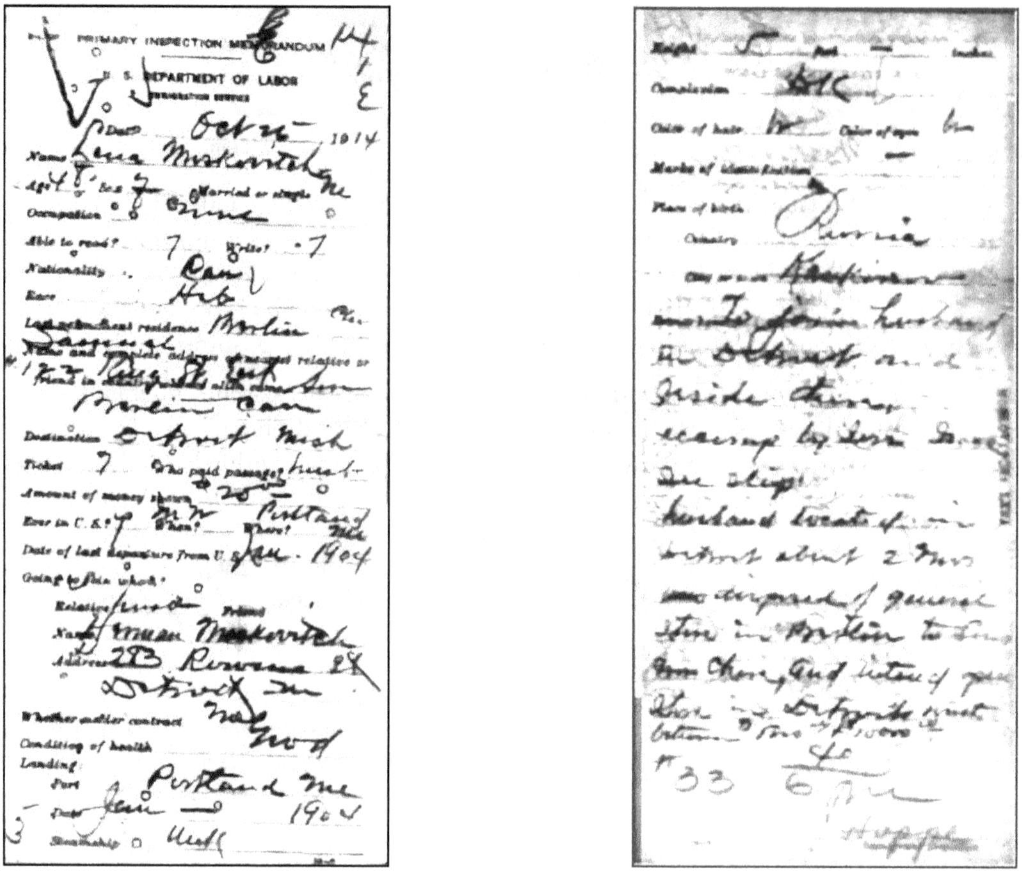
PRIMARY INSPECTION MEMORANDUM

U. S. DEPARTMENT OF LABOR

Figure 14 Record for Lena Moskevitch, dated Oct 26, 1914
Primary Inspection Memorandum, Dept. of Labor

***

Lena and Isaac Follow (Oct. 1914)

On Oct. 26, 1914, just two days after Hyman made his way to Detroit, his wife Lena apparently filled out what's called "A Primary Inspection Memorandum," from the US Department of Labor, which includes personal information and appears to document the belongings she was shipping or taking to her husband in Detroit. The document is difficult to read but includes some useful information. As we shall see, her son Isaac (aka Frank Moss) filled out the same form for himself on the same day.

Lena Moskovitch is listed as 48 years old. Her nationality is described as Canadian and Race as Hebrew. Her last address is Berlin [Ontario] Can. Her closest relative there is her son Samuel at 122 King Street East. Her ticket was paid by her husband, and she was carrying $25.

She was headed to her husband Himan [or Herman] Moskovitch at 283 Rowena Street in Detroit, the same address where Hyman headed before her. Of significance is her answer to the question, whether she had ever been in the US previously? "Yes," she wrote, and the place of last departure was Portland Me [Maine] in Jan. 1904. The answer was consistent with the record of her husband Hyman but provided more detail. The implication is that Hyman and Lena landed in or passed through Portland, Maine in Jan. 1904 on their way to Canada.

Isaac's (aka Frank Moss) information is similar. He is described as age 17, a machinist and single. He lists the same last address in Berlin and the same destination in Detroit as his mother. He also answered "Yes" to being in the US previously.

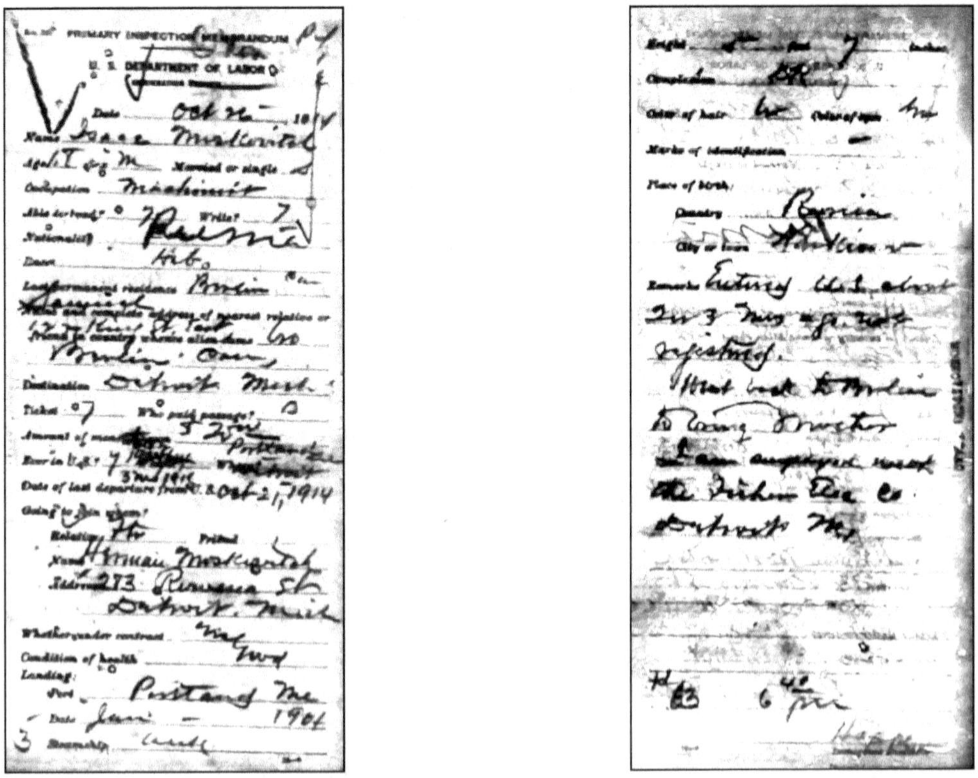

Figure 15 Primary Inspection Memorandum for Isaac Moskovitch

Isaac's document is nearly illegible but appears to say his first time in the US was in 1904 Portland [Me] and then more recently for three months in Detroit which he left only one day earlier [presumably to help his mother]. At the bottom, he again indicates he landed at Portland, Me in June 1904. He gives the name of the steamship, but the writing is illegible. We shall see that Isaac goes back to Berlin in 1915 to accompany his disabled brother Harry to Detroit during his migration.

The second page of the two Memoranda are very difficult to read but in lightening up the images some words are discernible. The back of Lena's appears to describe what is being shipped to her husband in Detroit. What I can discern is this:

> Place of Birth appears to be Kashinev.....To join husband in Detroit and ? ...In ship husband went [to son?] in Detroit about 2 months dispa[tach? dispersal?] of general item in [Briton? Sons?] to L? from [China? Or contains china?], and inter c/[o] ? item in Detroit with between $500 ? $1,0000.00.

The back of Isaac's record seems to read "[went to Detroit] 2 to 3 months ago [illegible] went back to Berlin to help mother [illegible] worked ? Electric Co."

It seems that Lena was shipping goods to her husband and only joined him a month later, or perhaps she was going back and forth between her husband and children back in Canada. On Nov. 24, 1914, Lena Moskovitch appears on a list of aliens crossing the border into the US at Port Huron, Michigan.

List of aliens entering Port Huron on Nov. 24, 1914, including Lena Moskovitch

Page 2 of Lena's record showing she had previously been in Portland [Me] in Jan. 1904

The personal information on the manifest matches what Lena wrote on the Inspection Memorandum a month earlier. In columns about any previous stay in the US previously, the document indicates Portland [Me], Jan. 1904 and appears to say "[in] trans[it]" in the column labeled "duration."

The same information is repeated in the far right columns of page 2. Lena is headed to her husband "Herman" at 283 Rowena in Detroit. And she lists her birthplace again as "Kashinow," which I take to be a transliteration of how she pronounced Kishinev. Perhaps this lends some further support to her husband Hyman's birth there as well.

***

Ben Moskovitch Heads to Detroit (Nov. 1914)

Hyman and Lena's son, Benjamin, migrated next, although he apparently went back and forth a couple times in 1916 to bring his wife and children, as we shall see. A Primary Inspection Memorandum dated Nov. 23, 1914, provides details.

He is listed as Ben Moskovitch, age 26, a wood finisher. His last residence is 122 King St. in Berlin, Canada and his closest relative [wife] Nellie. In answer to the question whether he had ever been in the US before he wrote, "no." Adding detail below he clarifies that he landed in Quebec in April 1899 on the Steamship Canada. The implication is that he did not come through Portland Maine, like his parents or brother. His answers align with the record we looked at previously of Benjamin and Samuel arriving in Quebec from England (on page 11 above).

Ben's destination is also 283 Rowena Street in Detroit. Instead of listing his father at that address, however, he lists "his uncle Max Panik." Max Panik, I thought to myself, must be the husband or father of the woman described as "daughter Mrs. M. Panish" on his father's record a month before. Max Panik was also the man traveling with Benjamin and Samuel to Quebec from England.

***

Who Was the Panick Family?

A Detroit City Directory for 1914 shows a listing of people by addresses. There I found a Morris Panick living at 283 Rowena. A deeper dive into his background indicated that he and his wife Anna (née Lebowitz, also spelled Libowitz, Lebovitsh, and Libuvitch) were also living in Berlin, Ontario in the 1911 census with Anna's father and two brothers who were lodging with them.

, City Directories, 1822-1995 for Brush Rowena
chigan › Detroit › 1914 › Detroit, Michigan, City Directory, 1914

283 Kelfer Margaret E
" Lacher Jacob
" Jassy Henry, extracts
" Winistka Samuel
" Panick Morris

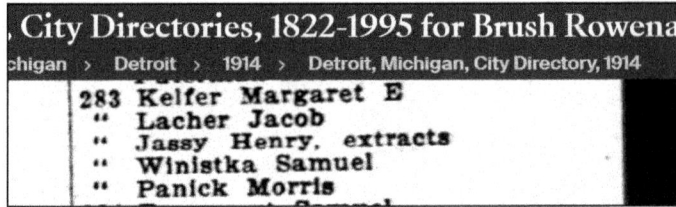

Figure 16 1914 Detroit City Directory for Morris Panick at 283 Rowena

Anna was obviously not the daughter of Hyman Moskovitch since she had a different surname at birth. How then did they know each other? Anna and her husband Morris Panick were both from Kishinev based on their immigration records. Morris migrated from Berlin, Ontario to Detroit in July 1913 a bit before Hyman and Anna followed him in August.

Clearly the Moskovitch family knew the Panick family in Berlin, Ontario, and followed them to Detroit. A later Naturalization Petition from May 1940 indicates that Anna Panick was born in "Kalarech, Rumania" (i.e., Kalarash, Russia when she was born), the same place where several of Hyman and Lena's sons were born (see discussion above page 7). Perhaps they knew each other from Kalarash as well. The Panick's 1911 census in Canada says they arrived in 1907 so it seems they migrated to Canada about the same time as Hyman and Lena Moskovitch. Could Morris or Anna have also been related to Hyman's wife Lena (Wolpinsky)?

Name of Bride. 1. Lebovitsh Anna
Rank, or Profession. 3.
Spinster, Widowed or Divorced. 4. S
Age. 5. 20
Religious Denomination. 6. Jewish
Usual Residence. 7. Berlin
Name and Surname of Father. 8. Joseph Lebovitsh
Rank or Profession of Father. 9.
Name, and Maiden Name of Mother. 10. Bessie Volpanski
When, where and how married. License, or Banns. 23 day of June 1908 at Berlin (County of). by L (License or Banns).

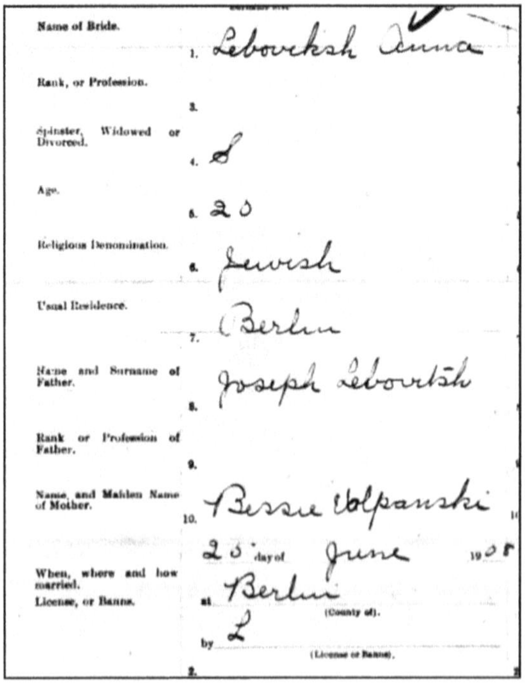

Figure 17 Marriage Certificate of Anna Lebovitsch, 1908

It appears so. Hyman's great-granddaughter, Sharon Moss, helped me find the revealing record: Anna and Morris's marriage certificate from Berlin, Ontario in 1908. The record shows that Anna's mother's surname was Bessie "Volpanski." Anna Panick's mother and Hyman's wife, Lena, were apparently sisters.[5] It seems Anna Panick was the niece of Hyman's wife, Lena.

---

[5] Hyman's great-granddaughter Sharon shared photos of her grandfather Samuel with a first cousin Jack Leibof (see photo page 18) who was a brother of Anna Panick. It is also interesting that one of Anna's other brothers, Samuel, married a woman named Julia Wolpinsky in Brooklyn, NY, possibly another cousin of theirs. A 1913 border crossing

It is notable too perhaps that the news article about Samuel Moskovitch's wedding in 1913 in Berlin Ontario (see p. 21) mentions telegrams being received from Mr. and Mrs. Harry Wolpinski from Brooklyn, perhaps another sibling of Lena as well. In any case, what is clear is that the Panick household in Detroit was the landing place of the Moskovitch family when they arrived.

***

Harry and Isaac Go Together (Mar. 1915)

The brothers Harry and Isaac Moskovitch (aka Frank Moss) appear traveling to Detroit together in March 1915. Isaac was previously in Detroit and went back to accompany his older brother for reasons that will become clear shortly. There are several kinds of revealing records documenting the brothers' arrival. In a Border Crossing record from March 29, 1915, Harry is listed as age 19 and Isaac is 17. According to the record, both were born in Odessa [which conflicts with other records]. Harry is described as having red hair and gray eyes and as 5' 0". Isaac had brown hair and brown eyes and was taller at 5' 6 ½".

Although Harry was older than Isaac, Isaac paid the way for his brother. Isaac is listed as a machinist, but Harry has no occupation. Both listed their last permanent residence as Berlin, Ontario, and their closest relative their brother Samuel Moskovitch at 124 King Street East. They are both headed to their father Hyman Moskovitch now at 117 Benton Street, which is close to the river and the ferry to Windsor, showing that their parents did not stay long with the Panick family on Rowena.

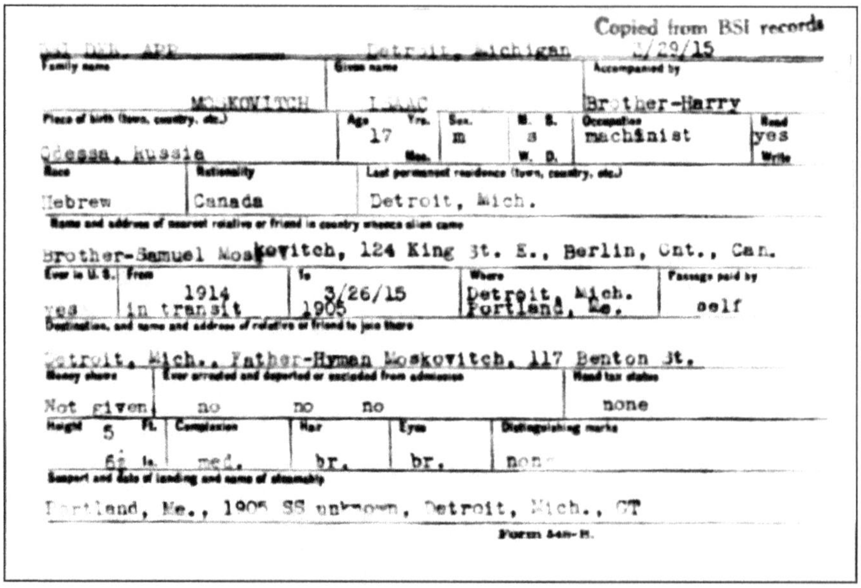
Copied from BSI records
Detroit, Michigan 3/29/15
Family name: MOSKOVITCH
Given name: ISAAC
Accompanied by: Brother-Harry
Place of birth (town, country, etc.): Odessa, Russia
Age: 17 Yrs.
Sex: m
M. S.: s
Occupation: machinist
Read: yes
Write:
Race: Hebrew
Nationality: Canada
Last permanent residence (town, country, etc.): Detroit, Mich.
Name and address of nearest relative or friend in country whence alien came: Brother-Samuel Moskovitch, 124 King St. E., Berlin, Ont., Can.
Ever in U.S.: yes
From: 1914 / in transit
To: 3/26/15 / 1905
Where: Detroit, Mich. / Portland, Me.
Passage paid by: self
Destination, and name and address of relative or friend to join there: Detroit, Mich., Father-Hyman Moskovitch, 117 Benton St.
Money shown: Not given
Ever arrested and deported or excluded from admission: no no no
Head tax status: none
Height: 5 Ft. 6½ In.
Complexion: med.
Hair: br.
Eyes: br.
Distinguishing marks: none
Seaport and date of landing and name of steamship: Portland, Me., 1905 SS unknown, Detroit, Mich., GT
Form 548-B.

Figure 18 Border Crossing records of Isaac Moskovitch (March 1915)

Isaac's record indicates he was in the US twice before, once recently in Detroit from 1914 until March 26, 1915, apparently returning to Canada only days before to accompany his brother Harry to Detroit. He also indicated he was in the US earlier in 1905, in transit from Portland, Me., the name of his steamship unknown. This record is inconsistent with his March 1914 record which indicates he landed in

---

record for Julia's mother, Sarah Wolpianski, shows her heading back to her husband Louis in New York after visiting her married daughter, Julia Libowitz, in Berlin, Ontario in 1913.

Portland, Me. in 1904. Harry's record indicates he was in the US only once before in 1905 in transit from Portland, Me. His steamship is no longer known.

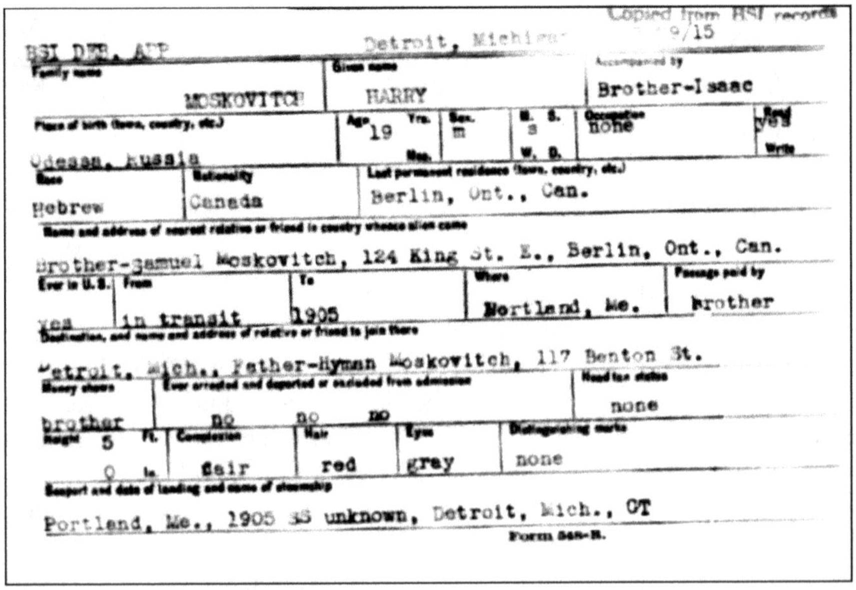
Copied from BSI records 9/15
BSI DET. APP — Detroit, Michigan
Family name: MOSKOVITCH — Given name: HARRY — Accompanied by: Brother-Isaac
Place of birth (town, country, etc.): Odessa, Russia — Age: 19 Yrs. — Sex: m — M. S.: s — Occupation: none — Read: yes
Race: Hebrew — Nationality: Canada — Last permanent residence (town, country, etc.): Berlin, Ont., Can.
Name and address of nearest relative or friend in country whence alien came: Brother-Samuel Moskovitch, 124 King St. E., Berlin, Ont., Can.
Ever in U.S.: yes — From: in transit — To: 1905 — Where: Portland, Me. — Passage paid by: brother
Destination, and name and address of relative or friend to join there: Detroit, Mich., Father-Hyman Moskovitch, 117 Benton St.
Money shown: brother — Ever arrested and deported or excluded from admission: no no no — Head tax status: none
Height: 5 ft. 0 in. — Complexion: fair — Hair: red — Eyes: grey — Distinguishing marks: none
Seaport and date of landing and name of steamship: Portland, Me., 1905 SS unknown, Detroit, Mich., CT
Form 548-B.

Figure 19 Border Crossing record of Harry Moskovitch (March 1915)

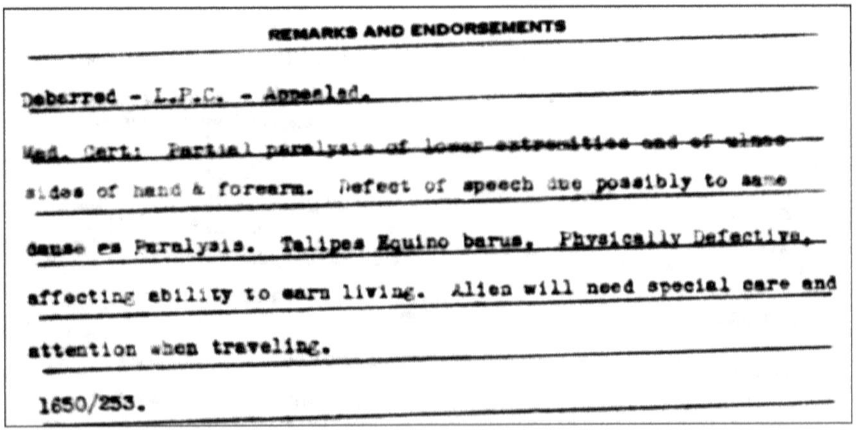
REMARKS AND ENDORSEMENTS
Debarred - L.P.C. - Appealed.
Med. Cert: Partial paralysis of lower extremities and of [illegible]
sides of hand & forearm. Defect of speech due possibly to same
cause as Paralysis. Talipes Equino barus. Physically Defective,
affecting ability to earn living. Alien will need special care and
attention when traveling.
1650/253.

Back of Harry's Record

The comments on the back of Harry's card are revealing and explain why Isaac paid for Harry and went back to Berlin to accompany him to Detroit. Harry was disabled with a clubfoot, a speech impediment, and some paralysis. Because of his disability he was initially prevented from entering the US.

The back of Harry's border crossing card reads:

> Debarred–L. P. C [Likely public charge]– Appealed. Med. Cert: Partial paralysis of lower extremities and of [word illegible] sides of hand & forearm. Defect of speech due possibly to same cause [es?] Paralysis. Talipes Equino barus [=clubfoot]. Physically Defective, affecting ability to earn living. Alien will need special care and attention when traveling.

The appeal must have succeeded which explains why the two brothers show up on a border crossing list on Detroit on April 24, 1915, and then again on June 24, 1915. The records again show that Harry was "debarred," that it was appealed April 2, 1915 and dismissed [i.e., successful] on April 8, 1915. A few weeks later the brothers arrived in Detroit together and possibly returned to Berlin and came back in again.

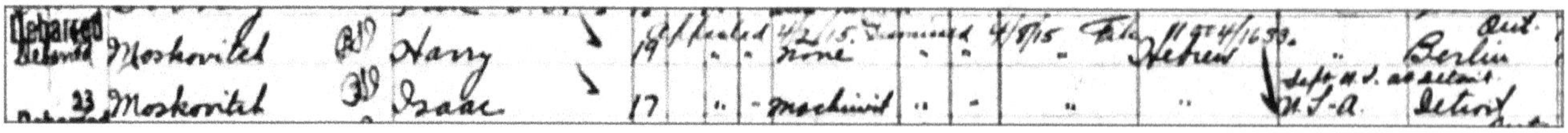
Debarred Moskovitch Harry 19 none Hebrew Berlin
33 Moskovitch Isaac 17 machinist Detroit

Figure 20 Border Crossing List for Isaac and Harry (April 24, 1915)

***

The Migration of Ben's Wife and Children (Nov. 1915)

In November 1915, with his brothers settling in Detroit, Ben went back to Berlin and brought his wife, Nellie, and their three children to Detroit. A record dated Nov. 16, 1915, shows Nellie and the three children crossing with her husband "Beryl." They are headed to a rented house on Benton Street. The family apparently went back and forth between Berlin and Detroit over the next year. Several additional records of Ben and Nellie appear in 1916. The first is dated Mar. 23, 1916, indicating Ben was accompanied by his wife and three children. Some of the information is consistent with his earlier 1914 record. He is age 29 now, and again lists his birthplace as "Kisarnuf, Bassarbia."

While Ben's earlier record indicated he arrived in Quebec the first time in 1899 and was never in the US before, this record indicates he landed in Quebec on Aug. 24, 1902, on the SS Canada and was in the US in 1908 through July 1909 in New York and Baltimore. He may have visited his Baltimore cousins during this time.

A record dated March 28 records Nellie's crossing with her husband and three children again.

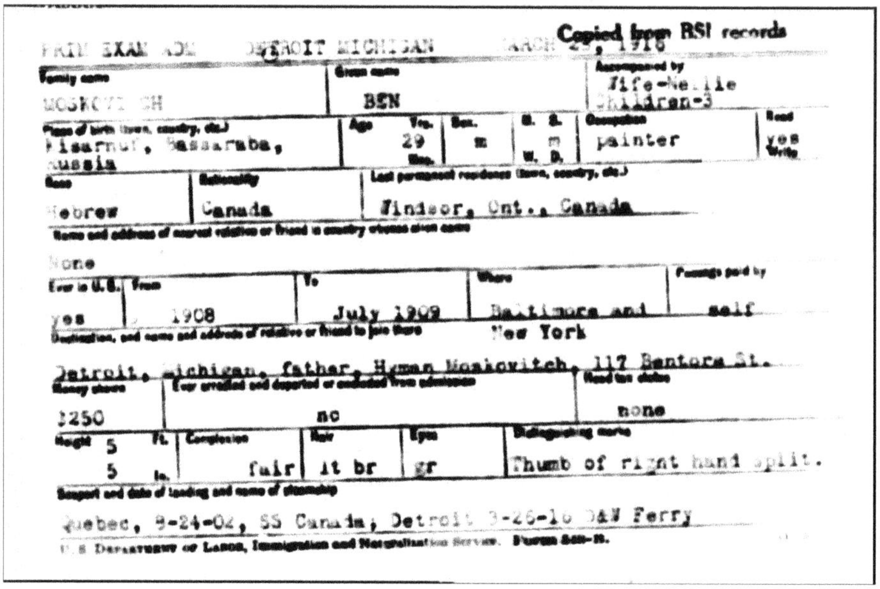
Copied from RSI records
Family name: MOSKOVITCH — Given name: BEN — Accompanied by: Wife-Nellie, Children-3
Place of birth: Kisarnuf, Bassaraba, Russia — Age: 29 — Sex: m — S. M. W. D.: m — Occupation: painter — Read: yes
Race: Hebrew — Nationality: Canada — Last permanent residence: Windsor, Ont., Canada
Name and address of nearest relative or friend in country whence alien came: None
Ever in U.S.: yes — From: 1908 — To: July 1909 — Where: Baltimore and New York — Passage paid by: self
Destination, and name and address of relative or friend to join there: Detroit, Michigan, father, Hyman Moskovitch, 117 Bentore St.
Money shown: $250 — Ever arrested and deported or excluded from admission: no — Head tax status: none
Height: 5 ft. 5 in. — Complexion: fair — Hair: lt br — Eyes: gr — Distinguishing marks: Thumb of right hand split.
Seaport and date of landing and name of steamship: Quebec, 9-24-02, SS Canada; Detroit 3-26-16 D&W Ferry
U. S. Department of Labor, Immigration and Naturalization Service.

Figure 21 Border Crossing Record for Ben and family (March 23, 1916)

***

Migration of Israel (Jan. 1916)

Israel's migration was captured in a Border Crossing record from Jan. 12, 1916. He is described as 26 years-old, 5' 7", with dark brown hair and brown eyes. His birthplace is "Speishinef [Kishinev] Bassarabia, Russia." Like his brothers, he too was headed to his father "Himan Muskovitch" at 117 Benton Street.

Israel's last residence was Windsor, Ontario and his closest relative there was his brother "[D?]aniel Muskovitch." I suspect the official copying his original record mistakenly wrote "Daniel" instead of Samuel. Israel had $200 in his possession.

The record indicates he was in the US from 1912 to July 1915, in Baltimore Md. and Detroit, which probably explains why he was headed to Detroit after his other brothers. Perhaps he visited with the Baltimore branch of his family when he was there. His initial port of landing in the US is listed as Halifax, Nova Scotia in December 1906, but the name of his steamship is no longer remembered. A later naturalization record shows he had British citizenship, which may have been part and parcel of his naturalization in Canada or earlier in England.

***

Arrival of Samuel and Family (Feb. 1916)

While Israel was settling in, his brother Samuel made the move to Detroit with his family. He was the last of the brothers to do so. The record shows "Shmel (Sam) Mowkewich, age 29, his wife Vitte [spelled Vita elsewhere], age 24 and their son, Joseph, age 1 and 6 months, crossing together into Detroit on Feb. 24, 1916. They list their last residence as Windsor. His occupation is difficult to read but probably says "barber" which is his occupation in his US Draft registration card filled out not long afterwards. His granddaughter, Sharon Moss, tells me that he was a fine violinist but couldn't make a living that way and became a barber to support the family (see the photo of him in Russia with violin on p. 8)

Samuel's record confirms he was the last of his family to migrate and thus says "no relatives" left in their last residence. More revealing is his wife's Vitte's answer. Her closest relative was her Uncle Leib Chernikoff living at 114 Albert St. in Berlin, Ontario. Just a few months later, Samuel's brother, Israel, married a daughter of this very same man. In other words, the wives of the brothers, Israel and Samuel, were first cousins.[6]

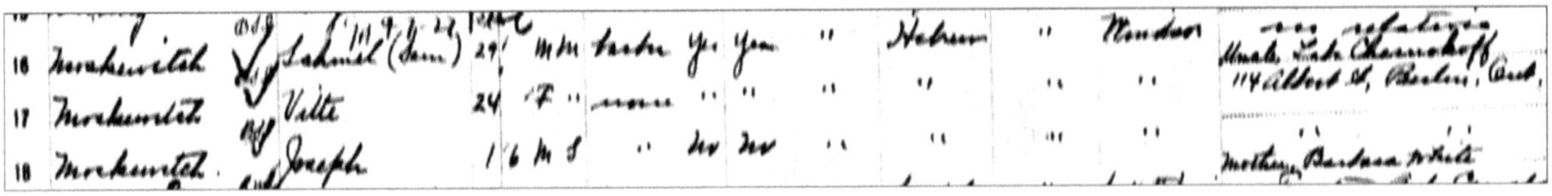

Figure 22 Border Crossing of Samuel and Vita (Feb. 1916)

The second page of Samuel and Vita's passenger list includes several interesting pieces of information. The record shows they were headed to 59 Benton Street. Samuel's birthplace is listed as Kalarash, Basarabia. In the column for "Seaport of Landing" is written D&W [Detroit & Windsor] for his entrance to Detroit and then underneath that "Quebec" for his original entrance to Canada. The name of the vessel is listed as SS "Canada." The date of landing is April 14, 1905. The passenger manifest looked at earlier which we suspect belonged to Samuel and Benjamin shows them arriving in 1906 (see Figure 4 on p. 11). It is possible that Samuel mixed up the year of his migration or perhaps as they were settling in Canada he went back and forth to England to help his family with the migration.

---

[6] The wife of Leib/Louis in other records is called Fannie Lebow or Leboy. It appears she is the sister of Vitte's mother.

Vita's birth location is listed as the region Chernekov [Chernigov], and the town Staridob [today Starodob], Russia. Her surname, Chernekov, was probably derived from the family's geographical origin. Her port of landing is listed as D&W, NY, on the [SS] Finland, July 1910.

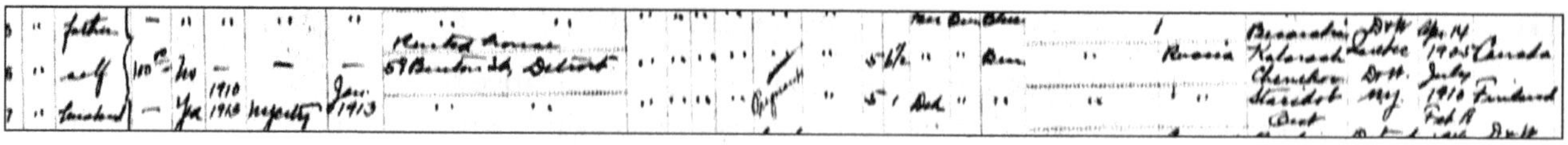

Page 2 of Border Crossing manifest for Samuel and Vita

***

Photo 8 Samuel in Toronto Symphony Orchestra

***

Israel Gets Married (June 1916)

A few months after Samuel and his family arrived in Detroit, his brother Israel got married. A marriage record shows Israel Moskovitch, a peddler, age 26, married Anna Chernokow, age 26 on June 11, 1916, in Detroit.[7]

Anna's surname is spelled Chernikoff among several variations in the records (Chernokow, Chernikov, Cherney). She was born in Russia and lived with her family in Berlin, Ontario. Israel and Anna

---

[7] Apparently, Anna (Hannah Zlata) should not be confused with her sister, Henya, who is also misleadingly called Anna Chernekov in the records. An online family tree shows them as sisters. Both women appear as Anna Chernikov daughters of Louis and Fannie. Henya/Anna Chernikov married Abram Klein in Aug. 1916 that same summer in Berlin, Ontario. They too migrated to Detroit at a later date.

must have met there, but not married until Israel settled into Detroit. As noted above, she was probably the first cousin of Samuel's wife. The marriage record seems to have some misinformation about Anna. Her parents' names are listed as David and Jennie. But in records of Anna crossing into Detroit, her father's name is listed as Louis Chernekov.

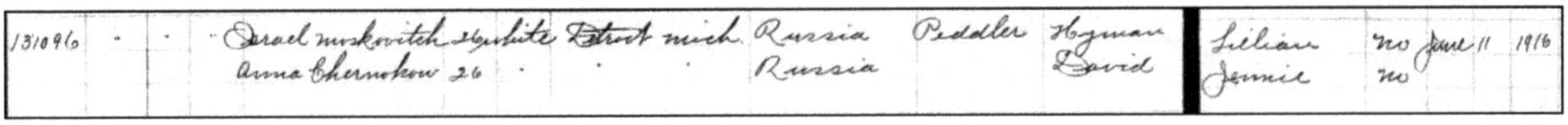
131096 Israel Moskovitch 26 white Detroit Mich. Russia Peddler Hyman Lilian no June 11 1916
Anna Chernokow 26 Russia David Jennie no

Figure 23 Marriage record of Israel Moskovitch and Anna Chernokow (June 1916)

There are two records of Anna crossing into Detroit that summer indicating she was going back and forth from Detroit to Berlin, Ontario where she was living. A Border Crossing List from June 24, 1916, just weeks after their wedding shows "Annie" arriving in Detroit. Her last residence was Berlin, Ontario where her father Louis Chernikow was living at 114 Albert Street. She is headed to husband Israel Moskovitch at 258 Adelaide Street. A record from August shows her entering Detroit again with the same information.

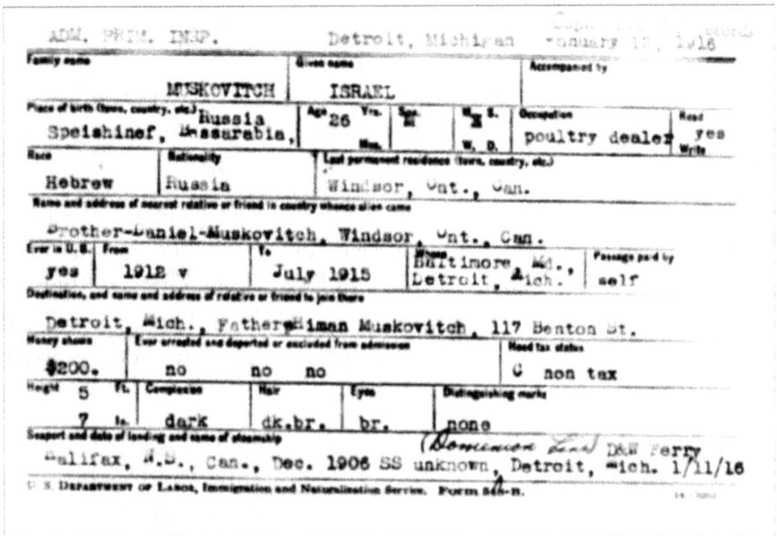
ADM. PRIM. INSP. Detroit, Michigan January 12, 1916
Family name: MUSKOVITCH Given name: ISRAEL Accompanied by:
Place of birth (town, country, etc.): Speishinef, Bessarabia, Russia Age: 26 Yrs. Sex: M M.S. Occupation: poultry dealer Read: yes Write
Race: Hebrew Nationality: Russia Last permanent residence (town, country, etc.): Windsor, Ont., Can.
Name and address of nearest relative or friend in country whence alien came: Brother-Daniel-Muskovitch, Windsor, Ont., Can.
Ever in U.S.: yes From: 1912 To: July 1915 Where: Baltimore, Md., Detroit, Mich. Passage paid by: self
Destination, and name and address of relative or friend to join there: Detroit, Mich., Father-Himan Muskovitch, 117 Benton St.
Money shown: $200. Ever arrested and deported or excluded from admission: no no no Head tax status: C non tax
Height: 5 Ft. 7 In. Complexion: dark Hair: dk.br. Eyes: br. Distinguishing marks: none
Seaport and date of landing and name of steamship: Halifax, N.S., Can., Dec. 1906 SS unknown, (Dominion Line) D&W Ferry Detroit, Mich. 1/11/16
U. S. Department of Labor, Immigration and Naturalization Service. Form 548-B.

Figure 24 1916 Border Crossing Record of Israel (Jan. 12) and Annie (Jun. 22)

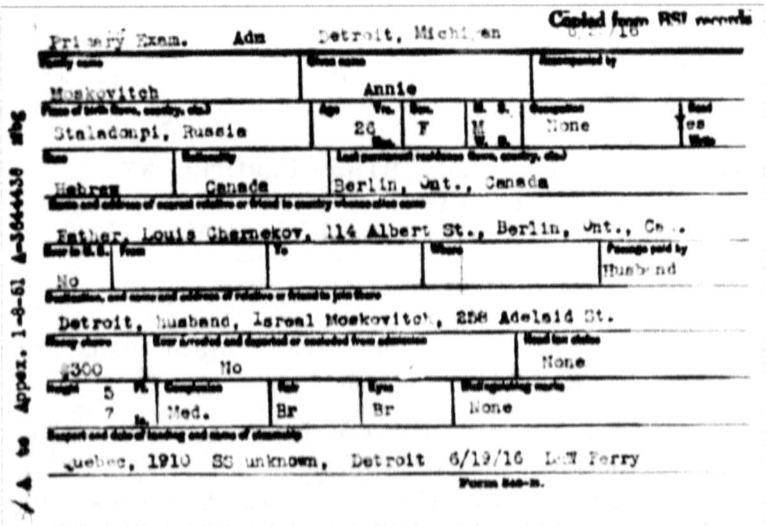
Copied from RSI records
Primary Exam. Adm Detroit, Michigan
Family name: Moskovitch Given name: Annie Accompanied by:
Place of birth (town, country, etc.): Staladonpi, Russia Age: 26 Yrs. Sex: F M.S.: M Occupation: None Read: Yes Write
Race: Hebrew Nationality: Canada Last permanent residence (town, country, etc.): Berlin, Ont., Canada
Name and address of nearest relative or friend in country whence alien came: Father, Louis Charnekov, 114 Albert St., Berlin, Ont., Ca.
Ever in U.S.: No From: To: Where: Passage paid by: Husband
Destination, and name and address of relative or friend to join there: Detroit, husband, Isreal Moskovitch, 258 Adelaid St.
Money shown: $300 Ever arrested and deported or excluded from admission: No Head tax status: None
Height: 5 Ft. 7 In. Complexion: Med. Hair: Br Eyes: Br Distinguishing marks: None
Seaport and date of landing and name of steamship: Quebec, 1910 SS unknown, Detroit 6/19/16 D&W Ferry
Form 548-B.
Appex. 1-8-51 A-3644438

***

Life in Detroit: 1917 and Beyond

By the end of 1916, Hyman's family was firmly settled in Detroit, though the spelling of the family surname and their addresses remained fluid for some time to come. In the 1916 City Directory, Hyman, Isaac [Frank], and Israel are living at 176 Brady St. Isaac is a machinist, Hyman and Israel are peddlers. Samuel is living at 58 Benton and working as a barber at 519 Hastings. Benjamin is not listed in the directory and Harry was disabled and living with his parents. Since he was not working, he didn't need his own listing.

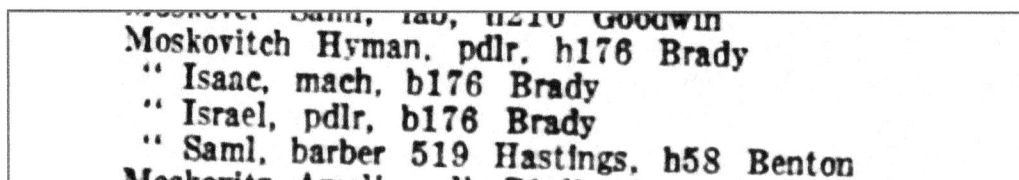

Figure 25 1916 Detroit City Directory with Hyman, Isaac [Frank], Israel, and Samuel

Not long after arriving, Isaac (Frank Moss), age 21, got married to Agnes Cohen in Detroit on March 4, 1917. The first compulsory draft since the Civil War began that summer and registration records for two of the sons have been located.

Ben was in the first registration on June 5, 1917, for men between the ages of 21 and 31. He was 30 at the time and listed as a painter for a business called "Siever and Hurtman." The record says he was 5'5", with red hair and brown eyes. His name is spelled "Ben Moskovitz," though he signed formally as "B. Moskovitch." His place of birth is Kolorash [Kalarash] and his birthdate is Mar. 23, 1887. The family's address appears to be in transition: 178 Wilkins is scratched out and a second address is written which is difficult to read.

Ben's brother, Samuel, filled out his draft card during the third registration on September 12, 1918, for men between the ages of 18 and 45. Samuel was 33 at the time and lists his birthday as Oct. 8, 1884. The record describes him as medium height and build, with blue eyes and light hair. He was still living at 56 Benton Street and was working as a barber at 519 Hastings Street. He remained a barber for most of his career, with one short exception discussed below, making it easy to track him in the records. The boys' father, Hyman, is listed as their closest relative, living at 176 Brady which remains Hyman's address in the 1920 census.

The online 1918 City Directory is missing the last third of its pages, so it is impossible to tell where anyone was living that year. By 1919, however, we can see that Isaac started to informally use the name Frank.

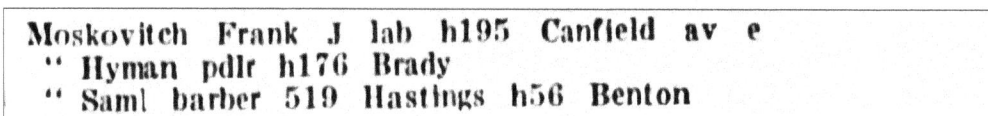

Figure 26 1919 City Directory for Frank, Hyman and Samuel

During the 1920s, the Moskovitch brothers expanded their families, tried their hand in the auto industry and made progress on their naturalization.

In 1920, the brothers' parents, Hyman, now 55 and Leah [a new variation of Lena], age 52, were still living at 174 Brady Street. Hyman was working as a fruit peddler, and already submitted first papers ("PA") towards his naturalization. Their disabled son Harry, age 23, was also living with them and had no occupation. The record indicates they migrated to the US in 1900, a detail inconsistent with their earlier border crossing records and the 1911 census in Canada. Another man was also boarding with them, with the last name apparently of Couzin.

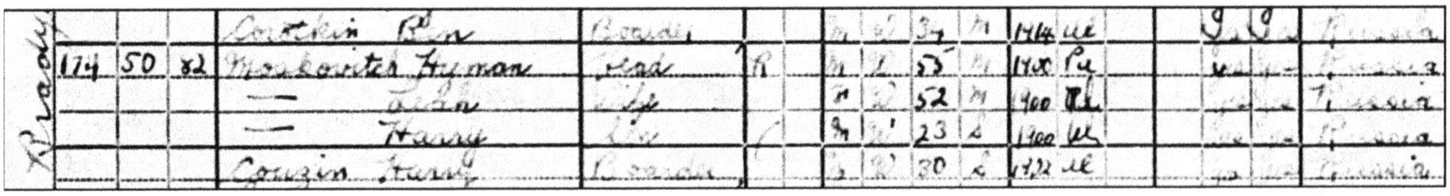

Brady				Cortkin Ben	Boarder		M	W	34	M	1914	Al	Russia
	174	50	82	Moskovitch Hyman	Head	R	M	W	55	M	1900	Pa	Russia
				— Lena	Wife		F	W	52	M	1900	Pa	Russia
				— Harry	Son		M	W	23	S	1900	Al	Russia
				Couzin Harry	Boarder		M	W	30	S	1912	Al	Russia

Figure 27 1920 Census of Hyman, Leah, and Harry

Hyman and Lena both passed away in the middle of the decade. Hyman's death was ruled a homicide. An astonishing news article in the *Lansing State Journal*, discovered by his great-granddaughter Sharon Moss, recorded what happened.

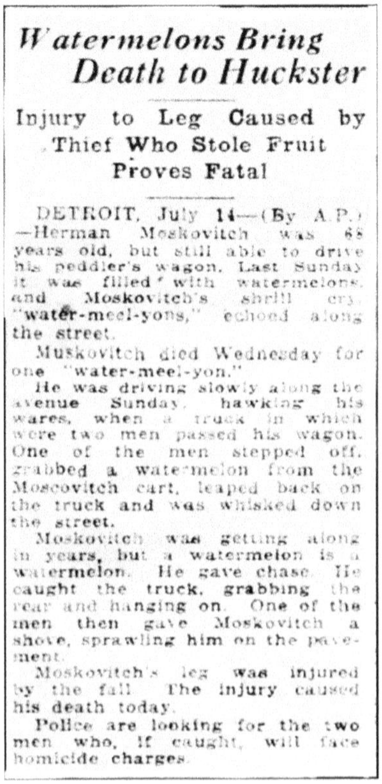

Watermelons Bring Death to Huckster

Injury to Leg Caused by Thief Who Stole Fruit Proves Fatal

DETROIT, July 14—(By A.P.)—Herman Moskovitch was 68 years old, but still able to drive his peddler's wagon. Last Sunday it was filled with watermelons, and Moskovitch's shrill cry, "water-meel-yons," echoed along the street.

Muskovitch died Wednesday for one "water-meel-yon."

He was driving slowly along the avenue Sunday, hawking his wares, when a truck in which were two men passed his wagon. One of the men stepped off, grabbed a watermelon from the Moscovitch cart, leaped back on the truck and was whisked down the street.

Moskovitch was getting along in years, but a watermelon is a watermelon. He gave chase. He caught the truck, grabbing the rear and hanging on. One of the men then gave Moskovitch a shove, sprawling him on the pavement.

Moskovitch's leg was injured by the fall. The injury caused his death today.

Police are looking for the two men who, if caught, will face homicide charges.

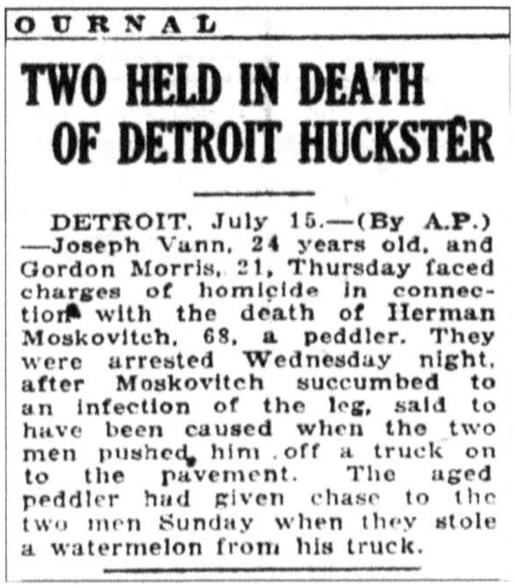

OURNAL

TWO HELD IN DEATH OF DETROIT HUCKSTER

DETROIT, July 15.—(By A.P.)—Joseph Vann, 24 years old, and Gordon Morris, 21, Thursday faced charges of homicide in connection with the death of Herman Moskovitch, 68, a peddler. They were arrested Wednesday night, after Moskovitch succumbed to an infection of the leg, said to have been caused when the two men pushed him off a truck on to the pavement. The aged peddler had given chase to the two men Sunday when they stole a watermelon from his truck.

Figure 28 Hyman's Death Over Watermelon Theft

On July 14, 1926, at the age of 68, Hyman was still a "huckster" and peddling watermelons on the city streets. Two men in a truck pulled up alongside him and one snatched a watermelon. "Herman" gave chase and grabbed the back of the truck. One of the men gave him a shove and he fell to the pavement and injured his leg. His death certificate indicates he died from an infection caused by the injury. The next day the police arrested the two men involved and charged them with homicide.

Lena passed away a year later in 1927. By 1930, their disabled son Harry moved into the home of his brother Samuel.

***

Samuel Moskovitch, the Barber and Violinist

In the 1920 census, Samuel and Vita are still living at 56 Benton Street. Samuel is 33, his wife Vita [called Dora in this record] is 27, and their son Joseph who was born in Berlin, Ontario is now 6. The couple has two additional sons who were born in Michigan: Jacob—3 years and 7 months and Solomon—1 year and 8 months.

Living with them (and appearing on the next page) is Dora's mother, Mary Levitt, now 63 and Dora's brother, Maurice (Morris), age 35. Samuel must have given the auto industry a try during this time. He is described as an autobody assembly laborer.

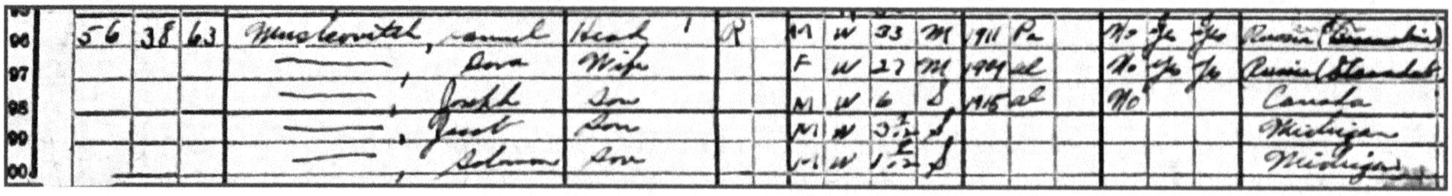

Figure 29 1920 Census of Samuel "Muskovitch" and family

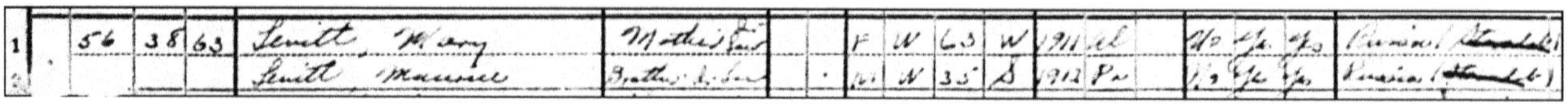

Next page of 1920 Census showing Vita's mother and brother in the household

Samuel's stint in the auto industry did not last long. He was back to being a barber again by the time he declared his naturalization intention on June 10, 1925. He is described as 39 years old, 5'5" with brown hair and hazel eyes. His birthday is listed as Oct. 8, 1886. His Declaration renounces his loyalty to King of Great Britain and Ireland which could indicate he had been earlier naturalized in the UK or in Canada which was still part of Great Britain until 1931.[8] The family is now residing at 648 Hendrie Street in Detroit.

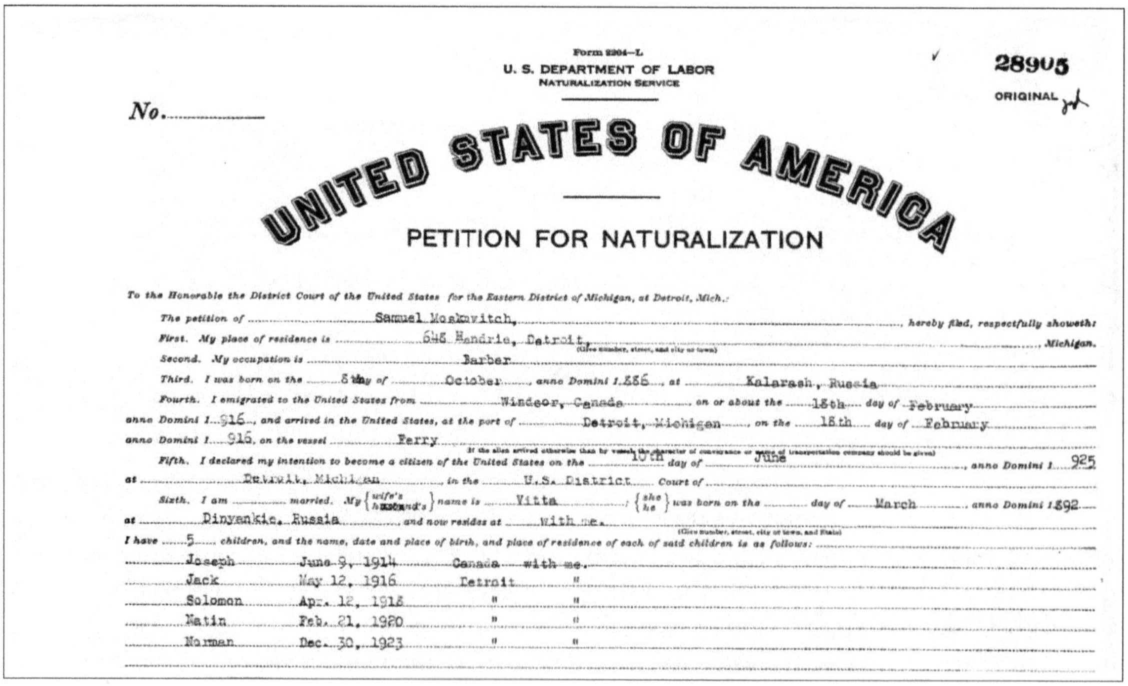

Form 2204–L
U. S. DEPARTMENT OF LABOR
NATURALIZATION SERVICE

28905
ORIGINAL

No.

UNITED STATES OF AMERICA

PETITION FOR NATURALIZATION

To the Honorable the District Court of the United States for the Eastern District of Michigan, at Detroit, Mich.:

The petition of Samuel Moskovitch, hereby filed, respectfully showeth:

First. My place of residence is 648 Hendrie, Detroit, Michigan.

Second. My occupation is Barber.

Third. I was born on the 8 day of October, anno Domini 1886, at Kalarash, Russia.

Fourth. I emigrated to the United States from Windsor, Canada on or about the 18th day of February anno Domini 1916, and arrived in the United States, at the port of Detroit, Michigan, on the 18th day of February anno Domini 1916, on the vessel Ferry.

Fifth. I declared my intention to become a citizen of the United States on the 10th day of June, anno Domini 1925 at Detroit, Michigan in the U.S. District Court of

Sixth. I am married. My wife's name is Vitta; she was born on the day of March anno Domini 1892 at Dinyenkie, Russia and now resides at with me.

I have 5 children, and the name, date and place of birth, and place of residence of each of said children is as follows:

Joseph June 9, 1914 Canada with me.
Jack May 12, 1916 Detroit "
Solomon Apr. 12, 1918 " "
Natin Feb. 21, 1920 " "
Norman Dec. 30, 1923 " "

Figure 30 Samuel's Naturalization Petition

Samuel subsequently signed his Naturalization Petition on Feb. 9, 1928. His personal information is consistent with his Declaration, but this time the form required him to provide his birthplace: Kalarash, Russia. Samuel lists the birthdates of his five children. Joseph born June 9, 1914 in Canada. The other four

[8] I am grateful to David Chapin for pointing out this ambiguity to me.

were born in Detroit: Jack (May 12, 1916), Solomon (Apr. 12, 1918), Nathan (Feb. 21, 1920) and Norman (Dec. 30, 1923).

Photo 9 Samuel Moskovitch in Acme Barber Shop Detroit
Courtesy of Sharon Moss

Because US naturalization rules for women changed under the Cable Act of 1922, Vita had to fill out her own Petition, which she did a year later on May 1, 1928. In the interim, a new son was born named Herman (Mar. 25, 1929). Interestingly, Vita listed a different birth year for their son Norman who was born on Dec. 30, 1922 (not 1923) according to the information on her record.

Figure 31 Vita Moskovitch's Citizenship Certification
Courtesy of Sharon Moss

In the 1930 census, Sam, Vita and their six sons are living together at 646 Hendrie St. Sam is still a barber in a barbershop. Vita's widowed mother, Marsha Levitt, age 75, is still living with them as is Samuel's disabled brother Harry, now age 35. Next door at 648 Hendrie Street is Vita's brother Morris Levitt, now married with three children.

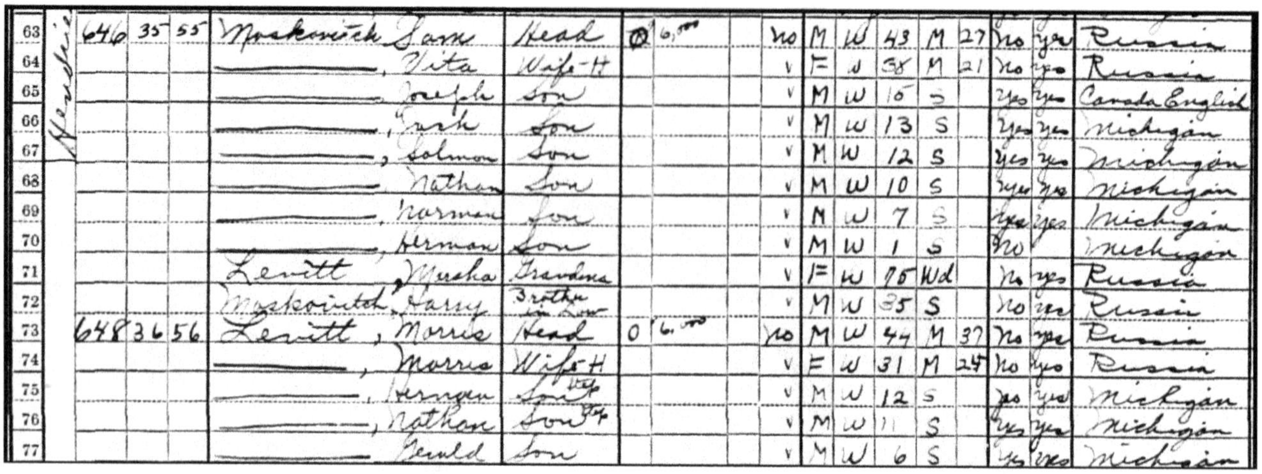

63	Hendrie	646	35	55	Moskovitch, Sam	Head	O	6,000	no	M	W	43	M	27	No	yes	Russia
64					——, Vita	Wife-H			v	F	W	38	M	21	No	yes	Russia
65					——, Joseph	Son			v	M	W	16	S		Yes	Yes	Canada English
66					——, Jack	Son			v	M	W	13	S		Yes	yes	Michigan
67					——, Solomon	Son			v	M	W	12	S		Yes	yes	Michigan
68					——, Nathan	Son			v	M	W	10	S		Yes	yes	Michigan
69					——, Norman	Son			v	M	W	7	S		Yes	yes	Michigan
70					——, Herman	Son			v	M	W	1	S		No		Michigan
71					Levitt, Masha	Grandma			v	F	W	75	Wd		No	yes	Russia
72					Moskovitch, Harry	Brother in Law			v	M	W	35	S		No	yes	Russia
73		648	36	56	Levitt, Morris	Head	O	6,000	no	M	W	44	M	37	No	yes	Russia
74					——, Morris	Wife-H			v	F	W	31	M	24	No	yes	Russia
75					——, Herman	Son			v	M	W	12	S		yes	yes	Michigan
76					——, Nathan	Son			v	M	W	11	S		Yes	yes	Michigan
77					——, Gerald	Son			v	M	W	6	S		Yes	yes	Michigan

Figure 32 1930 census of Sam, Vita and family

A death certificate signed by Samuel on Jan. 10, 1934, indicates that his brother Harry, who was living with them at the time, came down with pneumonia and died within 24 hours.

In the 1940 census, Sam is no longer listed as a barber. He is described instead as a proprietor of a retail shop. The family is living at 3711 Duane Avenue and five of the sons are still living at home. "Sol" (Solomon) is 22 and working as an apprentice in a printing shop that was servicing the auto industry, Nathan is 20 and working in a laundry. Norman is 17 and Herman is 11.

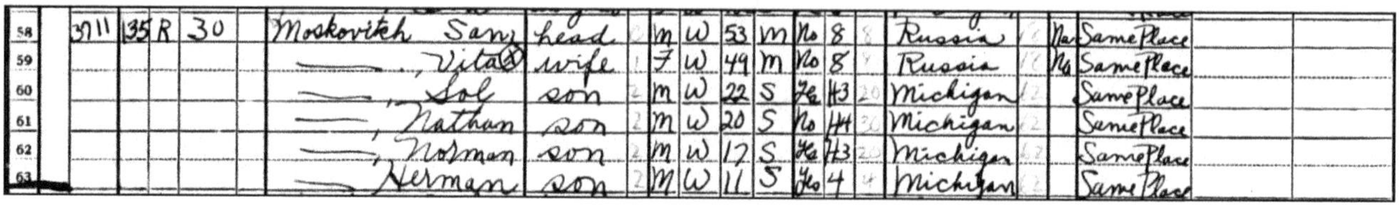

58	3711	35	R	30	Moskovitch Sam	head	M	W	53	M	No	8	Russia	No	Same Place
59					——, Vita	wife	F	W	49	M	No	8	Russia	No	Same Place
60					——, Sol	son	M	W	22	S	Yes	H3	Michigan		Same Place
61					——, Nathan	son	M	W	20	S	No	H4	Michigan		Same Place
62					——, Norman	son	M	W	17	S	Yes	H3	Michigan		Same Place
63					——, Herman	son	M	W	11	S	Yes	4	Michigan		Same Place

Figure 33 1940 census of Sam and family

Joseph and Jack, the two eldest sons of Samuel and Vita, were both married and living with in-laws in 1940. Joseph, the eldest, married in May 1939 and was living with his wife Gertrude and her parents Max and Goldie Chaben. He passed away not long afterwards in 1940. A death certificate indicates he was in the local hospital, St. Joseph's Sanitarium, for six weeks following a sinus surgery and died of meningitis. His photo, perhaps of his wedding day, appears on his tombstone. Gertrude subsequently married a man named Leon Paul and they had one child.

Photo 10 A photo of Joe Moskovitch
on his tombstone

The other son, Jack, who married in 1938, was living with his wife Sonya, and her parents, Abe and Sonya Petuch. Jack and Sonya had a daughter, Marsha Jean, before they divorced on May 5, 1944. Jack (1916-1990) remarried but did not have other children. His daughter Marsha married Larry Cohen and they had two sons, Ian and Joel.

A divorce record shows that the boys' parents, Sam and Vita, divorced on March 29, 1949, not long before Sam, the head of the family, passed away (Oct. 2, 1950). In the 1950 census, Vita is listed as head of her household living with her two sons Herman (1929-2014) and Norman (1922-1991) still at the same address as in 1940. Norman's new wife, Anita (Steinfeld), appears listed on the next page living with them.

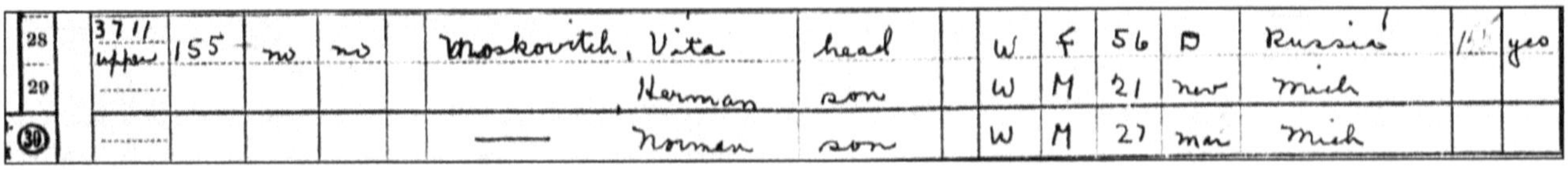

28	3711 upper	155	no	no		Moskovitch, Vita	head		W	F	56	D	Russia	14	yes
29						Herman	son		W	M	21	now	Mich		
30					———	Norman	son		W	M	27	mar	Mich		

Figure 34 1950 Census of Vita and two sons

Sam and Vita's granddaughter, Sharon Moss, tells me how she learned the story behind Sam and Vita's sad divorce. She had been delving into the history of the Moskovitch family when she discovered the record of Sam and Vita's divorce record. Not knowing they had divorced she asked her brother and her cousins about it. No one knew about it. Finally, she asked her uncle Herman (her father's brother and one of Sam and Vita's sons) about it. The story and family secret came tumbling out.

Sam had been depressed after the death of his son Joseph and was not functioning well. Vita was listed as head of the household that year in the census. Vita was advised to get a divorce so that Sam would be cared for by the State, at a time when depression was not well understood and medications for its treatment not yet routinely available. Sam spent the last year of his life institutionalized at Eloise Hospital. Sharon's uncle Herman told her that the memory of the divorce and Sam's final stay in Eloise was a painful one in the family and that he and his siblings didn't talk about it. It was too painful to discuss.

This was the period of large institutionalization—Detroit being famous for leading the way through the development of Eloise Hospital documented by a reporter Sam Luxenberg in Annie's Ghost, A Journey into a Family Secret. The book tells the story of how the author, Steve, discovered that his mother had a sister named Annie he never knew about. No one in the family seemed to know anything about her or her fate. Steve tells the story of his journey to learn Annie's story. It turns out that Annie had a disability and that she was incarcerated in Eloise for most of her adult life. In 1940, Eloise was a sprawling hospital of about 75 buildings and 9,000 residents (not all of whom were mentally ill).

When Sharon heard about *Annie's Ghost:* she ordered the book in hopes of learning more about the institution where her great-grandfather had lived the last year of his life. She was in for a big surprise as she read the book. An old photo that the author, Steve, discovered of his mother and some friends led him eventually to a woman named Millie Brodie who was still alive and who knew his mother and his aunt Annie before the latter was incarcerated in Eloise. This Millie Brodie was born Mildred Moskovitch and was the daughter of Frank Moss (aka Hyman's son Isaac Moskovitch). Millie lived for a time in Ypsilanti before moving back to Detroit with her family. She and her brother Martin Moss remembered Annie and the disability that led to her incarceration, and they supplied key details that ultimately helped recover her story. I wonder if Millie also knew that her grandfather, Samuel, spent a year of his life in Eloise too. The two Detroit family stories intersected in multiple ways.

Vita passed away in 1955. Norman and Anita subsequently had three children Sheryl, David, and Victor. Samuel and Vita's son "Sol" Moss [Solomon] (1918–2000) married Helen Baker and they had two children, Barry Moss and Sharon Moss. Sharon is the cousin from the Detroit line who helped with my knowledge of this branch of the family. Samuel and Vita's son Nathan Moss (1920–1993) married Alice Weinger in 1944 and they had two children Marsha (married name Fischel) and Sidney Paul Moss.

***

Ben Moskovich and Family

Samuel's brother, Benjamin "Moskowitch" and his wife, Nellie, and their three children were living at 182 Rowena Street in the 1920 census, a block from where their father Hyman first stayed in 1914 with the Panick family. Benjamin is called "Barmud" in this record, probably a variation on Bernard, which appears as we have seen in his daughter's birth record (see Figure 10 on p. 6). During this time, Benjamin was working as a carpenter in the auto industry.

In the 1920 census record, "Barmud" is 32, his wife Nellie 27, and their children Esther 7, David 5, and Jack 3 years, 9 months. Their youngest son, Jack, was five months older than his first cousin, also called Jack, who was son of Benjamin's brother Samuel. This Jack (Ben's son) was born in Canada and that Jack (Samuel's son) was born in Detroit.

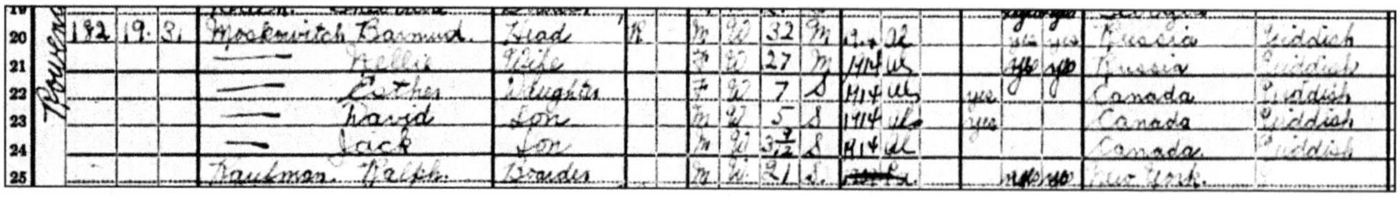

20	Rowena	182	19	31	Moskowitch Barmud	Head	M	32	M	Russia	Yiddish
21					— Nellie	Wife	F	27	M	Russia	Yiddish
22					— Esther	Daughter	F	7	S	Canada	Yiddish
23					— David	Son	M	5	S	Canada	Yiddish
24					— Jack	Son	M	3 9/12	S	Canada	Yiddish
25					Kaufman Ralph	Boarder	M	21	S	New York	

Figure 35 1920 Census of Benjamin, Nellie and children

In 1920, Benjamin and family still have the naturalization status of "aliens." A few weeks after the census was taken, Benjamin declared his intention to become a citizen. He wrote his name as "Bayril [Beryl] Moskovitch" and described himself as a merchant. The record lists his birthplace as Kalarash and his birthdate as Feb. 25,1887 (which differs from the Dec. 1887 on the 1911 census in Canada). His record indicates he was previously a British citizen, perhaps through his earlier Canadian naturalization.

It seems that Benjamin had a serious accident back in Canada later that year. He was lucky to be alive by the reports of it. He was apparently back in Ontario, a bit north of Berlin, when he drove his car across the train tracks and got hit by a train. The engine was thrown from the car and Ben suffered severe head lacerations. He was transported to the train station and then to the hospital. The article concluded that "it is believed he will recover."

Indeed, Ben did recover. On Aug. 22, 1922, he filled out his Naturalization Petition, again using his Yiddish name Bayril. By then the family was living at 130 Superior Street in Detroit. The records provides the birthdates of the three children who were all born in Canada: Esther (Nov. 16, 1912), David (April 15, 1914), and Jack (Jan. 20, 1916). One of the witnesses on Ben's Petition was his sister-in-law, Agnes (Cohen) Moskovitch, wife of his brother Isaac (Frank Moss).

AUTO CRASHES INTO TRAIN

Ben Moskovitch Severely Injured Near St. Jacobs In Collision With Elmira Train.

In an endeavor to cross the tracks ahead of the train at the crossing about a half mile above St. Jacobs, on the road to Hawkesville, about 8 o'clock this morning, Ben Moskovitch, a Russian, of Detroit, drove his motor car into the Elmira train bound for Kitchener. The radiator of the car crashed into the engine and the machine was hurled out and when Moskovitch was picked up he was found to be suffering from severe head laceration.

The train was brought to a sudden stop and the crew went back to the scene. The injured man was carried into the train and a wire sent at once to Kitchener requesting the ambulance to meet the train at Waterloo. When the train pulled into Waterloo at about 8.30 o'clock, J. Philip Weber, jr., was waiting at the station to convey the victim of the accident to the K.-W. hospital. Dr. Livingston of Waterloo was waiting with the ambulance and administered every possible medical aid to the injured man while on the way to the hospital.

At the hospital it was found that the man had several serious cuts about the head. He had practically no bodily injuries. It is believed he will recover.

Figure 36 Ben Moskovitch Crashes
Waterloo Region Record, Nov. 20, 1920, page 1.

Benjamin and Nellie and family were still living in Detroit in the 1930 census at 6115 Hazlett Ave and sharing a home with one other family. Benjamin is 41 and working as a painter for a contractor. Nellie is 37, Esther, 17, David 15, and Jacob (Jack) 14.

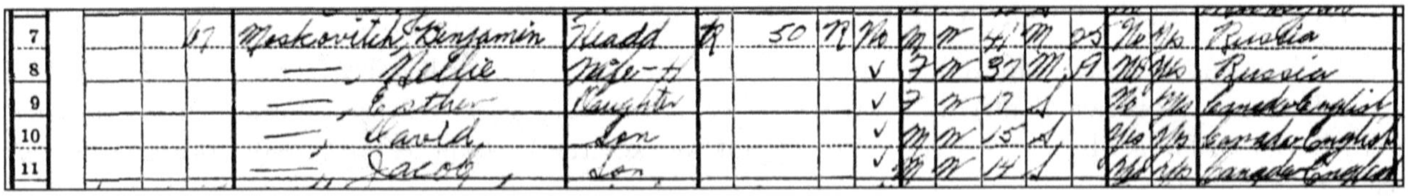

7	67	Moskovitch, Benjamin	Head	R	50	N	No	M	W	41	M	25	No	Yes	Russia
8		—, Nellie	Wife-H				✓	F	W	37	M	19	No	Yes	Russia
9		—, Esther	Daughter				✓	F	W	17	S		No	Yes	Canada English
10		—, David	Son				✓	M	W	15	S		Yes	Yes	Canada English
11		—, Jacob	Son				✓	M	W	14	S		Yes	Yes	Canada English

Figure 37 1930 Census for Ben and Family

By the 1940 census, Ben and Nellie moved to 3735 Glynn Court where they shared a home with another family. By this point, their daughter Esther (1912–1985) has married and her husband Sydney Micon and their 7-year-old daughter Lorraine (married name Shiffman) (1933–2020) are part of the household.

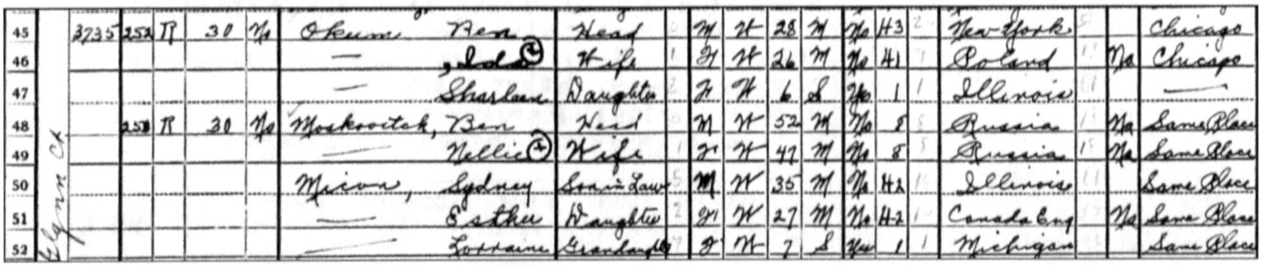

45	Glynn Ct	3735	252	R	30	No	Okum, Ben	Head	M	W	28	M	No	H3	New York		Chicago
46							—, Ida ⓧ	Wife	F	W	26	M	No	4I	Poland	Na	Chicago
47							—, Sharlene	Daughter	F	W	6	S	Yes	1	Illinois		—
48			253	R	30	No	Moskovitch, Ben	Head	M	W	52	M	No	8	Russia	Na	Same Place
49							—, Nellie ⓧ	Wife	F	W	47	M	No	8	Russia	Na	Same Place
50							Micon, Sydney	Son-in-Law	M	W	35	M	No	H2	Illinois		Same Place
51							—, Esther	Daughter	F	W	27	M	No	H2	Canada Eng	Na	Same Place
52							—, Lorraine	Grandaughter	F	W	7	S	Yes	1	Michigan		Same Place

Figure 38 1940 Census for Benjamin, Nellie and family.

By 1940, Ben and Nellie's two sons were already married and living elsewhere, and both were using the surname "Moss." Their son, David "Moss" (1914–1995) was living with the family of his wife Beulah

(Korn) (1917–2002) with their newborn daughter Judith (married name Urdan) (1940–2010). David and Beulah go on to have three more children: Daniel, Robert and Shelly (married name Borsuk).

Ben and Nellie's third child, Jacob/Jack "Moss" (1916–1994), is married in the 1940 Detroit census to Esther (Wold) and they have one son, Jerry [Jerome], who is 1 year's old at the time. They subsequently have two additional children: Lawrence and Phillip.

By the 1950 census, Ben and Nellie are using the Moss surname as well. Ben passed away in 1971 and Nellie in 1972.

***

Isaac Moskovitch (aka Frank Moss) and Family

Isaac was calling himself "Frank" by at least 1916 soon after he arrived in Detroit. He was also apparently the first of the Detroit brothers apparently who started using "Moss" as a surname.

In the 1920 census, "Frank Muskovitz" is 22 and living at 195 Canfield Ave where he and his family have been since at least 1919. His wife, Agnes, is 21 and they have a son Joseph (referred to as Martin J. in later records) who is two years old and was born January 4, 1918. Frank is described as a laborer in "Ford's" [plant].

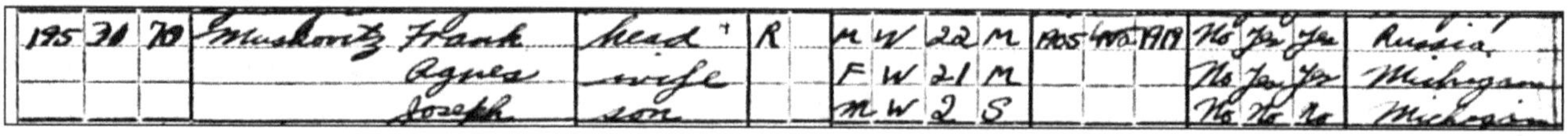

Figure 39 1920 Census of Frank (Isaac) "Muskovitz"

Through most of the 1920s, Frank and Agnes lived in Detroit. Frank is described as a "machinist" in the City Directory, living at 988 Farnsworth (Agnes's address too when she signed as a witness on her brother-in-law's Petition). They were at that address in 1921 when their second child was stillborn. On the death certificate, the child is simply called Baby Moskovitch.

A second daughter, Mildred, was born in 1924. In 1925, Frank is listed as a machinist at 8328 12th Ave. That year his father Hyman is listed in the City Directory as a "Huckster" and is living at 1004 Farnsworth as is Frank's brother Harry. In 1927, Frank Moskovitz appears at 8435 12th Ave working at Renier Garage.

1922 Detroit City Directory

Moskovitz Abr slsmn Moss Furniture Co h615 Hancock av e
" Frank mach h988 Farnsworth av
" Geo plmbr r623 Hancock av e

1925 Detroit City Directory

Moskowitch David meats r526 Mt Vernon av
" Saml barber h618 Hendrie av
Moskovitch Benj poultry h388 Belmont av
" Frank mach h8328 12th
" Harry r1004 Farnsworth av
" Hyman huckster h1004 Farnsworth av

1927 Detroit City Directory

" Florence sten r260 Rosedale ct
" Frank (Agnes; Renier Garage) h8435 12th apt 2
" Geo (Fannie) plmbr h12027 Broadstreet av

By the 1930 census, Frank and family have moved to Ypsilanti, Michigan and are living next to the family of his brother, Israel. Frank has adopted the "Moss" surname, though his brother is still listed as

"Moskovitch" in that census. In the Baltimore branches of the family, the "Moss" variation begins showing up in about 1923, as we shall see.

91	512	60	67	Moskovitch,	Israel	Head	O	15000		No	O	W	39	m	26	No	Yes	Roumania	Roumania
92				—	Annie	Wife-H				v	F	W	39	m	26	No	Yes	Russia	Russia
93				—	Sonia	Daughter				v	F	W	6	S		Yes		Michigan	Roumania
94			672	Moss,	Frank	Head	O	6000		No	M	W	32	m		No	Yes	Roumania	Roumania
95				—	Agnes	Wife-H				v	F	W	31	m		No	Yes	Michigan	Russia
96				—	Martin	Son				v	M	W	12	S		Yes	Yes	Michigan	Roumania
97				—	Mildred	Daughter				v	F	W	6	S		Yes		Michigan	Roumania

Figure 40 1930 Census for Frank Moss and his brother Israel Moskovitch

Ypsilanti is 35 miles West of Detroit and 14 miles from Ann Arbor. In 1829, the town was named Ypsilanti after Demetrios Ypsilantis, a hero in the Greek War of Independence. In the 1920s, the town played an important role in the automobile industry. From 1920 to 1922, Apex Motors produced the "ACE" car there.

In the census, both families were living at 512 S. Washington Street, and they owned the home which they shared. The brothers were both working in "BottleWorks"—it may have been the business that brought them to Ypsilanti. In the record, Israel is 39 and Frank 32. Both brothers wrote that they were born in "Roumania," which was unified with Bessarabia in 1918. Israel is listed as a manager in BottleWorks (more on this business below). His wife, Annie, is 39 and their daughter, Sonia, is 6. Frank is listed as a proprietor in "BottlingWork." His wife Agnes is 26, his son, Martin (called Joseph in 1920), is 12 and his daughter Mildred 6.

The 1940 census indicates that Frank and the family moved back to Detroit and were at that address by 1935. The record indicates they are living at 1956 Pingree St., not far from the house that became famous as home to Motown. Frank is now listed as a truck driver.

36	1956	455	R	45	Moss,	Frank	8	Head	0	M	W	43	M	No	8		Russia		Na	Same Place
37					—	Agnes		Wife	1	F	W	42	M	No	6		Michigan			Same Place
38					—	Martin		Son	2	M	W	22	S	No	H4		Michigan			Same Place
39					—	Mildred		Daughter		F	W	15	S		H1		Michigan			Same Place

Figure 41 1940 Census for Frank (Isaac) Moss

Frank and Agnes's son, Martin (1918-2011) married Rosaline Craine in 1947. They had a daughter Marlene (married name Fogelman). Frank and Agnes's daughter Mildred (1924-2021) married Sidney Brodie in 1943. (This is the same Mildred Brodie who was an informant in the book *Annie's Ghost*). They had two daughters, Caryn (married name Jaeger) and Laurie (married name Green). Caryn's husband, now deceased, was the family historian who documented the Detroit branch of the family. Agnes passed away in 1963 and Frank passed away in 1983.

***

Israel Moskovitch and the Ypsilanti Bottling Company

Israel, like his brother, Frank, ended up in Ypsilanti by the 1930 census. Although Israel's 1920 census has not been located at the time of this writing, it is clear that in 1919 he was still living in Detroit, as evident by a border crossing record showing his return from Canada to Detroit. The record is dated June 24, 1919. "Isreal" Moskovitch, age 30, a poultry dealer, is on his way back to Detroit. His wife Annie is still back in Kitchener (the new name for Berlin). His destination is his "Home 56 Benton Street," the address also of his brother Samuel in 1919 and 1920.

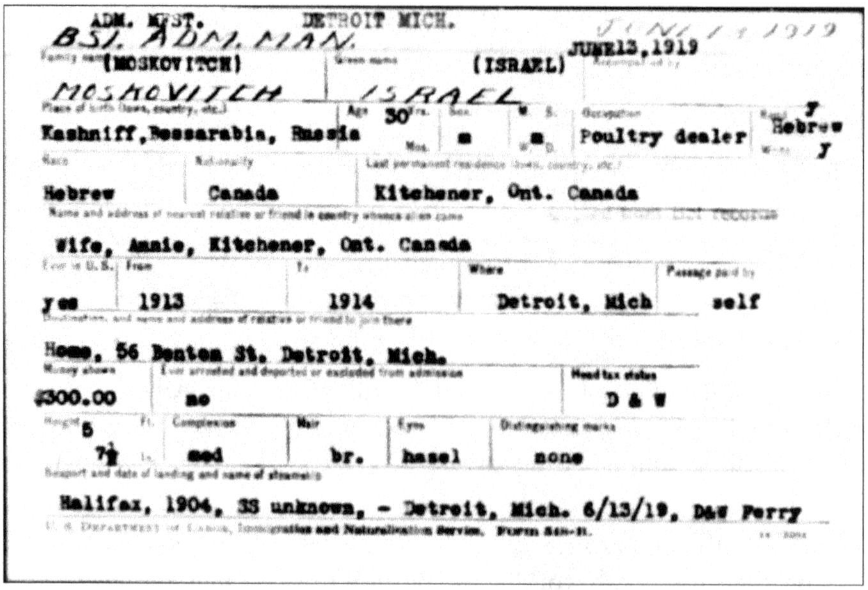
ADM. MYST. DETROIT MICH.
B51. ADM. MAN. JUNE 13, 1919
(MOSKOVITCH) (ISRAEL) JUNE13,1919
MOSKOVITCH ISRAEL
Place of birth (town, country, etc.) Age 30 yrs. Sex m S. Occupation Poultry dealer Hebrew
Kashniff, Bessarabia, Russia
Race Hebrew Nationality Canada Last permanent residence (town, country, etc.) Kitchener, Ont. Canada
Name and address of nearest relative or friend in country whence alien came
Wife, Annie, Kitchener, Ont. Canada
Ever in U.S. yes From 1913 To 1914 Where Detroit, Mich Passage paid by self
Destination, and name and address of relative or friend to join there
Home, 56 Benton St. Detroit, Mich.
Money shown $300.00 Ever arrested and deported or excluded from admission no Head tax status D & W
Height 5 ft. 7½ in. Complexion med Hair br. Eyes hazel Distinguishing marks none
Seaport and date of landing and name of steamship
Halifax, 1904, SS unknown, - Detroit, Mich. 6/13/19, D&W Perry
U. S. Department of Labor, Immigration and Naturalization Service. Form 548-H.

Figure 42 June 1919 border crossing record for Israel Moskovitch

Israel declared his intention to become a citizen on Oct. 24, 1924, but the form did not ask for his address. According to his later Naturalization Petition from 1929, they moved to Ypsilanti by 1925. The first record located that reflects their new address is from 1926. The record captures Israel and Annie attempt to go back to Kitchener on Jan. 31, 1926. The record is interesting for several reasons.

Israel, Annie, and a business colleague named Ben Hoffman show up on a border crossing record trying to cross from Detroit into Windsor to visit Annie's mother. We know that the man named Ben, age 32, is a business partner because Israel and Ben both list their occupation as involved in Bottling in the right-hand columns. Israel's record indicates that he had been in Kitchener (the new name for Berlin) from 1906–1919, perhaps because he had been traveling back and forth all that time. Annie's record indicates she had been in Windsor from 1909 to 1916. They appear to be fudging the dates of their entrance to Detroit.

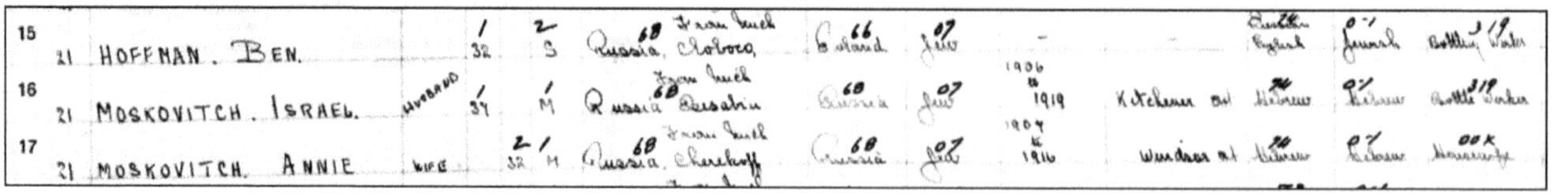
15 21 HOFFMAN. BEN.
16 21 MOSKOVITCH. ISRAEL. Husband
17 21 MOSKOVITCH. ANNIE Wife

Figure 43 1926 Israel and Annie's Attempted Border Crossing to Canada

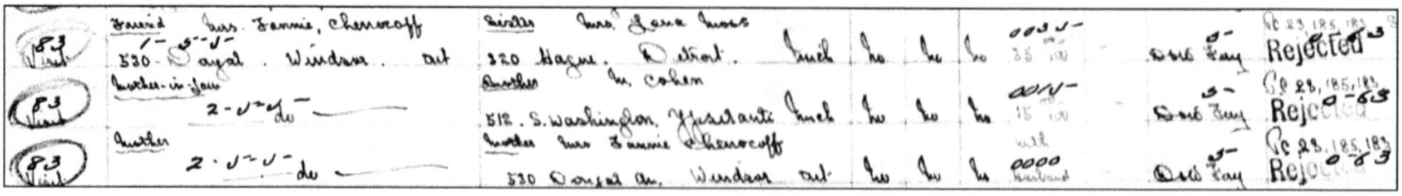

Right-hand columns specifying current address in Ypsilanti and their destination

The border crossing record indicates their destination is Israel's brother-in-law (Annie's brother) at 2-5-5[?] "do" meaning "ditto," the same address to which their business partner Ben was going. He was headed to 530 Dougal Street in Windsor to see his "friend" Fannie Chernocoff, i.e., Annie's mother.

Annie's parents in fact were still living at 530 Dougal still in the 1931 Canadian census. However, it seems implausible that Fannie Chernocoff was a friend of Israel's business associate Ben Hoffman. Perhaps this was one reason their admission to Canada was "rejected" as can be seen on the right side of the record. The record indicates they could make no appeal.

For current address, Ben Hoffman writes that he is living with his "sister Mrs. Lena Moss, at 320 Hague" in Detroit. Despite the name, Lena Moss was not a relative of the Moskovitch family nor married to one.[9] She was born Lena Hoffman. She married Jacob Moss, whose parents were Nathan and Fannie Moss, and who apparently were originally from the Lithuanian area of Russia. In any case, Ben Hoffman, does show up in 1928 in the City Directory at the same address as Israel and working for the Ypsilanti Bottling Co. He was clearly a business partner living for a time with Israel and involved in the bottling operation.

For his current address and closest relative in this record, Israel listed his "brother, M. Cohen, 512 S. Washington, Ypsilanti Michigan." The address is the one Israel and Annie appear at in the 1930 census with his brother Frank Moss (see page 45). As noted earlier, Israel indicated on his Petition that he moved to Ypsilanti in 1925, though it is not clear in this border crossing record who he means by "brother M. Cohen." I suspect M. Cohen is the brother-in-law of his wife Annie, a man named Mores Cohen, who married her sister Bertha, though no record of them in Ypsilanti has turned up to date.

It seems odd that Annie gave a different current address than her husband Israel. She listed her address and closest relative, as her mother Mrs. Fannie Chernocoff in Windsor, as if she was still living there. Perhaps the inconsistency in their story was also responsible for them being "Rejected" and having "no appeal" as the record makes plain in the right-hand columns.

In any case, records make clear that Israel is living in Ypsilanti by 1926 at 512 S. Washington. They appear at the same address in the Ypsilanti City Directory of 1928 and, as we have seen already, in the 1930 census living with Israel's brother, Frank Moss. The 1928 directory implies that the name of the business was Ypsilanti Bottling Works. Although Israel appears in the 1930 census as Israel Moskovitch, he also shows up with the surname Moss that same year in the city directory.

1928 *Ypsilanti City Directory*	**YPSILANTI CITY DIRECTORY (1928)** **153** **Moskovitch Israel (Anna; Ypsilanti Bottling Works h512 S Washington**
1930 *Ypsilanti City Directory*	**Moss Frank I (Agnes; Ypsilanti Bottling Wks) h512 S Washington** **Moss Israel (Anna L; Ypsilanti Bottling Wks) h512 S Washington**

Israel filled out his Naturalization Petition in 1929. That record includes an amendment which indicates he was living in Ypsilanti continuously since Sept. 30, 1925. His typed name and signature are spelled "Isreal" with the "e" before the "a." This is the same way his name appeared in his 1919 border crossing record and 1950 census, though it appears the normal way "Israel" in his 1930 census and city directories. This could just be an artefact of officials not knowing how to spell "Israel" rather than Israel's own inconsistency.

---

[9] Lena Moss was born Lena Hoffman. She married Jacob Moss whose parents were Nathan and Fanny Moss and who are not related to our Moskovitch family and appear to be from Lithuania.

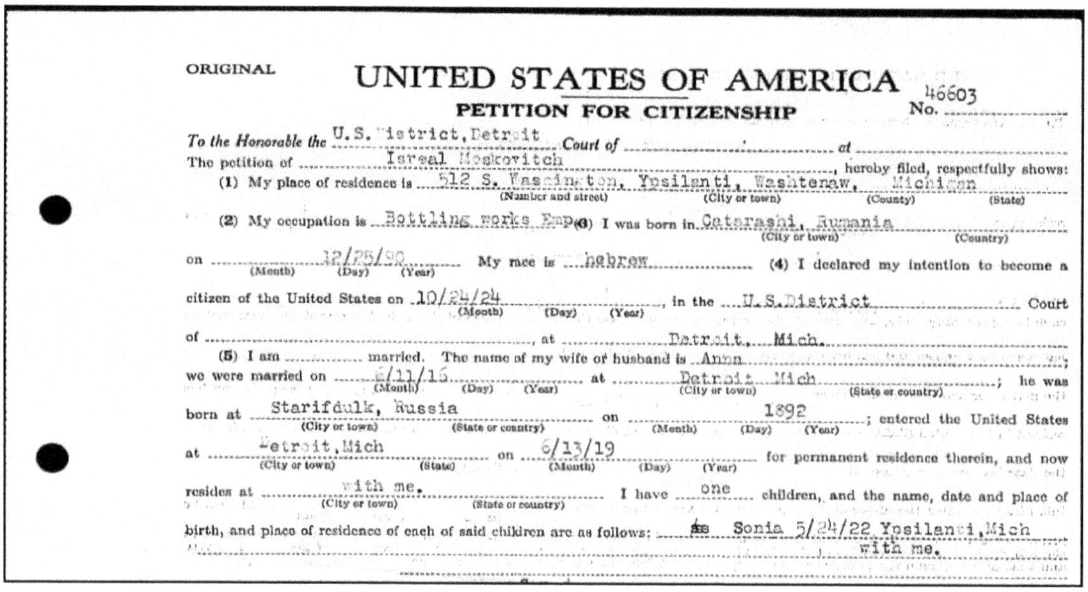

Figure 44 Naturalization Petition of Isreal Moskovitch

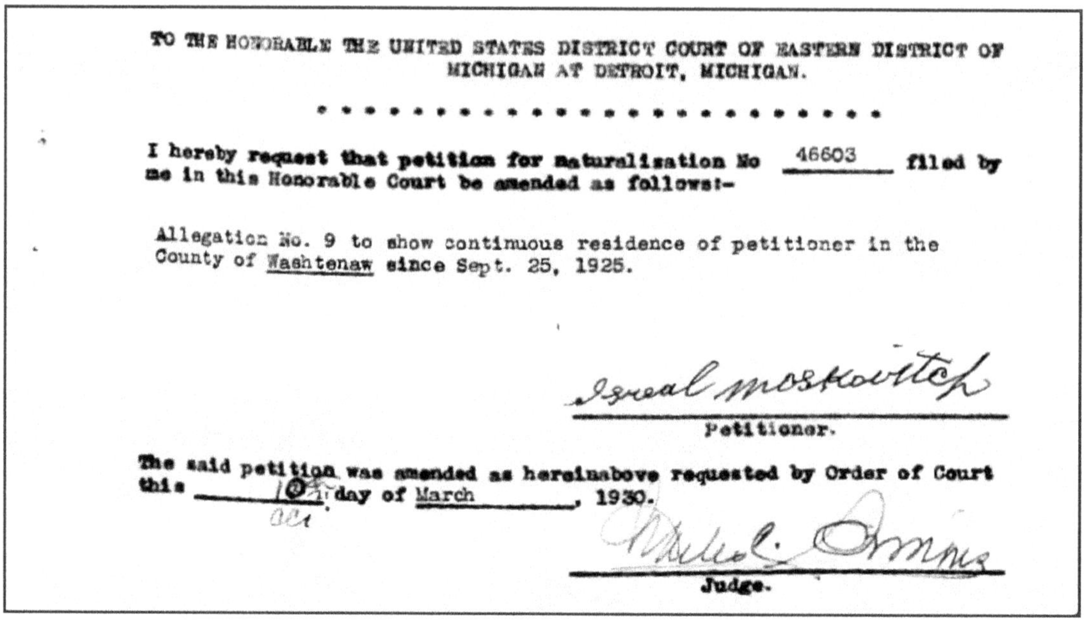

In his Petition, Israel lists his birthplace as Catarashi Rumania [Kalarash, Russia when he was born] and his birthdate as Dec. 25, 1890. The birthdate of their daughter, Sonia, is listed as May 24, 1922.[10] On subsequent pages, Israel renounced his citizenship to Great Britain as part of taking his oath on March 10, 1930, his British citizenship probably conferred as part of his earlier Canadian naturalization.

Israel and Annie's daughter, Faye, who is in her 90s as this narrative is being written, filled in some details about life in Ypsilanti when she was a young girl. She explained to me by phone that her father and "uncle Frank" were living in separate units above the Ypsilanti Bottling company. The company would bottle sodas and other drinks. At some point, they also had an orchard on their property that they leveraged for cider as well. Eventually, her father Israel got into distribution of drinks as well.

---

[10] Though Israel wrote Ypsilanti, Mich, next to Sonia's name, the intent appears to be referring to her current address, not where she was born.

In the 1940 census, "Israel and Annie Moss" are still living at 512 S. Washington in Ypsilanti. They did not head back as quickly to Detroit like Israel's brother, Frank. In the record, their daughter Sonia is 16 and their second daughter Fannie (Faye) is 9. Israel's occupation is described as a "wholesale manager" in a wholesale beverage business.

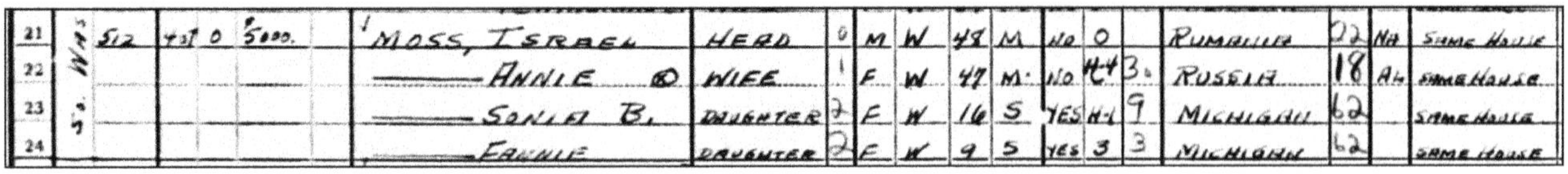

21	512	4??	0	5000	MOSS, ISRAEL	HEAD	0	M	W	48	M	NO	0	RUMANIA	22	NA	SAME HOUSE
22					——— ANNIE	WIFE	1	F	W	47	M	NO	H 4	3	RUSSIA	18	AL	SAME HOUSE
23					——— SONIA B.	DAUGHTER	2	F	W	16	S	YES	H 4	9	MICHIGAN	62		SAME HOUSE
24					——— FANNIE	DAUGHTER	2	F	W	9	S	YES	3	3	MICHIGAN	62		SAME HOUSE

Figure 45 1940 census for Israel and Annie Moss

By the 1950 census, the family is back in Detroit. Their daughter Faye recalls that Ypsilanti was small, and they may have been the only Jewish family in town, or at least one of the few. When she and her sister got older, her parents wanted to give them more exposure, so they moved back to Detroit.

In the 1950 census, Israel and Anna's daughter, Sonia, is married. She and her husband Nathan Tenenbaum are living above her parents at 3825 Tyler St. in Detroit. Israel is still a proprietor in a bottling company and Nathan is a jewelry salesman.

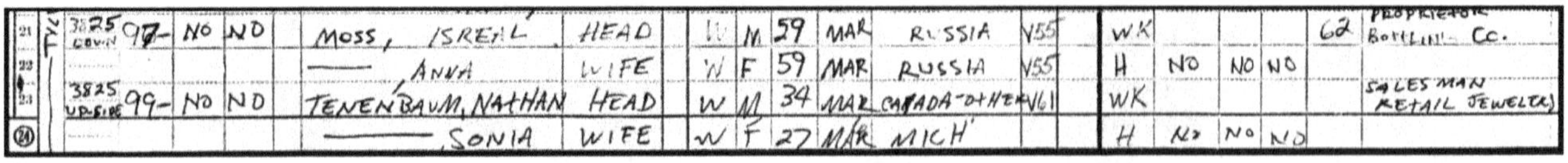

21	3825	97-	NO	ND	MOSS, ISREAL	HEAD	W	M	59	MAR	RUSSIA	Y55	WK			62	PROPRIETOR BOTTLING CO.
22					——— ANNA	WIFE	W	F	59	MAR	RUSSIA	Y55	H	NO	NO	NO	
23	3825 UPSIDE	99-	NO	ND	TENENBAUM, NATHAN	HEAD	W	M	34	MAR	CANADA-OTHER	V61	WK				SALESMAN RETAIL JEWELRY
24					——— SONIA	WIFE	W	F	27	MAR	MICH		H	NO	NO	NO	

Figure 46 1950 Census for "Isreal" and Anna Moss

A 1947 Central high school yearbook shows their daughter Fay Moss (right) in the same row with her first cousin Herman Moskovitch (youngest son of Samuel).

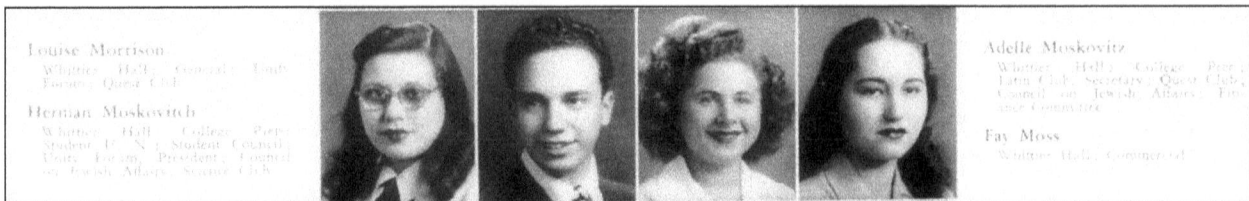

Photo 11 High school photo of Fay Moss (right)

Fay married Freddie Sweet in 1949 and in the 1950 census they are living close to her folks at 3816 Tyler Street. They subsequently had two children, Mark and Lisa (married name Tobis). Fay subsequently married Marvin Kreske. Fay and her sister Sonia are both alive in their 90s as I document this story.

Israel, passed away in 1978. His wife Annie passed away in 1983.

***

Records for Hyman Moskovitch and Family

This is a summary of records unambiguously identified for the family of Hyman and Lena Moskovitch and their sons: Sam, Benjamin, Israel, Harry, Isaac (Frank Moss).

1911 Census Berlin, Ontario	**Himan Moskovitch**, [address] 30 Stahl, [birthdate] June 1863 [age] 47 [Country / place of birth] Russia [year of immigration to Canada] 1907, [year naturalized] 1910, [Racial or tribal origin] Russian, [Nationality] Canadian, [Religion] Jewish, [Chief occupation] laborer, [works at] buildings; **Lena**, wife, birthdate: July 1868, Russia, [year of immigration] 1907, NA[turalized]; **Sam**, birthdate: August 1886, age 24, immigration: 1906, naturalization: 1911, occupation: shoemaker; **Israel**, birthdate: Dec 1890, age 20, immigration 190?, naturalized 1911, occupation: shoemaker; **Harry** birthdate: Aug 1895, age 18, immigration: 1906, NA[turalized] occupation: none; **Isaac** birthdate: June 1896, age 14, immigration 1906, NA[turalized], occupation: machinist, foundry; Barnhurst? [**Benjamin**, Berel] birthdate: Dec 1887, age 23, immigration 1906, naturalized 1910, occupation: Finisher, industry Factory
Aug. 9, 1913 (signed) Marriage Record	Bridegroom **Samuel M. Moscowitz** (also appears as Samuel Morris Moshkovitch), age 27 [implied birth year 1886], 30 Stahl Av. Berlin, Place of birth: Russia, occupation shoemaker, Religion Hebrew, Name of father Hyman Muscowitz, name of Mother Leah Muscovitz; Bride **Vieta Levitin**, age 21, 156 Church St. Berlin Place of birth: Russia, Religious denomination: Hebrew, name of Father Joseph Levitin, Maiden Name of Mother: Mariam Levitin. Signature of bridegroom: Samuel signed in Hebrew. Stamped received Aug 25, 1914
June 9, 1914 Birth Records County of Waterloo / Division of Berlin	For **Joseph Moskovitch** [son of Samuel and Vita Moskovitch]. Surname: Moskovitch, Christian name: Joseph, Date of birth June 9/14, Address 124 King St. E, Are parents married? Yes, Where and when married: Berlin, Aug. 16, 1913, name of Father: Samuel Moshkovitch, Address 124 King St. E., Occupation: Shoe worker, Maiden name of mother: Veta Levittn
Oct. 24, 1914 Passenger List	For **Hyman Moskovitz/Moskowitch**, age 49, merchant, last residence Berlin [Ontario] closest relative: wife, Leah Moskowitz 122 King St E. Berlin Ont[ario], destination daughter Mrs M. Panish [i.e., Panick] 283 Rowena St, Detroit Mich[igan], Kishev [Kishinev], arrived in D&W Quebec Aug 1904 name of SS: unknown
Oct. 26, 1914 Primary Inspection Memorandum [Immigration / Shipping record]	**Lena Moskovitch** age 48, occupation: none, nationality Can[adian] Race: Heb, Last residence: Berlin, name and address of nearest relative: Samuel 122 King St. East, Berlin Can[ada], Destination: Detroit Michigan, who paid passage husb[and] Ever in the US? Y[es], Where?: Portland Me, Date of last departure from US: Jan. 1904; Going to whom? Relative: husband Herman Moskovitch 283 Rowena, Detroit Mich[igan]
Oct. 26, 1914 Primary Inspection Memorandum [Immigration record]	**Isaac Muskovitch** (aka Frank Moss), age 18 [implied birth year 1896], Occupation: Machinist, nationality: Russia, Race: Hebrew, Last permanent residence: Berlin Can, Name and address of nearest relative: Samuel 122 King St. East, friend in country whence alien came (?) bro, Berlin Can., Destination: Detroit Mich, amount of money $25, ever in US? Where [date scratched] Portland, Me, 3 mo 1914, Detroit, date of last departure from US Oct. 2, 1914, Going to join whom? Relative: ftr [father], Name

	Herman Moskovitch 283 (Russia? St. Detroit Mich, Landing: port Portland Me, Date: June 1904, Steamship: (illegible) 4-5 letters
Oct. 26, 1914 Border Crossing Card Primary Inspection Memorandum	**Lena Moskovitch** (aka Leah Hyman's wife) traveling **with Isaac (her son)** age 48, Occupation: none, nationality: Cana[da], Race: Hebrew, Last permanent residence: (?) Berlin Can[ada], Name and address of nearest relative: [son] Samuel 122 King St. East, friend in country whence alien came (?) Samuel, Berlin Can. Destination: Detroit Mich, amount of money $25, ever in US? Yes, where Portland Me, date of last departure from US Jan. 1904, Going to join whom? husband, Name Herman or Himan (=Hyman) Moskovitch 283 Rowena, St. Detroit, Landing Port: Portland Me, Date: Jan. 1904 Steamship: (illegible) 4–5 letters
Nov. 24, 1914 US Border Crossing / Manifest	For **Lena Moskovitch**, arriving in Port Huron, Michigan. **Lena Moskovitch** age 48 [implied birth year 1865], Hebrew, Berlin, destination Son, Samuel 122 King East Berlin Can, page 2, date of last departure from US: Jan. 1904; destination headed to Husb[and] Himan 283 Rowena, Detroit, place of birth Kashinow [Kishinev?] Russia, seaport of landing: Portland [Me], Jan. 1904, name of vessel [illegible]
Nov. 23 1914, Arriving Passengers, Port Huron Michigan Primary Inspection Memorandum	**Benj[amin] Moskovitch**, occupation wood finisher, age 26 [implied birth year of 1888] nationality Can., Race Hebrew, last permanent residence, Berlin Can, name and address of nearest relative Nelli 122 King St, wife, Berlin Can, destination Detroit Mich, [page 2]: who paid? self, Ever in US? No, going to join Relative Uncle Max Panek 283 Rowena St. Ontario Michigan, Landing: Port Quebec, date Apl 24 1899, Steamship Canada place of birth Kischineff
Mar. 29, 1915 Immigration card [Copied from BSI records]	**Harry Moskovitch**, accompanied by: Brother-**Isaac**, Place of birth: Odessa, Russia, Age 19 [implied birth year 1895/96], Occupation: none, Race Hebrew, Nationality Canada, Last Permanent Residence Berlin, Ont., Can[ada], Name and address of nearest relative or friend in last residence: Samuel Moskovitch, 124 King St. E., Berlin, Ont. Can., Ever in US?-yes, From: in transit, To: 1905, Where Portland, Me. Destination: Detroit, Mich., Father-Hyman Moskovitch, 117 Benton St. Ever arrested: no..., Height 5' 0" red hair, gray eyes, Seaport and date and name of steamship, Portland, Me. 1905 SS unknown, Detroit, Mich., OT (?)
Mar. 29, 1915 Immigration card [Primary Inspection Memorandum]	**Isaac Moskovitch**, accompanied by brother Harry, Place of birth Odessa, Russia, age 17 [implied birth year 1897-98], machinist, can read, Race: Hebrew, Nationality: Canada, last residence, Detroit, Mich. name and address of relative from when alien came: Brother-Samuel Moskovitch, 124 King St. E, Berling, Ont., Can, Ever in the US? yes, from 1914 to 3/26/15 Detroit underneath it is written in transit 1905 Portland, Me. Paid by self, destination: Detroit, Mich, Father-Hyman Moskovitch, 117 Benton St. height 5' 6" hair br. eyes br., Seaport and date of landing: Portland, Me., 1905 SS unknown, Detroit, Mich. OT?
Apr. 24, 1915, Border Crossing List, Port of Detroit	For brothers Harry and Isaac. **Moskovitch, Harry,** "Debarred" Appealed 4/2/15 Dismissed 4/8/15 File 11004/1633, age 19 [implied birthyear 1895/96], last residence Berlin Ont. closest relative there, Brother Samuel Moskovitch 124 King St. E Berlin Ont, [page 2] Harry is listed as LPC [Likely Public Charge], passage paid by brother, ever in US before if so where? 1905 trans[it], Portland Me, year 1905, destination Father Hyman Moskovitch 117 Benton Ave. Detroit Michigan, birthplace Odessa, date of land 1905, seaport of landing Portland [Me] name of ship [illegible but maybe] Michigan; [listed next to brother]

	Isaac Moskovitch [Frank Moss], age 17 [implied birth year 1897-98], machinist, last residence USA Detroit, same as above, paid for self, ever in US before if so where? trans[it] 1905 6 months, Portland [Me], and 1914–15 Detroit, March 26, 1915, headed to same address and same landing date and ship
May 25, 1915 Immigration card Copied from BSI records	For **Harry Moskovitch**, Place of birth: Odessa, Russia, age 19 [implied birth year 1895/96], Race: Hebrew, Nationality: Canada, Last permanent residence: Berlin, Ont., Can., Name and address of nearest relative: Brother, Samuel Moskovitch, 124 King St. E., Berlin, Ont., Can. Ever in the US: from: in transit, To: 1905, Where Portland, Me. Passage paid by: father. Destination: Father, Hyman Moskovitch 117 Benton St., Detroit, Mich., height, 5", 0", complexion: fair, Hair: red, Eyes: gray, Seaport and date of landing and name of steamship: Portland, Me., 1905-ex SS unknown-Detroit Mich. D&W Ferry [Detroit and Windsor] [page 2] Debarred - L.P.C.- Appealed, (excluded, Mar. 29, 1915-L.P.C) Med. Cert: Paralagia of lower extremities and ulpas side of hands and arms, defects of speech, physically defective, talipses equina varus (club foot) affecting earning ability.
June 24, 1915 Border Crossing	Isaac and Harry crossing again. Information similar to their April record above.
Nov. 16, 1916 Immigration Card Copied from BSI Records	**Beryl (Ben) Moskovitch**, accompanied by 3 children & Wife, Nellie, place of birth Kolarasz, Bessarabia, age 28 [implied birth year 1887-88], painter and Decorator, Race Hebrew, Nationality Canada, Last permanent residence Windsor, Ont. Can. Name and address of relative or friend in country when alien came? None, Ever in the US? Yes, from 1908 to Dec. 1909, Where Baltimore, Ohio, paid for by self, Destination Detroit, Mich., Rented House, 220 Benton. Money $250, 5'5" hair li. br. eyes br. Distinguishing marks None, Seaport and date of landing and name of steamship: Quebec, 1901, SS Canada; Detroit, Mich., D&W Ferry
Jan. 12, 1916 Immigration Record Copied from BSI Records	**Israel Muskovitch,** Accompanied by: -, Place of Birth: Speishinof [Kishinev], Bassarabia, Russia, Age: 26, Occupation: poultry, Race Hebrew, Nationality: Russia, Last Permanent Residence: Windsor, Ont., Canada. Name and address of nearest relative or friend in country when alien came: Brother-[D?]aniel-Muskovitch, Windsor, Ont. Can., Ever in US?:yes, From 1912 to July 1915, Where: Baltimore, Md. / Detroit, Mich, Destination: Detroit, Michigan, Father Himan Muskovitch, 117 Benton St. Height 5" 7" complexion: dark, Hair dk br. Eyes: br. Distinguishing marks: none, Seaport and date and name of steamship: Halifax, N.S. [Nova Scotia], Can. Dec. 1906 SS Unknown; Dominican Line: Detroit, Mich., D&W [Detroit and Windsor] Ferry 1/11/16
Mar. 23, 1916 Immigration Record (Prim Exam Adm Copied from BSI records)	**Ben Moskovitch,** accompanied by wife-Nellie, Children-3, Place of birth Kisarnuf, Bassarabia, Russia, age 29 [implied birth year 1886-87] , painter, Race Hebrew, Nationality Canada, Last residence Windsor, Ont. Canada, Ever in US? yes from 1908-July-1909 where, Baltimore and New York, passage paid by self, Destination Detroit, Michigan, father, Hyman Moskovitch, 117 Bentora [Benton] St. Money $250, ever arrested or deported? no, 5'5", hair lt br, eyes green, distinguishing marks Thumb of right hand split, Seaport and date of landing and name of Steamship: Quebec, 8-24-02, SS Canada; Detroit 3-26-16 D&W Ferry
June 11, 1916 Marriage Record	**Israel Moskovitch,** [bridegroom], 26, Peddler, father Hyman, mother Lilian [Lena/Leah], place of marriage Detroit, [bride] Anna Chernokow, 26, father David, mother Jennie [see narrative for discussion of her parents' names]

Mar. 4, 1917 Michigan Marriage Register	Marriage certificate for Isaac Moskovitz and Agnes Cohen. **Isaac Moskovitz,** age 21 [implied birth year 1895-96], birthplace Russia, occupation Machinist, father's name Herman, mother's name Lena; Agnes Cohen, age 18, birthplace Mich, father's name: Louis, mother's name Fannie
June 5, 1917 WWI Draft Registration Card	**Ben Moskovitz,** age 30 [scratched out:] 178 Wilkins St. and instead 1315 and 176 Forady, date of birth March 23, 1887, status alien, born Kolorash-Russia-Jew Painter, employer Siever Hurtmans, family wife and children 3 -4 years, married, signed B Moskovitch
Sept. 12, 1918 WWI Draft Registration Card	**Samuel Moskovitch** 56 Benton St. Detroit Wayne Mich, age 33, birthdate Oct. 8, 1884, naturalization status: Non-declarant [i.e., has not started process], occupation Barber, Nearest Relative: Hyman Moskovitch (father) 176 Brady Detroit, Wayne Mich
June 24, 1919 Border Crossing from Canada to Port of Detroit	"Isreal" Moskovitch age 20 poultry dealer, wife Annie was back in Kitchener, Ontario. He has $300 in his possession. He is 5'7" hazel eyes brown eyes, birthplace Kshinef [Kishinev], Bessarabia, Russia, destination home 56 Benton Stret. He was in the US 1913-1914. His date of last departure from US was 1914.
Jan. 3, 1920 US Federal census	**Hyman Moskovitch,** Detroit Ward 3, 174 Brady Street, Head, age 55, Immigration year 1900, PA [naturalization pending] 1900, fruit peddler on the street; Leah, wife, age 52, 1900, Al[ien], Harry age 23 [implied birth year 1896] immigration year 100, Al[ien], occupation: none; Harry couzin, boarder, age 30.
Jan. 3, 1920 US Federal Census	**Samuel Muskovitch,** 56 Becton Street, Head, R[ents home], age 33 [implied birth year 1887], Year immigration [to Canada] 1911, PA[naturalization pending], birthplace Russia (Bessarabia scratched out), occupation: body assembly, Factoriy (auto); Dora, wife, age 27, Year immigrated 1909, Al[ien], birthplace Russia (something scratched out); Joseph, son, age 6, birthplace Canada; Jacob son, age 3, 1/12 birthplace Michigan; Solomon son, age 1 8/12, birthplace Michigan;
Jan. 3, 1920 US Federal census	**Barmud [Benjamin] Moskovitch,** 182 Rowena Street, Head, Renting home, age 32 [implied birth year 1887], immigration 1914 [from Canada to Detroit], Al[ien], birthplace Russia, occupation: fruit peddlar on street; Nellie, wife, age 27, immigration 1914, Al[ien], birthplace Russia, occupation: none; Esther, daughter, age 7, immigration 1914, Al[ien], birthplace: Canada, David, son, age 5, immigration 1914, Al[ien], birthplace: Canada; Jack, son 3 9/12, immigration 1914, Al[ien], birthplace: Canada;
Jan. 31, 1920 Declaration of Intention	**Bayril [Benjamin] Moskovitch,** age 32, merchant, 5'5" 145 lbs, hair brown, eyes Gray, born in Kalarash Russia on Feb. 25, 1887, now resides at 182 Rowena St Detroit, emigrated from Windsor on vessel Ferry former residence Canada, wife Nellie, born Russian, arrived at Detroit, Mich Nov. 20 1916, signed Jan. 31, 1920
Jan. 3, 1920 US Federal Census for Detroit	**Frank (Isaac) Muskovitz,** head, residence 195 Canfield Ave, Renting, age 22 [implied birth year 1897], year immigrated 1905, Na[turalized] Year naturalized 1919, birthplace Russia, occupation laborer, industry Ford's [auto], Agnes, wife, age 21, Year immigrated -, Naturalized -, Birthplace Michigan; Joseph son age 2, birthplace Michigan
Aug. 23, 1922 Naturalization Petition	**Bayril [Benjamin] Moskovitch,** residence 1308 Superior street, Detroit, occupation auto [illegible] Feb. 25th, 1887 Russia, emigrated to US from Windsor, Canada Nov. 16, 1916 on Ferry, declared intention to become citizen on March 31, 1920 at Detroit,

	Mich in ? Court of Wayne County, wife Nellie born Dec. 25, 1893 in Russia, 3 children: Esther born Nov. 16, 1912, in Canada, **David** born April 15, 1914 in Canada, **Joseph** born Jan. 20, 1916 in Canada, [document signed:] Aug. 23, 1922 witnesses Jacob Gobinpon [?] salesman and Agnes Moskovitch [his sister-in-law, Isaac's wife], housewife, 988 Farnsworth
June 10, 1925 Declaration of Intention	**Samuel Moskovitch**, age 39 (implied year of birthyear of 1885], occupation: barber, complexion: fair, height 5' 5", weight 160 pounds, hair color: brown, eyes color: hazel. born in Russia, on Oct. 8, 1886, resides now 658 Hendrie Street, Detroit, Emigrated to the US from Windsor, Canada on the ferry, last foreign residence was Canada, name of wife: Vitta, she was born in Russia, I arrived at the port of Detroit, Michigan on Feb. 18, 1916 [inconsistent with records]
Jan. 31, 1926 Border Crossing from US *to Canada*	**Israel Moskovitch** and wife Annie trying to go into Canada from the US. Entrance Rejected. Israel Moskovitch, age 34, birthplace Besaia [Bessarabia] Russia [someone wrote] "From Mich[igan", period in Canada previously- 1906 to 1919 in Kitchener, Ont[ario], occupation Bottle Worker, [purpose] visit, headed to mother-in-law, [address notation is not clear], nearest relative in US—brother M. Cohen 512 S. Washington, Ypsilanti, Mich; **Annie** age 32, birthplace Cherekoff Russia Russia [someone wrote] "From Mich[igan]", period in Canada previously–1904 to 1916, headed to mother [address notation is not clear], nearest relative in US–Mother Mrs Fannie Chernocoff 530 Dougat Av Windsor Ont. Rejected no Appeal
Oct. 24, 1924 Declaration of Intention	**Israel Moskovitch**, age 33, occupation merchant, 5" 8", born in Russia Rumania British Subject on Dec. 25, 1890 now reside at 211 Eliot st., Detroit, emigrated to US on Ferry, my last foreign residence wsa Rumania, wife Anna, born at Russia arrived at port of Detroit on June 13, 1919,
Feb. 9, 1928 Naturalization Petition	**Samuel Moskovitch**, address 648 Hendrie, Detroit, occupation Barber, born Oct. 8, 1886 at Kalarash, Russia. Emigrated to US from Windsor, Canada on Feb. 18, 1916 and arrived at Detroit, Michigan on Feb. 18, 1916 on Ferry, declared intention on May 10, 1925 in Detroit; wife **Vitta** born March 1892 in Dinyankie, Russia. children: **Joseph** born 6/9/14 in Canada, **Jack** 5/12/16 in Detroit, **Solomon** 4/12/18 in Detroit, **Natin** 2/21/20 in Detroit, **Norman** 12/30/23 in Detroit, **Herman** 3/25/29 in Detroit
Nov. 29, 1929 Naturalization Petition	**Isreal Moskovitch** 512 S. Washington, Ypsilanti, Washtenaw, Michigan, occupation Bottling works Emp, born in Catarashi, Rumania on Dec. 25, 1890, race Hebrew, declared intention on 10/24/24, wife Anna, married on 6/11/16 at Detroit Mich, she was born at Starifdulk, Russia on 1892, entered the US at Detroit, Mich on 6/13/19. One child: Sonia 5/24/22 Ypsilanti, Mich,
Jan. 31, 1926 Port of Windsor Border Crossings	**Israel Moskovitch**, husband 39 [implied birth year 1887], from Mich / Russia Besabia [Bessarabia], if in Canada before? 1906 to 1919, Kitchener [previously called Berlin], Ont, Bottle Worker, Visit, mother-in-law / mother M. Cohen / also written Fannie Chenocoff, 512 S. Washington, Ypsilanti, MIch, rejected No appeal Annie Moskovitch, wife, 32, from Mich[igan] Russia Cherekoff, if in Canada before 1904 to 1916, Windsor Ont

May 23, 1929 Petition for Naturalization	**Vita Moskovitch** [Samuel's wife] residence 648 Hendrie, Detroit, occupation: Housewife, born Feb. 1892 at Hemianka [Kishinev?][11] Russia, (Husband nat[turalized] in Canada], I emigrated to the US from Windsor, Canada, on Feb. 18, 1916 on the Ferry. husband Samuel, born on Oct. 8th, 1885, at Kalarash, Russia, children: Joseph born 6/9/14 in Canada, Jack 5/12/16 in Detroit, Solomon 4/12/18 in Detroit, Nathan 2/21/20 in Detroit, Norman 12/30/22 in Detroit, Herman 3/25/29 in Detroit, Husband nat. 5/14/28 at Detroit, Married 8/16/13
Apr. 12, 1930 US Federal Census Detroit	**Sam Moskowitch**, head, living at 646 Hendrie St., age 43, age first marriage age 27, Barber in Barbershop Vita, wife, 38, age at first marriage 21, Joseph, son, age 16, born in Canada, Jack son, age 13, born in Michigan, Solomon, son, age 12 born in Michigan, Nathan son, age 10 born in Michigan, Norman, son age 7 born in Michigan, Herman, son, age 1 born in Michigan, Marsha Levitt, grandma, 75, widowed born in Russia, Harry Moskewitch, brother in law [sic], age 35, born in Russia
Mar. 10, 1930 US Federal Census Ypsilanti	**Isreal Moskovitch**, 512 S. Washington, Ypsilanti, Washtenaw, Michigan, occupation Bottling works Emp, born in Catarashi, Rumania on 12/15/90, race is Hebrew, Declared intention on 10/24/24 in Detroit, wife is Anna, married on 6/11/16 in Detroit, she was born at Starifdulk, Russia on 1892, she entered the US at Detroit, Mich on 6/13/19, one child, Sonia born 5/24/22 in Ypsilanti, Michigan [resides] with me. Record shows he renounced British citizenship.
Jan. 10, 1934 Certificate of Death	**Harry Moskovitch**, 8932 Linwood Ave, single, age 38, trade:none birthplace Russia. Father Hyman Moskovitch, birthplace Russia, Mother maiden Name Lena Wal[illegible], birthplace Litvia, informant Sam Moskovitch, 3832 Linwood
Apr. 19, 1940 US Federal Census, Detroit	**Sam Moskovich**, head, age 53, Na[trualized' Proprietor, Retail Dept Store, Vita, age 49, Na[turalized], Sol, son, 22, apprentice in printer/Printing shop, Nathan, son, 20, laundry worker in laundry, Norman son, 17, Herman son, 4.
1942 WWII Draft Registration Card	**Isreal [Israel] Moss** 512 So Washington - Ypsilanti-Washtenaw-Mich age 51, date of birth 10/10/1891, place of birth Besarey [Bessarabia] Russia
Mar. 29, 1949 Divorce Decree	**Samuel and Vita Moskovitch**. Wayne Michigan. Divorce Granted. No further details
Oct. 2, 1950	**Samuel Moskovitch**, marital status, divorced, birthdate Oct. 8, 1885, deathplace Eloise, Wayne, Michigan, USA, father Chaim Moskovitch, Leah Tsivia Wolpinsky

---

[11] Perhaps a Yiddish pronunciation and/or transliteration of Kishinev.

***

3.

FAMILY OF AARON MOSHKEVICH AND SOPHIE (NAUSECHA)

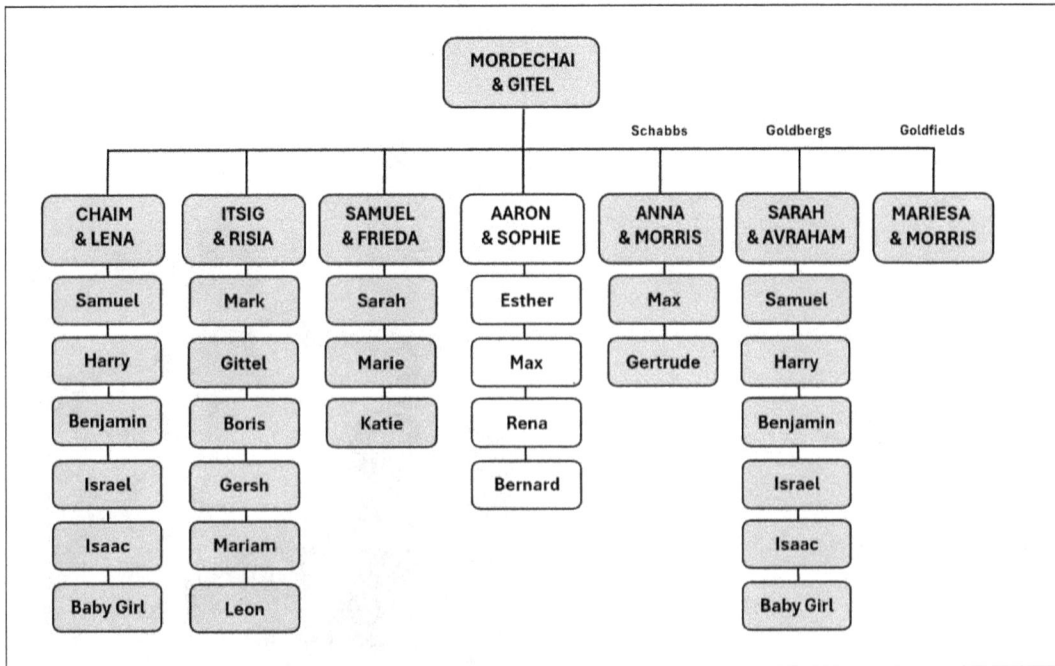

Figure 47 Family of Aaron Moskevich and Sophie (Nausecha)

***

Arriving in Baltimore

Aaron Moshkevich and his wife Sophie were the first of the Moskovitch siblings to arrive in Baltimore. As discussed earlier, Aaron was the fourth in the birth order of the "Moskovitch Seven." We can speculate that Aaron left Russia before most of his siblings because he and his wife Sophie were less encumbered. Their first child Esther, who was born in 1900, died in 1903. A photo of Aaron and Sophie in Ekaterinoslav with Esther was taken during this time (see Photo 12 below). The young woman holding the toddler was Aaron's younger sister Mariesa. Perhaps they embraced the opportunity to leave Russia and their sadness behind.

Aaron and Sophie may have had other motivations to leave as well. There were signs on the horizon of possible new violence that might arise in the wake of the Kishinev pogrom of April 1903, which shocked the Russian Jewish population and helped erode hope about achieving civic equality.[1] An academic writing about the violence in Ekaterinoslav in1905 noted that the signs were present earlier:

> By 1905, both middle-and working-class Jews in Ekaterinoslav were well warned of impending trouble. In 1883 the city had been the site of one of the pogroms following Alexander II's assassination. More recently, anti-Jewish violence had begun to rise anew following the Kishinev pogrom of April 1903. The Kishinev events sent waves of fear throughout the Pale of Settlement and produced responses of both flight and fight. The politics of Zionism suddenly made sense to more people, as the election of Rabbi Levin indicated, but so did the politics of revolution. The growth of Zionism and socialism marked a heightened self-awareness among all strata of Jews in Ekaterinoslav as elsewhere in the Pale. By 1905 Paole-Zion and other Jewish radicals had organized armed self-defense groups in the city, sometimes funded by anxious and well-off members of the Jewish community...[2]

Photo 12 Aaron, Sophie (right) and baby Esther in Ekaterinoslav ˜ 1900–1903.

The woman holding the baby is Aaron's youngest sister Mariesa. Courtesy of David Chapin.

According to their passenger manifest, "Aron Moschkewitch" and his wife "Sore" (Nausecha) left Bremen on the SS Main on January 29, 1904. They arrived in New York on Valentine's Day, February 14th. The record indicates that Aron was 34 years old, "md" [married], and an optician.

---

[1] See Gerald Surh, "Ekaterinoslav City in 1905: Workers, Jews, and Violence." *International Labor and Working-Class History*, No. 64. (Fall, 2003), pp. 139-166. See especially p. 143. https://www.jstor.org/stable/27672887. There were forty-three pogroms in Russia m 1904 and fifty-four in 1905 prior to October. See Shlomo Lambroza, "The Pogroms of 1903-1906," *Pogroms: Anti-Jewish Violence in Modern Russian History*, ed. John D Klier & Shlomo Lambroza (Cambridge, UK, 1992), pp. 213, 223.

[2] Surh, "Ekaterinoslav City in 1905," pp. 139-66.

Photo 13 Aaron Moshkevich as a young man in military uniform
First photo ca. 1886; Second photo ca. 1895, the uniform indicates he was a Dragoon officer.
Courtesy of David Chapin.

The journey that Aaron and Sophie made to Bremen was impressive. On contemporary maps the distance is 1400 miles and would take 27 hours of driving today. We can assume that they caught trains to make the journey from Ekaterinoslav (today Dnipro) through Brody (then Austria) to the port of Bremen, Germany where much of immigration to the US began. Up until 1914, Jewish migration was relatively unfettered. Many of the Jews who left Russia for the United States had to wait in Brody before boarding sealed trains or transports organized by the shipping companies to get the immigrants to the ports. Germany eventually introduced sophisticated screening measures. Many immigrants had to go through a disinfection process in small towns along the way. Mass transit migration was a highly lucrative business for the rail and steamship companies.[3]

Figure 48 Contemporary map showing distance from Dnipro (Ekaterinoslav) to Bremen

---

[3] See for example https://archives.history.ac.uk/history-in-focus/Migration/articles/brinkmann.html. Accessed Feb. 20, 2024. I'd like to thank David Chapin for this reference.

Aaron and Sophie's last residence before leaving is difficult to read on the manifest but is probably Yakaterinoslav [Ekaterinoslav] which is also listed as Aaron's birthplace in his 1911 Naturalization Petition. As noted earlier, birthplaces on such records need to be taken with a grain of salt since immigrants often oversimplified their life stories to avoid confusing officials with multiple locations. Aaron's wife, Sore [called Sophie and Sophia in later records] is listed as 30 years old, f[emale] and has no occupation indicated.

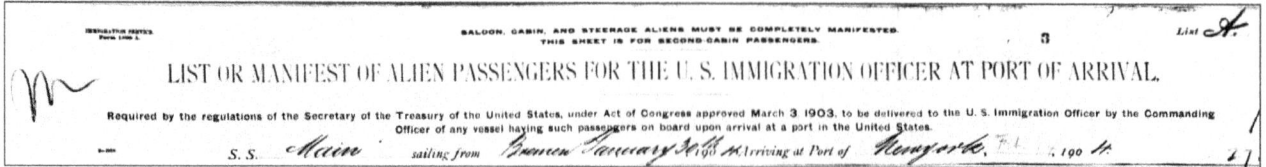

Photo 14 Manifest of Aaron and Sophie Moschevitch on SS Main Feb. 1904

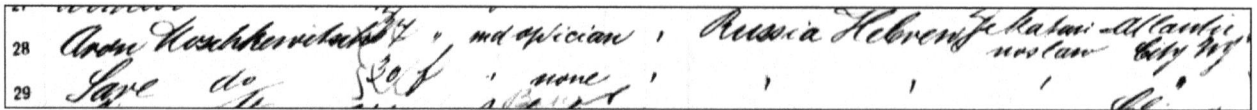

Aron Moschkewitch, age 37, optician, last residence Yekateri-noslav, headed to Atlantic City, NY

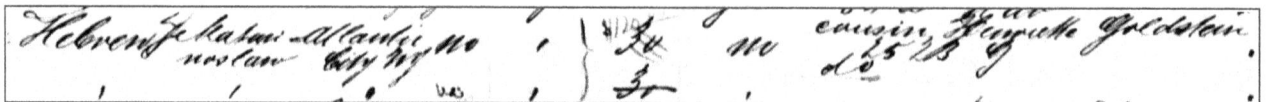

Right-hand columns showing Aaron and Sore's destination of cousin Henriette (?) Goldstein 2523 [NJ?] do

Someone scratched out $30 as the amount of money Aaron was carrying and wrote $120 over it. This is the second largest sum being carried by anyone on that page of the manifest, indicating they were better off than most of the immigrants. The couple's destination listed in the right-hand columns was a cousin in Atlantic City by the last name of Goldstein. The first name appears to be Henriette or something like that.

A 1904 City Directory for Atlantic City lists twelve Goldstein families. I confirmed that Aaron and Sophia headed towards the couple listed as Mark (Katherine) Goldstein at 2523 Atlantic Avenue, their address matching the number "2523" written as the destination on Aaron and Sophie's manifest. I suspect the first name of their cousin, which looks like Henriette, is some version of Katherine, whose Yiddish name was Gitel.

Figure 49 1904 Atlantic City Directory showing Mark Goldstein at 2523 Atlantic Ave

Research on this family indicates that Mark (Morris) Goldstein and Katherine (Gitel) (nee Goldberg) were in the US in the 1880s and in Atlantic City by the late 1890s when they started having children. I confirmed with one of Aaron and Sophie's great-grandsons, David Chapin, that Sophie was indeed related somehow to the Goldstein family, though the exact relationship is no longer remembered. It seems likely that Sophie's relationship to the Goldstein family in Atlantic City was one reason why she and Aaron did not head to Canada where Aaron's older brother Hyman was settling with his family.

In the next generation, a marriage took place between the Goldstein and Moskevitch families. Aaron and Sophie's daughter, Rena Moshkevich, married her cousin William Chapin, a nephew of Morris Goldstein.[4] The couple first met one another at a wedding of Morris and Katherine Goldstein's daughter, according to their grandson, David Chapin.

David also explained to me why Aaron and Sophie ended up in Baltimore, rather than Atlantic City where they were first headed. Aaron was drawn to Baltimore for work opportunities following the Great Baltimore Fire which took place Feb. 7-8, 1904, just a week before Aaron and Sophie landed in New York. The massive destruction of the City created well-paid cleanup opportunities that didn't require English skills, drawing Aaron to the area.

Figure 50 Sophie (Nausecha) (right) with her cousin Katie Goldstein, 1925
Courtesy of David Chapin

While Aaron and Sophie left Russia a year after the loss of their daughter, Sophie must have already been pregnant with Max who was born in Baltimore on May 29, 1904, only five months after they landed.

***

Settling in Baltimore, 1910–1920

By 1910, Aaron, Sophie and their two children were living at 316 S. High Street in downtown crowded East Baltimore, an area filled with Jews and other immigrants from Eastern Europe. During this period, city officials in Baltimore studied the squalor of four tenement neighborhoods including one on East Pratt Street, just a block away from where Aaron and Sophie were living.[5]

---

[4] William was son of Morris Goldstein's sister, Reba (Goldstein) Chapin.

[5] See *Housing Conditions in Baltimore*. Report submitted by Association for the Improvement of the Condition of the Poor and the Charity Organization Society. Submitted by Janet E. Kemp, 1907. See also Antero Pietila, *Not in My Neighborhood: How Bigotry Shaped a Great American City*, Chicago: Ivan R. Dee, 2010, pg. 15.

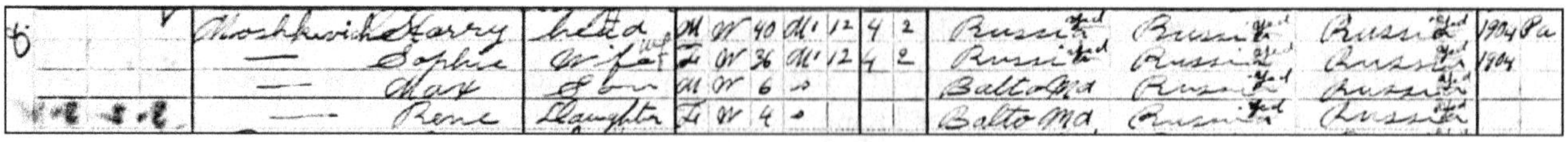

Moshkevich Harry	Head	M	W	40	M1	12			Russia	Russia	Russia	1904
— Sophie	Wife	F	W	36	M1	12	4	2	Russia	Russia	Russia	1904
— Max	Son	M	W	6	S				Balto Md	Russia	Russia	
— Rene	Daughter	F	W	4	S				Balto Md	Russia	Russia	

Figure 51 1910 US Federal Census for Harry (Aaron) and Sophie Moshkevich on S. High St.

In the 1910 census, Aaron appears under the name "Harry," is age 40 and has been married for twelve years, placing the date of his marriage to Sophie in circa 1898. Harry still has the occupation of optician. Sophie is 36, Max is 6, and Rene (Rena) is 4. Rena is the one who later marries a nephew of their Goldstein cousins in Atlantic City (i.e., William Howard Chapin).

The numbers "4" and "2" in the center columns of the census indicate that Aaron and Sophie had 4 children, only 2 of whom were still living. Great-grandson David Chapin knows of only one child who died back in Russia before they came. He speculates that the census taker also counted their son Bernard with whom Sophie was three-months pregnant at the time of the census in April that year. Perhaps, but how would the census taker have known she was pregnant at three months? Was Sophie showing or did she tell him?

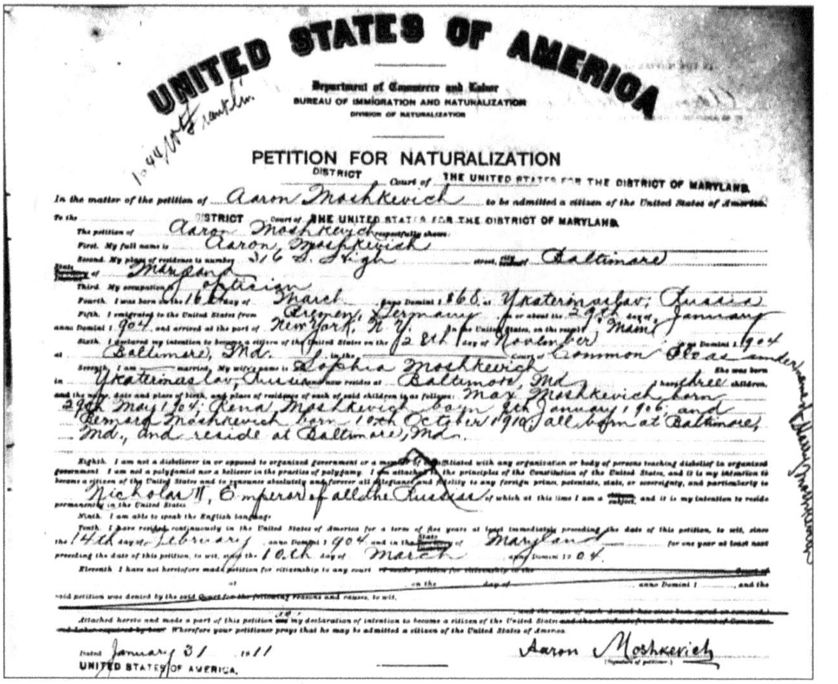

UNITED STATES OF AMERICA

Department of Commerce and Labor
BUREAU OF IMMIGRATION AND NATURALIZATION
DIVISION OF NATURALIZATION

PETITION FOR NATURALIZATION

In the matter of the petition of Aaron Moshkevich to be admitted a citizen of the United States of America.

First. My full name is Aaron Moshkevich
Second. My place of residence is number 316 S. High street, Baltimore, Maryland
Third. My occupation is Optician
Fourth. I was born on the 16th day of March anno Domini 1868 at Ykaterinaslav, Russia
Fifth. I emigrated to the United States from Bremen, Germany on or about the 29th day of January anno Domini 1904, and arrived at the port of New York, N.Y.
Sixth. I declared my intention to become a citizen of the United States on the 12th day of November anno Domini 1904 at Baltimore, Md. in the Common Pleas
Seventh. I am married. My wife's name is Sophia Moshkevich. She was born in Ykaterinaslav, Russia and now resides at Baltimore, Md. I have three children, and the name, date and place of birth, and place of residence of each of said children is as follows: Max Moshkevich born 29th May 1904; Rena Moshkevich born 9th January 1906; and Bernard Moshkevich born 10th October 1910, all born at Baltimore, Md., and reside at Baltimore, Md.

Eighth. I am not a disbeliever in or opposed to organized government or a member of or affiliated with any organization or body of persons teaching disbelief in organized government. I am not a polygamist nor a believer in the practice of polygamy. I am attached to the principles of the Constitution of the United States, and it is my intention to become a citizen of the United States and to renounce absolutely and forever all allegiance and fidelity to any foreign prince, potentate, state, or sovereignty, and particularly to Nicholas II, Emperor of all the Russias, of which at this time I am a subject, and it is my intention to reside permanently in the United States.
Ninth. I am able to speak the English language.
Tenth. I have resided continuously in the United States of America for a term of five years at least immediately preceding the date of this petition, to wit, since the 14th day of February anno Domini 1904, and in the State of Maryland for one year at least next preceding the date of this petition, to wit, since the 10th day of March anno Domini 1904.
Eleventh. I have not heretofore made petition for citizenship to any court.

Attached hereto and made a part of this petition are my declaration of intention to become a citizen of the United States and the certificate from the Department of Commerce and Labor required by law. Wherefore your petitioner prays that he may be admitted a citizen of the United States of America.

Dated January 31 1911

Aaron Moshkevich (Signature of petitioner)

UNITED STATES OF AMERICA

Figure 52 Aaron's Naturalization Petition Jan. 31, 1911

By January 1911, Aaron filled out his Naturalization Petition. The family was still living at 316 S. High St. in Baltimore. Aaron's occupation was still listed as optician and his birthday recorded as Mar. 16, 1868, in Ykaterinaslav [Ekaterinoslav]. Ykaterinaslaw is also listed as the birthplace of Aaron's wife "Sophia." The birthdays of their three [living] children are now listed: Max—May 29, 1904, Rena—Jan. 9, 1906, and Bernard— Oct. 10, 1910.

"My Uncle Bernie loved to brag about his birthday," David Chapin shared with me. "10-10-10. When the movie Rin-Tin-Tin came out, he joked that he was the original Ten-Ten-Ten."

It appears that Aaron abandoned his profession of optician within a few years. He appears in the 1912 City Directory at a new home address and as a grocer at 1044 W Franklin St. His brother, Samuel, who arrived in 1906 (discussed below) appears next to him in the directory. The two brothers appear again at the same addresses in 1913. Then in 1914 Aaron is listed as a grocer at 1206 Poplar Grove St. where the family was still living in the 1920 Census.

1913 Baltimore City Directory

> Moshkevich Aaron, grocer, 1044 w Frank-
> lin, h do
> Moshkevich Saml, men's furngs, 923 e
> Balto, h 1729 do

1914 Baltimore City Directory

> Moshkevich Aaron grocer 1206 Poplar
> Grove h do
> " Saml dry gds 923 e Balto h 1729 do

Photo 15 Aaron Moshkevitch and son Bernie in his dry goods store on Poplar Grove St.

Photo 16 Max and Aaron Moshkevich, 1912

Photo 17 Gertrude Schabb, Rena Moshkevich

with unknown (l to r) circa 1920

***

Rena Marries William Howard Chapin

In the 1920 census, Aaron and Sophie's three children are still living at home at 1204 Poplar Grove St. Aaron is 52, Sophia 48, Max 15, Rena 14, and Bernard 9 years, 7 months.

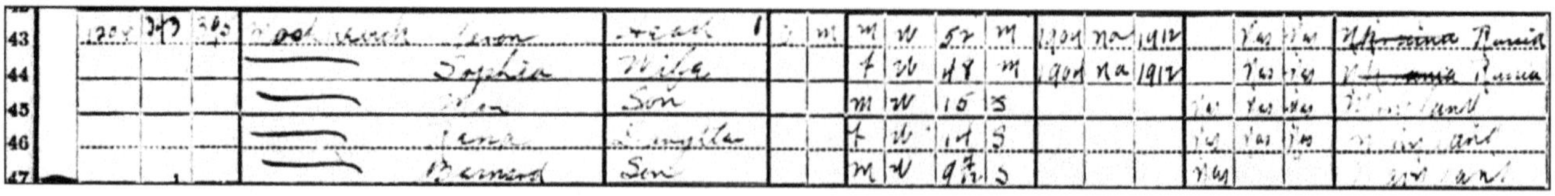

1920 Census for Aaron and Sophia Moshkevich

By 1922, the family appears in the Baltimore City Directory at 423 Norman Ave and is listed at that same address in 1924 and 1928. Their grandson, David, believes this listing was a typo and the address was actually 423 *Normandy* Avenue which is where they appear in the 1930 census. It seems odd though that the same mistake would have been repeated on three different years and that someone would not have caught the mistake, especially since there was also a street called Norman Ave across town.

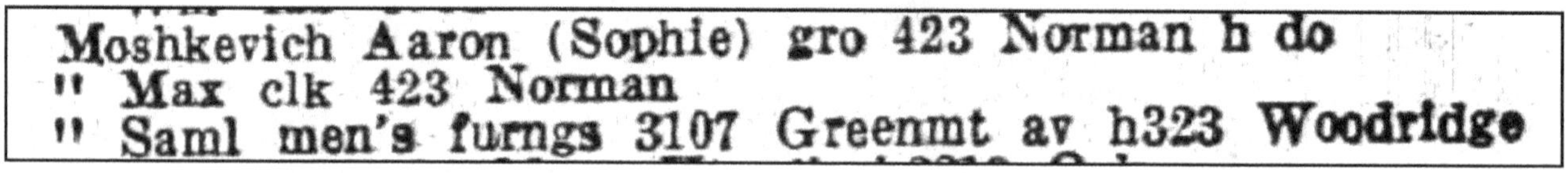

Moshkevich Aaron (Sophie) gro 423 Norman h do
" Max clk 423 Norman
" Saml men's furngs 3107 Greenmt av h323 Woodridge

Figure 53 1922 Aaron and Sophie in Baltimore City Directory

During this same period, Aaron and Sophie's daughter, Rena, married her cousin William Howard Chapin. William was born in Pennsylvania in 1891 with the surname "Goldstein." As noted earlier, he was a nephew of the family with whom Aaron and Sophie stayed in Atlantic City when they first arrived.[6] According to the 1900 census, William's parents arrived in the US with his eldest sister in 1886. Rena and William's grandson, David Chapin, tells me that his grandfather's family adopted "Goldstein," the surname of William's mother, because William's father, Israel, was avoiding conscription.

William's family moved to Atlantic City by the 1900 census and were still there in the 1920 census. The family name in all these censuses is "Goldstein." From an announcement in the Atlantic City Gazette-Review in May 1923, we know William initiated his surname change to "Chapin" just a few years before he married Rena. He was reverting to an anglicized version of his father's original surname back in Lithuania (Chapeikin /Chapekinen). Perhaps the pending wedding was part of the catalyst.

---

[6] William's mother, Reba /Rebecca, was the sister of Morris Goldstein whose home in Atlantic City was the destination of Aaron and Sophie when they arrived in 1904.

Figure 54 Name Change of Goldstein to Chapin
Atlantic City Gazette-Review,
May 12, 1923, p. 13.

6a—Classified Legal

TO WHOM IT MAY CONCERN—
Take notice that the undrsigned
will apply to the Atlantic County
Common Pleas Court on the 11th
day of June next, at 19 o'clock in
the forenoon, or as soon thereafter
as I can be heard, at the Court
House at Mays Landing, New Jersey,
for an order authorizing me to assume another name to wit, the name
of William Howard Chapin, pursuant of the statute made and provided.
  Dated May 11, 1923,
  MEYER WEILMAN
    Attorney.
      WILLIAM H. GOLDSTEIN
          201 Atlantic Ave.,
          Atlantic City, N. J.

In 1923, the year William changed his name, he and his two siblings are listed in the City directory as Chapins living at 201 Atlantic Avenue in Atlantic City. William is listed as a musician. He appears consistently at that address, though in the 1928 directory he is listed twice, once as a musician and once in dry goods, apparently trying to expand his source of income. His sister Kate appears episodically.

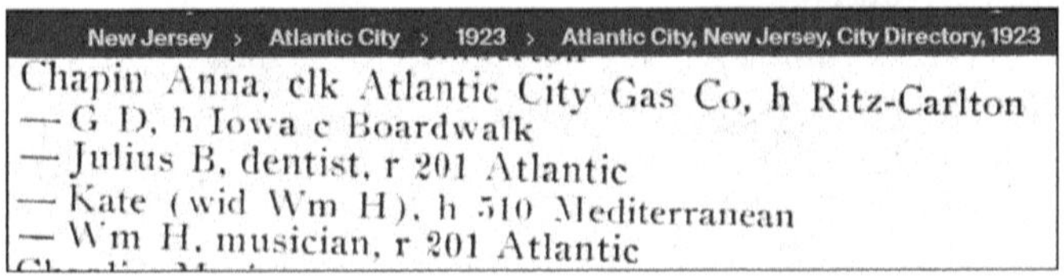

New Jersey > Atlantic City > 1923 > Atlantic City, New Jersey, City Directory, 1923

Chapin Anna, clk Atlantic City Gas Co, h Ritz-Carlton
— G D, h Iowa c Boardwalk
— Julius B, dentist, r 201 Atlantic
— Kate (wid Wm H), h 510 Mediterranean
— Wm H, musician, r 201 Atlantic

Figure 55 Atlantic City Directory 1923

On January 11, 1927, William and Rena's son, Norman Jerome ("Jerry") Chapin, was born while they were living in Atlantic City. Jerome was the first grandchild of Aaron and Sophie Moshkevich.

Photo 18 Rena (Moshkevich) Chapin, 1926
Courtesy of David Chapin

Photo 19 Sophie and Aaron (front) with sons, Bernie (center) and Max (right), 1927

***

Sophie Dies and Aaron Remarries

On April 21, 1927, just two months after Aaron and Sophie's first grandchild was born, Sophie passed away. She was 52 years old and died of appendicitis, which was treatable at the time. According to oral tradition in the family, she was too proud to go to a doctor. Sophie's death was totally unexpected and shocked the family.

Figure 56 Tombstone of Sophie Moshkevich

Here lies
our honorable mother, Sosia Gitel,
daughter of R. Naftali Herz the Levi,
passed the 19th of Nissan 5687,
May her soul be bound up in the bond of life.

Died April 21, 1927, Age 52 Years

By the 1930 census, Aaron has remarried and is listed with his second wife, Helen. His two sons, Max and Bernard, are also still in the household and Max is now listed as a lawyer. The census indicates they are living at 423 *Normandy* Ave. Aaron's new wife, Helen, was previously married to a man named Hersch Myers and already had two grown daughters, Aida/Ada (married name Golberg) and Fannie (married name Goodman); both were living elsewhere in 1930.

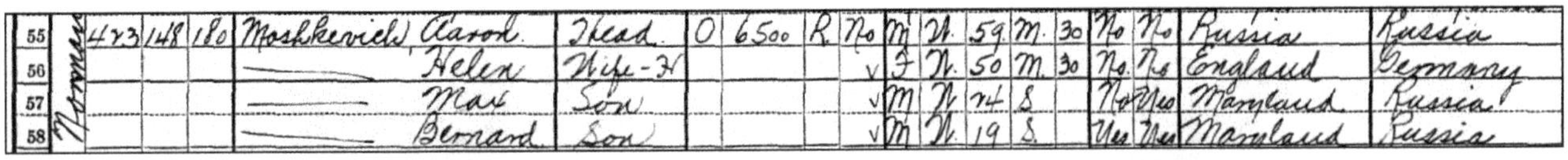

55		4x3	148	180	Moshkevich, Aaron	Head	O	6500	R	No		M	W	59	M	30	No	No	Russia	Russia
56					" Helen	Wife-H						F	W	50	M	30	No	No	England	Germany
57					" Max	Son					✓	M	W	24	S		No	No	Maryland	Russia
58					" Bernard	Son					✓	M	W	19	S		Yes	Yes	Maryland	Russia

Figure 57 1930 Census for Aaron Moshkevich and family

When the 1930 census was taken, Aaron's daughter, Rena, with her new husband, William Chapin and their young son, were at the Greenbrier Hotel resort in West Virginia, on April 26, 1930. Their names appear with other lodgers at the luxury resort located in the Allegheny Mountains near White Sulphur Springs in Greenbrier County, West Virginia. The document indicates that William H. "Chafin" [Chapin] was age 36 and married at age 32. Rena is 24 and was 20 when married. Their son Norman Jerome is 3.

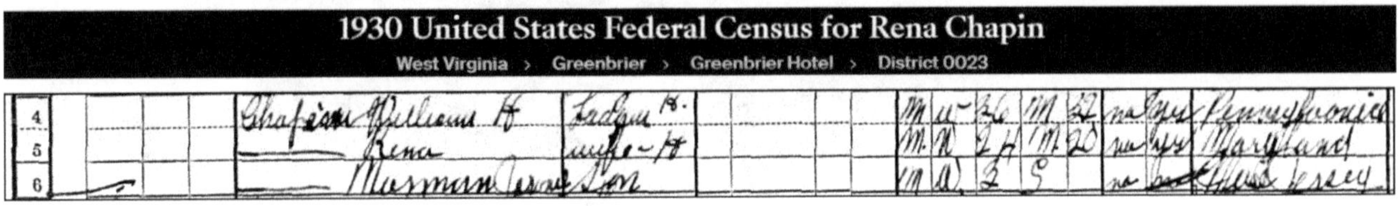

1930 United States Federal Census for Rena Chapin
West Virginia › Greenbrier › Greenbrier Hotel › District 0023

4				Chafin, William H	Lodger	H						M	W	36	M	32	na	Yes	Pennsylvania
5				" Rena	Wife-H							M	W	24	M	20	na	Yes	Maryland
6				" Norman Jerome	Son							M	W	3	S		na		New Jersey

Figure 58 1930 Census for William, Rena and Jerome

When I first found this record, I suspected that Rena and William were at the Greenbrier Hotel on vacation and were in fact still living in Atlantic City with his family. I learned the real reason they were at the Greenbriar resort from their grandson, David, who informed me that William was a concert violinist. David writes:

> When he was first married in the mid-1920s he had a very lucrative job as the head of the Meyer Davis Orchestra at the Greenbrier resort in WVA. His salary included lodging and food. During the offseason he was an orchestra leader aboard luxury cruises to places like Havana Cuba.
>
> He became very wealthy. But most of his money went into banks. When the banks failed in the early 1930s, he got a double whammy—the Greenbrier terminated the contract with Meyer Davis, firing all the musicians and he lost his savings because of a run on the bank. Fortunately [his father-in-law] Aaron Moshkovich squirreled away a portion of his salary literally in a cookie jar. That money helped him pay for a grocery store that he ended up owning and running until he retired.

Figure 59 Greenbrier Hotel in West Virginia, Photo by Richard Rosendale.[7]

---

[7] By Richard Rosendale - Own work, CC BY-SA 3.0, https://commons.wikimedia.org/w/index.php?curid=15776447

Photo 20 William Chapin (far right) at the Greenbrier 1926
Courtesy of David Chapin

Photo 21 Rena (Moshkevich) Chapin with father
Aaron and son Jerry Chapin, 1930

***

Back in Baltimore, 1940 and Beyond

A City directory shows William and Rena still living in Atlantic City in 1931. By 1935 they moved to Baltimore and were residing at 421 Normandy Ave, in a house next to where Rena's father, Aaron and his second wife, Helen, were living.

The 1940 census taker apparently recorded the names incorrectly that day. After listing William, Rena, and Jerome at 421 Normandy, the census worker incorrectly listed "Max Moshkevich" [rather than Aaron] as head of household at 423 Normandy. Rena's brother, Max, had in fact already moved elsewhere as we shall see shortly. And the personal details attributed to Max clearly belong to his father Aaron: age 70 and married to a Helen.

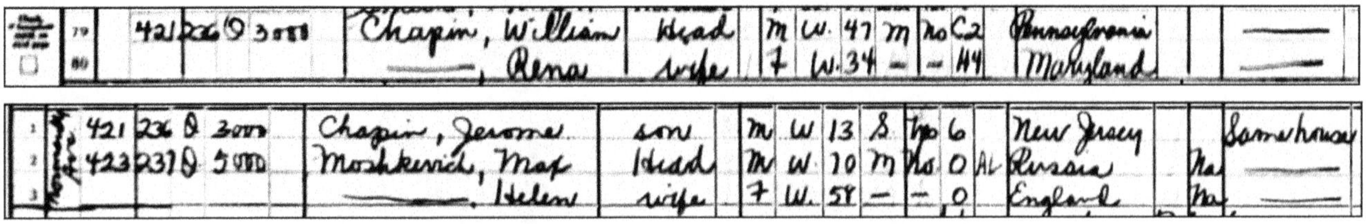

79	421	226	9	3000	Chapin, William	Head	M	W	47	M	No	C2	Pennsylvania					—
80					—, Rena	wife	F	W	34	—	—	H4	Maryland					—
1	421	236	8	3000	Chapin, Jerome	son	M	W	13	S	Yes	6		New Jersey				Same house
2	423	237	0	5000	Moshkevich, Max	Head	M	W	70	M	No	0	AL	Russia		Na		—
3					—, Helen	wife	F	W	58	—	—	0		England		Na		—

Figure 60 1940 Census incorrectly listing Max rather than Aaron next to Rena and family

Max was living elsewhere by 1935 with his new wife, Hildegarde (Fox). They married in the District of Columbia on May 24, 1932. Hildegarde appears in the 1910 census as "Hilda Fox," one of the younger daughters of a large Jewish family. Her parents Harris and Ester Fox immigrated in 1888 and 1889.

By 1935 Max and Hildegarde settled in Baltimore at 511 N. Loudon Street, one block away from Max's father Aaron and his sister Rena on Normandy Ave. Max and Hildegarde are still there in the 1940 census. By the time of the 1950 census, Max has anglicized his name appearing now as M. Richard Moss. He also used M. Richard Moss as his professional name as an attorney and signed documents that way. He probably kept the "M" [Max] initial to distinguish himself from another Richard Moss who appears in records.

***

Bernard Gets Married

In the meantime, Aaron's youngest son, Bernard, got his marriage certificate to marry Rose Caruso on Sept. 12, 1932, in Wilmington, Delaware. The marriage certificate indicates Bernard was living in Wilmington at 725 9th Street and was an office manager. He was 21 and Rose was 20. Both of Rose's parents were born in Italy to Italian families. A record shows Bernard and Rose were married by Roman Catholic Reverend Leonard Walter. David Chapin recalls hearing that "marriage was a big scandal in those days for both sides of the aisle, Jew and Catholic. Their marriage soon fell apart, and they had a stormy divorce. It was rare to get divorced in those days, so it tainted both of them."

Bernard and Rose's son, Gerald, was born in 1936. The 1940 census indicates they were living in the household with Rose's family in Wilmington at 100 Tatnall Street and their son Gerald was 4 years old. Bernard is listed as a plant supervisor in a wholesale oil business–oil refineries and other chemical plants being prominent in Wilmington, Delaware at the time.

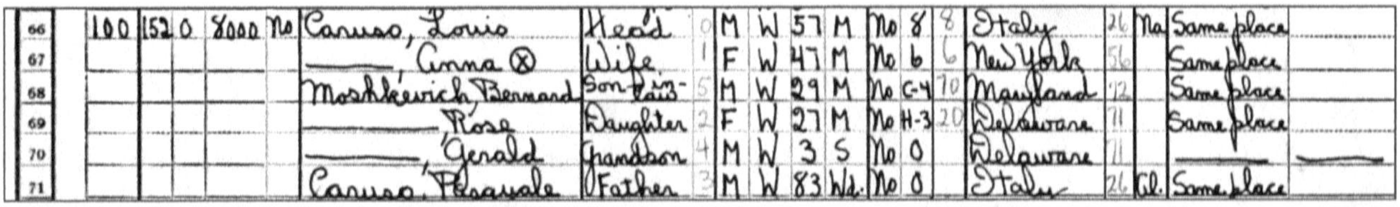

66	100	152	0	8000	No	Caruso, Louis	Head	0	M	W	57	M	No	8	8	Italy	26	Na	Same place
67						—, Anna ⊗	Wife	1	F	W	47	M	No	6	6	New York	56		Same place
68						Moshkevich, Bernard	Son-in-law	5	M	W	29	M	No	C-4	10	Maryland	12		Same place
69						—, Rose	Daughter	2	F	W	27	M	No	H-3	20	Delaware	11		Same place
70						—, Gerald	Grandson	4	M	W	3	S	No	0		Delaware	11		—
71						Caruso, Pasquale	Father	3	M	W	83	Wd	No	0		Italy	26	Al	Same place

Figure 61 1940 Census of Bernard Moshkevich and wife Rose and son Gerald

Sometime between 1940 and 1950, Bernard shortened his surname to Moss, which is the spelling in the 1950 census after the family moved to Baltimore. The transition from Moshkevich to Moss was captured vividly on Bernard's WWII Draft Registration Card, which he initially filled out on Oct. 16, 1940. Bernard initially signed the card with the name "Bernard Moshkevich" and his address in Wilmington. Someone, perhaps an official, scratched out "Moshkevich" and wrote "Moss." His address is also scratched out twice and someone in a different hand wrote his address as 26 S. Catherine Street in Baltimore. His employer is American Oil Company in Wilmington.

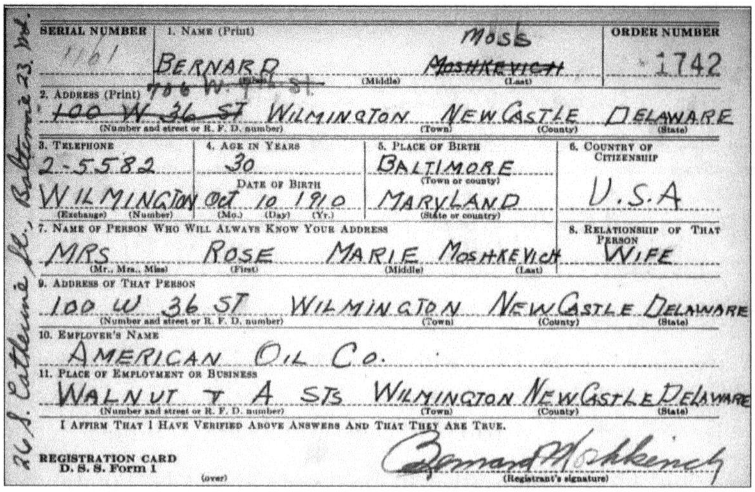
SERIAL NUMBER 1161
1. NAME (Print) BERNARD (Middle) ~~MOSHKEVICH~~ MOSS (Last)
ORDER NUMBER 1742
2. ADDRESS (Print) ~~706 W. ... St.~~ ~~100 W 36 ST~~ WILMINGTON NEW CASTLE DELAWARE
(Number and street or R. F. D. number) (Town) (County) (State)
3. TELEPHONE 2-5582 WILMINGTON (Exchange) (Number)
4. AGE IN YEARS 30 DATE OF BIRTH Oct 10 1910 (Mo.) (Day) (Yr.)
5. PLACE OF BIRTH BALTIMORE (Town or county) MARYLAND (State or country)
6. COUNTRY OF CITIZENSHIP U.S.A
7. NAME OF PERSON WHO WILL ALWAYS KNOW YOUR ADDRESS MRS ROSE MARIE MOSHKEVICH (Mr., Mrs., Miss) (First) (Middle) (Last)
8. RELATIONSHIP OF THAT PERSON WIFE
9. ADDRESS OF THAT PERSON 100 W 36 ST WILMINGTON NEW CASTLE DELAWARE
(Number and street or R. F. D. number) (Town) (County) (State)
10. EMPLOYER'S NAME AMERICAN OIL CO.
11. PLACE OF EMPLOYMENT OR BUSINESS WALNUT & A STS WILMINGTON NEW CASTLE DELAWARE
(Number and street or R. F. D. number) (Town) (County) (State)
I AFFIRM THAT I HAVE VERIFIED ABOVE ANSWERS AND THAT THEY ARE TRUE.
REGISTRATION CARD D. S. S. Form 1 (over)
Bernard Moshkevich (Registrant's signature)
26 S. Catherine St., Baltimore 23, Md.

Figure 62 WWII Draft Registration for Bernard Moshkevich Moss

***

Jerry Chapin Lands in Nagasaki

When Rena and William's son, Jerry, graduated high school in 1944, he entered the army. He was 17 years old. I learned the story of those years from his son, David.

In the spring of 1945, Jerry was assigned to the chemical warfare unit of the massive force assembling in the Philippines to invade Japan scheduled for the fall of 1945 (Operation Olympic). He would have been cannon fodder in the first wave. But the war ended before then.

He was thus part of the occupation forces. His unit landed in Nagasaki about 8 weeks after the atom bomb leveled it. They came in full battle dress ready for hostilities, but none took place. Part of his job in the chemical warfare unit was to survey with the Geiger counter and rope off the radioactive areas. In letters home, he wrote about how he didn't understand why members of his unit were still "seasick" even when off the ship—we now know this was radiation sickness.

Not long afterwards, he was assigned to a supply unit in Kobe Japan. They were tasked with rebuilding the harbor for US military supply shipments to alleviate food shortages facing the Japanese population. At the time it was cheaper to keep the supplies flowing into Japan rather than return the excess to America. Jeeps kept coming in, all filled with gasoline ready to go. Every man in his unit got a jeep which they would drive until empty and then swap it out for a new one.

His supply unit was also tasked with confiscating Japanese weapons. They had a warehouse full of samurai swords. Jerry picked out 3 of the best and shipped them home. His son David still has them today.

By the end of 1946, his tour was over, and he returned home. The GI bill then got him into dental school as he transitioned into civilian life. Around 1978, he was diagnosed with a type of non-Hodgkins lymphoma, a type of cancer obtained from exposure to radiation. When he passed away, the government considered him statistically as a casualty of WWII.

Photo 22 Jerry Chapin and friend Irv Dubick Tokyo, Japan, June 1946
Imperial Palace grounds. Later, Jerry introduced his friend Irv to a cousin, Bella Moss, Irv's future wife.
Courtesy of David Chapin

In the 1950 census, after Jerry returned home, his grandfather Aaron and his wife Helen were still living at 421 Normandy Ave. Aaron is listed as 80 years old and Helen is 70. Jerry's family was still at 423 Normandy Ave. Aaron passed away on Sept. 18, 1952, in Baltimore. His wife Helen passed away in 1967.

Jerry (son of Rena and William Howard Chapin), subsequently married Pauline Zimmerman. They had four children: Roni Ann Chapin (married name Udoff), David Alan Chapin (the Moss family historian), Julie Lynn (married name Janofsky) and Margie who never married. Jerry's father, William Howard Chapin passed away in 1978 and his mother, Rena (Moshkevich), passed away in 1984. His daughter, Margie, passed away in 2016.

Jerry's dental office played a role in introducing his "Uncle Bernie" (his mother's brother Bernard Moss) to his second wife, Marie Wade. David tells me the following story:

> My dad had a dental assistant by the name of Marie Wade, from Anniston, Alabama. She ended up in Baltimore because a Baltimore Jew by the name of Bernard Abrams went to basic training in WWII in Anniston, where they met and got married. Soon they had a baby, but he got shipped off to war, never to return.

> She was a young single mom, a war widow, stuck in Baltimore. My dad employed her, starting around 1955. This was shortly after my Uncle Bernie and Rose divorced. Matchmaker dad fixed up [his uncle] Bernie and Marie and eventually they married.

> They had a wonderful life together with an amazingly blended family. Marie was quite an amazing lady; I knew her well. Even though she wasn't born Jewish, she embraced Judaism. While she was an outsider to the family, to Baltimore, and to the religion she adopted, she didn't view it that way. My father and her were close in age, yet he called

her Aunt Marie out of respect to whom she married. She was an avid Orioles fan, to my father's delight. They had season tickets to baseball games together. After Marie got married, she moved on from my father's dental practice to become a radiological tech, which was quite a good job— she was the primary breadwinner in the family. This would have been circa 1961.

When my youngest sister Margie was in college, Marie mentored her into also becoming a radiological tech. Margie and Marie remained very close through the rest of their lives.

Marie died in 2012 and had a Jewish funeral. The two, Margie and Marie, are buried just a few feet away from one another—Marie next to Bernie; Margie who died in 2016, next to my dad, perhaps 10 feet from each other.

Bernard's son from his first marriage, Gerald ("Jerry") Moss, married Joann Hagner and they had two sons, Barry and Rudy. Jerry was an electrician for the Baltimore Gas and Electric Company. Sometime in the 1970s he suffered a terrible accident when he slipped down a telephone pole, broke some bones and got awful splinters in his chest. He was in the hospital for a long time. In those days they used to climb up the pole using spiked boots. He ended up receiving disability from the power company. Jerry and Joann subsequently divorced, and Joann raised Rudy and Barry as a single mom, eventually becoming a highly successful real estate broker. Jerry subsequently remarried Beulah Corkran. Rudy died in Florida in 2011 – he owned a nursery and a hardware store. His father, Jerry, passed away in 2015.

Aaron and Sophie's other son, Max Richard Moss, had no children. He passed away in 1978.

***

Some Memories of Max Richard Moss

Although Max had no children, he left a vivid impression in the family. Because he had no other family, he was close to the family of his nephew, Jerry. Some stories recounted in the words of Jerry's son David:

> When I was maybe 6 or 7, Uncle Max and Aunt Hildegarde took me and my sister Julie for a day at the beach. He took us to Bay Ridge beach on the Chesapeake Bay, at the foot of the Bay Bridge near Annapolis. It was a beach that probably had better times in the past, maybe when he was growing up. It had broken glass strewn on the beach and jellyfish in the water. Both my sister and I got all cut up on our feet and stung. We were a mess and hated it there. Uncle Max and Aunt Hildegarde cut it short and brought us home.

> A few months later, looking back I think it must have been to make up for the fiasco at Bay Ridge, Uncle Max and Aunt Hildegarde wanted to take me with them to Atlantic City. They chose a day in March. It was cold and it was also during Passover week. We kept Pesachdik, so my mother gave them strict instructions not to feed me anything with bread. It was a long 3-hour drive in the back seat of their decrepit old car that didn't have any heat. Not only that, Uncle Max and Aunt Hildegarde were constantly bickering and sometimes in a full-out screaming match. I said nothing and was bored to death, hoping it would be over soon. They didn't talk to me at all because they were not kid-friendly people. At one point I told them I had to go to the bathroom. They just pulled the car over and told me to pee in the bushes by the side of the road. It was so embarrassing because I had never done that before. When we finally made it to Atlantic City, it was miserable weather—very cold and windy. Not a good day to go to the beach. We walked a little on the Boardwalk, walked one of the amusement piers—I think maybe the Steeplechase. They fed me hot dogs. We didn't stay too long and then we returned to

Baltimore. In the evening when we arrived home, my mother quizzed them on what we did. She was appalled to find out they fed me hot dogs and really let them have it that they should have known better because it was Passover.

When I was just a kid in our new house, this must have been 1965 or 1966, my parents sponsored the Moss Family Cousins Club meeting. There was an adult-only dinner meeting held in different people's houses every other month. It was a business meeting — they actually had a president, treasurer, and budget. Afterwards, they served dinner and played cards. (Once a year, typically around the 4th of July or Labor Day, they would rent a place for a picnic and organized kid-friendly activities). It was a Sunday, and my mother was very nervous trying to get the setup just right and was cooking for the large group of perhaps 30–40. Everything had to be just right. Not to mention, my mother had to deal with 4 kids and keep us out of harm's way. That was more or less the responsibility of my dad, who kept us in the basement clubroom watching TV and playing board games.

At about 2 in the afternoon, we heard the doorbell. It was Uncle Max and Aunt Hildegarde! They said that they were in the neighborhood. "Would we mind if they hung out with us for 4 hours until the meeting?" My father complied and took them down to our clubroom. Aunt Hildegarde didn't lift a finger to help my mother who was scurrying around the kitchen. They just sat around watching TV. Eventually, my mother blew her stack and told my father to send them away until meeting time. Reluctantly, he told them to leave us and return at the right time. They got very mad and, in a huff, stomped out, apparently highly insulted. They never returned later that evening.

Years later, it was probably in the early 1970s, Uncle Max and Aunt Hildegarde got divorced. By then, Hildegarde had some type of dementia and was now in a nursing home. Though divorced, Max still visited her every single day.

One day he suffered a massive stroke and almost didn't survive. He was in the hospital for a long time, several months. It became apparent that he could no longer practice law anymore and bills were mounting. They were going to evict him from his law office.

Since we were among his closest relatives, Dad and I went to clean out and pack his office. He dragged me there because my dad had a bad back. Max's office was located in the basement of an ancient ornate office building on Calvert Street next to the Baltimore courthouse. It was a scene straight out of a 1940s film noir. The place was poorly lit. Walls painted dark industrial green. Green speckled linoleum tiles lined the floor, with some tiles cracked and others missing. Bare lightbulbs hanging from wires going up to an immensely high ceiling. Vertical steam pipes everywhere wrapped with asbestos. It was echoey and smelled musty, from another era.

Uncle Max's office was a small, two room office midway down the basement corridor. It had a frosted glass door with black stencils "M. Richard Moss, esquire Attorney-at-Law." I didn't know what esquire meant at the time. Once through the door, we were met with the waiting room/secretarial. It was cluttered beyond belief. It had an overstuffed leather sofa that had seen better days. No one could sit there anymore because it was covered in legal documents. File cabinets lined the walls. There was an old-fashioned secretary typing stool and an antique manual typewriter. It was obvious that he hadn't been able to afford a secretary for many years and Max learned to type his own documents, which was unusual at the time. But those typing days were now gone. Behind the area for the secretary was a hand-carved wooden door that led to his private office. Inside was more clutter, lots more file cabinets, and a giant fancy wooden desk with a glass top. His executive leather chair was creaky and wobbly to sit in. My dad and I packed up the loose items and supervised the movers. They put it all into storage as we stripped the office bare.

After Max got out of the hospital, he was paralyzed on one side of his body and walked with a cane. Somehow, he had a relationship with a woman he did legal work for years before–actually her divorce. Her name was Lillian James–Aunt Lil to us. She was a very sweet gentile lady who brought out the best in Uncle Max. He was a changed man who no longer had the hard edge to him. They got married quickly, but the marriage didn't last very long. She died about a year later, I believe, from lung cancer (she was a heavy smoker).

After that, my father got him into the Concord—one of the first assisted living facilities in Baltimore. It was associated with Levendale and Sinai Hospital. It was Jewish-owned and brand new. He had a small efficiency apartment in a high-rise that overlooked the Pimlico racetrack. We once visited and watched the Preakness from his apartment.

He stayed there for a few years but eventually he suffered another massive stroke from which he didn't recover. But he hung on for several months in a partial coma at Sinai. At the same time, my grandmother (his sister) Rena fell and broke her hip. She, too, was in the hospital for a long time. They were literally one hospital room apart from one another, brother and sister. My grandfather William, Rena's husband, died on Mar 6, 1978. One day later Max died. My grandmother Rena, who was now very frail, attended both funerals on the very same day.

Records Summary for Family of Aaron and Sophie Moshkevich

Feb. 14, 1904 Passenger Manifest	Departing Bremen Jan. 30, 1904 on SS Main arriving in NY on Feb. 14, 1904; **Aron Moschkewitch**, age 34 [implied birth year 1870], md [married], [nationality] Russia [Race] Hebrew, [last residence] illegible, [destination] Atlantic City, NJ, $120 [in possession], Sore [Sophie] age 30, md [married] no occupation, destination cousin [illegible Henriette?] Goldstein 25 2B[?] NJ [*see narrative for discussion of cousin Katherine Goldstein]
Nov. 28, 1904 Declaration	No detail included in the record except that his name is Harry
Apr. 23, 1910 US Federal Census	316 S. High Street **Harry [=Aaron] Moshkivich**, head, age 40 [implied birth year 1870], years married 12, children 4, 2 living, birthplace Russia, parents' birthplace Russia, immigration year 1904, PA (naturalization papers submitted), speaks English, occupation-optician, store, rents home; **Sophie**, wife, age 36, years married 12, children 4, 2 living, parents' birthplace: Russia, immigration year 1904, speaks English; **Max**, son, age 6, speaks English; **Rene**, age 4, speaks English.
Jan. 31, 1911 Naturalization Petition District Court of Maryland	**Aaron Moshkevich**, address 316 S. High, Baltimore Maryland, occupation: optician, born Mar. 16, 1868 at Ykaterinaslav [Ekaterinoslav], Russia, emigrated from Bremen, Germany on Jan. 29, 1904 arrived New York on vessel Main, declared intention Nov. 28, 1904, wife's name **Sophia** Moshkevich, born in Ykaterinaslav [Ekaterinoslav], Russia, and now resides at Baltimore. 3 children all born in Baltimore: Max Moshkevich, born May 29, 1904, **Rena** Moshkevich, born Jan. 9, 1906, **Bernard** Moshkevich born Oct.. 10, 1910; witnesses: Jacob W. Lubchansky, physician, residing at 145 N. Exeter and William Schevker residing at 904 Fawn St.
Jan. 15, 1920 US Federal Census for Baltimore	1206 Poplar Grove St. **Aaron Moshkevich**, Head, Home owned, Mortgage, age 52, year immigrated 1904, na[turalized], year naturalized 1912, birthplace [illegible but perhaps Ukraina] Russia occupation: Grocerman, grocery store; **Sophia**, wife, age 48, year immigrated 1904, na[turalized], year naturalized 1912, birthplace [illegible but perhaps Ukraina] , occupation none; **Rena**, daughter, age 14, birthplace Maryland, occupation none; **Banard**, son 9 7/12, born in Maryland.
Apr. 21, 1927 Obituary	Obituary published in *The Baltimore Sun* on Apr. 21, 1927 reads: On February [sic-should be April] 20, 1927 at 8.18 P. M., Sophia beloved wife of **Aaron Moshkevich**. Funeral from her late residence, 423 Normandy avenue, of which due notice will be given.
Apr. 21, 1927 Tombstone, Adath Yeshurun Cemetery	Tombstone of Sophia Moshkevich. Tombstone reads: Here lies our honorable mother, Shashia Gitel, daughter of R. Naftali Herz, passed the 19 of Nissan 5687, May her soul be bound up in bond of life. Died April 21, 1927, Age 52 Years
April 7, 1930 US Federal Census for Baltimore	**Aaron Moshkevich** 423 Normandy Ave, Head, O[wns home], Value 6500, age 59, age at first marriage 30, born in Russia, father born in Russia, mother born in Russia, language spoken in home before coming to US Russian, Year of immigration 1904, Na[turalized], Yes Able to speak English, retired; **Helen** wife, age 50, age at first marriage 30, born in England, father and mother born in Germany, year of immigration 1904, Na[turalized], Yes able to speak English, no occupation; **Max Moshkevich**, age 24, single, born in Maryland, father born in Russia, mother born in England, occupation legal attorney;

	Bernard Moshkevich, age 19, single, born in Maryland, father born in Russia, mother born in England, clerk Oil and Gas
April 26, 1930 1930 US Federal Census	For family of **William H. Chapin**, **Rena Chapin**, and **Norman Jerome**. Greenbrier West Virginia, Greenbrier Hotel, **William H. Chafin** [sic] Lodger, age 36, age at marriage, 32, born in Pennsylvania, parents born in Russia, occupation Director? Music?, **Rena**, wife, age 24, age at marriage 20, born in Maryland, parents born in Russia: Norman Jerome, age 3, born in New Jersey, father born in Pennsylvania, mother born in Maryland
May 24, 1932 Marriage Record	**Max Moshkevich**, age 27, married Hildegarde G. Fox. District of Columbia
Oct. 11 1932 Marriage Certificate State of Delaware	**Bernard Moskewich**, groom 725 W. 9th St. Wilmington New Castle, Delaware, age 21, occupation office manager, born in Baltimore, father Aaron born in Russia, mother Sophie born in Russia, **Rose Caruso**, bride, residence Wilmington, New Castle, Del. age 20, born Waterbury, Conn., father's name Louis born in Italy, mother's name Anna Fischer, born in Italy, married by Rev. Leonard Walter, a Roman Catholic clergy.
April 11, 1940 US Federal Census Wilmington, DE	100 West 36th Street, Wilmington DE. **Bernard Moshkevich,** son-in-law, was living with his wife's parents Louis and Anna Caruso and her grandfather Pasquale Caruso. Bernard is 29 and listed as a plant superintendent in wholesale oil, Rose is 27 and working as a hairdresser in a beauty parlor. Gerald is age 3.
April 24, 1940 US Federal Census Baltimore	For Rena Chapin's family and her father Aaron Moshkevich 421 Normandy Ave. **William Chapin**, head, owns home, value $3000, age 47, born in Pennsylvania, at same place in 1935, retail grocer in his own business. **Rena** age 34, born in Maryland, working as grocer clerk in Retail Grocery, **Jerome**, son, age 13, born in New Jersey. Also includes: 423 Normandy Ave, **Max Moshkevich** [sic-this was really Aaron] Owns home valued at $5,000, age 70 born in Russia, lived in same house in 1935, Na[turalized], No occupation listed, wife **Helen**, age 58, born in England, Na[turalized]
Oct. 16, 1940 WWII Draft Registration	**Bernard Moshkevich** [Moshkevich is scratched out] and Moss is written above it. Address 100 W. 36 st Wilmington New Castle [100 W. 36 St] is scratched out, down the side the address reads 26 S Catherine St. Baltimore, age 30, date of birth Oct 10, 1910 in Maryland. name of person who will know your address: Mrs. **Rose Marie Moshkevich**, wife, 100 W 36 Street New Castle, Employer Name American Oil Co, place of employment Walnut & A Sts Wilmington, New Castle

***

4.

FAMILY OF ANNA (MOSHKEVICH) AND MORRIS SCHABB

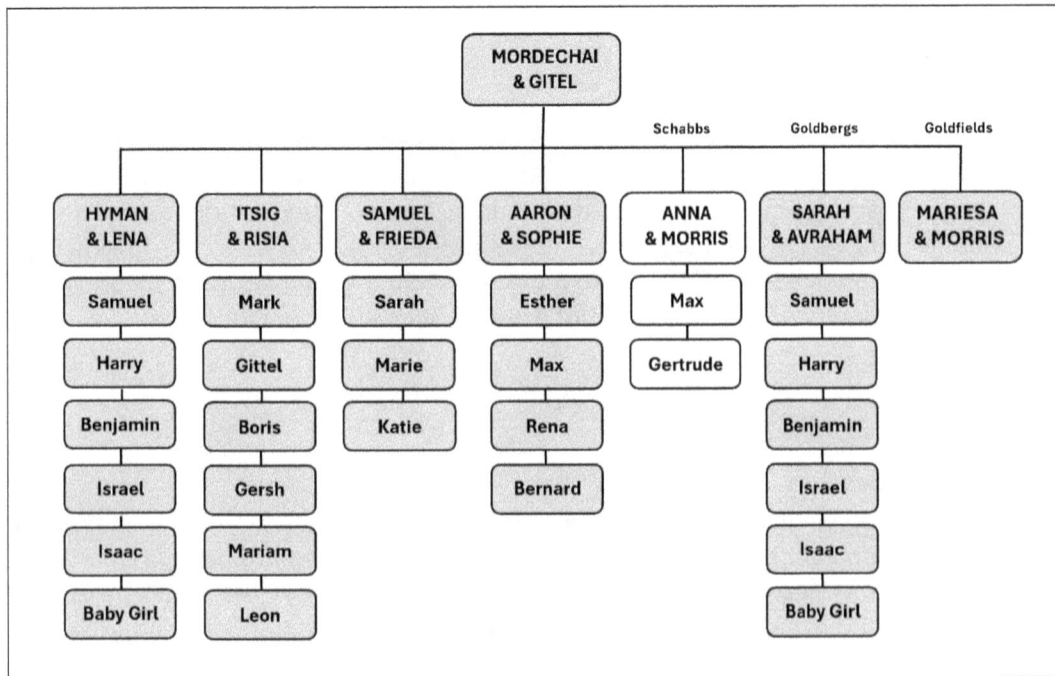

Figure 63 Family of Anna (Moskovitch) and Morris Schabb

***

Two years after Aaron and Sophie Moshkevich arrived in Baltimore, Aaron's sister **Anna (Moskevitch) Schabb** arrived with her family. If they weren't already planning to follow her brother, the October 1905 pogrom in Ekaterinoslav and the events leading up to it would have given them sufficient cause.[1]

Morris and Anna's granddaughter Marie (Schabb) Schwartz,[2] recalls learning that her grandparents lived in an apartment house in Ekaterinoslav and were middle class. Marie is in her 90s and I spoke to her by phone. She recalls that her grandmother, Anna, never learned to read or write but that she was good with numbers. She also heard that her grandparents put crosses in their window to survive. Marie's father, Max,

---

[1] See, for example, accounts in the Yizkor book, https://www.jewishgen.org/yizkor/ekaterinoslav/Ekaterinoslav.html and Surh, "Ekaterinoslav City in 1905: Workers, Jews, and Violence."
[2] Marie is the daughter of Max Schabb and Dora (Matz).

who was eight years old when he arrived in the US, used to reminisce later in life about skating on the Dnieper River in the winter when he was a child. During winters in Baltimore, he used to regularly take Marie and her brother Oscar ice skating and recall those times in Russia when he was young.

The causes behind the Ekaterinoslav pogrom were complex and varied. In 1904–1905, the Russian Empire fought a brutal military conflict against Japan over control in Manchuria, which provided an immediate backdrop to the events in the period. January 1905 began in Russia with "Bloody Sunday" when a group of workers led by the radical priest Georgy Apollonovich Gapon marched to the Tzar's Winter Palace in St. Petersburg to make their demands. Imperial forces opened fire on the demonstrators, killing and wounding hundreds. Riots and strikes broke out across the country sparking the first Russian revolution; the Tsar promised reforms.

By mid-1905, as noted earlier, both middle- and working-class Jews in Ekaterinoslav were warned of impending trouble. "In the course of 1905, these simmering fears and expectations of conflict were realized in several attacks on Jews and their property, attacks to which individual Jews and self-defense groups responded vigorously, if not as violently."

On June 20, a small pogrom broke out in which several shops were damaged, people were injured, and a Jewish art student named Goldberg was killed. Eight hundred persons turned out for his funeral at a Jewish cemetery and the event itself turned into a political demonstration. On July 20, another one-day pogrom took place that vandalized Jewish homes and small businesses. Discontent fomented among workers at the end of summer followed by an increase in political meetings. On October 11, three demonstrations took place in the city that ended in violence, death and injury. The violence against Jews began Oct. 21 and continued for two days. Sixty-seven Jews and over 30 Russians were killed and more than 189 wounded.[3]

***

The Schabb Migration, Jan. 1906

On Jan. 19, 1906, Anna left Bremen with her husband Morris Schabb and two children on the SS Frankfort and landed in Baltimore on Feb. 1, 1906. On their manifest, the family name appears as "Sabosowitz," and I confirmed with their granddaughter, Marie, that the surname was indeed shortened upon their arrival. Sabosowitz may mean "child of the Sabbath" and may indicate an ancestor was born on the Sabbath day.

The record indicates that "Mathes" (Morris) was 33 and a shoemaker. Henie (Annie) was 34, Mottl (Max) was 9, and Gitel (married name Gertrude Cohn) was 8. Their last residence, like Aaron and Sophie's, was Ekaterinoslav. Someone crossed out $25 and wrote $60 as the amount of money in Morris's possession. The right-hand columns indicate they were headed to Morris's "Bro-in-law Aron Moschewitz at 316 S High St." Aaron, of course, was Anna's brother who arrived in 1904.

SALOON, CABIN, AND STEERAGE ALIENS MUST BE COMPLETELY MANIFESTED.
THIS SHEET IS FOR STEERAGE PASSENGERS.
List 6

LIST OR MANIFEST OF ALIEN PASSENGERS FOR THE U. S. IMMIGRATION OFFICER AT PORT OF ARRIVAL.

Required by the regulations of the Secretary of Commerce and Labor of the United States, under Act of Congress approved March 3, 1903, to be delivered to the U. S. Immigration Officer by the Commanding Officer of any vessel having such passengers on board upon arrival at a port in the United States.

S. S. Frankfurt sailing from Bremen Jan 19, 1906 Arriving at Port of Baltimore FEB 01 1906

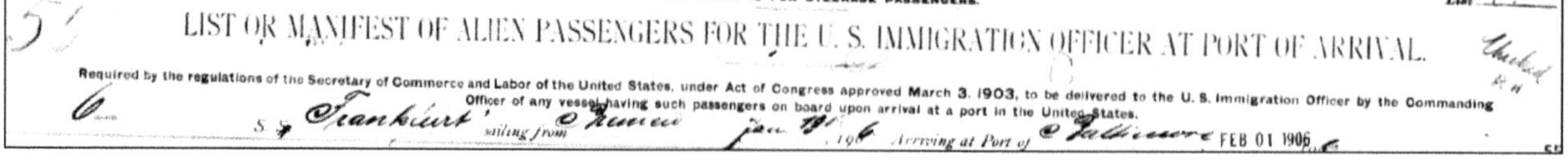

Figure 64 Schabb Family on SS Frankfurt, arriving Feb. 1, 1906

[3] See Surh, "Ekaterinoslav City in 1905," pp. 143, 145, 151.

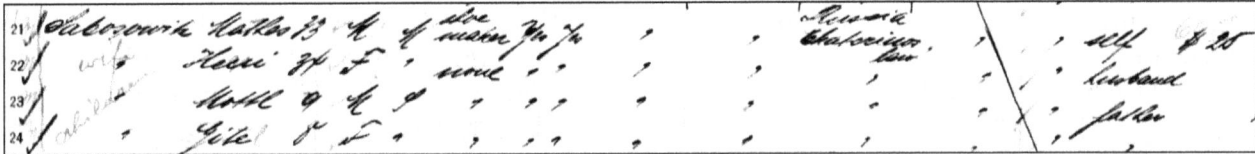

"Mathes" and "Henie" Sabosowitz (Morris and Anna Schabb) and children

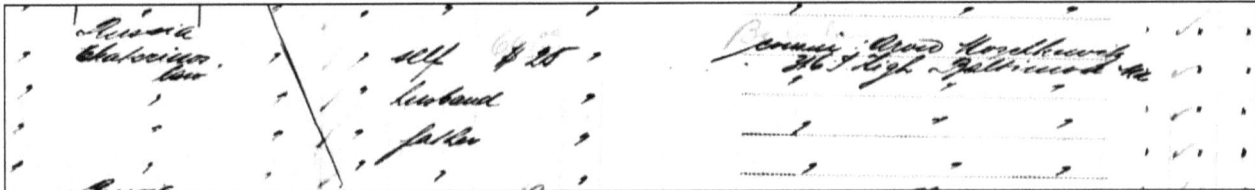

Right-hand columns of manifest showing destination is Bro-in-law Aron Moschewitz at 316 S. High St.

Morris "Chaub" declared his intention to become a citizen soon after arriving on April 10, 1906. The Declaration contains no further information about Morris or where he was living at the time, nor does the 1907 Baltimore City Directory. In 1908, the family was living close to Anna's brother, Aaron Moshkevich, at 313 S. High St. (Aaron and family were still at 316 S. High St.)

In 1909, Morris is listed in the City Directory at 2470 Greenmount Avenue which was apparently the location of his shoe repair store and the future street where his family and other Moshkeviches would settle, as we shall see. At this point, however, their home address was still at 1635 E Fayette Street, in downtown East Baltimore, as evident in the 1910 census and on Morris's 1911 Petition for Naturalization.

Photo 23 Gertrude and Max Schabb, 1907–1908[4]
Courtesy of Oscar Schabb

In the 1910 census, Morris S. Schabb is age 37. His wife "Jennie" (Anna) is 39, and her implied birth year is 1871/1870. They have been married 15 years, indicating their marriage took place in 1894/95. The census incorrectly lists their immigration year as 1905 (as noted above it was 1906). Their daughter, Gitel, now called Gertrude, is 12 and their son Mottle, now called Max, is 13.

---

[4] Max's daughter, Marie, believes these photos may have been taken at Max's bar-mitzvah

A nephew Max Goldberg, age 16, was also living with them. Max Goldberg was the son of Anna's younger sister, Sarah (Moskevitch) Goldberg (discussed later, p. 118ff). Max arrived in 1909 with his sister Gitel Goldberg (later married name Gertrude Kauff). Where Gitel was living in 1910 is not known.

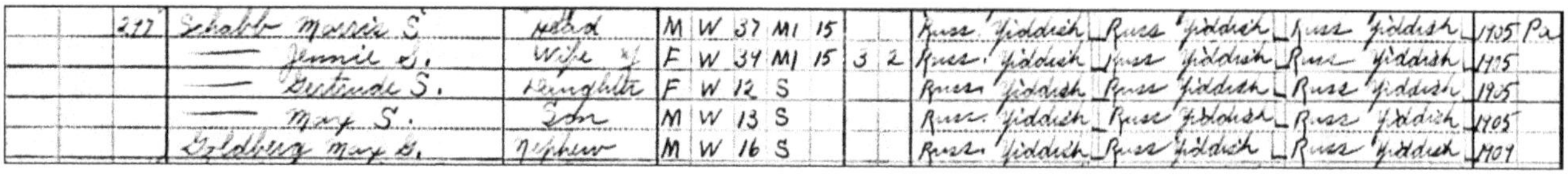

217	Schabb Morris S.	Head	M	W	37	M1	15			Russ	Yiddish	Russ	Yiddish	Russ	Yiddish	1905	Pa
	— Jennie S.	Wife	F	W	34	M1	15	3	2	Russ	Yiddish	Russ	Yiddish	Russ	Yiddish	1905	
	— Gertrude S.	Daughter	F	W	12	S				Russ	Yiddish	Russ	Yiddish	Russ	Yiddish	1905	
	— Max S.	Son	M	W	13	S				Russ	Yiddish	Russ	Yiddish	Russ	Yiddish	1905	
	Goldberg Max G.	Nephew	M	W	16	S				Russ	Yiddish	Russ	Yiddish	Russ	Yiddish	1909	

Figure 65 1910 Census for Morris Schabb and Anna (Moskevitch)

According to Morris's Petition from August 9, 1911, the family was still living in Baltimore at 1635 E. Fayette Street. Morris's birthdate is listed as March 27, 1873, and his occupation is "shoemaker." His birthplace is recorded as "Museer, Russia." The name "Museer" was used for multiple locations (such as Mazyr Russia now in Belarus) and it is not certain where Morris was born or how he and Anna met. If Mazyr, Russia was Morris's birthplace, he traveled quite a distance (544 – 744 km) to meet Anna whose hometown is listed as Kremenchuk or to Ekaterinoslav where their children were born. His granddaughter, Marie, tells me she never heard any town mentioned besides Ekaterinoslav.

The document indicates that Morris and Anna's son Motel, called Max Schabb, was born on May 26, 1896, in Ekaterinoslav Russia. Their daughter, Gitel, called Gertrude Schabb in the Petition, was born Oct. 11, 1898, in Ekaterinoslav. Both are living at home in Baltimore.

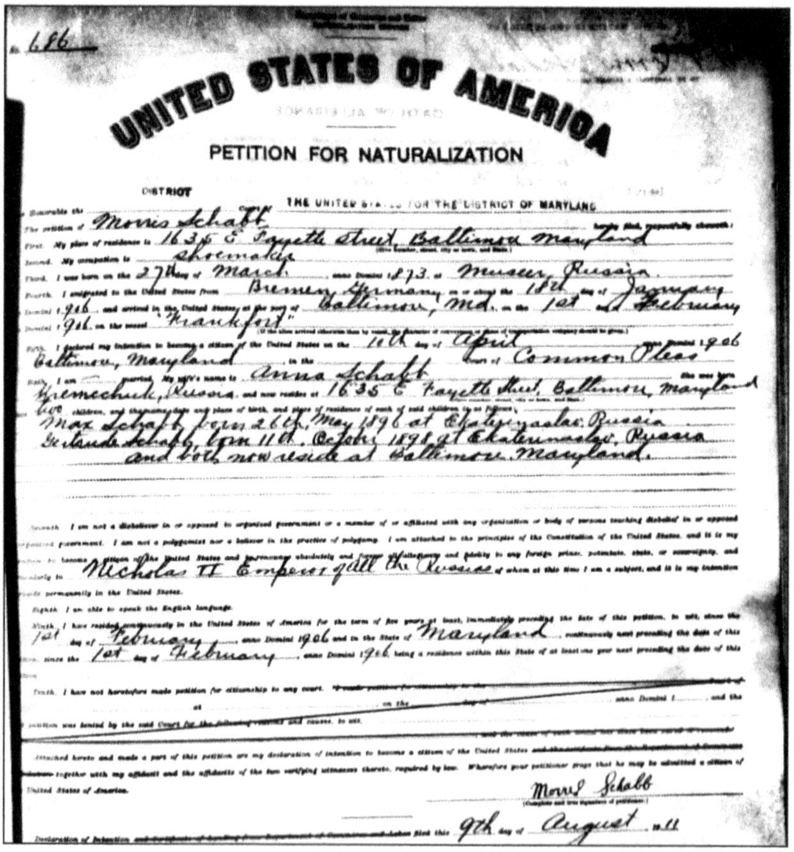

UNITED STATES OF AMERICA

PETITION FOR NATURALIZATION

The petition of Morris Schabb

First. My place of residence is 1635 E. Fayette Street, Baltimore Maryland

Second. My occupation is shoemaker

Third. I was born on the 27th day of March anno Domini 1873 at Museer, Russia.

Fourth. I emigrated to the United States from Bremen, Germany on or about the 18th day of January anno Domini 1906 and arrived in the United States at the port of Baltimore, Md. on the 1st day of February anno Domini 1906 on the vessel "Frankfort"

Fifth. I declared my intention to become a citizen of the United States on the 10th day of April anno Domini 1906 at Baltimore, Maryland in the Court of Common Pleas

Sixth. I am married. My wife's name is Anna Schabb she was born at Kremechuk, Russia and now resides at 1635 E Fayette Street, Baltimore, Maryland

I have two children, and the name, date and place of birth, and place of residence of each of said children is as follows: Max Schabb, born 26th May 1896 at Ekaterinoslav Russia. Gertrude Schabb, born 11th October 1898 at Ekaterinoslav, Russia and both now reside at Baltimore Maryland.

Seventh. I am not a disbeliever in or opposed to organized government or a member of or affiliated with any organization or body of persons teaching disbelief in or opposed to organized government. I am not a polygamist nor a believer in the practice of polygamy. I am attached to the principles of the Constitution of the United States, and it is my intention to become a citizen of the United States and to renounce absolutely and forever all allegiance and fidelity to any foreign prince, potentate, state, or sovereignty, and particularly to Nicholas II Emperor of all the Russias of whom at this time I am a subject, and it is my intention to reside permanently in the United States.

Eighth. I am able to speak the English language.

Ninth. I have resided continuously in the United States of America for the term of five years at least, immediately preceding the date of this petition, to wit, since the 1st day of February anno Domini 1906 and in the State of Maryland continuously next preceding the date of this petition, since the 1st day of February anno Domini 1906, being a residence within this State of at least one year next preceding the date of this petition.

Tenth. I have not heretofore made petition for citizenship to any court.

Attached hereto and made a part of this petition are my declaration of intention to become a citizen of the United States together with my affidavit and the affidavits of the two verifying witnesses thereto, required by law. Wherefore your petitioner prays that he may be admitted a citizen of the United States of America.

Morris Schabb

Declaration of Intention filed this 9th day of August 1911

Figure 66 Aug. 9, 1911, Naturalization Petition of Morris Schabb

By June 5, 1917, when Morris and Anna's son, Max, filled out his Draft Registration Card, the family was living at 2468 Greenmount Ave just doors away from his father's shoe repair shop. Max is listed as a shoemaker working at 2470 Greenmount Ave. The family appears at the same address in the 1920 census. Greenmount Ave was about 4 miles East across town from where Aaron Moshkevich settled with his family at 1206 Poplar Grove Street by this point. Morris's granddaughter, Marie, recalls Morris's shoe repair shop, which she described as a standalone between the house they lived in and stores on other side.

Today Greenmount Ave is known as a violent area and as a dividing line between rich and poor and white and black Baltimore.[5] At the time when the Schabb's moved here, it was a major commercial corridor in Baltimore running north-south from the downtown area to the city limits. The introduction of the automobiles and trolleys was speeding up the migration out of crowded downtown.

The area was also the emerging site of racial tension and segregation as some white residents here (and elsewhere in Baltimore) formed a neighborhood association in 1924 to prevent Blacks from buying or renting in the area. Informal gentlemen's agreements also kept Jews from moving to Northeast Baltimore, which is why so many Jews were moving up the Northwest corridor.[6]

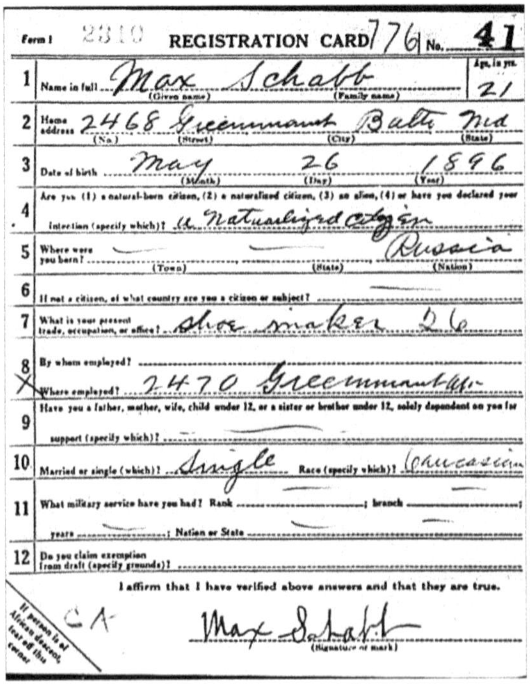
Form 1 2310 REGISTRATION CARD 776 No. 41

1 Name in full Max Schabb (Given name) (Family name) — Age, in yrs. 21

2 Home address 2468 Greenmount Balto Md (No.) (Street) (City) (State)

3 Date of birth May 26 1896 (Month) (Day) (Year)

4 Are you (1) a natural-born citizen, (2) a naturalized citizen, (3) an alien, (4) or have you declared your intention (specify which)? a Naturalized citizen

5 Where were you born? (Town) (State) Russia (Nation)

6 If not a citizen, of what country are you a citizen or subject?

7 What is your present trade, occupation, or office? shoe maker 26

8 By whom employed? Where employed? 2470 Greenmount Ave

9 Have you a father, mother, wife, child under 12, or a sister or brother under 12, solely dependent on you for support (specify which)?

10 Married or single (which)? Single Race (specify which)? Caucasian

11 What military service have you had? Rank ; branch ; years ; Nation or State

12 Do you claim exemption from draft (specify grounds)?

I affirm that I have verified above answers and that they are true.

If person is of African descent, tear off this corner

C A

Max Schabb (Signature or mark)

Figure 67 WWI Draft Registration Card of Max Schabb with address on Greenmount Ave

Based on a military record, it appears that Max was inducted on October 5, 1917, and placed in a "school for bakers and cooks" at Camp Meade in Maryland. "I knew my father was a cook in the army," Marie his daughter recalls. "He was stationed in Plattsburgh, NY near the Canadian border." Max was honorably discharged on June 14, 1919, after the War ended.

As noted above, the Schabbs were still living at 2468 Greenmount Ave in the 1920 Census. Morris was 47, Anna 45, Max 23 and Gertrude 22. The census correctly identifies their year of immigration as 1906—

---

5 For a visual reflection on Greenmount Ave, see https://www.youtube.com/watch?v=Jw3fMxKz-0g

6 See Garrett Power, "The Residential Segregation of Baltimore's Jews." In *Generations*, Fall 1996, 5–7. On the history of neighborhood and racial segregation in Baltimore, see Antero Pietila, *Not in My Neighborhood: How Bigotry Shaped a Great American City*.

they were all naturalized through Morris's process in 1911. The column for birthplace lists Southern Russia but the word "Southern" is scratched out.

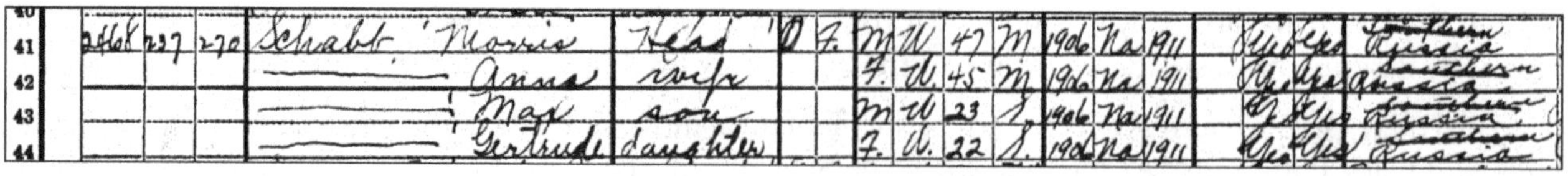

41	2468	237	270	Schabb, Morris	Head	O	F.	M	W	47	M	1906	Na	1911		Yes	Yes	~~Southern~~ Russia
42				—, Anna	wife			F.	W.	45	M	1906	Na	1911		Yes	Yes	~~Southern~~ Russia
43				—, Max	son			M	W	23	S	1906	Na	1911		Yes	Yes	~~Southern~~ Russia
44				—, Gertrude	daughter			F.	W.	22	S	1906	Na	1911		Yes	Yes	~~Southern~~ Russia

Figure 68 1920 census for the Schabb family

A perusal of their page in the 1920 census shows that everyone else listed nearby was born in the US as were their parents. This was not an immigrant neighborhood. The Schabbs had moved from crowded East Baltimore filled with immigrants to a block where most of the residents were second generation.

Anna was apparently hurt in an accident in 1920 for which Morris sued United Railways for $10,000. United Railways was a street railway company in Baltimore from 1899–1935.

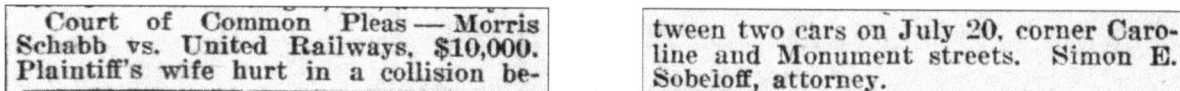

Court of Common Pleas — Morris Schabb vs. United Railways, $10,000. Plaintiff's wife hurt in a collision between two cars on July 20, corner Caroline and Monument streets. Simon E. Sobeloff, attorney.

Figure 69 Morris sues United Railways
The Baltimore Sun, Aug. 3, 1920, p. 7.

The announcement of the lawsuit indicated that Anna was hurt in a collision between two cars at the Corner of Caroline and Monument Streets. Morris was asking for a significant sum of money in compensation. Accidents must have been common since Morris's lawsuit is listed among ten others that day.

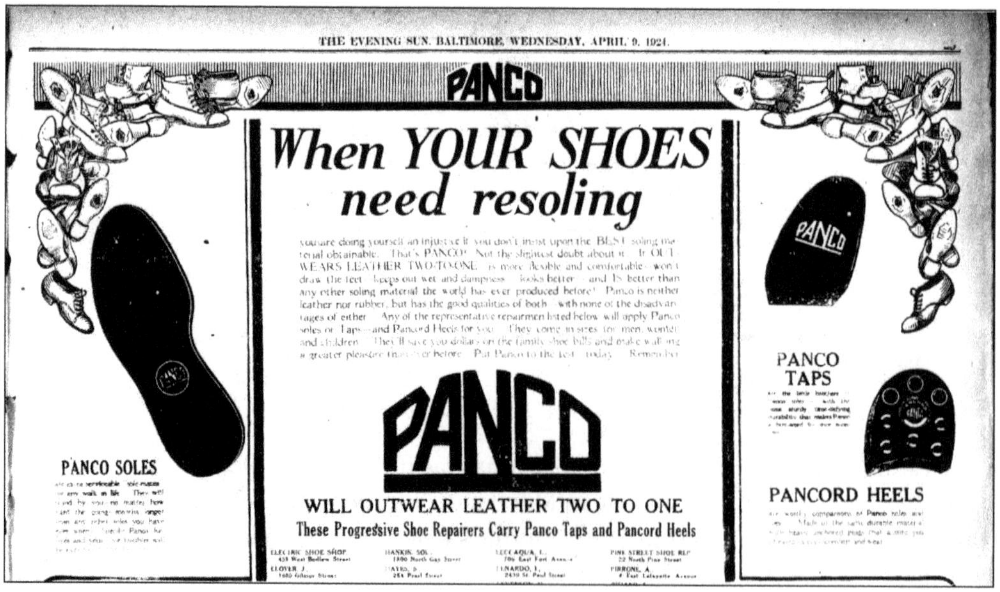

Figure 70 Morris Schabb was one of the signers of this ad for resoling shoes
The Evening Sun, Apr. 9, 1924, page 25

Max's daughter Marie recalls the shoe repair shop growing up.

> We would go there all the time; I would play with his leather and nails, and glue. He was also involved in selling real estate and from one house, he got antique chairs and he put them in his store. My aunt [Gertrude Schabb] said, "You can't have them in the shop." She took them and did the needlepoint for all the chairs. My mother eventually got two and my aunt had two, and I eventually inherited two.

Morris (seated) and wife Anna (standing)
with Max (left) and Gertrude, (right)

Gertrude Schabb circa 1920

Photo 24 The Schabb Family 1918
Courtesy of Oscar Schabb

Photo 25 Engagement photos of Max Schabb and Dora Matz circa 1919
Courtesy of Marie (Schabb) Schwartz

***

Max and Gertrude Get Married

The marriage license of Max and his finance Dora Matz was recorded in *The Baltimore Sun* on June 27, 1924. Max was no longer living in his parents' home by this time and had relocated to 1609 Eastern Avenue close to Fell's Point. Fiancée, Dora, was the daughter of Oscar Matz and Frieda (Kaplan). They arrived in the US from Russia in 1891 with Dora's three older siblings according to their 1900 census. Dora was born in Maryland in April 1895 according to the same document. Her father Oscar died in 1919 and Max and Dora named their first child, Oscar, after Dora's father. He was born on Aug. 26, 1925.

SCHABB—MATZ.—Max, 28, 1609 Eastern avenue; Dora, 26.

Figure 71 Listing of Max and Dora's Marriage License
The Baltimore Sun, June 27, 1924, p. 21

In the 1930 census, Max and Dora are listed at 726 Hilton Street in Baltimore (near Denison) and not far from Max's uncle Aaron. Their daughter, Marie Schabb (married name Marie Schwartz) was born in 1931. In the 1940 census, the family is still residing at 726 Hilton Street. Max is working in produce and owns his own business.

1930 census for Max, Dora and Oscar

***

A Memory of Dora Schabb by David Chapin

> She was affectionately nicknamed "Dee." She was a wonderful person, never had a bad word to say about anyone, and an absolutely terrific cook and baker who made everything from scratch. She lived to be 100 years old and was sharp as a tack till the day she died. Her grandkids wrote a cookbook of their favorite Dee recipes. Family history is more than just the facts in documents, it is also the cultural stuff, including in this case what they cooked.

GRANDMA DEE'S RECIPES

a collection of recipes from the kitchen of

DORA MATZ SCHABB

compiled by her daughter

Marie Schabb Schwartz

drawings by her granddaughter

Beth Schabb

April 25, 1988
Silver Spring, Maryland

Copyright 1988 Marie Schwartz

Figure 72 Cookbook cover of recipes of Dora Matz Schabb

Morris and Anna's daughter, Gertrude Schabb, was still living with her parents in 1925 when she and Alexander Cohn got their marriage license, recorded in *The Baltimore Sun* a day before their wedding.

COHN—SCHABB.—Alexander, 31, Pinkney road and Wirt avenue; Gertrude,
27.

Figure 73 Marriage License Gertrude and Alexander Cohn
The Baltimore Sun, Sept. 4, 1925, p. 19

An article in *The Baltimore Sun* a week later covered the wedding. The article mentions the presence of Gertrude's aunt, Mrs. A. Moshkevich [i.e., Aaron's wife, Sophie] as well as their daughter Rena (not yet married). Gertrude's brother, Max Schabb, was there, as well as his new mother-in-law, Mrs. F. [Freda] Matz (mother of Dora Matz) as well as Dora's sister Fannie Matz.

Gertrude's first cousin, Gersh I. Moss (son of Itsig /Isaac Moshkevich) was also present. As we shall see below, Gersh arrived in 1914, and had already shortened his name to Moss (p. 145ff) by this time. Also present was the groom's sister, Mrs. B. Rosenberg from Roanoke, Virginia.[7]

Figure 74 Wedding,
Gertrude Schabb and Alexander Cohn
The Baltimore Sun, Sept. 13, 1925, p. 82

The marriage of Miss Gertrude Schabb, daughter of Mr. and Mrs. Morris Schabb, to Mr. Alexander Cohn, of this city, took place at the home of the bride's parents, 2468 Greenmount avenue, on Saturday, September 5, at 8.30 P. M. The Rev. Dr. S. Schaffer officiated.

The guests were Mr. and Mrs. S. Moskalik and Miss Fannie Moskalik, of New York city; Mrs. B. Rosenberg, of Roanoke, Va.; Miss Mary Silverman, of North Carolina; Mrs. A. Moshkevich, Mrs. F. Matz, Mrs. E. Thomas, Mrs. Ella M. McNamar, Mrs. H. Kohn, Mrs. I. Barnett, Mr. and Mrs. J. Rudolph, Mr. and Mrs. S. Hurwitz, Misses Ida Potterfield, Lillie Levin, Mary Levin, Minnie Pasternack, Rena Moshkevich and Fannie Matz, Messrs. Max Schabb and Gresh I. Moss, all of Baltimore. Mr. and Mrs. Cohn are spending their honeymoon in Atlantic City, N. J.

Gertrude's husband, Alexander Cohn, was born in Chicago on Dec. 2, 1893. It is unclear when he arrived in Baltimore. His Draft Card from June 5, 1917, shows he was already living in Baltimore by that point on 2003 E. Pratt Street and working for the Bethlehem Steel Co as a "ship fitter" at Sparrows Point.[8] In the 1926 City directory, not long after they got married, Alex is listed working at National Pharmaceutical Manufacturing and the couple is living at 208 Pickney Road. With that clue, we can trace Alex's history back for several years before he married Gertrude.

The Baltimore City Directory indicates Alex Cohn was working at National Pharmaceutical from 1921-1924, living first at 1925 E. Baltimore St. and then moving to 2243 Eutaw Place where he lived until he and Gertrude married. Alex doesn't appear in the 1920 City directory, and I suspect he may have gone to pharmaceutical school during that time, though this is not certain. In 1918 he is listed as a clerk at the same E. Pratt address that appears on his 1917 WWI Registration Card. Before 1917, there is more than one man named "Alex Cohn" in the City directory, but it is not possible to disambiguate them and identify the Alex Cohn that Gertrude married. From obituaries it appears Alex came from a large family.

---

[7] In Alexander Cohn's obituary, his sister is listed as Mrs. Lake Rosenberg from Roanoke. Her name growing up was Bessie Cohn. His brother's name in the obituary is Charles Cohn.

[8] It is clear this Alexander Cohn is the man whom Gertrude married because the birthdate matches the information on his later WWII Draft Registration card in which he explicitly mentions Gertrude.

By the 1930 census Alex and Gertrude moved to 3306 Pickney Road, northwest of downtown and not far from Park Heights Ave and the neighborhood of Falstaff. The couple owned their house there which had a value of $10,000.

The record indicates Alexander was 36 and a pharmacist in a drugstore and Gertrude was 31 and a manager in a hosiery shop. The couple never had children. They are still at the same address on Pinkney Road in the 1940 census. Gertrude rather than Alex is listed as "head" of household in this census. Gertrude's niece, Marie, recalls that Alex was sickly and speculates that perhaps the cause was his earlier work as a ship fitter at Sparrows Point.

Figure 75 1930 Census for Gertrude (Schabb) and husband Alexander Cohn

Figure 76 1940 Census for Gertrude (Schabb) and husband Alexander Cohn

Gertrude and Max's mother, Anna (Moshkevich) Schabb, passed away on Jan. 22, 1947. She was buried in the Adath Jeshurun Cemetery. Their father, Morris, waited a year longer before passing away on Jan. 23, 1948.

Morris's tombstone reads:

Father

Morris

Jan 23, 1948

Matiyahu son of R. Yitzhak Isaac

passed away the 12 of Shevet, 5708.

Anna's tombstone reads:

Mother

Anna

Jan 22, 1947

Henia daughter of Mordechai the Cohen

Passed away the first of the New Month Shevet [year is effaced but was 5707].

Gertrude's husband, Alexander Cohn, passed away on May 11, 1956. Gertrude lived for almost 30 more years and passed away on May 3, 1984.

Gertrude's brother, Max, passed away in 1955. His daughter Marie tells me he passed on the second day of Rosh Hashanah. Everyone was in shul when he was taken to the hospital. Marie went to see him and recalls that he was the best he had been in a long time. But by the time she got home, he had passed away. Max's wife Dora lived another 40 years and passed away in 1995 on the seventh night of Chanukah. She was 100 years old. Their son, Oscar Schabb, who is still living as I write, married Evelyn Chantel. They had two sons, Mark and Richard, and two daughters, Joan (married name Bellhouse) and Beth (married name Williams). Joan Schabb Bellhouse passed away in 2002. Evelyn passed away in 2003.

Max and Dora's daughter, Marie Schabb (my informant), married Seymour Schwartz and they had two sons, Steve and Martin. Marie is still alive in her 90s and I consulted her while working on this narrative. Her husband Seymour passed away in 2012.

Photo 26 Oscar Schabb, 1943
Baltimore Polytechnic Institute

Figure 77 Marie (Schabb) Schwartz (center)
University of Maryland College Park 1951

Records Summary for Anna (Moshkevich) Schabb and Family

Feb. 1, 1906 Passenger Manifest	Sailing on SS Frankfort from Bremen on Jan. 19, 1906 arriving at Baltimore Feb. 01, 1906. **Sabosowitz, Mathes** [i.e., Morris] age 33, shoe maker, last residence Ekaterinoslaw, who paid? self, possesses $25 [written faintly and overwritten with $60] destination [faint] Br. in law [brother-in-law] cousin Aron Moschkewitz 316 S. High Street, Baltimore Md, **Henie [i.e., Anna],** wife, age 34, occupation none.... **Mottl [Max]** age 9, and **Gitel [Gertrude]** age 8.
1908 Baltimore City Directory	Morris Schabb is listed 313 S High St.
1909 Baltimore City Directory	Morris Schabb is listed at 2470 Greenmnt ave
Apr. 29, 1910 US Federal Census	1635 E Fayette St. (3 families at the address) **Morris S. Schabb** Head, age 37, years married 15, Birthplace Russ[ia] Yiddish, immigration year 1905, naturalization PA[first papers submitted] Speaks English, shoemaker, store; **Jennie S.** wife, 39 [implied birth year 1871], years married 15, children born 3, living 2, immigration year 1905, Speaks English; Gertrude S. Daughter, age 12, Birthplace Russ[ia] Yiddish, immigration year 1905, Max S, Son, age 13, Birthplace Russ[ia] Yiddish, immigration year 1905; **Max Goldberg** nephew age 16, immigration year 1906, naturalization status Al[ien]
Aug. 9, 1911 Naturalization Petition	**Morris Schabb**, 1635 E. Fayette Street, Baltimore, occupation shoemaker, born March 27, 1873 at Museer [uncertain reference], Russia, emigrated from Bremen Germany on Jan. 18, 1906 and arrived in Baltimore, Md on Feb. 1, 1906 on the vessel "Frankfort", declared intention April 10, 1906 in Baltimore, wife's name **Anna Schabb**, she was born Kremechuk, Russia and resides same address. Two children: **Max Schabb** born May 26, 1896 at Ekaterinaslav Russia, **Gertrude Schabb** born Oct. 11, 1898 at Ekaterinaslav both reside in Baltimore. Witnesses Israel Markowitz, merchant 1635 E. Fayette St. and witness Abraham Levin 219 S. Bond St.
Sept. 12, 1918 WWI Draft Registration Card	Max Schabb, 2468 Greenmount Balto Md, date of birth May 26, 1896, a naturalized citizen, born in Russia, shoe maker 2470 Greenmount ave, nearest relative Anna 2468 Greenmount Ave
Maryland Military Men, 1917–1918	Age 21, address 2468 Greenmount. Records reads as follows: Ind [Inducted] 10/5/17 pvt [private]; cook 6/1/19, Co F 313 Inf [Infantry?]; Sup Co 313 Inf 12/31/17; School for Bakers & Cooks Camp Meade Md. 3/18/18; Overseas Repl Draft Camp Meade Md. 4/29/19, Hon disch [honorable discharge] 6/14/19
Jan. 16, 1920 US Federal Census Baltimore	Living at 2468 Greenmount Ave, **Morris Schabb**, Head, Owns home, age 47, year immigrated 1906, Na[turalized], Year Naturalized 1911, Birthplace Russia [Southern scratched out], Occupation Proprietor Shoemaker Store, wife **Anna**, age 45, year immigrated 1906, Na[turalized], Year Naturalized 1911, Birthplace Russia [Southern scrated out], occupation none, son **Max**, age 23, year immigrated 1906, Na[turalized], Year Naturalized 1911, Birthplace Russia [Southern scratched out], occupation Salesman Shoe Co, daughter, **Gertrude**, age 22, year immigrated 1906, Na[turalized], Year Naturalized 1911, Birthplace Russia [Southern scratched out], occupation none

Apr. 7, 1930 US Federal Census Baltimore	Living at 2468 Greenmount Ave., **Morris Schabb**, Head, Home Owned, Home Value $3000, age 55, marriage age, 22, birthplace Russia, Immigration year 1905, Na[turalized], occupation shoe repairing, Shoe Repair Shop, wife **Annie** age 54, marriage age 20, birthplace Russia, year immigrated 1905, Na[turalized], occupation None
Apr. 7, 1930 US Federal Census Baltimore	Living in 3306 Pinkney Road, **Alexander Cohn**, Head, owns home, value $10,000, age 36, age at marriage 31, born in Illinois, occupation pharmacist in drug store, wife **Gertrude**, age 31, age at marriage 26, born in Russia, occupation manager in hosiery shop
Apr. 14, 1930 US Federal Census Baltimore	Living at 726 Hilton Street, **Max Schabb**, Head, owns home, value $7,400, age 33, age at marriage 27, Born Russia, immigration year 1906, NA[turalized], Proprietor in Produce, wife **Dora**, age 31, age at marriage 26, born in Maryland, son **Oscar I.** , age 4m born in Maryland.
Apr. 5, 1940 US Federal Census Baltimore	Living at 2468 Greenmount Ave., **Morris Schabb**, head, 67, born in Russia, Na[turalized], Same House in 1935, occupation Repairer / Shoemaker, **Annie**, wife, age 67, born in Russia
Apr. 11, 1940 US Federal Census Baltimore	Living at 3306 Pinkney Road, owns home, value $6,000 **Gertrude Cohn** Head, 42, born in Russia, same house in 1935, no occupation, husband **Alexander**, age 47, born in Illinois, occupation: Pharmacist in Drug Store
Apr. 11, 1940 US Federal Census Baltimore	Living at 726 Hilton Street, **Max Schabb**, Head, age 43, born in Russia, same house in 1935, occupation Produce jobber, owns produce business, wife **Dora**, age 41, born in Maryland, son **Oscar I**, age 14, Maryland, daughter **Marie P**, age 8, born in Maryland

***

5.

FAMILY OF SAMUEL MOSHKEVICH AND FRIEDA (SHPETNER)

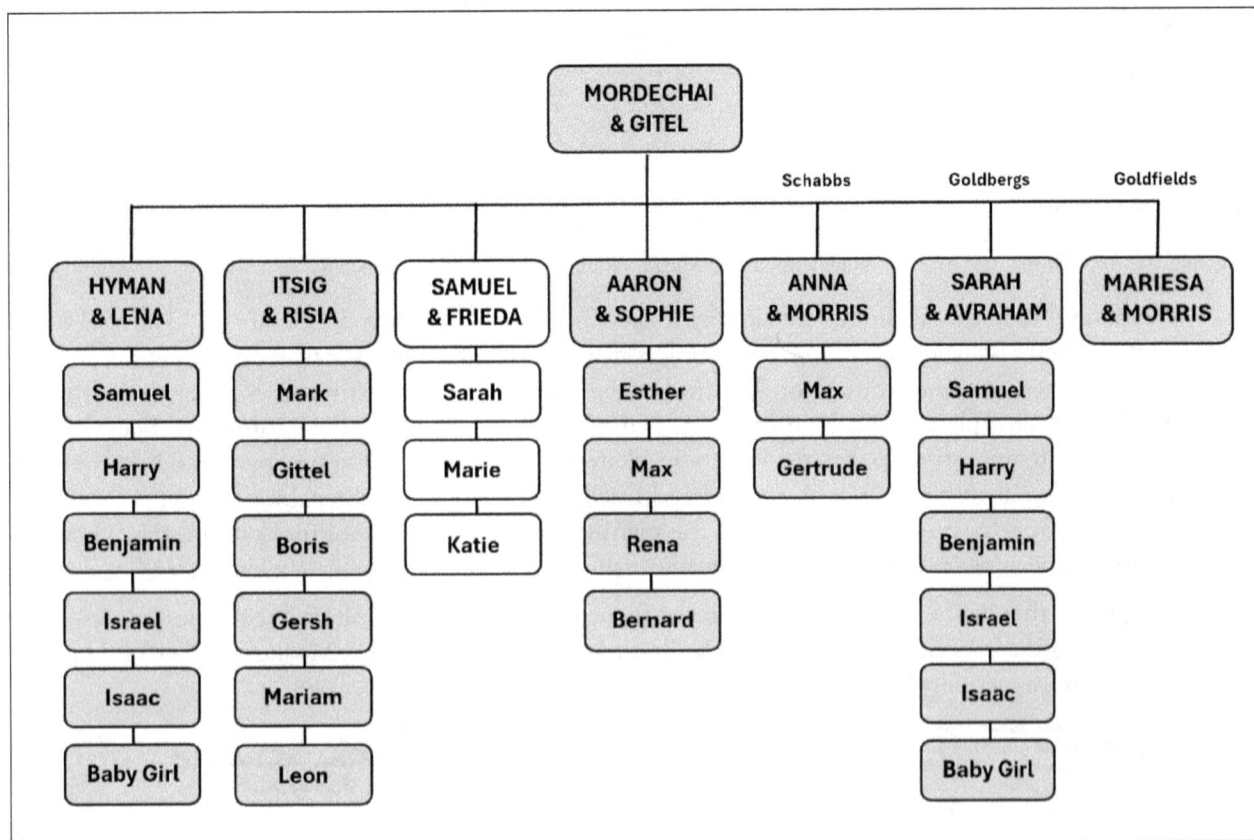

```
                              MORDECHAI
                               & GITEL
                                                Schabbs      Goldbergs    Goldfields

   HYMAN      ITSIG      SAMUEL     AARON      ANNA        SARAH        MARIESA
   & LENA     & RISIA    & FRIEDA   & SOPHIE   & MORRIS    & AVRAHAM    & MORRIS

   Samuel     Mark       Sarah      Esther     Max         Samuel
   Harry      Gittel     Marie      Max        Gertrude    Harry
   Benjamin   Boris      Katie      Rena                   Benjamin
   Israel     Gersh                 Bernard               Israel
   Isaac      Mariam                                       Isaac
   Baby Girl  Leon                                         Baby Girl
```

Figure 78 Family of Samuel Moshkevich and Frieda (Shpetner)

***

Arrival of Samuel and Frieda Moshkevich and Family

Almost a month after Anna (Moshkevich) and Morris Schabb and family left for Baltimore (on Jan. 19, 1906), Anna's brother Solomon followed with his family. He would soon be known as "Samuel" in Baltimore and remembered that way by his descendants. Solomon was third in the birth order of the "Moskovitch Seven." By the time he left Russia with his family, his older brother Hyman was already in Canada, and his younger brother Aaron and younger sister Anna Schabb were already in Baltimore.

On Feb. 15, 1906, Solomon, his wife "Fanny" (also called Frieda and Freda) (née Shpetner), and their three daughters departed Bremen on the SS Roland and landed in Baltimore on March 3, 1906.

The writing on the manifest is difficult to decipher but we know the record belongs to Solomon/Samuel Moshkevich because the information matches that on his naturalization Petition from 1912, and because their destination is Samuel's brother, Aaron Moskevitch at 316 S. High Street in Baltimore where Aaron and his family were then residing.

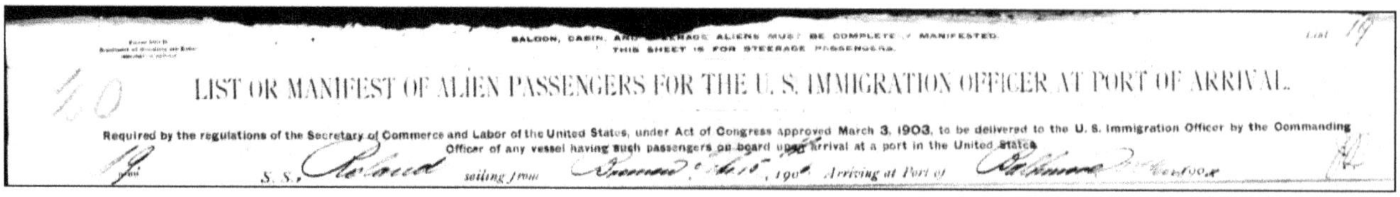

Figure 79 Manifest of Solomon and Frieda and children on SS Roland, arriving March 3, 1906

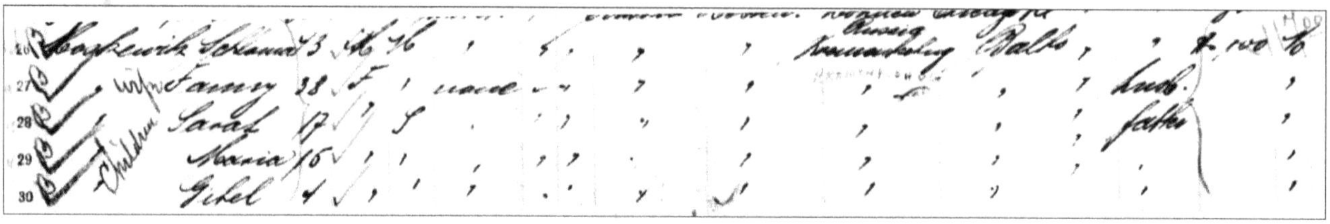

"Schlame" age 43, "Fanny" age 38 with daughters, Sarah, Maria, Gitel, last residence Kremenchug

"Schlame" (Solomon/Samuel) Moskewitz is age 43, "Fanny," his wife, 38, Sarah 17, "Maria" 15 and Gitel (Kate) 4. Their last residence before migrating is nearly unreadable but starts with a K. Underneath it someone has written "Kremenkohug" or "Kremenkchug," presumably referring to Kremenchuk, Russia, which matches the birthplace Samuel wrote on his Naturalization Petition in 1912 (discussed below). As is evident from a contemporary map, Kremenchuk and Ekaterinoslav were not that far apart, and both were on the Dnipro River (see map Figure 3 p. 6). Samuel and Frieda's great-granddaughter, Linda Rose,[1] tells me her grandmother, Sarah, who is listed as age 17 on the manifest, was in high school in Ekaterinoslav when the family departed. She appears in a photo with her high school class in Ekaterinoslav below (p. 94).

It appears that in the right-hand columns of their manifest, "$100" dollars in Solomon's possession is scratched out, and someone wrote $117.00. His destination is "brother Aron Moskewitz," 316 E High St. Baltimore. Aaron was actually living at 316 *South* High Street, but the intent is clear.

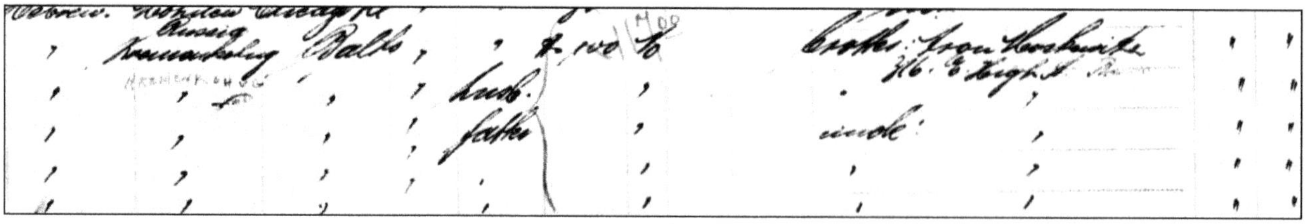

Right-hand columns of manifest showing destination: brother: Aron Moskevitz 316 E High St Balto

Solomon started his naturalization process almost immediately upon arrival, signing his Declaration of Intention on April 11, 1906. He did so just five days after his brother-in-law, Morris Schabb signed his Petition, probably inspired by his brother-in-law's progress. The Declaration has little information but shows he was still using the name "Solomon Moskevitch."

---

[1] Linda Rose is a great-granddaughter of Samuel and Frieda Moshkevich. Her mother was Gertrude (Haberer) Rose, who was the daughter of Sarah (Moskevitch) Haberer, one Samuel and Frieda's daughters.

Photo 27 Moshkevich Family Reunion in Baltimore, circa 1906[2]
Families of siblings Anna (Moshkovich) Schabb, Samuel Moshkovich and Aaron Moshkovich.
Courtesy of David Chapin, Sharon Moss and Linda Rose

1) Aaron Moshkevich and wife 2) Sophie (Nausecha)

3) Morris Schabb and wife 4) Anna (Moshkovich) Schabb, their daughter 5) Gertrude Schabb, and their son 6) Max Schabb

7) Freida (Shpetner) with her husband 8) Samuel Moskevitch, their daughter 9) Sarah, 10) Marie 11) Kate

---

[2]Some descendants believe this photo was taken in Russia. See discussion in the next footnote for its probable dating.

A family reunion of sorts apparently took place in Baltimore not long after Samuel arrived with his family. Three Moshkovich siblings (Aaron, Anna, and Samuel) and their families were now living in Baltimore. A photo (Photo 27 above) shows Aaron and Sophie (#1 and #2) standing in the back, Anna's family—her husband Morris Schabb and children Max and Gertrude (#3 #4, #5, #6) and Samuel's family — his wife Frieda and their children, Sarah, Marie and Katie (#7, #8, #9, #10, #11).

Katie Moshkevich (#11), who is the youngest in the photo, was born in 1901 and appears to be about 4 or 5 years old. Gertrude Schabb (#5) was born in 1898 and appears to be 8 or 9 in the photo. I suspect this photo was taken in 1906 not long after Samuel's family arrived and showing the three siblings' families together in Baltimore, to send to family still back to Russia and to their brother Hyman living in Canada.[3]

Photo 28 1905 High School class of Sarah Moskevitch in Ekaterinoslav
Sarah is second row from the bottom to the left. Courtesy of Linda Rose.

---

[3] The family photo taken above appears to be a Moshkevich reunion of sorts in Baltimore in 1906, not back in Russia as at least one descendant believes. Since the photo includes three Moshkevich siblings (Aaron Moshkevich, Anna Schabb, Samuel Moskevich), it must have been taken when they were all together—either before 1904 (when Aaron and Sophie left for Baltimore) or after March 1906 (after Anna and Samuel arrived with their families). If this photo was taken in Russia before 1904, we would expect to see Aaron and Sophie's daughter who was born in 1900 and who died in 1903. We would also expect to see the younger Moskovitch sibling, Mariesa. The only person missing from this photo if it was taken in Baltimore is Aaron and Sophie's son, Max, who was born in 1904. He would have been about two at this point.

Photo 29 Samuel and Frieda's daughter
Sarah Moshkevich as baby in Russia
Courtesy of Linda Rose

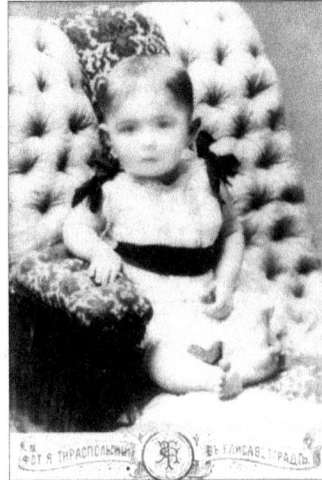

By 1907, Solomon is listed as "Saml Moskovitch" in the Baltimore City Directory as a straw hatmaker at 36 S. High St., a block away from his brother Harry (Aaron) "Moshkievich," who is also listed in the Directory as an optician residing at 316 S. High St. Notice that Harry (Aaron) appears as "Moshkievich" and Samuel as "Moskovitch." The spelling of the surname had not yet stabilized.

Moshkievich Harry, optician, 316 s High
Moskawicz Julius, lab, 506 s Bethel
Moskovetz Chas H, barber, 2312 Boston
Moskovetz Max, barber, 1742 Aliceanna
Moskovitch Saml, straw hatmkr, 36 s High
Moskovitz David, mattressmkr, 17 s Exeter
Moskovitz Max, tailor, 1524 e Madison
Moskowitz Morris, clk, 223 w Franklin
Moskowitz Saml, tailor, 123 s Spring

Figure 80 Samuel Moskovitch, 1907 Baltimore City Directory

By 1909, *The Baltimore Sun* published an announcement that leaves no doubt that by this time Solomon had begun using the name "Samuel" at least outside of official records. The announcement involved the engagement of his eldest daughter Sarah, as we shall now see.

***

The Daughters Start Marrying

I suspect that Samuel and Frieda were surprised, if not shocked when—just one year after their arrival—their daughter Sarah became engaged to Mr. Berthold Benjamin Haberer. "B. B.", as he was called in the engagement announcement and other news articles from the same decade, was a young Jewish man who was born in Baden Baden, Germany and 10 years Sara's senior.

ENGAGEMENT ANNOUNCED.
The engagement has been announced of Miss Sarah Moshkevich, daughter of Mr. and Mrs. Samuel Moshkevich, to Mr. B. B. Haberer, of Baltimore.

Figure 81 Engagement of Sarah Moshkevich
The Baltimore Sun, Aug. 5, 1907, page 6

"B. B." was 28 years old at the time of their engagement and Sarah just 18, still reasonably fresh off the boat a year and a half after her arrival. They married on Jan. 12, 1908.

According to records, Berthold Haberer was born in Germany on March 22, 1878, and arrived in the US at the age of 20 on Jun. 7, 1898. He declared his intention to be a citizen on Sept. 4, 1903, and he signed his Petition on April 11, 1906, just a month after Sarah landed in Baltimore with her parents and ironically the same day that Sarah's father, Samuel, signed his Declaration of Intention. I like to imagine that Samuel met his future son-in-law that day in line. Their granddaughter, Linda Rose, tells me the story she heard. Because Sarah spoke many languages, she was hired to work in one of Berthold's stores at the docks in Baltimore. That's how they met. Berthold's photo posted online shows a dashing young man. The rest is history.

Perhaps Samuel and Frieda felt relieved that their daughter Sarah was marrying an immigrant who was already established and acclimated to being a US citizen. Sarah and B. B. married in Baltimore on Jan. 12, 1908. We return to their story below.

***

"Came to Buy; Won Bride"

An even bigger surprise greeted the family in September 1909. Even *The Baltimore Sun* was taken with the love story between Samuel and Frieda's middle daughter, Marie, and Morris Cooper, a prominent Jewish merchant from Petersburg, Virginia. Morris met Marie at a dance during a business trip to Baltimore to purchase goods for his department store in Petersburg. Morris and Marie were engaged two weeks later. "Came to Buy; Won Bride" read the title of the article announcing their wedding plans just three months after they met.

Figure 82 "Came to Buy; Won Bride"
The Baltimore Sun, Sept. 1, 1909, p. 14

> **CAME TO BUY; WON BRIDE**
>
> **Mr. Cooper, Virginia Merchant, Weds Miss Moshkevich.**
>
> After a courtship of less than three months, Miss Marie Moshkevich, daughter of Mr. Samuel Moshkevich, 726 East Baltimore street, was married last night at Fink's Hall, Bond and Pratt streets, to Mr. Morris Cooper, a prominent business man of Petersburg, Va.
>
> The ceremony was performed under a bower of roses in the big hall by Rabbi B. Bleiberg, of Eden Street Synagogue, and was witnessed by nearly 200 friends of the bride and groom.
>
> Less than three months ago Mr. Cooper came to this city to make purchases to stock his department store, and several friends invited him to a dance. Mr. Cooper went to the dance and met Miss Moshkevich. It was love at first sight, and in two weeks the couple were engaged.
>
> Miss Mollie Applefeld was the maid of honor, and Mr. Samuel Applefeld was the best man.
>
> After the ceremony a reception in honor of Mr. and Mrs. Cooper was held in the hall, and late last night they departed on their honeymoon.

After the two daughters, Sarah and Marie, were married, the 1910 census shows the now shrunken "Moschkevich" family still living at 36 S. High St. with two other families. Samuel is age 42, Frieda age 40 and Katie, their youngest daughter, age 8. The 1910 census also notes that Samuel and Frieda had 3 children and that all 3 were still living (in contrast to Aaron and Sophie who lost a child).

Samuel's naturalization status, which at this time in the US conferred a husband's status on his wife and children, is "Pa," indicating his "first papers" were submitted but he was not yet a citizen. The census lists their date of migration correctly as 1906 and that Samuel worked in a "dry goods" store. The record also indicates the couple Samuel and Freida were married for 15 years. This is obviously a mistake, since it implies their marriage took place in 1895, which was after their daughters Sarah and Marie were born.

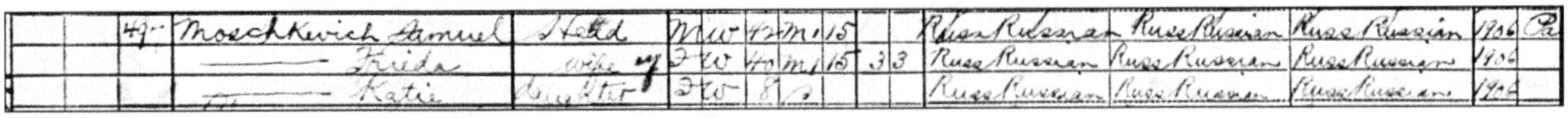

47	Moschkevich Samuel	Head	M	W	42	M1	15			Russ Russian	Russ Russian	Russ Russian	1906	Pa
	—— Freida	Wife	F	W	40	M1	15	3	3	Russ Russian	Russ Russian	Russ Russian	1906	
	—— Katie	Daughter	F	W	8	S				Russ Russian	Russ Russian	Russ Russian	1906	

Figure 83 1910 Census for Samuel Moschkevich and family at 36 S. High St.

On Jan. 5, 1912, with two daughters married-off and gone from their home, Samuel filled out his Naturalization Petition. The record shows he continued to list his formal name as "Solomon Moshkevich," using his first name to match his earlier records and the spelling of the surname as it was starting to stabilize in Baltimore. They are still living in crowded East Baltimore at 923 E. Baltimore Street and Solomon is a merchant.

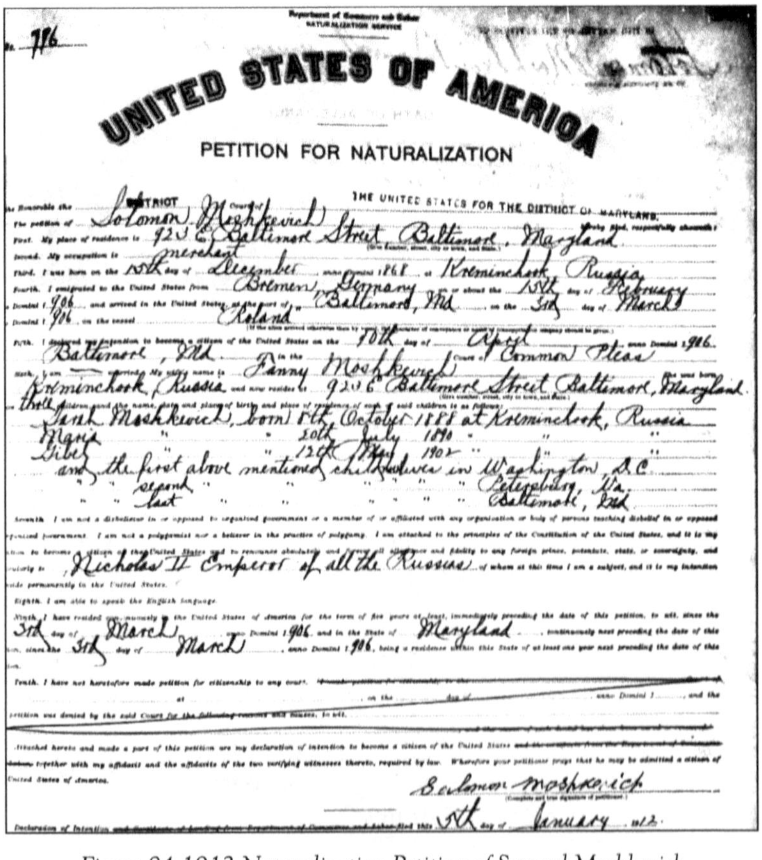

Figure 84 1912 Naturalization Petition of Samuel Moshkevich

Samuel lists his birthplace as "Kreminchook" [Kremenchuk] and his birthdate as Dec. 15, 1868. The three daughters are also listed, but the Petition indicates that Sarah had gone to live in Washington, DC and Marie was in Petersburg, Va. Only Gitel (Kate) still remained in the home with them.

According to this record, all the girls were born in "Kreminchook." The Petition also records birthdates of the daughters: Sarah was born Oct. 8, 1888, Marie on July 20, 1890, and Gitel (Katie) on May 12, 1902. The record does not align with oral traditions passed on in the family. Sarah's granddaughter, Linda Rose, was told Sarah was born in Ekaterinoslav, where she also attended a Russian Orthodox High

School in 1905. They also used to celebrate her birthday on Oct. 21 (not Oct. 8) and Sarah was never sure if she was born in 1888 or 1889.

In the meantime, Samuel and Frieda's two eldest daughters got started on their families. Sarah and her new husband, B. B., moved to the District of Columbia where their first daughter Gertrude Haberer was born on Oct. 2, 1909.[4] Their second daughter Claire Haberer was born on Jan. 27, 1913. A son Berthold was born in Virginia after they relocated there, a story to which we return.

Photo 30 Wedding photo of Sarah Moshkevich
and Berthold "B. B." Haberer
Courtesy of Harry Tankin

Meanwhile, Marie and her new husband Morris Cooper had their first child, Grace Cooper, on Oct. 30, 1911. Grace was followed by Beatrice on March 3, 1916, and Harriet on Nov. 5, 1918. A daughter Shirley was born in 1922 after the family relocated to Michigan (discussed later).

Samuel, Frieda and youngest daughter Kate remained at 923 E. Baltimore for most of the decade. In the 1915 City Directory Samuel is still listed in "dry goods." In 1919, Kate got engaged to Thomas Shpetner of New York, who was also a relative of her mother Frieda.[5] In the engagement announcement, Samuel, Frieda and Kate are living at 3122 Calvert Street which was about 4 miles north of where they lived earlier and was still their address in the 1920 census.

Kate and her new husband moved to New York initially where their first daughter, Norma Shpetner was born on March 10, 1922. By 1925, they moved to Springfield, Mass where their son Stanley was born on March 5, 1925.

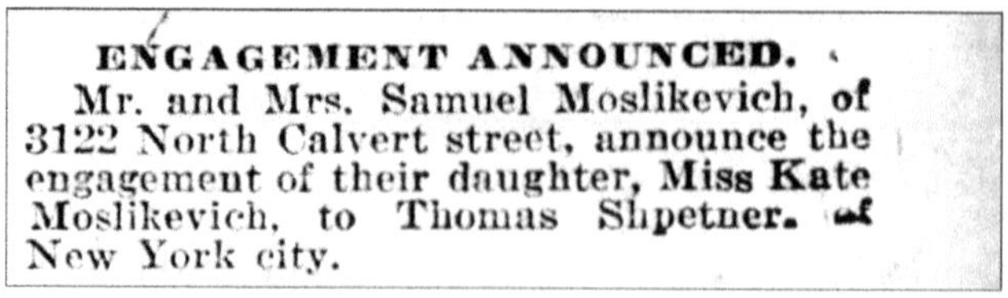

ENGAGEMENT ANNOUNCED.
Mr. and Mrs. Samuel Moslikevich, of 3122 North Calvert street, announce the engagement of their daughter, Miss Kate Moslikevich, to Thomas Shpetner, of New York city.

Figure 85 Kate's Engagement Announcement
The Baltimore Sun, Dec 7, 1919, p. 13

---

[4] A mistake was made on her tombstone listing her birth year as 1908. Her birth certificate says 1909.
[5] According to notes David Chapin made, Thomas was a first cousin once removed of Kate's mother, Frieda.

Photo 31 1913 Families of Samuel Moshkevich and Anna (Moshkevich) Schabb

(1) Anna (Moshkevich) Schabb, her husband (2) Morris Schabb, their daughter Gertrude (3) and their son (4) Max.

(5) Samuel Moshkevich and his wife (6) Frieda (Shpetner),

(7) Samuel and Frieda's daughter Sarah (Moshkevich) holding her baby Clair Haberer born in 1913, with her husband (8) "B. B." Haberer and (9) their daughter Gertude Haberer (born in 1909)

(10) Samuel and Frieda's daughter, Marie, and her husband (11) Morris Cooper holding their daughter Grace

(12) Samuel and Frieda's youngest daughter, Kate
(13) Frieda (Shpetner's) brother, Joseph Spetner, (14) his son Saul Spetner and his daughter (15) Rose Spetner, and (16) Leon Spetner (17) unidentified

The photo above of the Schabb family and Samuel and Frieda's family was taken in 1913, the year that Sam and Frieda's granddaughter Clair was born and is a baby in the photo.

Sam and Frieda are in the center with their daughter Sarah to the right next to her husband B. B. with her new baby Clair. Their daughter Gertrude Haberer is sitting in front of them. Sam and Frieda's second eldest daughter, Marie, is sitting left of Freida. Marie's husband Morris Cooper is behind her holding their first-born Grace.

To the left side of the photo is Samuel's sister Anna (Moshkevich) Schabb and her husband Morris Schabb standing behind. Their daughter Gertrude Schabb is standing all the way to left, bow in hair, and their son Morris is standing in the center. Frieda's brother, Joseph, and his two children are also in the photo.

Figure 86 Sam Moskevich in shoe store, date unknown
Courtesy of Linda Rose

***

Sarah Moshkevich and B. B. Haberer, 1910–1918

Sarah's 1910 census with her husband "B. B." Haberer has not been located. They had moved by this time to the District of Columbia, where "B. B." was involved in expanding his business and where, as noted above, their first child Gertrude Haberer (married name Gertrude Rose) was born on Oct. 2, 1909. On January 27, 1913, Samuel and Sarah's second daughter, Clair Haberer (married name Katz) was born in the District of Columbia.

Later that same year, an article appeared in *The Washington Times* indicating B. B. was busy expanding his business, "Newport Stores," on Seventh Street and agitating in D. C. for an upgrade of that area of the City. The article indicates his business started in April 1910 just two years after he and Sarah married. In September 1915, B. B. participated in two committees that were planning a celebration in honor of completing the paving of Seventh Avenue,[6] the same initiative he supported back in 1913. Then in 1915, B. B.'s name appears joining a Public Health committee in an article about the Midcity Citizens' Association coming out against Prohibition.[7]

FRIDAY, JUNE 13.

Stores on Seventh Street Enlarged

Growth of the northern part of Seventh street and its development as a retail center is evidenced by the announcement of the enlargement of the Newport stores, of which B. B. Haberer is proprietor. The business was begun as a men's furnishing store April 16, 1910, and has been enlarged several times since on account of the growth of trade. A short time ago the Singer Sewing Machine Company vacated a large adjacent store building and this was immediately procured for the Newport stores and a line of furnishings and merchandise for women and children was put in. The Newport stores are located at 1514 and 1516 Seventh street northwest.

Up to ten years or so ago there was no business whatever in this part of the city, but six new stores have replaced the Johnson coal yard, and a number of other shops and stores have been opened.

Figure 87 B. B. Stores Enlarged
The Washington Times, June 13, 1913, p. 4

***

Marie and Morris Cooper

While B. B. and Sarah were in DC, her sister Marie and her husband, "Morriss" Cooper, were living in Petersburg, Virginia. A 1910 census shows the young husband and wife living at 120 Sycamore Street in Petersburg. Morris is 26 and a merchant in dry goods. Marie is listed as age 18.

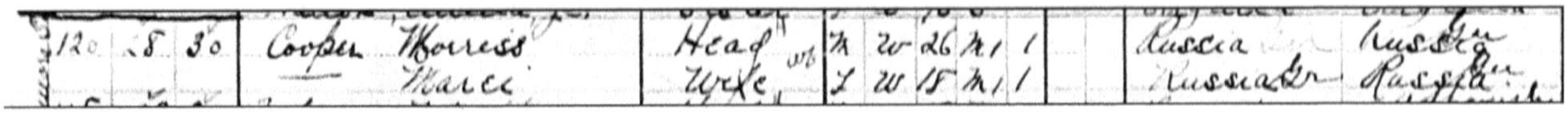

Figure 88 1910 Census for Morris Cooper and Marie (Moshkevich)

By 1918, when Morris filled out his WWI draft registration card, the family had moved to 12 S. Adams Street in Petersburg, though his business address is still on Sycamore. The record indicates Morris was now 34 and that his birthdate was April 23, 1884. Morris is listed as a fully naturalized citizen.

---

[6] "Gala Day Is Planned By Mid-City Citizens," *The Washington Times*, Sept, 8, 1915, p 5.

[7] "All Decry Prohibition," *The Washington Post*, Nov. 23, 1915, page 12.

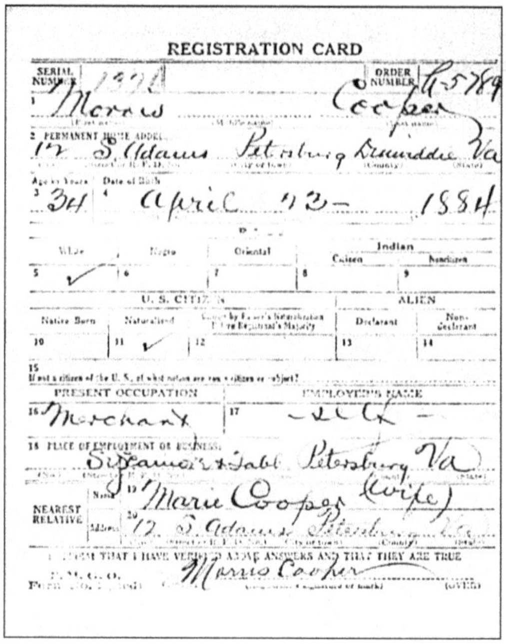

REGISTRATION CARD

SERIAL NUMBER 1398 — ORDER NUMBER A-5789

1 Morris Cooper

2 PERMANENT HOME ADDRESS: 12 S. Adams Petersburg Dinwiddie Va

Age in Years 3 34 — Date of Birth 4 April 23 – 1884

White 5 ✓

U. S. CITIZEN — Naturalized 11 ✓

PRESENT OCCUPATION 16 Merchant — EMPLOYER'S NAME 17 self

18 PLACE OF EMPLOYMENT OR BUSINESS: Sycamore & Tabb Petersburg Va

NEAREST RELATIVE — Name 19 Marie Cooper (wife) — Address 20 12 S. Adams Petersburg

I AFFIRM THAT I HAVE VERIFIED ABOVE ANSWERS AND THAT THEY ARE TRUE

Morris Cooper

Figure 89
WWI Draft Registration Card of Morris Cooper
Sept. 12, 1918

***

The Move to Hopewell and the Passing of B. B.

Tragically, Sarah's husband "B. B." Haberer died prematurely in March 1918, leaving Sarah with three children, including a son born July 7th that same year, just months after his father passed away; the child was named Berthold for his deceased father. A record of his birth indicates he was born in Petersburg Hospital in Virginia. On the birth certificate someone wrote "died" after the name of the newborn's father. The record gives Sarah's address as "Newport Stores" in Hopewell, Virginia.

B. B. and Sarah's granddaughter, Linda Rose, confirmed the general outlines of the story. The family apparently moved to Hopewell, Virginia sometime in 1915 where B. B. opened another one of his "Newport Stores." Linda tells me there was a Dupont plant and army base nearby in the Hopewell vicinity and the area was booming at that time. It seems probable too that the move from D. C. to Hopewell was influenced by the presence of Sarah's sister, Marie Cooper, who earlier settled with her husband Morris in Petersburg, VA, which was very close to Hopewell.

An article in the *Richmond Times-Dispatch* in Nov. 1916 indicates that Sarah and B. B. and family were already in Hopewell when B. B. was elected secretary for a new Hebrew Congregation that was forming.[8] Then in January 1918, B. B. was elected to a new board of trade officers in Hopewell. He clearly was still full of energy and going strong. He died within two months of that election. According to his granddaughter, B. B. died quickly of spinal meningitis. Sarah was pregnant at the time of her husband's death and named her baby boy "Berthold" when he was born.

Sarah and her daughters were quarantined and not allowed to attend Berthold's funeral. An article on the front page of the Hopewell Record about him and his death (Mar. 5, 1918) indicates he owned "one of the largest retail businesses in the city," and was also a member of the school board, board of trade and other civic bodies.

---

[8] "Hebrew Congregation Formed," *Richmond Times-Dispatch* (Nov. 23, 1915, p. 10)

Sarah's parents, Samuel and Frieda, who were still living in Baltimore at this time, must have been worried sick about their eldest daughter after her husband died leaving her single with three children.

Then on a happier note their youngest daughter Kate announced her engagement to Thomas Shpetner in 1919. As noted, oral family tradition indicates Thomas Shpetner was a relative of Katie's mother, Frieda (Shpetner) Moshkevich.[9] Thomas was born in 1899 in the Bronx. The 1900 census of his family shows their name was originally spelled "Slipetren" and was shortened to Shpetner by the time of the 1910 census. Other relatives spelled their surname "Spetner." Thomas's father Henry arrived in NY in 1894. He was born in Kremenchuk, the same town where Samuel and Frieda Moshkovitch were born as well.

Meanwhile in Viriginia, Sarah—now widowed with three children—must have had a terrible time coping. On Jan. 27, 1920, she remarried and tied the knot with Louis J. Haberer, age 26. Her granddaughter (Linda Rose) tells me that Louis J. Haberer wanted to provide a home for the young two-year old toddler Berthold, who was the namesake of the child's deceased father. Tragically, within six months of Sarah's second wedding, the young Berthold passed away of diphtheria.

Photo 32 Three Moshkevich Cousins April 13, 1919
(Right to left): First cousins Gersh Moshkevich [son of Itsig Moskevitch], Gertrude Schabb (later Gertrude Cohn), Kate Moshkevich
(soon to be Kate Shpetner), with friend Sam Smulian, and (in front) Louis Rubin [soon to marry Rose Spetner]

***

Louis Haberer and the Move to Cleveland Heights

That Sarah and her new husband Louis J. Haberer both had the same surnames was not serendipitous. Louis J. Haberer was the son of B.B.'s half-brother (called Louis Haberer without the "J" middle initial). Sarah's new husband, Louis J., was thus a half-nephew of B. B. Judging from family trees it appears Louis J. was born the year his own father died. The situation of Sarah and the toddler Berthold must have hit close to home.[10]

---

[9] Information shared with me by Linda Rose, granddaughter of Katie's sister, Sarah.

[10] The complicated family tree was documented by Harry Tankin, a grandson of Bertha (Haberer) and Harry Jacob Tankin. Harry Tankin's grandmother, Bertha, was a sister of Louis Haberer. According to Harry Tankin's research, B. B. Haberer and Louis Haberer were both sons of Isaac Haberer with different mothers. B. B. was the son of Isaac Haberer and his third wife, Helena Braum. Louis Haberer was the son of Isaac and his first wife Sara Lay. This Louis Haberer had a son Louis J., the man Sarah married.

MARRIAGE LICENSES

Louis J. Haberer, 26, of Cleveland, Ohio, and Sarah Haberer, 28, of Baltimore, Md. The Rev. G. Silverstone.

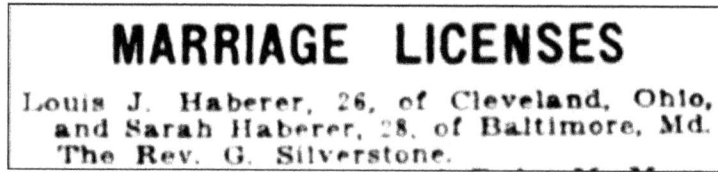

Figure 90 Marriage License of Louis Haberer and Sarah
Washington Times, Jan 28, 1920, p. 19

Louis J. was born in Arkansas in 1895. A 1914 DC city directory indicates that he came to DC by that year and was living with Sarah and B. B. while he worked as a clerk in B. B.'s store. Sarah's granddaughter, Linda Rose, heard that B. B. was helping to relocate some of the young people in his family from the South to the Baltimore/Washington area where there was greater opportunity.

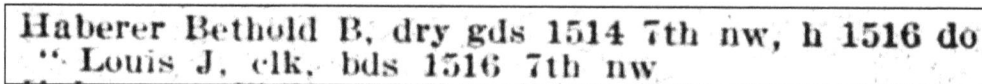

Haberer Bethold B, dry gds 1514 7th nw, h 1516 do
" Louis J. clk, bds 1516 7th nw

Figure 91 1914 City Directory showing Louis J. Haberer and his half-uncle Berthold

Louis apparently accompanied B.B. and Sarah to Hopewell, Virginia. He was living in Hopewell when he filled out his WWI Draft Registration Card on June 5, 1917. The card indicates that his employer was B. B. Haberer and that he was managing the Newport Store.

Figure 92
Draft Registration Card of Louis J. Haberer
June 5, 1917

Once married, Sarah and Louis J. did not remain long in Hopewell, Virginia. They moved to Cleveland, Ohio by Aug. 28, 1922, where their own daughter, Betty, was born. Her niece, Linda, tells me that in her teens, Betty changed the spelling of her name to "Bette" after Bette Davis.

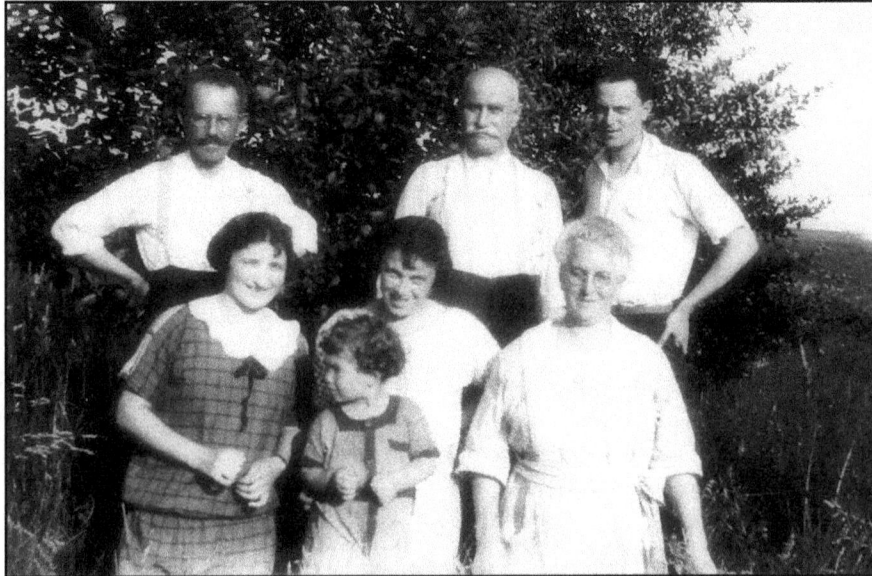

Photo 33 Sam Moshkevich (back center) with wife Frieda (Shpetner) (front right) with relatives circa 1922.[11] Courtesy of Linda Rose

It seems likely that Sarah and Louis's decision to move to the Midwest was influenced by the recent move of her sister Marie and the Cooper family to the Midwest as well, just as she had followed her family to Virginia. By 1920, Marie and Morris Cooper, had relocated from Virigina to Flint, Michigan, an area north of Detroit, about 3 hours from where Sarah and Louis soon settled in Cleveland Heights.

In the 1920 census, Morris and Marie Cooper were living at 1902 Detroit Street in Flint and they owned their home. Morris is listed as 35 and a businessman in real estate; Marie is age 27. The daughter Grace is 8, Beatrice 3 and 10 months, and Harriet 1 ½, all born in Virginia. Their fourth daughter Shirley was born in Flint a few years later, on April 23, 1922.

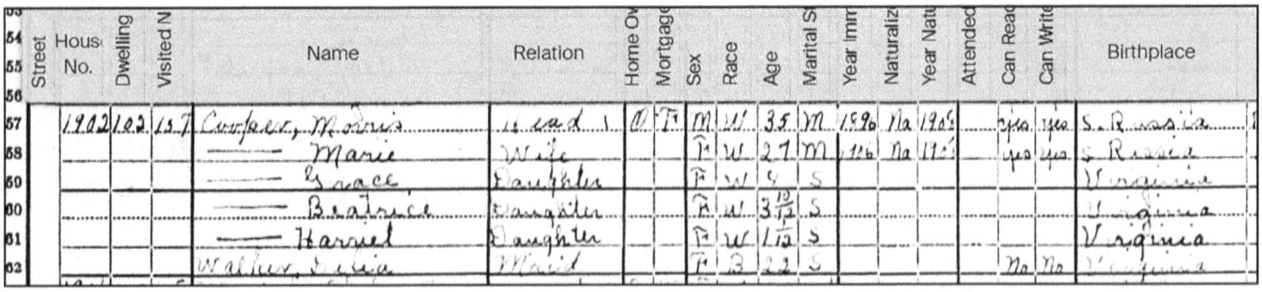

	Street	House No.	Dwelling	Visited N	Name	Relation	Home Ow	Mortgage	Sex	Race	Age	Marital S	Year Imm	Naturaliz	Year Natu	Attended	Can Read	Can Write	Birthplace
57		1902	102	137	Cooper, Morris	Head	O	F	M	W	35	M	1896	Na	1905		yes	yes	S. Russia
58					—— Marie	Wife			F	W	27	M	1906	Na	1905		yes	yes	S. Russia
59					—— Grace	Daughter			F	W	8	S							Virginia
60					—— Beatrice	Daughter			F	W	3 10/12	S							Virginia
61					—— Harriet	Daughter			F	W	1 [illegible]/12	S							Virginia
62					Walker, Delia	Maid			F	B	22	S					No	No	Virginia

Figure 93 1920 Census of Cooper Family in Flint Michigan

In the 1930 census, the Cooper family is still in Flint, Michigan, living at 1624 Lyons Street. They own their home which is valued at $16,000. Morris is age 44, still in real estate, Marie is 34, Grace 18, Beatrice 14, Harriet 11, and Shirley who was born in Flint is now age 9. A "servant," Florence Wilson, age 21, is part of their household.

[11] Back row (left to right): Joseph Shpetner (Frieda's brother), Samuel Moshkovich, Joseph's son Saul Spetner. Front row (left to right): Saul's wife, Sarah Spetner, Joseph's daughter Rose (Spetner) Rubin, her son Paul Rubin, Frieda (Shpetner) Moskovitch

Line No.	Street	House No.	Dwell No.	Famil No.	Name	Relation	Home O	Home Value	Radio	Farm	Sex	Race	Age	Marit Statu	Marriage	Atten Scho	Read & Write	Birthplace
33	16 24	4/7	575		Cooper, Morris a.	Head	O	6000	R	no	m	W	44	M	24	no	ye	Russia
34					Marie	wife			V		F	W	37	M	17	no	ye	Russia
35					Grace	daughter			V		F	W	18	S		ye	ye	Virginia
36					Beatrice	daughter			V		F	W	14	S		ye	ye	Virginia
37					Harriet	daughter			V		F	W	11	S		ye	ye	Virginia
38					Shirley	daughter			V		F	W	7	S		ye		Michigan
39					Wilson, Florence	servant			V		F	W	21	S		no	ye	Michigan

Figure 94 1930 Census for Cooper Family

Sarah and her second husband Louis, for their part, are listed in the 1930 census with their three girls in Cleveland Heights, Ohio at 1000 Greyton Rd. The record shows Louis is 35 and Sarah 39, though the true gap in ages was six or seven years. Gertrude is listed as age 20, Clair 17, and Betty 7. Louis is described as a proprietor of a commercial advertising business and Sarah is a proprietor of a beauty shop. Their granddaughter, Linda Rose, tells me Louis produced large-scale billboard-style ads in his business.

Line No.		House No.	Dwell No.	Famil No.	Name	Relation	Home O	Home Value	Radio	Farm	Sex	Race	Age	Marit Statu	Marriage	Atten Scho	Read & Write	Birthplace
60		1000	260	278	Haberer, Louis	Head	O	11500	R	No	M	W	35	M	22	No	Yes	Arphanroma
61					Sarah	Wife-H			V		F	W	39	M	18	Ye	Yes	Russia
62					Gertrude	Daughter			V		F	W	20	S		Ye	Ye	District Co
63					Clair	Daughter			V		F	W	17	S		Yes	Ye	Columbia
64					Betty	Daughter			V		F	W	7	S		Yes		Ohio
65		261	279		Ko___ M__	Head	O				M	W		M	27	No	Ye	Ohio

Figure 95 1930 Census for family of Sarah and Louis Haberer in Cleveland Heights

Sarah and Marie's younger sister, Kate and her husband Thomas Shpetner are living with their two children in Springfield, MA, in the 1930 Census. Their address is 126 Woodlawn Street. Kate's husband Thomas is 29, and a leather worker in a leather factory. Kate is 27, incorrectly listed as born in New York. [Was she hiding her birth in Russia or was this just a mistake?] Their daughter Norma was 8 and born in New York, and their son Stanley was 5 and born in Massachusetts.

Line No.	Street	House No.		Famil No.	Name	Relation	Home O	Home Value	Radio	Farm	Sex	Race	Age	Marit Statu	Marriage	Atten Scho	Read & Write	Birthplace
5		126		639	Shpetner, Thomas	Head	R		50	R	no	M	W	29	M	19	No	Yes	New York
6					Kate	Wife-H				V		W	27	M	17	No	Yes	New York
7					Norma	Daughter				V		W	8	S		Yes		New York
8					Stanley	Son				V		M	W	5	S		Yes		Massachusetts
9					Hagling, Emma	Servant				V		W	49	S		No	No	Sweden

Figure 96 1930 Census of Kate and Thomas Shpetner and children in Springfield, MA

By the late 1920s, the girls' parents, Samuel and Frieda Moshkevich, followed their two daughters (Sarah and Marie) to the Midwest. The Cleveland City directory from 1926 shows a Samuel Moshkevich (with the Baltimore surname spelling) in men's furnishing living at 3339 E 142nd street. Their 1940 census shows them living in Cleveland at 3413 139th Street, just six miles away from where their daughter Sarah was living. The record indicates they had been living there already by 1935.

Line No.	Street	House No.	Visited N	Home Ov	Home Value	Farm	Name	Relation	Code A	Sex	Race	Age	Marit Statu	Attended	Grade	Code B	Birthplace	Code C	Citizensh	City
7		-p	3809	78		No	Moshkevich, Samuel	Head	2	M	W	69	M	No	0		Russia	18	No	Same Place
8							Frieda	Wife	1	F	W	67	M	No	0		Russia	18	No	Same Place

Figure 97 1940 Census of Samuel Moshkevich and wife Frieda in Cleveland

***

Charles Rose and the Medicine Man

Sometime in the 1930s, Sarah's daughter, Gertrude Haberer, met Charles Rose, a young man who was lodging with Chief Thunderwater (1865-1950), a native American entertainer, businessman and political activist who worked to protect the rights of indigenous peoples (more on the Chief below).[12] This is one of the more interesting stories in the Moshkevich family saga. When I first heard this story from Gertrude and Charles' daughter, Linda, who lives not far from me in the Bay Area, I began trying to learn more about her father's background.

Gertrude's husband, Charles Rose, was born Charles Rosenzweig in Chicago; a 1910 census shows the eight-year-old Charlie living with his parents Israel and Rose Rosenzweig and five siblings in Cleveland that year. Charles's father is called Isaac and Isadore in other records.

Charles shows up for the first time with the Chief in the 1920 Cleveland City Directory under the name "Chas Rose" with the occupation "medicine" and living at 6716 Baden Court, where the Chief Thunderwater had a 17-room dwelling. The Chief began selling herbal cure-alls in Cleveland in the early 1900s. His products—including "Mohawk Penetrating Oil," "Thunderwater Tonic Bitters," "Seminole Sweet Gum Salve," and "Jee-wan-ga tea,"—were supposedly derived from traditional medicines.

Charles apparently moved in with Chief Thunderwater and became business partners sometime after the 1920 census (in which he is not present). By 1922, Charles and the Chief had clearly gone into business together and he appears in the Cleveland Directory under the entry "Rose, Chas B (Thunderwater and Rose) 6716 Bade Ct," the name of the business seemingly indicating that his surname had been added to the business name.

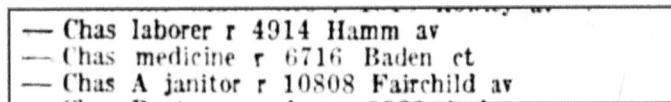

Figure 98 1920 City Directory showing Chas Rose in medicine at 6716 Baden Ct

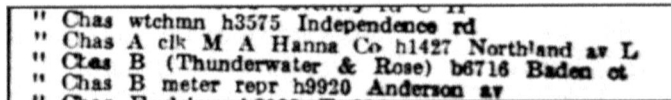

Figure 99 1922 City Directory showing Chas B involved with "Thunderwater & Rose"

A 1928 invoice posted online shows Kit Carson (son of the famous frontiersman) ordering herbs from the Thunderwater & Rose business. The involvement of Charles with Chief Thunderwater was deep enough that one historical website mistakenly concluded that the Chief had "joined forces with *fellow Indian Charlie Rose* to start several businesses [italics mine]."[13]

In the 1930 census, Charles, now age 27, is still living at 6716 Baden Court with the Chief "Thunderbolt" (a variation on Thunderwater) along with five other young twenty-something-year-old men.

---

[12] See "Chief Thunderwater," https://case.edu/ech/articles/c/chief-thunderwater (accessed 12/23/2023) https://clevelandhistorical.org/items/show/275. See the recent biography, *Chief Thunderwater: An Unexpected Indian in Unexpected Places.* By Gerald F. Reid.

[13] See discussion on Cleveland History. https://clevelandhistorical.org/items/show/275 Accessed 12/20/2023.

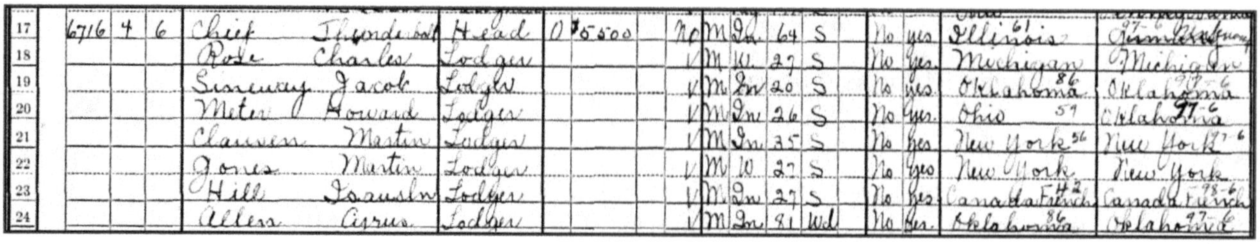

17	6716	4	6	Chief	Thunderbolt	Head		O 5500		no	M	Th	64	S		No	yes	Illinois	61	Penn. Sylvania
18				Rose	Charles	Lodger				V	M	W	27	S		No	yes	Michigan		Michigan
19				Sincury	Jacob	Lodger				V	M	In	20	S		No	yes	Oklahoma	86	Oklahoma
20				Meter	Howard	Lodger				V	M	In	26	S		No	yes	Ohio	59	Oklahoma	97-6
21				Clausen	Martin	Lodger				V	M	In	35	S		No	yes	New York	56	New York	76
22				Jones	Martin	Lodger				V	M	W	27	S		No	yes	New York		New York
23				Hill	Joaquin	Lodger				V	M	In	27	S		No	yes	Canada French	42	Canada French	98-6
24				Allen	Cyrus	Lodger				V	M	In	81	Wd		No	yes	Oklahoma	86	Oklahoma

Figure 100 1930 Census showing Charles Rose lodging with Chief Thunderbolt

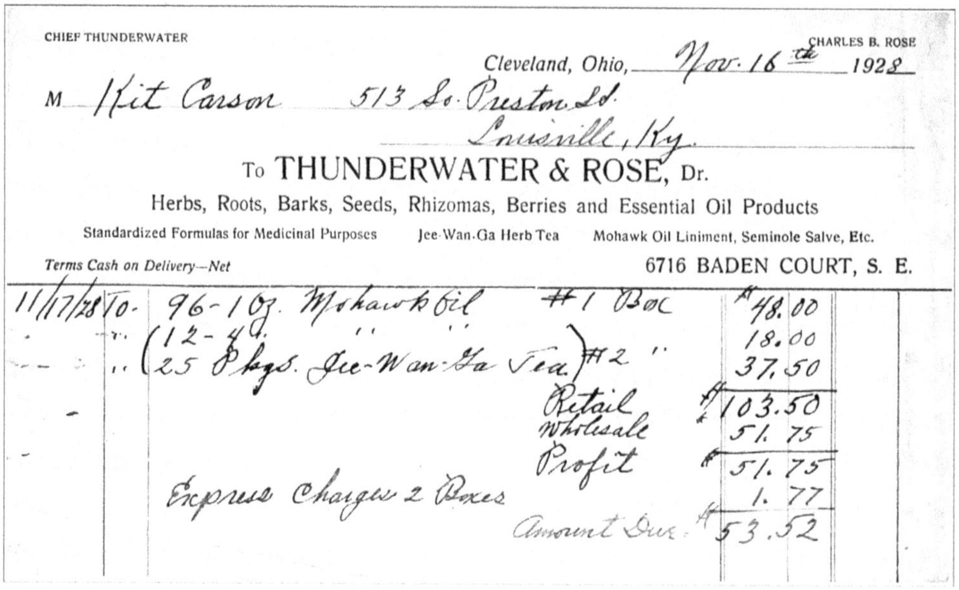

Figure 101 An invoice by Kit Carson sent to Thunderwater and Rose

According to his daughter Linda Rose, Charles was living with Chief Thunderwater when he spotted her mother, Gertrude Haberer, while she was working in a department store. He came up to her and said, "I'm going to marry you." They were married by a minister on May 2, 1937, and subsequently married again by a rabbi in Cleveland on May 17, 1937.

In the 1940 census, Gertrude appears alongside husband, Charles, Chief Thunderwater, and another roomer. The Chief's birth name, Oghema Niagara, is squeezed in line next to Thunderwater on the record. The Chief is 74, Charles is 37 and Gertrude is 30. By this point, Charles had been living with the Chief for twenty years.

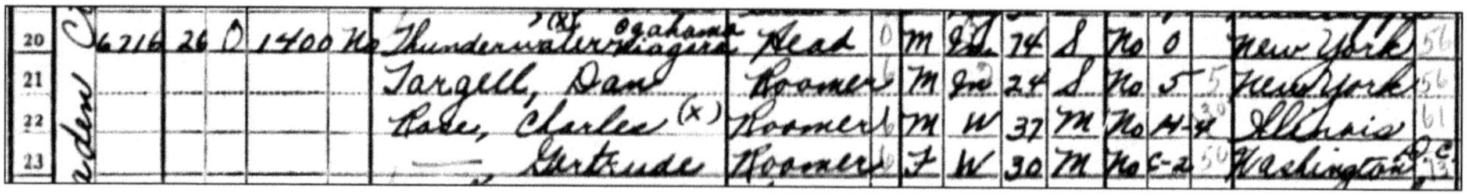

20	6716	26	O	1400	No	Thunderwater, Niagara Ogahama	Head	O	M	W	74	S	No	O		New York	56
21						Targell, Dan	Roomer		M	In	24	S	No	5	5	New York	56
22						Rose, Charles (x)	Roomer		M	W	37	M	No	H-4	30	Illinois	61
23						Gertrude	Roomer		F	W	30	M	No	C-2	50	Washington	29

Figure 102 1940 Census–Charles Rose and Gertrude living with [Chief] Thunderwater

Sometime before Gertrude moved in with Charlie Rose and the Chief, her younger sister Clair Haberer decided to make a move to Washington DC. She was there by the 1940 census in which she is described as single, a typist, working as a court reporter. She was living at 1901 R. Street in D.C. with twelve other individuals described as lodgers.

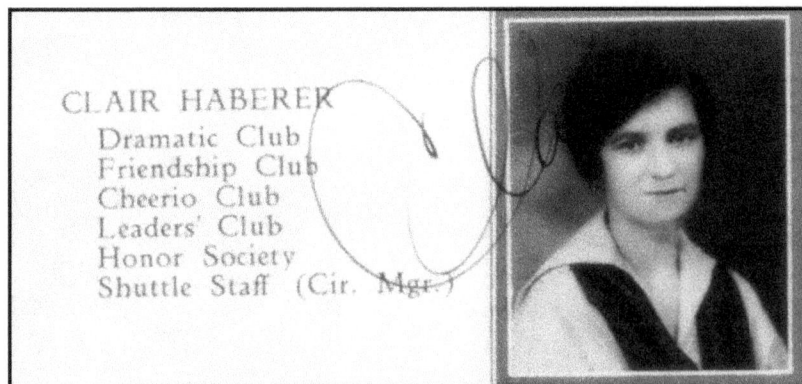

Photo 34 A photo of Clair Haberer in 1930 High School Yearbook

Meanwhile, back in Cleveland, it seems plausible that Gertrude's pregnancy or the birth of their son Robert Arthur Rose on Apr. 30, 1941, made it impossible for her and Charles to continue living with the Chief. They left downtown Cleveland at this time for a rural address, where they were living when Linda, their daughter and my informant, was born in 1943. Within two years of her birth, her father Charles died of TB, which Linda believes he picked up living with the Chief. Unfortunately, Linda's mother Gertrude suffered mental health issues with the consequence that Linda and her brother were raised by their grandmother, Sarah Haberer and her second husband Louis.

I try to imagine how Sarah and Louis were coping with the complex situation. Her life was repeating itself in the life of her daughter. Sarah lost her first husband B. B. when she was a young mother. Now her daughter, Gertrude, lost her husband as a young mother. To add more loss to the situation, Sarah's parents soon passed away too. Samuel passed away on June 14, 1943. Frieda [Shpetner] Moshkevich passed away on Dec. 12, 1943.

Figure 103 Tombstone of Samuel and Frieda

Father Samuel 1864–1943, Shlomo son of Mordechai, the Cohen, expired on 11th of Sivan 5703 [June 14, 1943]

Mother Frieda 1872–1943, Henia Hudah son of R. Yitzchak Isaac, expired 5th of Kislev, 5704 [Dec. 12, 1943]

A classic family drama unfolded related to Samuel and Frieda's tombstone, as recounted to me by their great-granddaughter, Linda Rose. Apparently, their eldest daughter, Sarah, was responsible for the funeral arrangements and tombstone. Without Sarah's knowledge, her younger sister, Kate, arranged to have their parents' photo placed on their tombstone, violating Jewish norms to keep images off tombstones. The incident led to a falling out of the sisters for many years, until it was later patched up on a vacation in the Virgin Islands, where Kate had developed a real estate business.

Photo 35 Samuel Moshkevich
and Frieda (Shpetner)

As a court recorder, Claire Haberer apparently got to travel around the country. A photo of her recording witness testimony about the shocking crash of an Eastern DC-4 appeared in dozens of newspapers across the country in 1947. Her name also appears in two articles recording testimony for a hearing on claims of the Ute Indians in Colorado. I find it interesting—if not coincidental—that Clair's sister, Gertrude, married a man who lived with a native American activist for Indian rights. I wonder if Clair discussed the case with her sister.

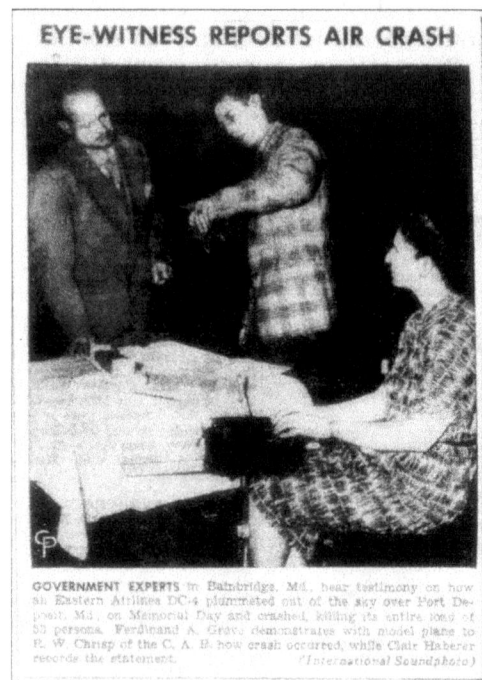

Photo 36 Clair Haberer recording expert witness testimony
about the crash of Eastern Airlines DC-4

This photo appeared in dozens of papers across the country.
This example from The Tipton Daily Tribune [Indiana]
July 08, 1947, page 4

Clair married Milton Katz before 1952 when their son Bert B. Katz was born. He was named for Clair's father, "B. B." Haberer. They also had a daughter, Mella, in 1955.

Gertrude and Clair's half-sister, Bette Haberer, married Lawrence Berk on Jan. 22, 1944. They were married by a justice of the peace in Alabama where Larry was stationed. Her niece, Linda Rose, tells me the version of the events that unfolded according to the family oral tradition.

Bette's sister Claire was in town for the wedding. So Bette and Clair went looking for a rabbi and couldn't find one nearby. As a result, Bette and Larry went to the justice of the peace. According to the story, Larry's mother was so upset that she locked herself in the bathroom and wouldn't come out. Apparently, in all the commotion, the justice of the peace forgot to put his signature on the document and Clair had to run outside to get him after he left. They had been distracted, so the story goes, by his glasses sliding down his nose and didn't immediately notice the omission. Family pressured Bette to get married with a rabbi, like her sister Gertrude did; she unhappily complied a few months later.

The 1950 census shows Bette and husband in Ohio with two children, Gary and Johnnie. At some point Bette moved to California. She was followed by her parents, Sarah and Louis.

Sarah passed away in 1976 and is buried in San Jose. Sarah's second husband, Louis Haberer, passed away in 1989. Sarah's eldest daughter, Gertrude, passed away in 1996 in Ohio but was buried in San Jose, CA. Sarah's second daughter, Clair (Haberer) Katz, passed away in 1988. Bette (Haberer) Berk passed away in 2011.

***

The Cooper Family Detroit and Beyond

As discussed earlier, Samuel and Frieda's second daughter, Marie Cooper, settled with her husband in Flint, Michigan with their daughters after leaving Petersburg, VA. By 1935, the family moved from Flint, Michigan to Detroit. It is unknown if they contacted Marie's Moskovitch first cousins living there, children and grandchildren of her uncle Hyman, though one suspects they did. According to family oral traditions, Morris was in real estate and financially hurt during the Depression. Perhaps this was the reason they left Flint.

As evident from the 1940 census, they were living at 2690 Hogarth St. in Detroit. Morris Cooper is age 57, Marie is 48, Beatrice 24, and Shirley 17. Morris has no occupation listed here, though Marie is described as an assistant buyer for a Detroit Department Store. Their daughter, Beatrice, is a laboratory teaching assistant, and the record specifies "Dept. WPA student aid," presumably referring to her source of income as President Roosevelt's Work Progress Administration.

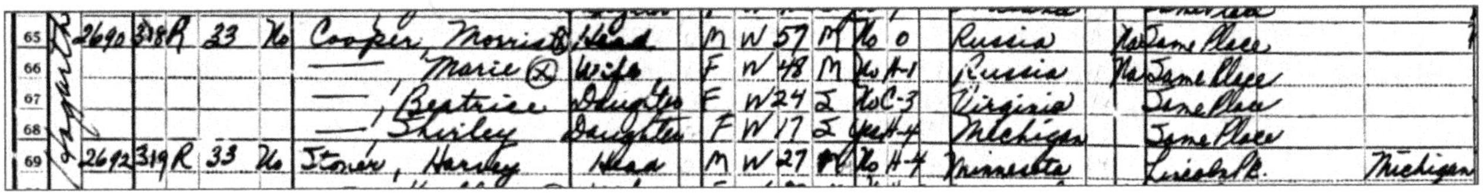

65	2690	318	R	33	No	Cooper, Morris	Head	M	W	57	M	No	0	Russia	No	Same Place	
66						— Marie ⊗	Wife	F	W	48	M	No	H-1	Russia	Na	Same Place	
67						— Beatrice	Daughter	F	W	24	S	No	C-3	Virginia		Same Place	
68						— Shirley	Daughter	F	W	17	S	Yes	H-4	Michigan		Same Place	
69	2692	319	R	33	No	Stoner, Harley	Head	M	W	27	M	No	H-4	Minnesota		Lincoln Pk.	Michigan

Figure 104 1940 Census of the Cooper Family

Morris and Marie's daughters, Grace and Harriet, are not listed with their parents in the 1940 census. Harriet is listed independently elsewhere, age 21, still single and working as a cashier while living on Adelaine St. By 1950, she is back living with her mother. According to a family oral tradition, Morris went bankrupt at some point and he and Marie divorced.

Morris and Marie's daughter, Grace, apparently went to live in Washington, DC in this period. On Feb. 18, 1950, she married John M. Fillner in Petersburg, Virgina, the city where she was born. The address on their marriage certificate indicates they were both living at that time in separate addresses on W. Clifton Terrace in Washington, DC and apparently met there. In 1950 they are still on Clifton Terrace. John is an accountant for a wholesale produce company and Grace is a research psychologist for the Dept. of Army. John and Grace had no children. At some point they moved to California. John passed away in 1965 and Grace in 1996.

Morris and Marie's daughter, Beatrice, married Roy J. Gillette—their marriage license listed in the St. Louis Globe-Democrat (p. 24) on Sep. 11, 1940. They appear in the 1950 census in Chicago at [1120?] E 61st Street. Roy is 32 and Beatrice 34. Their daughter, Susan age 8, was born in Missouri; daughter Jeane is 7 and was born in Maryland. They subsequently had another daughter Alice.

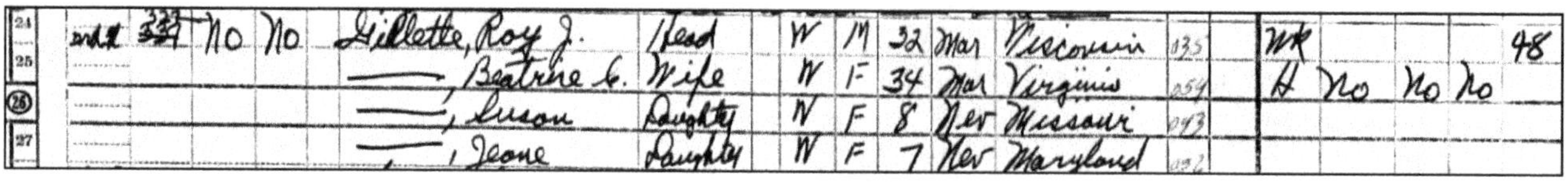

Gillette, Roy J.	Head	W	M	32	Mar	Wisconsin
Beatrice C.	Wife	W	F	34	Mar	Virginia
Susan	Daughter	W	F	8	Nev	Missouri
Jeane	Daughter	W	F	7	Nev	Maryland

Figure 105 1950 census of Beatrice (Cooper) and Roy Gillette

At some point, Marie moved to Berkeley. Her daughters, Shirley and Harriet, followed her to California. Marie passed away in 1983 in Santa Clara. Shirley had kidney disease and never married. She passed away in Santa Clara on Aug 27, 1989. Harriet at some point married Charles Heugley and moved to California too. They had no children. Harriet passed away in Santa Clara on Mar. 13, 1996.

***

Kate and Thomas Shpetner, 1930–1950

As noted earlier, Kate, the youngest of Samuel and Frieda's daughters, settled with her husband Thomas Shpetner in Springfield, MA by 1930. They are still in Springfield in 1940 living at 129 Vernon Ave. Thomas is 40, Kate 38, their daughter Norma is 18 and son Stanley 15. Thomas is working as a salesman in a wholesale ladies bag company.

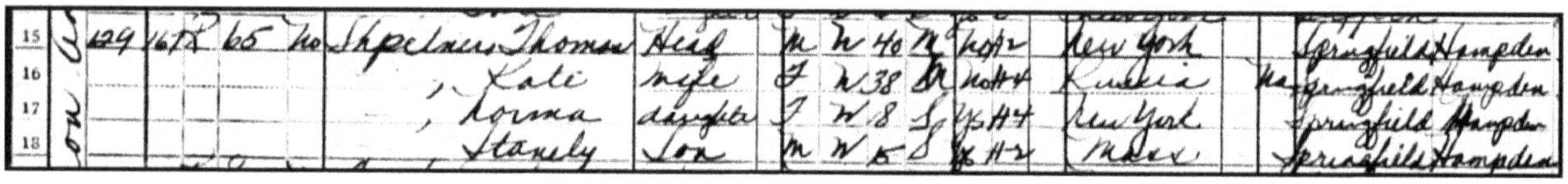

Shpetner, Thomas	Head	M	W	40	M	New York
Kate	wife	F	W	38	M	Russia
Norma	daughter	F	W	18	S	New York
Stanely	Son	M	W	15	S	Mass.

Figure 106 1940 Census of Thomas and Kate Shpetner's family

By 1943, they relocated to 616 East Lincoln Ave in Mount Vernon, New York, not far north of the City. This is their address in the engagement announcement of their daughter Norma to Arthur Levin who was then in the Army stationed at Camp Cooke, California

Photo 37 Norma Shpetner, Engagement Photo
The Daily Argus, Jul 17, 1943

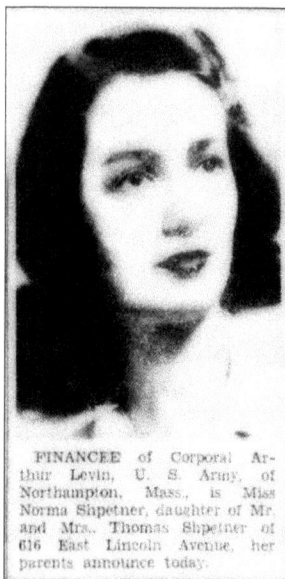

FINANCEE of Corporal Arthur Levin, U. S. Army, of Northampton, Mass., is Miss Norma Shpetner, daughter of Mr. and Mrs. Thomas Shpetner of 616 East Lincoln Avenue, her parents announce today.

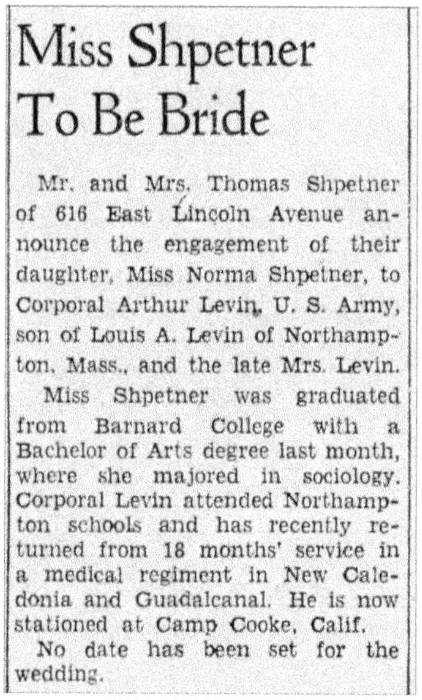

Miss Shpetner To Be Bride

Mr. and Mrs. Thomas Shpetner of 616 East Lincoln Avenue announce the engagement of their daughter, Miss Norma Shpetner, to Corporal Arthur Levin, U. S. Army, son of Louis A. Levin of Northampton, Mass., and the late Mrs. Levin.

Miss Shpetner was graduated from Barnard College with a Bachelor of Arts degree last month, where she majored in sociology. Corporal Levin attended Northampton schools and has recently returned from 18 months' service in a medical regiment in New Caledonia and Guadalcanal. He is now stationed at Camp Cooke, Calif.

No date has been set for the wedding.

By the 1950 census, Norma, age 28, is living with her husband Arthur Levin, age 30 back in Springfield, MA, at 249 Union St. Their son Mathew is a newborn. Arthur is listed as a business supervisor in a telephone company. They subsequently had a second daughter Martha.

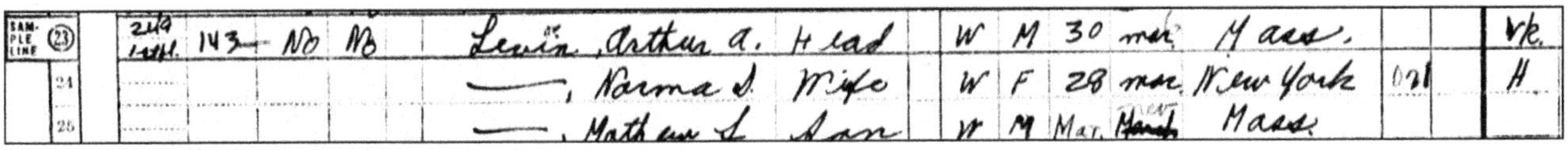

Figure 107 1950 Census of Norma (Shpetner) Levin and family

Norma's parents and brother (Kate, Thomas, and Stanley) that year were still at 616 East Lincoln Ave in Mount Vernon, in Winchester County, NY. [The street address notation is odd (C40 616) and may refer to an apartment number as well]. Thomas is 50, Kate 48, Stanley 25. Thomas is still in sales for ladies' shoes.

Kate and Thomas's son, Stanley, is now working in "television production" for an advertising agency. This must have been the start to what became an illustrious career in producing films. Between 1958 and 1984, Stanley Shpetner made more than a dozen films. According to his obituary, Shpetner is perhaps best remembered for producing the 1961 John Ford-directed cowboy film "Two Rode Together" and the 1971 paranormal drama "Sweet, Sweet Rachel," the pilot for the short-lived TV series "The Sixth Sense."[14] He was also a producer for "The Rat Patrol" in 1966, a favorite of young boys at that time (including myself).

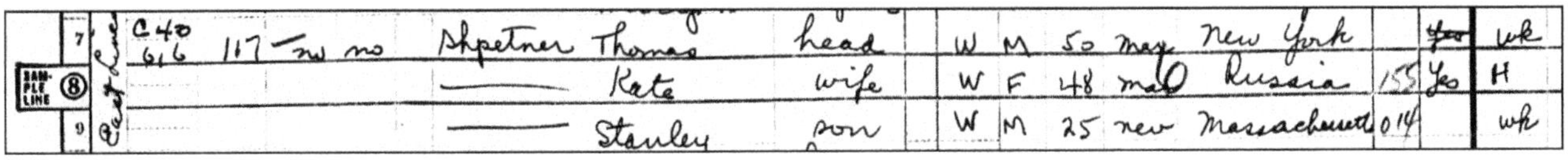

Figure 108 1950 Census of Thomas and Kate Shpetner

That April 1950, Thomas Shpetner passed away. His wife, Kate, lived another 40 years. Sometime in the 1950s, Kate moved to St. Thomas in the Virgin Islands. I understand from others in the family she established a thriving real estate business there. Eventually her daughter Norma and her husband settled there too. Norma and her husband had two children: Matthew and Martha Levin. Stanley also had two children, Patricia Shpetner-Lynch and a son, Stanley T. Shpetner.

Kate passed away in 1994. Stanley passed away in 2004. Norma passed away in 2018.

---

[14] https://lasvegassun.com/news/2004/jul/07/longtime-film-producer-shpetner-dies/

Records Summary for Samuel Moshkovich and Family

Mar. 3, 1906 Passenger Manifest	Manifest for family of Solomon/Samuel Moskevitch. Leaving Bremen, Germany on Feb. 15, 1906 on the SS Roland and arriving in Baltimore on March 3, 1906. to Baltimore on SS Roland. **Schlama Moskewitz** age 43, M[ale], last residence [writing illegible but looks like Kremanckalug] but someone hand printed Krzmenkohug,[15] destination Baltimore, possess $100, destination brother Aron Moshkevitz 316 E. High Str, wife **Fanny**, age 38, who paid?–husband; Sarah (married name Sarah Haberer) age 17, Maria (married name Marie Cooper) age 15, Gitel (married name Kate Shpetner) age 4
Apr. 11, 1906 Declaration	A record shows that "Solomon Moskevitch" signed his Declaration of Intention. No additional information is provided on this document.
Apr. 11, 1906 Petition for Naturalization	Petition of **Berthold Benjamin Haberer** ["B. B."] [soon engaged to Sarah Moshkevich, daughter of Samuel and Frieda], born in Germany March 22, 1878 and arrived in the US at the age of 20 on Jun. 7, 1898. He is living at 532 West Mulberry Street in Baltimore and has been living in Baltimore for 7 years [implied arrival in Baltimore 1899]. Indicates he declared his intention on Sept. 4, 1903.
Aug. 5, 1907 Engagement Announcement *The Baltimore Sun*, p. 6	Engagement announcement of Sarah Moshkevich, daughter of Mr. and Mrs. Samuel Moshkovich to Mr. B. B. Haberer of Baltimore
Sept. 1, 1909 *The Baltimore Sun*, p. 14	"Came to Buy, Won Bride" *The Baltimore Sun*, p. 14. After courtship of less than three months, Miss Marie Moshkevich, daughter of Mr. Samuel Moshkevich, 726 East Baltimore was married to Morris Cooper a prominent business man of Petersburg, VA.
Apr. 20, 1910 US Federal Census for Baltimore	Living at 36 S. High Street **Samuel Moschkevich** Head, age 42, years of marriage 15 [implied year of marriage 1895*], born in Russia, year of immigration 1906, naturalization PA [pending], occupation Dry goods in a store, **Frieda** wife, years of marriage 15, 3 children 3 alive, born in Russia, immigration 1906, **Katie**, daughter, age 8, immigration 1906 *this date of marriage has to be mistaken since their daughters Sarah and Marie were born before this date.
Apr. 15, 1910 US Federal Census for Petersburg, VA	[For Samuel and Frieda's daughter, Marie and new husband Morris Cooper] Living at 120 Sycamore Street, **Morriss Cooper**, Head, age 26, birthplace Russia, occupation Merchant, industry Dry Goods; Marci [Marie] wife, age 18, birthplace Russia
Jan. 5, 1912 Naturalization Petition	**Solomon Moshkevich,** 923 E. Baltimore Street, Baltimore, occupation merchant, born Dec. 15, 1868 at Kreminchook, Russia. Emigrated from Bremen, Germany on Feb. 15, 1906 arrived Baltimore on March 3, 1906 on the vessel Roland. Declared intention on April 10, 1906 in Baltimore, wife **Fanny Moshkevich**, she was born in Kreminchook [Kremenchuk], Russia, resides same address, three children: **Sarah** born Oct. 8, 1888 at

---

[15] The last residence on the manifest appears to be Kremenchuk. Sarah's granddaughter was told their last residence was Ekaterinoslav.

	Kreminchook lives in Washington, D. C., **Maria** born July 20th, 1890 at Kreminchook lives in Petersburg, Va. and Gitel born May 12, 1902 at Kreminchook lives in Baltimore Md, witnesses Adolph Nathanson and Harris Nachlas.
1912 Baltimore City Directory	Appears as Saml Moshkevich at 923 e Baltimore St.
1913	Article appears about B. B. Haberer expanding stores in the District of Columbia.
Mar. 5, 1918	Death of Sarah's husband, B. B. Haberer, in Hopewell, VA
Sept. 12, 1918 WWI Draft Registration Card	Draft Registration Card of Morris Cooper [Marie's husband], address 12 S. Adams Petersburg, Dinwiddie [County] Va, Age 34, birthdate April 23, 1884, occupation merchant, self employed, placed of employment Sycamore & Tabb [Streets] Petersburg VA, nearest relative Marie Cooper (wife)
Dec. 7, 1919 Engagement Announcement	{For Samuel and Frieda's daughter Kate]: Mr. and Mrs. **Samuel Moslikevich** of 3122 North Calvert Street, announce the engagement of their daughter, Miss Kate Moslikevich to Thomas Shpetner of New York City, *The Baltimore Sun*, page 13
Jan. 6, 1920 US Federal Census Flint, Michigan	Census for **Morris Cooper** and **Marie (Moshkevich)**. Living at 1902 Detroit Street, Morris, Head, Owns Home, age 35, year of immigration 1896, Na[turalized] in 1908, born in S. Russia, father and mother born in Russia, occupation business man in Real Estate, wife Marie, age 27, year of immigration 1906 Na[turalized] in 1908 [via her husband] born in Russia, father and mother born in Russia, daughter Grace, age 8, daughter Beatrice age 3 10/12, daughter Harrie 1 1/12, all born in Virgia, a maid Delia Walker living with them, age 22
Jan. 13/14, 1920 US Federal Census, Baltimore	**Samuel Moskevich**, 3122 Calvert Street, Head, Owns home, age 52, immigration year 1906, year naturalized 1919 [maybe 1914]? born in Russia, occupation Merchant in Dry Goods, own business; **Freda**, wife, age 46, immigration year 1906, year naturalized 1914, born in Russia; **Katie** (daughter), age 19, immigration year 1906, year naturalized 1914, born in Russia
Jan. 27, 1920 Marriage Index District of Columbia	Marriage index District of Columbia, **Sarah (Moshkevich) Haberer**, widowed, age 28, birthdate 1892 married date Jan. 27, 1920, spouse Louis J. Haberer
Apr. 16, 1930 US Federal Census Cleveland Heights, Ohio	[For **Sarah (Moshkevich) Haberer**, her second husband Louis J Haberer, and children] Living at 1000 Greyton Road, **Louis Haberer** Head, Owns home, Value 11,500, Has radio, age 35, Age at Marriage 25, birthplace Arkansas, father's birthplace Germany, mother's birthplace Arkansas, Proprietor in Com'l [Commercial] Advertising; **Sarah**, wife, age 39, age 18 at marriage [to first husband Berthold], Birthplace Russia, father and mother's birthplace Russia, proprietor in a Beauty Shop; **Gertrude**, [Sarah's] daughter age 20, single, birthplace District of Columbia, father's birthplace Arkansas [i.e. for her step-father], mother's birthplace Russia; **Clair**, [Sarah's]daughter, age 17, birthplace District of Columbia, father's birthplace Arkansas [for her step-father], **Betty**, daughter [of both Sarah and Louis], age 7, birthplace Ohio, father's birthplace Arkansas, mother's birthplace Russia

Apr. 17, 1930 US Federal Census Flint, Michigan	**For Morris and Marie Cooper.** Living at 1624 Lyons Street, **Morris A Cooper**, Head, Owns Home, Value $16000, age 44 wife, **Marie**, age 34, daughter Grace 18 born in Virginia, daughter **Beatrice** age 14 birthplace Virginia, daughter **Harriet** age 11, birthplace Virginia, daughter **Shirley** age 9, birthplace Michigan, servant Florence Wilson, age 21, birthplace Michigan
Aug. 22, 1940 US Federal Census, Cleveland Heights,	For **Louis Haberer, Sarah and Betty**. Living at 1000 Greyton Road. Louis Head, age 44, born in Arkansas, lived in same house in 1935, proprietor of a beauty shop, wife Sarah, age 50, born in Russia, daughter Betty, age 17, born in Ohio, Anna Ables, mother [of Louis], age 70 born in Arkansas
Apr. 2–3, 1940 US Federal Census for Cleveland City	For **Charles and Gertrude Rose**, living with Thunderwater "Ogaham Niagara" at 6716 Baden Ct. Chief is age 74, listed as Medicine Maker" in the medicine business. Charles Rose, Roomer, age 37, born in Illinois, was in same house in 1935, occupation salesman with partner [i.e. Chief Thunderwater] Gertrude, roomer, age 30, born in Washington DC, lived in same place in 1935, occupation Sales Clerk, in Retail Dept.
Apr. 17, 1940 US Federal Census, District of Columbia	For **Claire Haberer** Living at 1901 R. St. Claire is a "lodger", age 27, single, born in Dist. of Col[umbia], lived in Cleveland heights in 1935, occupation Typist for Court Reporting

***

6.

FAMILY OF SARAH (MOSHKEVICH) AND ABRAHAM GOLDBERG

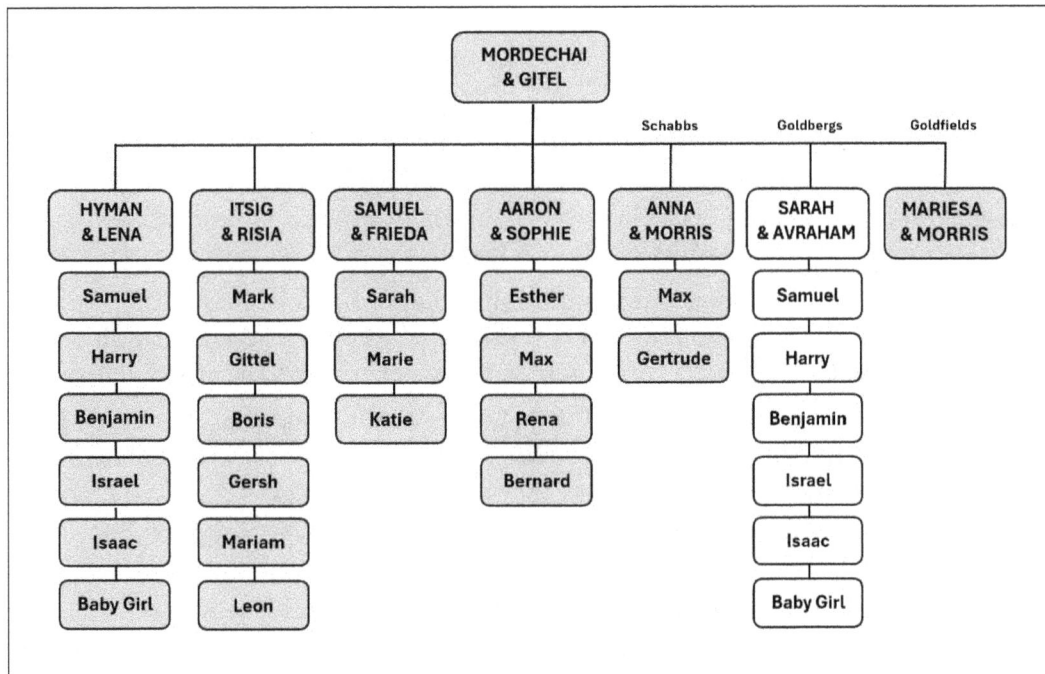

Figure 109 Family of Sarah (Moskovitch) and Avraham Goldberg

***

The Mystery of Sarah Moshkevich

Very little seems to be known about Sarah Moshkevich and a mystery surrounds part of her family's story. The family tree lists no birth year or date of death for Sarah, only the fact that she was born in Ekaterinoslav and married Abraham Goldberg in 1893. A marriage record of a woman named Sarah Moshkevich marrying Abraham Iossel Goldberg in Kishinev in 1893 is cited in Bessarabian records according to Ancestry and could belong to this Moshkevich sibling. Sarah and Abraham's oldest child, Max (Motel) was born in 1893 according to his US records and lends some credibility to this year being close to their date of marriage.

The family tree shows Sarah as next-to-last sibling in the birth order of the "Moskevitch Seven," younger than her sister Anna (Moshkevich) Schabb who was born in about 1876 but older than her sister Marie (Mariasha) Goldfield, who was born in about 1880. Given her position in the birth order, we could assume that Sarah was born in about 1878. But that would make her 15 years old at marriage which, though possible, seems unlikely and could suggest that she was born a few years earlier and held a different position in the birth order. As we shall see, the 1913 passenger manifest of Sarah's husband, Abraham Goldberg, describes his marital status as "wd" (widowed) thus indicating Sarah died before this date and never came to America. That is the reason we know so little about her.

While Sarah never made it to America, her husband and four of their children did. Two of her children, Ides (Edith Goldberg/ married name Kahn) and Gitel (Gertrude Goldberg/ married name Kauff) went on to marry and have children so that we know what became of them. The eldest son, Motel (Max Goldberg) was killed in an accident at the age of 19 in Baltimore and left barely a trace of his life. Sarah's husband Abraham and their other son Yankel disappeared completely after arriving in Baltimore. We don't know if Abraham remarried, returned to Russia as one descendent vaguely remembers hearing, or what became of him. What follows then is what we know and don't know about this Moshkevich family line.

***

The Arrival of Motel and Gitel Goldberg, 1909

Sarah and Abraham's children, Motel (Max Goldberg) and Gitel (married name Gertrude Kauff), sailed on the SS Chemnitz from Bremen on Oct. 21, 1909, and arrived in Baltimore on Nov. 5th. Motel and Gitel were listed as 17 and 16 years old respectively. According to the second page of their manifest, Motel was 5'2" with dark complexion, brown hair and grey eyes. Gitel was 4'6" also with a dark complexion, black hair and brown eyes. Written faintly to the left of the names on the first page, is the word "admitted" to the US.

Their last permanent residence is listed in the right columns as "Kolarasch" GB Bessarabia, referring to the town of Kalarash in the Gubernyia [Province] of Bessarabia. As noted earlier, Kalarash is now the town called Călăraşi in Moldova and is only 53 km (32 mi) on today's map from Chişinău (Kishinev).

Their closest relative in Kalarash is listed as their father "Abr. Goldberg." The second page of their manifest also lists "Kolarasch" as their places of birth. We have already seen that several of their uncle Hyman Moskevitch's sons were also born in Kalarash before they migrated to Canada.

By the time that Motel and Gitel landed in Baltimore, their mother's older brothers, Samuel and Aaron, and her sister, Anna (Moskevich) Schabb, were already settled in Baltimore, thus making it possible for the two teenagers to undertake the migration alone before their father and younger siblings. Still, it is impressive that they made their way as teenagers across Russia and Europe to Bremen in order to embark for Baltimore. Their destination was the home of their "uncle Sam Moskowitz 316 S High St. in Baltimore."

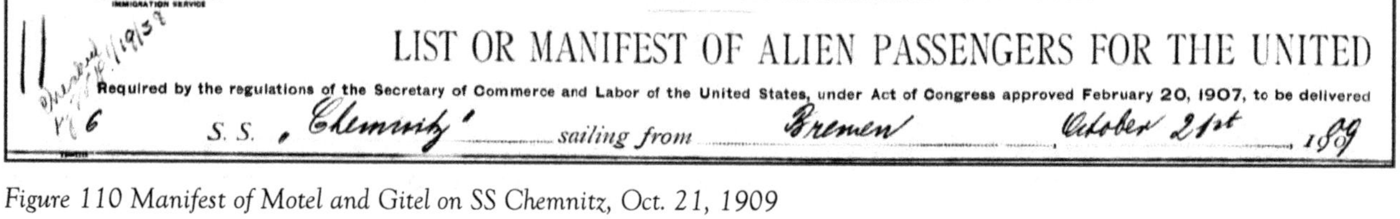
SALOON, CABIN, AND STEERAGE ALIENS MUST BE COMPLETELY MANIFESTED.

LIST OR MANIFEST OF ALIEN PASSENGERS FOR THE UNITED

Required by the regulations of the Secretary of Commerce and Labor of the United States, under Act of Congress approved February 20, 1907, to be delivered

S. S. Chemnitz sailing from Bremen October 21st 1909

Figure 110 Manifest of Motel and Gitel on SS Chemnitz, Oct. 21, 1909

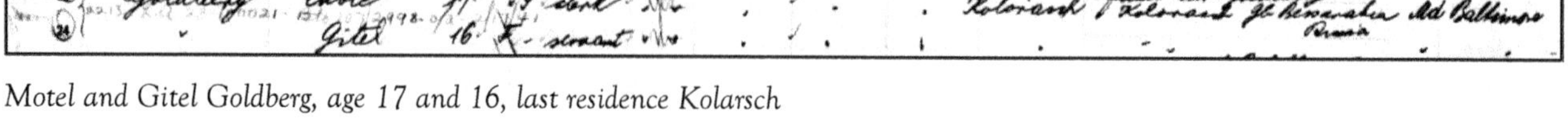
Goldberg Motel 17 ... clerk ... Kolarasch father Abr. Goldberg Kolarasch Gb Bessarabia Russia ... Baltimore

Gitel 16 ... servant

Motel and Gitel Goldberg, age 17 and 16, last residence Kolarsch

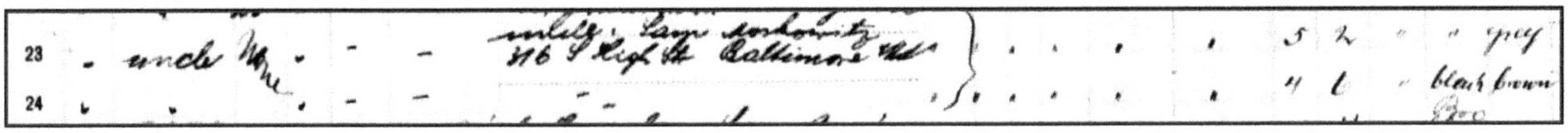
23	uncle	uncle, Sam Moskowitz 316 S High St Baltimore	5	2			grey
24				4	1		black brown

Page 2 of manifest with Motel and Gitel's destination uncle Sam Moskowitz

In the 1910 census, Motel, now called Max Goldberg, is living with his aunt Anna (Moshkevich) Schabb and her family at 1635 E. Fayette St. The record describes Max as 16 years old, a year younger than the age of 17, the age he earlier gave for his manifest in Oct. 1909. Presumably he claimed he was older than he was then to ease his way through customs. His occupation in 1910 is described as "slip cover maker."

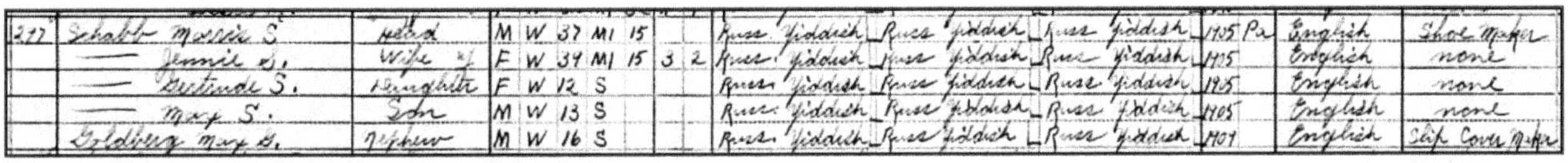
217	Schabb Morris S	Head	M	W	37	M1	15			Russ Yiddish	Russ Yiddish	Russ Yiddish	1905 Pa	English	Shoe Maker
	—— Jennie S.	Wife	F	W	34	M1	15	3	2	Russ Yiddish	Russ Yiddish	Russ Yiddish	1905	English	none
	—— Gertrude S.	Daughter	F	W	12	S				Russ Yiddish	Russ Yiddish	Russ Yiddish	1905	English	none
	—— Max S.	Son	M	W	13	S				Russ Yiddish	Russ Yiddish	Russ Yiddish	1905	English	none
	Goldberg Max G.	Nephew	M	W	16	S				Russ Yiddish	Russ Yiddish	Russ Yiddish	1909	English	Slip Cover Maker

Figure 111 1910 Census of Max Goldberg, son of Sarah

By Dec. 1911, Max declared his intention to become a citizen. His Declaration indicates that he was 18 at this point and born on Aug. 5, 1893. He again gives "Kalarasch," Russia as his birthplace. Max is living at this point at 1628 E. Fayette St., a few doors away from the home of his aunt Anna Schabb.

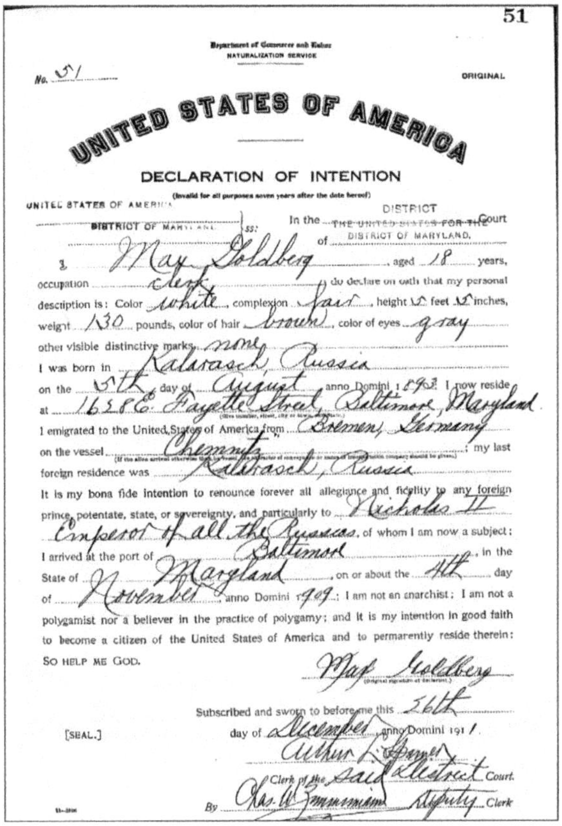
51

Department of Commerce and Labor
NATURALIZATION SERVICE

No. 51

ORIGINAL

UNITED STATES OF AMERICA

DECLARATION OF INTENTION

(Invalid for all purposes seven years after the date hereof)

UNITED STATES OF AMERICA, DISTRICT OF MARYLAND, ss: In the District Court of the United States for the District of Maryland.

I, Max Goldberg, aged 18 years, occupation clerk, do declare on oath that my personal description is: Color white, complexion fair, height 5 feet 5 inches, weight 130 pounds, color of hair brown, color of eyes gray other visible distinctive marks none

I was born in Kalarasch, Russia on the 5th day of August anno Domini 1893. I now reside at 1628 E. Fayette Street, Baltimore, Maryland

I emigrated to the United States of America from Bremen, Germany on the vessel Chemnitz; my last foreign residence was Kalarasch, Russia

It is my bona fide intention to renounce forever all allegiance and fidelity to any foreign prince, potentate, state, or sovereignty, and particularly to Nicholas II Emperor of all the Russias, of whom I am now a subject; I arrived at the port of Baltimore, in the State of Maryland, on or about the 4th day of November anno Domini 1909; I am not an anarchist; I am not a polygamist nor a believer in the practice of polygamy; and it is my intention in good faith to become a citizen of the United States of America and to permanently reside therein: SO HELP ME GOD.

Max Goldberg
(Original signature of declarant.)

Subscribed and sworn to before me this 26th day of December anno Domini 1911.

[SEAL.]

Arthur L. Spamer
Clerk of the said District Court.
By Chas. W. Zimmermann Deputy Clerk

Figure 112 Declaration of Max Goldberg

During this period, it is not clear where Max's sister Gitel/Gertrude was staying. She does not appear on the 1910 census with any of her aunts or uncles. Nor does she appear unambiguously in the city directory. In fact, the whole decade for this branch of the family is murky, as we shall now see.

***

The Arrival of Abraham, Yankel and Edith, 1913

Max and Gitel's father, Abraham, and their two siblings Yankel and Ides (married name Edith Kahn) arrived in Baltimore in July 1913. The travelers appear on the passenger manifest of the SS Breslau that sailed from Bremen on July 5, 1913, arriving in Baltimore on July 26th the same month. The names "Abram, Ides [Edith], and Yankel," match the members of Goldberg family in the circulating family tree. Their destination is the principal giveaway that this record belongs to them.

The notation on the second page is shorthand and a bit difficult to read: "br. i. l. [brother-in-law] A? Moszkowicz 1044 W. Franklin Str. Balto." They were going to the address of the children's uncle (and Abram's brother-in-law) Aaron Moshkevich at 1044 W. Franklin Street. As noted earlier, Aaron Moshkevich appears at that address on W. Franklin in the City Directory in 1913.

According to their passenger manifest, Abram Goldberg was a trader and 44 years old. His age implies his birth year was 1868–69, which would make him about 24 when he married Sarah in 1893. We can guess that his wife Sarah was probably not more than 5 years younger than him at the time.

Abram's daughter Ides (later Edith Kahn) is 15 years old. Her occupation is described as a "maid serv[ant]." Faintly underneath those words someone had written "seamstress." Ides is not the only young woman arriving in the US who presented herself as a maid or servant to strengthen the impression that she could assist the family with income and that she would not be a burden on society. To the left of their record, the official wrote "admitted."

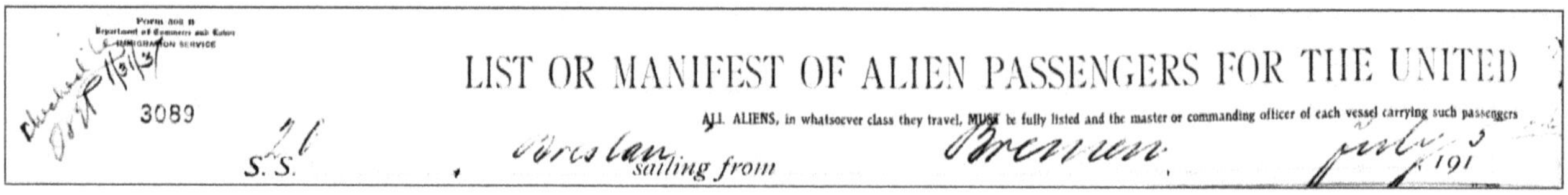
LIST OR MANIFEST OF ALIEN PASSENGERS FOR THE UNITED

ALL ALIENS, in whatsoever class they travel, MUST be fully listed and the master or commanding officer of each vessel carrying such passengers

3089

S.S. ... sailing from ... 191

Figure 113 Manifest of Abram, Ides (Edith) and Yankel Goldberg

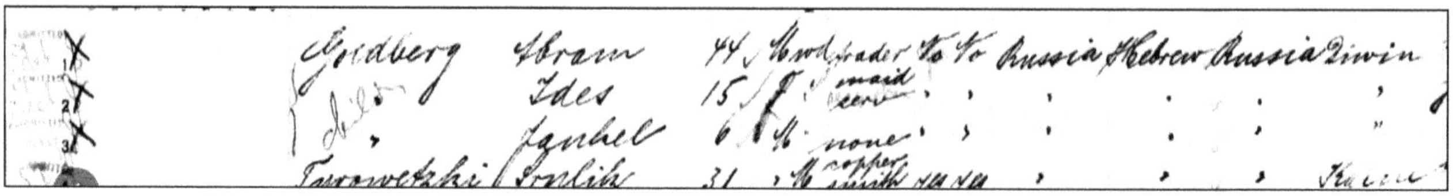

Arriving on SS Breslau July 1913

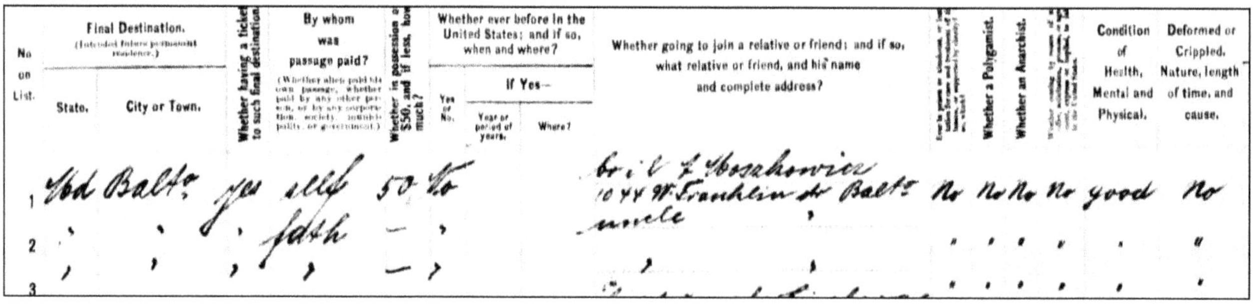
No on List.	Final Destination. (Intended future permanent residence.) State.	City or Town.	Whether having a ticket to such final destination.	By whom was passage paid?	Whether in possession of $50, and if less, how much?	Whether ever before in the United States; and if so, when and where? Yes or No.	If Yes— Year or period of years.	Where?	Whether going to join a relative or friend; and if so, what relative or friend, and his name and complete address?	Whether ever in prison	Whether a Polygamist.	Whether an Anarchist.	Whether coming by reason of any offer	Condition of Health, Mental and Physical.	Deformed or Crippled. Nature, length of time, and cause.

Page 2 of manifest showing destination of travelers to be "br i. l A? Moszkowicz 1044 W. Franklin Str"

The manifest also clears up one mystery about Abram's wife, Sarah. In the columns that list marital status (following age and sex), Abram is listed as "wd" [widowed]. Sarah died before 1913 when they left for Baltimore. This discovery explains why she is not listed as the travelers' closest relative in their last permanent residence, which the manifest identifies as Ziwin, Grodno, Russia.

The closest relative there is Abram's uncle and the children's great-uncle Hertz Bilwinsky (or something like that). We can guess that this might be the brother of Abram's mother or a husband of his father's sister. Perhaps after the death of his wife (Sarah), Abram left Kalarash where the children were born to live with family or he stopped to visit with family on the way to the port of Bremen. It is not clear what town "Ziwin" refers to, but Grodno was a region of Russia that is now in Belarus. Ziwin may be a transliteration or corruption of the name of some town there.

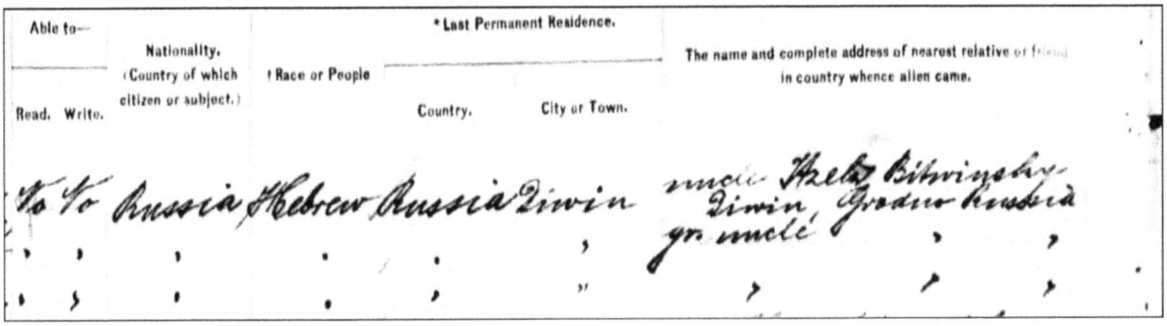
Able to— Read. Write. | Nationality. (Country of which citizen or subject.) | † Race or People | * Last Permanent Residence. Country. City or Town. | The name and complete address of nearest relative or friend in country whence alien came.

Yes Yes Russia Hebrew Russia Ziwin uncle Hertz Bilminsky Ziwin, Grodno Russia gr. uncle

Right-hand columns of page 1 showing the travelers last residence was Ziwin Russia and closest relative uncle Hertz Bilminsky

***

The Death of Max Goldberg

Tragically, Abraham, Edith and Yankel arrived too late in Baltimore to see Max (their brother/son), who apparently died in 1913 at the age of 19. The family tree lists Max's death in 1912, but a tombstone in the Yehuda Amachby Lodge Cemetery in Rosedale, Maryland, has a tombstone for a Max Goldberg, age 19, and a date of death of Feb. 12, 1913. I tracked down the death certificate of this Max Goldberg and confirmed it is Max son of Sarah (Moshkevich) and Abraham Goldberg, who arrived in 1909.

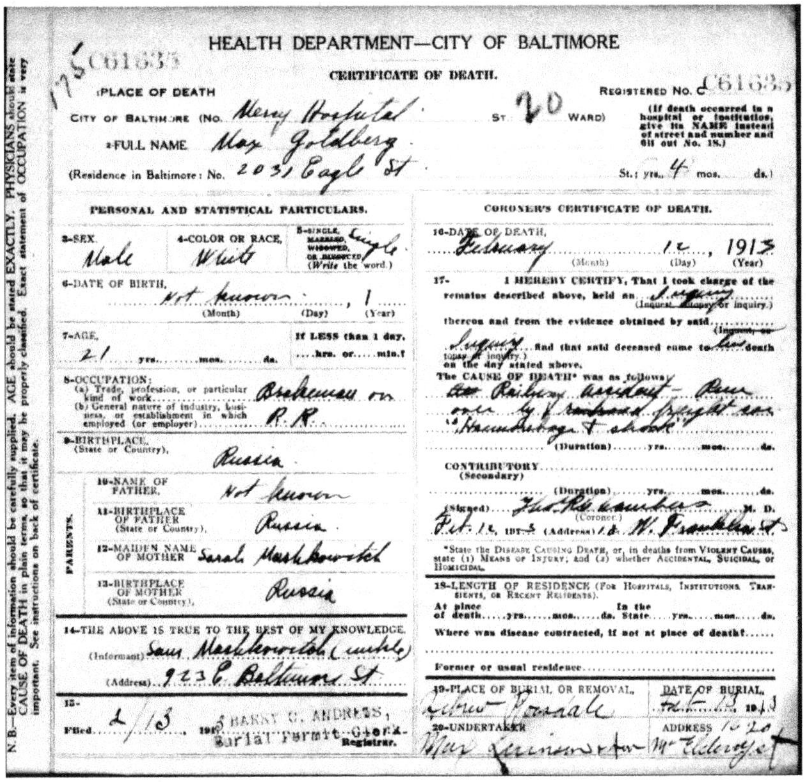
HEALTH DEPARTMENT—CITY OF BALTIMORE

CERTIFICATE OF DEATH.

1-PLACE OF DEATH — City of Baltimore (No. Mercy Hospital St. 20 Ward) — Registered No. C61635

2-FULL NAME Max Goldberg

(Residence in Baltimore: No. 2031 Eagle St. St.: yrs. 4 mos. ds.)

PERSONAL AND STATISTICAL PARTICULARS.

3-SEX Male — 4-COLOR OR RACE White — 5-SINGLE, MARRIED, WIDOWED, OR DIVORCED Single

6-DATE OF BIRTH Not known

7-AGE 21 yrs.

8-OCCUPATION Brakeman on R.R.

9-BIRTHPLACE Russia

10-NAME OF FATHER Not known

11-BIRTHPLACE OF FATHER Russia

12-MAIDEN NAME OF MOTHER Sarah Maschkowitch

13-BIRTHPLACE OF MOTHER Russia

14-THE ABOVE IS TRUE TO THE BEST OF MY KNOWLEDGE. (Informant) Sam Maschkowitch (uncle) (Address) 923 E. Baltimore St

15- Filed 2/13 1913 HARRY C. ANDREWS, Registrar.

CORONER'S CERTIFICATE OF DEATH.

16-DATE OF DEATH, February 12, 1913

17- I HEREBY CERTIFY, That I took charge of the remains described above, held an inquiry thereon and from the evidence obtained by said inquiry find that said deceased came to his death on the date stated above.

The CAUSE OF DEATH was as follows: Railway accident — Run over by Railroad freight car. Hemorrhage & shock

(Signed) M. D. (Coroner) Feb. 12, 1913 (Address) 1[illegible] N. Franklin St

18-LENGTH OF RESIDENCE

19-PLACE OF BURIAL OR REMOVAL Hebrew Rosedale — DATE OF BURIAL Feb. 13 1913

20-UNDERTAKER Max Levinson for McElderry St — ADDRESS

Figure 114 Death Certificate for Max Goldberg

Max's death certificate shows that he died in a railway accident when a freight car ran over him. It appears Max was working as a "brakeman" for the railroad. The informant for the certificate is listed as Max's uncle, Sam Moshkevich, who was then living at 923 E. Baltimore Street.

It is interesting that some of Max's personal details are unknown. Sarah Moshkewitch is listed as Max's mother. But "unknown" is written for the name of Max's father and date of Max's birth. Why this information was not provided by Max's uncle Sam is not clear. Did Sam not know the information or was he so shocked by the tragedy that he did not momentarily remember? Max's residence when he died is listed as 2031 Eagle Street in Baltimore. Perhaps he moved to the West side of the city to be closer to his work on the railways.

Accidental deaths involving train personnel were common at the time. In fact, just days before Max was killed, *The Baltimore Sun* had a big spread on the efforts of a Safety-First program that was modeled in Baltimore by the father of the "Safety First" movement. The article explains:

> Why the Baltimore and Ohio Railroad is doing all this is simple enough. During 1911, of the 60,000 employes [sic] 178 were killed and 10,000 injured. That meant the loss of trained services, practically; loss of the bread winner to widows and children; loss of profitable employment to the most seriously injured and impaired efficiency to all...The discovery that of these 178 killed and 10,000 injured fully 80 per cent. of the causes could have been avoided simply, easily, without the slightest inconvenience, was the reason for the safety first crusade. (*The Baltimore Sun*, Feb 9, 1913, p. 23 [see Part 3 page 7]).

An article that appeared 10 days after Max died indicated that 30 employees were fatally injured in 1913.

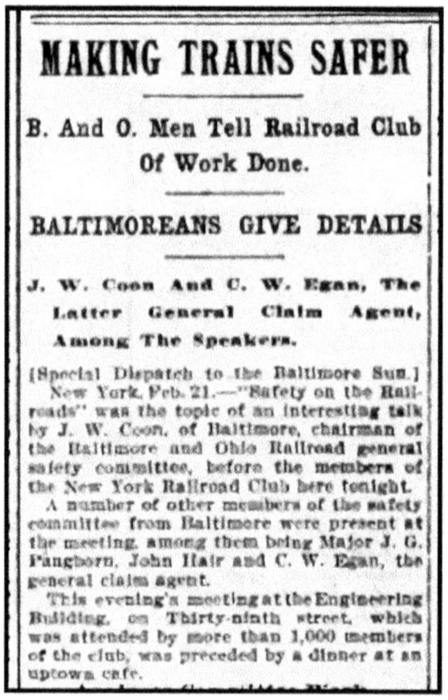

MAKING TRAINS SAFER

B. And O. Men Tell Railroad Club Of Work Done.

BALTIMOREANS GIVE DETAILS

J. W. Coon And C. W. Egan, The Latter General Claim Agent, Among The Speakers.

[Special Dispatch to the Baltimore Sun.]

New York, Feb. 21.—"Safety on the Railroads" was the topic of an interesting talk by J. W. Coon, of Baltimore, chairman of the Baltimore and Ohio Railroad general safety committee, before the members of the New York Railroad Club here tonight.

A number of other members of the safety committee from Baltimore were present at the meeting, among them being Major J. G. Pangborn, John Hair and C. W. Egan, the general claim agent.

This evening's meeting at the Engineering Building, on Thirty-ninth street, which was attended by more than 1,000 members of the club, was preceded by a dinner at an uptown cafe.

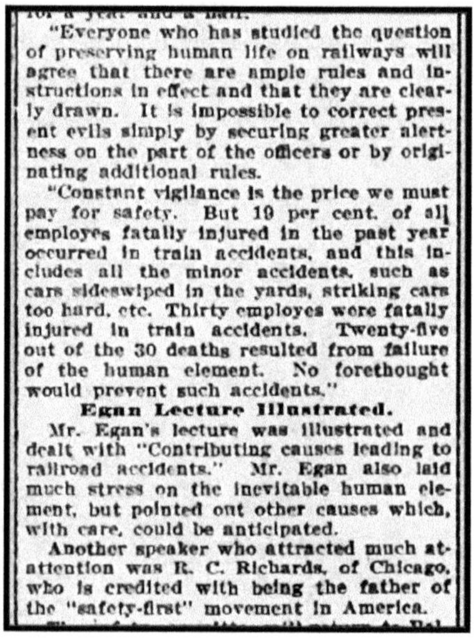

"Everyone who has studied the question of preserving human life on railways will agree that there are ample rules and instructions in effect and that they are clearly drawn. It is impossible to correct present evils simply by securing greater alertness on the part of the officers or by originating additional rules.

"Constant vigilance is the price we must pay for safety. But 19 per cent. of all employes fatally injured in the past year occurred in train accidents, and this includes all the minor accidents, such as cars sideswiped in the yards, striking cars too hard, etc. Thirty employes were fatally injured in train accidents. Twenty-five out of the 30 deaths resulted from failure of the human element. No forethought would prevent such accidents."

Egan Lecture Illustrated.

Mr. Egan's lecture was illustrated and dealt with "Contributing causes leading to railroad accidents." Mr. Egan also laid much stress on the inevitable human element, but pointed out other causes which, with care, could be anticipated.

Another speaker who attracted much attention was R. C. Richards, of Chicago, who is credited with being the father of the "safety-first" movement in America.

Figure 115 Train Safety Article
The Baltimore Sun, Feb. 22, 1913, page 2

> "Constant vigilance is the price we must pay for safety. But 19 per cent. of all employes [sic] fatally injured in the past year occurred in train accidents, and this includes all the minor accidents, such as cars sideswiped in the yards, striking cars too hard, etc. Thirty employes were fatally injured in train accidents. Twenty-five out of the 30 deaths resulted from failure of the human element. No forethought would prevent such accidents."

***

The Murky Years, 1913-1917

The years from 1913-1917 for the Goldberg family is a black hole. It appears that Edith and her sister "Gertie" (Gitel) may have been living together at 1200 e Baltimore Street, though we cannot be certain these City Directory listings belong to the sisters.

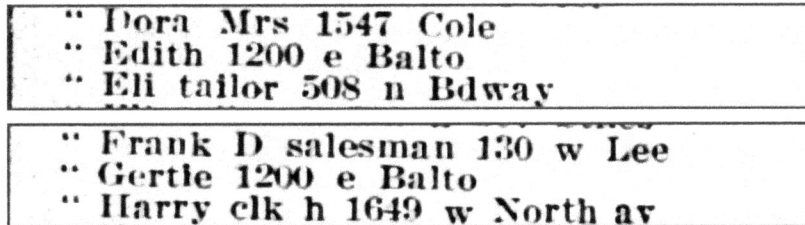

```
"  Dora Mrs 1547 Cole
"  Edith 1200 e Balto
"  Eli tailor 508 n Bdway
```

```
"  Frank D salesman 130 w Lee
"  Gertie 1200 e Balto
"  Harry clk h 1649 w North av
```

Figure 116 1914 City Directory Listing of Edith and "Gertie"

Though there were several men named Abraham Goldberg and Jacob (Yankel) Goldberg listed in the City directory for 1913-1917, it is not possible to identify which of them, if any, are the girls' father and brother. In fact, it is not clear what happened to either Abraham or Yankel. In the family tree, neither have a date of death.

I was told by Howard Green, a grandson of Edith (Goldberg) Kahn, that he has a vague memory that his grandmother (Edith) may still have had a brother still back in Russia. If so, it is possible Abraham and Yankel returned to Russia, perhaps prompted in part by the death of Max. If they did stay in the US, the Moskevitch family apparently lost track of them. They remain a mystery.

The lives of Edith and Gertrude begin to come into focus again around 1917. Both young women soon married and began a family. Tragedy beset Gertrude that decade in Detroit where she moved to be with her new husband as we shall see.

***

Gertrude and Samuel Kauff

It is not clear how Gertrude Goldberg met Samuel Kauff, an inspector of auto parts in an auto factory in Detroit, according to their 1920 census. It is tempting to think that Gertrude met Samuel through her Moskovitch Detroit cousins who started to arrive in Detroit in 1914, as discussed earlier. But we have no evidence this was the case or even that the cousins knew Gertrude had come to Detroit.

Gertrude and Sam got married in Detroit on Jan. 19, 1917, with a justice of the peace. On their marriage record, Sam is 24 and "Gurtrude" is 19. Sam's birthplace is simply "Russia" and Gertrude's is "Kischenoff," though she listed the nearby Kalarash, Russia, as her birthplace in subsequent records.

Samuel Kauff's surname, like so many Jewish immigrants, was a shortened anglicized version of a longer name that appeared on his immigration manifest as "Supkow" and also appears in various other spellings such as "Zoubcouff, Zubcof, Zubcoff" and was also shortened later by his brother to "Coff."

The year they married, Samuel and Gertrude lived in Detroit at 965 St. Antoine Street with Sam's mother, also called Gertrude or "Gussie" Kauff, his sister, and possibly with his brother Abe. The family was not listed in the Directory in 1915 or 1916 suggesting they recently moved to the city around 1917. In the 1917 Directory, Samuel's mother Gertrude Kauff is listed as a machine operator, boarding ("b") at 965 St. Antoine. Her son Samuel is an inspector, the directory cryptically indicating "h3" —"h" meaning house in the directory legend. Whether the boom in the auto industry or some other factor drew him to the city is not known. It appears that the family lived for several years in Waterbury, Connecticut before arriving in Detroit. Some of his siblings were still back East.

1917 Detroit City Directory

Kauff Gertrude, mach opr, b965 St Antoine
" Saml, inspr, h3, 965 St Antoine

On June 5, 1917, six months after Samuel and Gertrude married, Samuel filled out his WWI draft registration card. He was 24 years old. His address was still 965 St. Antoine Street and he was living there with his "dependents"—a mother, sister and wife. He is described on the second page as slender, dark brown hair, brown eyes and slightly bald. His occupation is inspector in the Ford Motor Co. Samuel's date of birth is listed as Nov. 12, 1892, though his later Declaration of Intention from Jan. 25, 1928, lists his birthdate as Nov. 5, 1892.

The Draft Registration card lists Samuel's birthplace cryptically as "Umion, Cieve, Russia." Samuel's brother listed "Uman, Kieff, Russia" on his Draft registration card a year later and "Immen Russia" on a Declaration he filled out later in California. I suspect they were referring to the town known today as "Uman Russia," south of Kiev, but this identification is not certain.

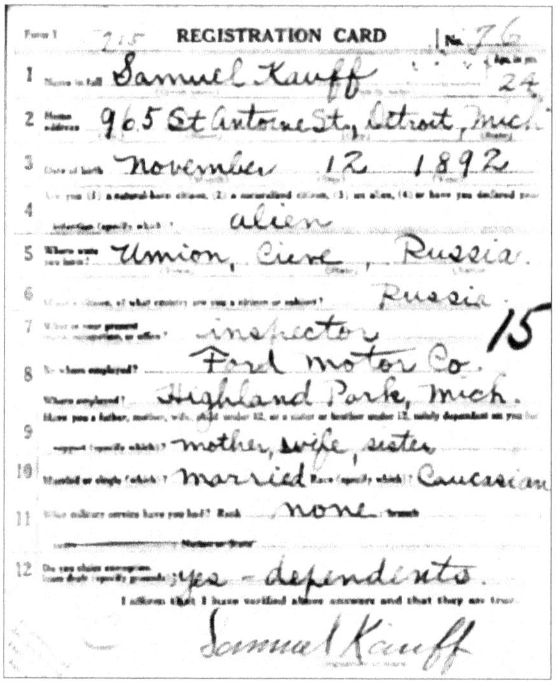
REGISTRATION CARD
1 Samuel Kauff 24
2 965 St Antoine St, Detroit, Mich.
3 November 12 1892
4 alien
5 Umion, Cieve, Russia.
6 Russia
7 inspector 15
8 Ford motor Co.
Highland Park, Mich.
9 mother, wife, sister
10 married Caucasian
11 none
12 yes - dependents.
I affirm that I have verified above answers and that they are true.
Samuel Kauff

Figure 117 WWI Draft Registration Card of Samuel Kauff

Samuel's later Naturalization Petition from 1928 indicates he arrived in the US 1901 on the SS "Gravalderzy" (Samuel's attempt to spell SS Graf Waldersee). I found "Schame" age 10 with his mother and siblings on the manifest of SS Graf Waldersee, sailing from Rotterdam and arriving in New York on Nov. 23, 1901.

The family's surname on the manifest is spelled "Supkow." He is traveling with his mother Gitel, his three sisters and his brother Abram. They are headed to his father, Froim (i.e., Ephraim and later Frank). A few lines above them in the manifest, there is also a brother-in-law of Froim Supkow, who was probably accompanying Gitel and her children on their journey.

Figure 118 1901 Manifest of Samuel Kauff ("Schame Supkow") and family on SS Graf Waldersee

It appears that Samuel's family moved at some point to Waterbury, Connecticut before coming to Detroit. By 1918, Samuel is listed as an inspector [in the auto industry] and is living with Gertrude at 209 Hendrie Avenue in Detroit. On Aug. 20th that year, Samuel and Gertrude had a son, Frank, who was apparently named for Samuel's father, Froim. By 1919 Samuel is listed as an autoworker boarding ("b") at 260 Westminster Ave.

It is tempting to imagine a connection between Gertrude who was living for a time on Hendrie Ave and her Detroit first cousin Samuel Moskovitch, the barber, who lived in the mid-1920s at 648 Hendrie Ave. However, they were on Hendrie at different times and it is possible they were like ships passing in the night.

1918 Detroit City Directory	**Kauff Gertrude, mach opr, b965 St Antoine** **" Saml, inspr, h3, 965 St Antoine**
1919 Detroit City Directory	Kauff Saml autowkr b260 Westminster av

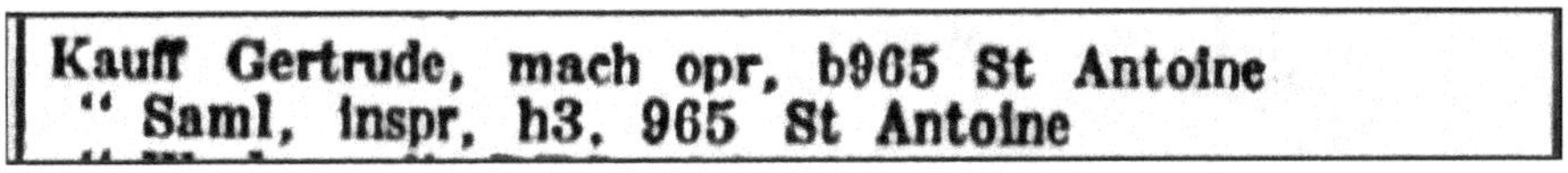

In the 1920 census, Samuel Kauff and Gertrude appear back at 965 St. Antoine, where Sam was living with his mother when he married Gertrude in 1917. We can guess that in the intervening years, Sam and Gertrude moved out to their own place and came back to live there after the birth of their son Frank. Samuel's mother and sister are no longer living at the St. Antoine address; their spaces filled by two roomers who are present. There are also several other families living at the same address according to the census.

Photo 38 Gertrude Kauff
Naturalization Petition Photo, 1941

In the 1920 census, Sam is 27 and his immigration is incorrectly listed as 1900 (he arrived in Nov. 1901). He is still an alien ("Al") and has not yet started his naturalization process. He is described as an inspector of auto parts in an auto factory, presumably still Ford. Gertrude is 22 and her immigration is listed as 1910 (we saw she came in 1909). Their son Frank is now 1 year and 4 months old.

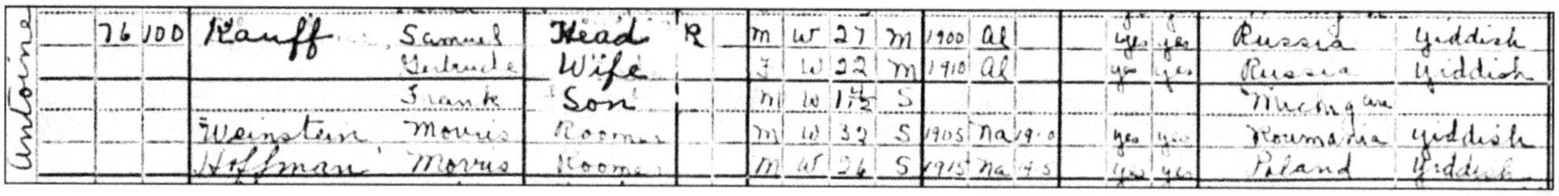

Antoine	76	100	Kauff	Samuel	Head	R	M	W	27	M	1900	Al		yes	yes	Russia	Yiddish
				Gertrude	Wife		F	W	22	M	1910	Al		yes	yes	Russia	Yiddish
				Frank	Son		M	W	1 4/12	S						Michigan	
			Weinstein	Morris	Roomer		M	W	32	S	1905	Na	[illegible]	yes	yes	Roumania	Yiddish
			Hoffman	Morris	Roomer		M	W	26	S	1915	Na	[illegible]	yes	yes	Poland	Yiddish

Figure 119 1920 Census of Samuel and Gertrude (Goldberg) Kauff at 965 St. Antoine

By Feb. 1926, Gertrude filed for a divorce which was granted on July 20, 1926. The justification of "extreme cruelty" on the record has to be taken with a grain of salt. The term evolved with new notions of autonomy that emerged in the late 19th century and took on a psychological meaning in the late 19th century. Today we would probably just say irreconcilable differences.[16]

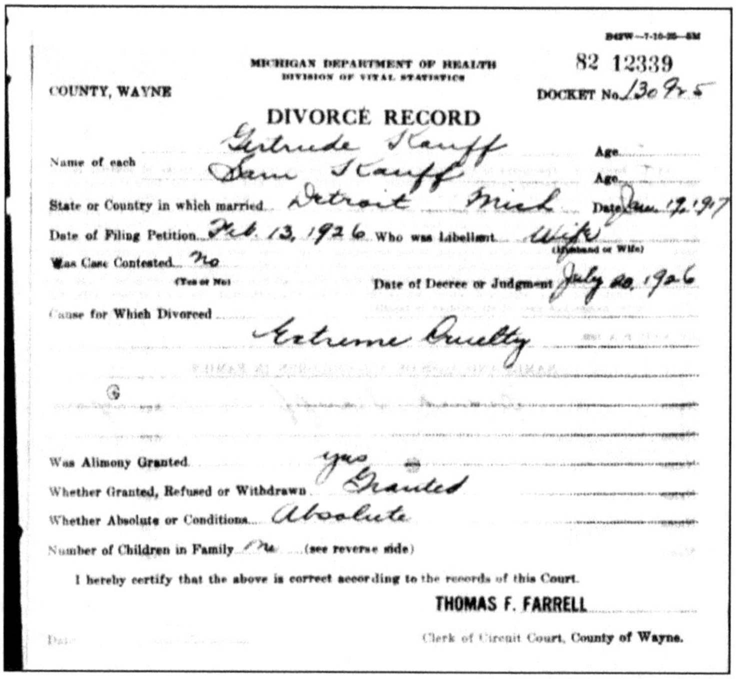

MICHIGAN DEPARTMENT OF HEALTH
DIVISION OF VITAL STATISTICS

82 12339

COUNTY, WAYNE

DOCKET No. 130975

DIVORCE RECORD

Name of each: Gertrude Kauff / Sam Kauff

Age / Age

State or Country in which married: Detroit Mich. Date: Jan. 19, 1917

Date of Filing Petition: Feb. 13, 1926 Who was Libellant: Wife (Husband or Wife)

Was Case Contested: No (Yes or No)

Date of Decree or Judgment: July 20, 1926

Cause for Which Divorced: Extreme Cruelty

Was Alimony Granted: yes

Whether Granted, Refused or Withdrawn: Granted

Whether Absolute or Conditional: Absolute

Number of Children in Family: No (see reverse side)

I hereby certify that the above is correct according to the records of this Court.

THOMAS F. FARRELL

Clerk of Circuit Court, County of Wayne.

Figure 120 Divorce Record of Gertrude and Sam Kauff

By the 1930 census, Samuel remarried a woman named Inez. He is living at 3017 Buena Vista Street in apartments. Sam's son Frank is living with him as is his niece, Selma Allison (daughter of his sister Betty Zubcoff Allison). A death record from 1933 records what became of Samuel Kauff.

On November 24, 1933, Samuel shot himself at his home at 2302 W. Grand Street. The informant was Jacob Winton, who was living at the same address, and may have been his brother-in-law. It was three years into the Depression, and we can guess that the economic suffering may have been a significant factor.

[16] Robert L. Griswold, "The Evolution of the Doctrine of Mental Cruelty in Victorian American Divorce, 1790-1900." Journal of Social History, vol. 20, no. 1, 1986, pp. 127–48. JSTOR, http://www.jstor.org/stable/3788279. Accessed 11 Jan. 2024.

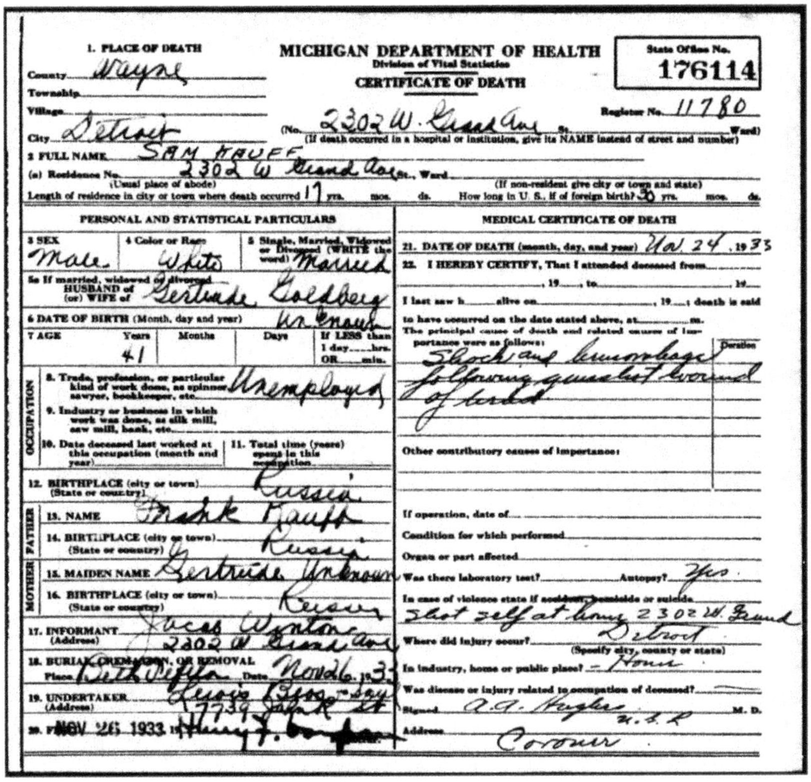

MICHIGAN DEPARTMENT OF HEALTH
Division of Vital Statistics
CERTIFICATE OF DEATH

State Office No. 176114
Register No. 11780

1. PLACE OF DEATH
County Wayne
Township
Village
City Detroit (No. 2302 W. Grand Ave St. Ward)
(If death occurred in a hospital or institution, give its NAME instead of street and number)
2. FULL NAME SAM KAUFF
(a) Residence No. 2302 W Grand Ave St., Ward
(Usual place of abode) (If non-resident give city or town and state)
Length of residence in city or town where death occurred 17 yrs. mos. ds. How long in U. S., if of foreign birth? 30 yrs. mos. ds.

PERSONAL AND STATISTICAL PARTICULARS
3 SEX Male
4 Color or Race White
5 Single, Married, Widowed or Divorced (WRITE the word) Married
5a If married, widowed or divorced HUSBAND of (or) WIFE of Gertrude Goldberg
6 DATE OF BIRTH (Month, day and year) Un Known
7 AGE Years 41 Months Days If LESS than 1 day ___hrs. OR ___min.
8. Trade, profession, or particular kind of work done, as spinner, sawyer, bookkeeper, etc. Unemployed
9. Industry or business in which work was done, as silk mill, saw mill, bank, etc.
10. Date deceased last worked at this occupation (month and year)
11. Total time (years) spent in this occupation
12. BIRTHPLACE (city or town) (State or country) Russia
FATHER 13. NAME Frank Kauff
14. BIRTHPLACE (city or town) (State or country) Russia
MOTHER 15. MAIDEN NAME Gertrude Unknown
16. BIRTHPLACE (city or town) (State or country) Russia
17. INFORMANT Jacob Winton
(Address) 2302 W Grand Ave
18. BURIAL, CREMATION, OR REMOVAL Place Beth Tefila Date Nov 26. 1933
19. UNDERTAKER Lewis Bros. Inc.
(Address) 7739 [illegible] St
20. FILED NOV 26 1933

MEDICAL CERTIFICATE OF DEATH
21. DATE OF DEATH (month, day, and year) Nov. 24, 1933
22. I HEREBY CERTIFY, That I attended deceased from ___, 19__, to ___, 19__
I last saw h__ alive on ___, 19__; death is said to have occurred on the date stated above, at ___m.
The principal cause of death and related causes of importance were as follows: Shock and hemorrhage following gunshot wound of head
Other contributory causes of importance:
If operation, date of
Condition for which performed
Organ or part affected
Was there laboratory test? Autopsy? Yes
In case of violence state if accident, homicide or suicide. Shot self at home 2302 W. Grand
Where did injury occur? Detroit (Specify city, county or state)
In industry, home or public place? Home
Was disease or injury related to occupation of deceased?
Signed A.G. Hughes M.D.
Address Coroner

Figure 121 Death Certificate for Sam Kauff

Gertrude has not been located in the 1930 census, and it is unclear whether she was still in Detroit at the time. She reappears in California in the 1940 census which indicates she was there at least since 1935. Her address is 745 S. Normandie Avenue in Los Angeles, and she was residing in an apartment which she rented and a lodger lived with her. She is described as a dressmaker and "wd" [widowed]. It is not known why Gertrude moved to California, though Samuel's brother, Abe, settled in LA by this time and perhaps his presence there was a reason she headed west, rather than to Baltimore where she still had family.

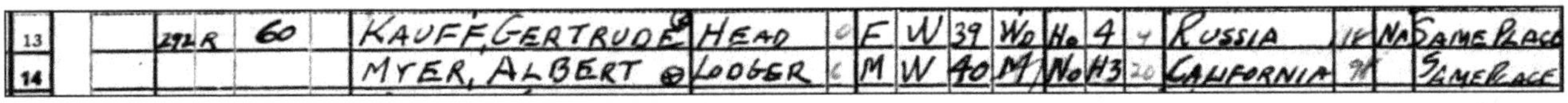

13		292R	60	KAUFF, GERTRUDE	HEAD	0	F	W	39	Wd	H0	4	4	RUSSIA	16	Na	SAME PLACE
14				MYER, ALBERT	LODGER	6	M	W	40	M	No	H3	20	CALIFORNIA	9		SAME PLACE

Figure 122 1940 Census of Gertrude Kauff

In 1941 while living at the same address, Gertrude declared her intention to become a citizen. She calls herself "Geetel Kauff aka Gertrude Kauff" and describes herself as 5'11" and 115 pounds. In the space to designate marital status, she indicated she "was" married and her husband "was Sam." She listed her age as 43, and her birthdate as March 27, 1898, in "Calaiash Bessaribia" [Kalarash, Russia]. She noted that her son Frank was living in Los Angeles as well. Her lodger in the 1940 census, Albert Meyer, reappears as a witness on Gertrude's Naturalization Petition in 1943. He was no longer lodging with her and described himself as a furniture store owner. In her Petition from 1943 she indicates her son Frank was currently in the reserves for the Navy.

Marie (Schabb) Schwartz (a first cousin of Gertrude's) recalls Frank Kauff visiting Baltimore or being stationed nearby possibly at Sparrows Point when he was in the Navy. "My father [Max Schabb] was very family minded, he would bring Frank to the house, around 1944. The Army and Navy football teams were playing, and my father got tickets. He didn't want to go, and he sent me with Frank to the game in Philadelphia. I was only 12."

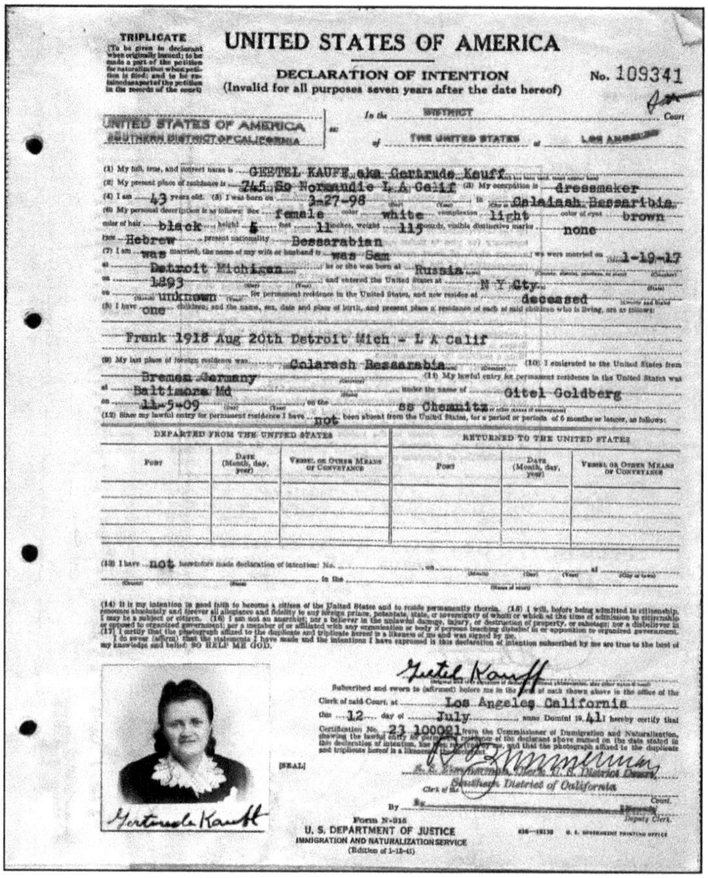

TRIPLICATE

UNITED STATES OF AMERICA

DECLARATION OF INTENTION

(Invalid for all purposes seven years after the date hereof)

No. 109341

UNITED STATES OF AMERICA, SOUTHERN DISTRICT OF CALIFORNIA — In the DISTRICT Court of THE UNITED STATES at LOS ANGELES

(1) My full, true, and correct name is GEETEL KAUFF aka Gertrude Kauff
(2) My present place of residence is 745 So Normandie L A Calif (3) My occupation is dressmaker
(4) I am 43 years old. (5) I was born on 3-27-98 in Calaiash Bessaribia
(6) My personal description is as follows: Sex female, color white, complexion light, color of eyes brown, color of hair black, height 5 feet 11 inches, weight 115 pounds, visible distinctive marks none, race Hebrew, present nationality Bessarabian
(7) I am was married; the name of my wife or husband is was Sam; we were married on 1-19-17 at Detroit Michigan; he or she was born at Russia on 1893 and entered the United States at N Y Cty on unknown for permanent residence in the United States, and now resides at deceased
(8) I have one children; and the name, sex, date and place of birth, and present place of residence of each of said children who is living, are as follows:
Frank 1918 Aug 20th Detroit Mich – L A Calif
(9) My last place of foreign residence was Colaresh Bessarabia (10) I emigrated to the United States from Bremen Germany (11) My lawful entry for permanent residence in the United States was at Baltimore Md under the name of Gitel Goldberg on 11-5-09 on the ss Chemnitz
(12) Since my lawful entry for permanent residence I have not been absent from the United States, for a period or periods of 6 months or longer, as follows:

DEPARTED FROM THE UNITED STATES			RETURNED TO THE UNITED STATES		
Port	Date (Month, day, year)	Vessel or Other Means of Conveyance	Port	Date (Month, day, year)	Vessel or Other Means of Conveyance

(13) I have not heretofore made declaration of intention: No. ...., on .... at .... in the ....

(14) It is my intention in good faith to become a citizen of the United States and to reside permanently therein. (15) I will, before being admitted to citizenship, renounce absolutely and forever all allegiance and fidelity to any foreign prince, potentate, state, or sovereignty of whom or which at the time of admission to citizenship I may be a subject or citizen. (16) I am not an anarchist; nor a believer in the unlawful damage, injury, or destruction of property, or sabotage; nor a disbeliever in or opposed to organized government; nor a member of or affiliated with any organization or body of persons teaching disbelief in or opposition to organized government. (17) I certify that the photograph affixed to the duplicate and triplicate hereof is a likeness of me and was signed by me.
I do swear (affirm) that the statements I have made and the intentions I have expressed in this declaration of intention subscribed by me are true to the best of my knowledge and belief: SO HELP ME GOD.

Geetel Kauff

Subscribed and sworn to (affirmed) before me in the form of oath shown above in the office of the Clerk of said Court, at Los Angeles California this 12 day of July anno Domini 1941. I hereby certify that Certification No. 23 100021 from the Commissioner of Immigration and Naturalization, showing the lawful entry for permanent residence of the declarant above named on the date stated in this declaration of intention, has been received by me, and that the photograph affixed to the duplicate and triplicate hereof is a likeness of the declarant.

[SEAL]

Clerk of the U. S. District Court, Southern District of California

By .... Deputy Clerk.

Gertrude Kauff

Form N-315
U. S. DEPARTMENT OF JUSTICE
IMMIGRATION AND NATURALIZATION SERVICE
(Edition of 1-13-41)

Figure 123 1941 Declaration of Geetel Kauff

By 1950, Gertrude and her son Frank moved to Miami Beach where they appear in the census at 920 Jefferson Ave. Gertrude is 50 and "wid[owed]". Frank is 32 and still single. Gertrude is described as a "sample maker" in a manufacturing business for ladies' clothing and Frank is a salesman in retail men's wear.

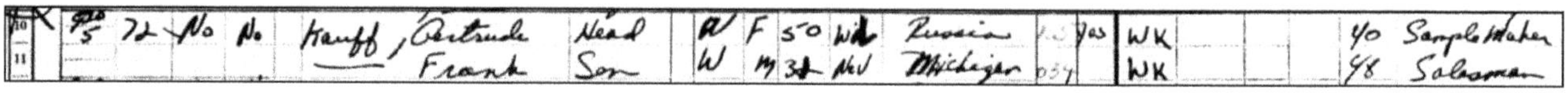

10	920 5	72	No	No	Kauff, Gertrude	Head	W	F	50	Wid	Russia	Yes	WK	40	Sample Maker
11					Frank	Son	W	M	32	Nev	Michigan		WK	48	Salesman

Figure 124 1950 Census in Miami for Gertrude and Frank

In May 1953, Frank married Ann C. Metzger. They subsequently had two children: Linda and Stephen. Gertrude passed away in 1975. Frank passed away in 1994.

***

Edith Goldberg and Hyman Kahn

A year after Gertrude married Samuel Kauff, her sister Edith married Hyman Kahn in Baltimore. Their marriage license was listed in *The Baltimore Sun* on July 25, 1918 (p. 8). Hyman was 23 and Edith 19. A friend of Hyman's named Nathan Land submitted the application for their marriage license. He was living at 2126 East Baltimore at the time. In the city directory a year earlier, Nathan Land was living at 117 N. Wolfe St., the same street address where Hyman was living with his family before he got married. I suspect that is how they knew each other.

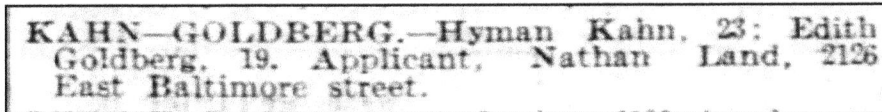

Figure 125 1918 Edith Goldberg and Hyman Kahn Marriage License

Hyman Kahn arrived in the US four years before Edith. He departed Liverpool England as "Chaim Kohn" age 14, with his mother and siblings on Dec. 28, 1908, on the SS Friesland, and arrived in Philadelphia on Jan. 10, 1909. Their destination was Baltimore where Hyman's father, Nathan, was living at 926 E Baltimore Street, "here 5 years" according to the second page of their manifest.

The Kohn's last permanent residence is described as "Disne" Wilna, where Hyman's maternal grandfather was living. It seems apparent that as his father Hyman was settling in Baltimore, Hyman's mother took the family back to her hometown, probably the town called Disna, Belarus today, which is not far from Kraslava, Latvia where Hyman was born.

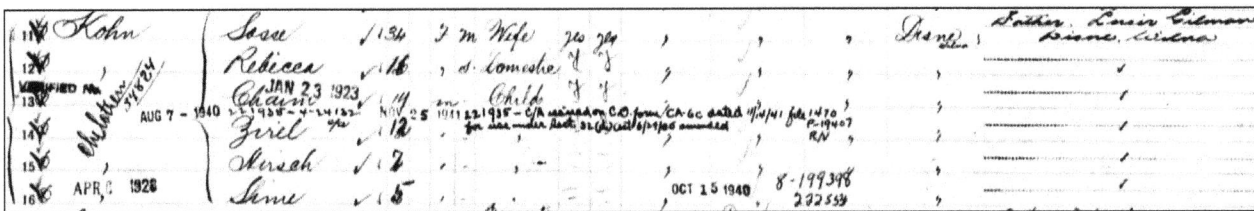

Figure 126 1909 Manifest of the Kahn family

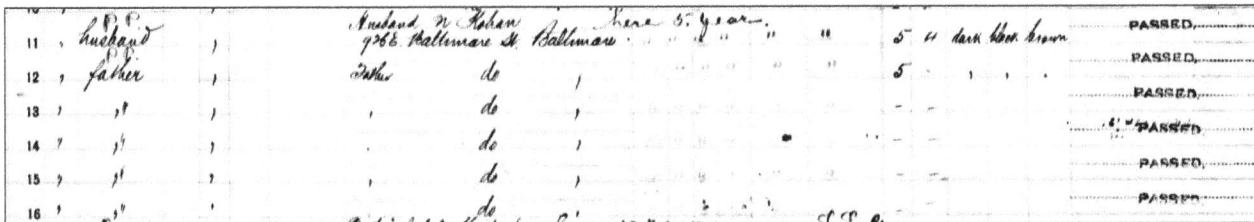

Page 2 of manifest, destination "husband N. Kohan 926 E Baltimore St.

A year after Edith and Hyman were married their son Morton was born, on May 13, 1919. The birth may have prompted Hyman to start his naturalization process. He filled out his Declaration of Intention on Nov. 20, 1919. The record describes him as 5'6" with dark brown hair and brown eyes. He is living at 2128 E. Lombard, the same address he and Edith were living in the 1920 census. His birthplace is listed as Kreslavki, Russia [today Kreslavka, Latvia[17]]. He listed his birthdate as Dec. 25, 1894.

These personal details differ a bit from those on his earlier WWI Draft registration card from June 5, 1917. At that point, he was still living with his parents at 117 N. Wolfe St. in Baltimore and listed his birthdate as *Sept. 25, 1894*, and his birth location Kreslavska, Russia. At the time he was working as a printer at Romm Press. He would remain in the printing business the rest of his life.

---

[17] Hyman's obituary lists his birth location as "Latvia" confirming the identification of his birthplace as formerly Kreslavska, Russia.

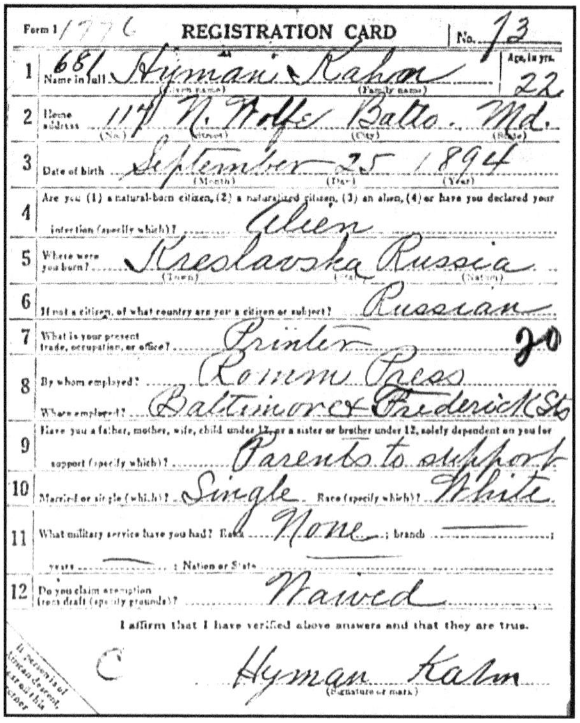

Form 1/776 REGISTRATION CARD No. 13

1 681 Name in full Hyman Kahn (Given name) (Family name) Age, in yrs. 22

2 Home address 117 N. Wolfe Balto. Md. (No.) (Street) (City) (State)

3 Date of birth September 25 1894 (Month) (Day) (Year)

4 Are you (1) a natural-born citizen, (2) a naturalized citizen, (3) an alien, (4) or have you declared your intention (specify which)? Alien

5 Where were you born? Kreslavska Russia (Town) (State) (Nation)

6 If not a citizen, of what country are you a citizen or subject? Russian

7 What is your present trade, occupation, or office? Printer

8 By whom employed? Romm Press

Where employed? Baltimore & Frederick Sts

9 Have you a father, mother, wife, child under 12, or a sister or brother under 12, solely dependent on you for support (specify which)? Parents to support

10 Married or single (which)? Single Race (specify which)? White

11 What military service have you had? Rank None; branch

years ; Nation or State

12 Do you claim exemption from draft (specify grounds)? Waived

I affirm that I have verified above answers and that they are true.

Hyman Kahn (Signature or mark)

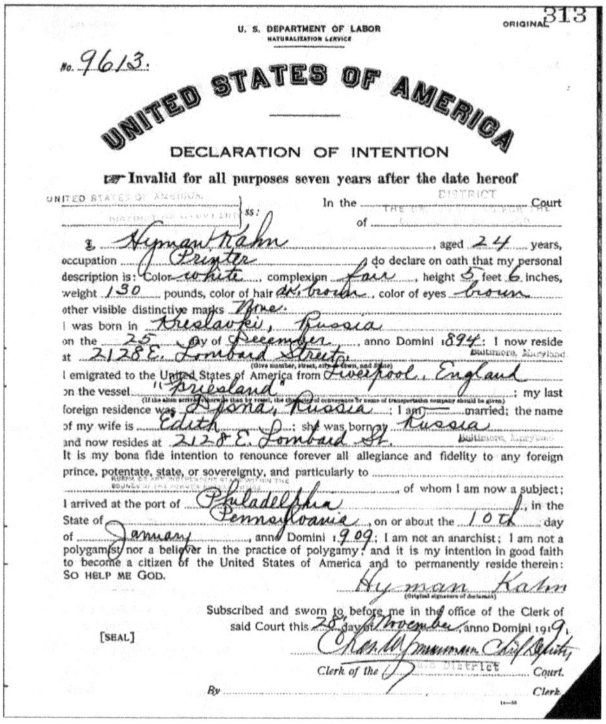

U. S. DEPARTMENT OF LABOR
NATURALIZATION SERVICE
ORIGINAL 313

No. 9613.

UNITED STATES OF AMERICA

DECLARATION OF INTENTION

Invalid for all purposes seven years after the date hereof

United States of America, District of Maryland, ss: In the District Court of the United States of

I, Hyman Kahn, aged 24 years, occupation Printer, do declare on oath that my personal description is: Color white, complexion fair, height 5 feet 6 inches, weight 130 pounds, color of hair dk. brown, color of eyes brown, other visible distinctive marks None. I was born in Kreslavki, Russia on the 25 day of December, anno Domini 1894; I now reside at 2128 E. Lombard Street, Baltimore, Maryland. I emigrated to the United States of America from Liverpool, England on the vessel "Friesland"; my last foreign residence was Dvinsk, Russia; I am married; the name of my wife is Edith; she was born at Russia and now resides at 2128 E. Lombard St. Baltimore, Maryland. It is my bona fide intention to renounce forever all allegiance and fidelity to any foreign prince, potentate, state, or sovereignty, and particularly to ... of whom I am now a subject; I arrived at the port of Philadelphia, in the State of Pennsylvania, on or about the 10th day of January, anno Domini 1909; I am not an anarchist; I am not a polygamist nor a believer in the practice of polygamy; and it is my intention in good faith to become a citizen of the United States of America and to permanently reside therein: SO HELP ME GOD.

Hyman Kahn (Original signature of declarant)

Subscribed and sworn to before me in the office of the Clerk of said Court this 28 day of November anno Domini 1919.

[SEAL]

Clerk of the District Court.

By ... Clerk.

Figure 127 Hyman Kahn's Draft Registration and Declaration

In their 1920 census, Edith and Hyman Khan are still at 2128 [E.] Lombard Street. They are renting ("R") their home and sharing the house with another family. Hyman is 25 and has submitted his first papers for naturalization ("PA"). He is described as a mechanic for a press.

Edith is age 20. Since they were married before the naturalization rules for women changed in 1922, Edith's naturalization status followed that of her husband. Their son Morton Kahn is listed as 8 months old. I suspect Morton was named after Edith's grandfather, Mordechai Moskovitch, making me think that her father, Abraham Goldberg, was still alive at that point or she would have named her son for him.

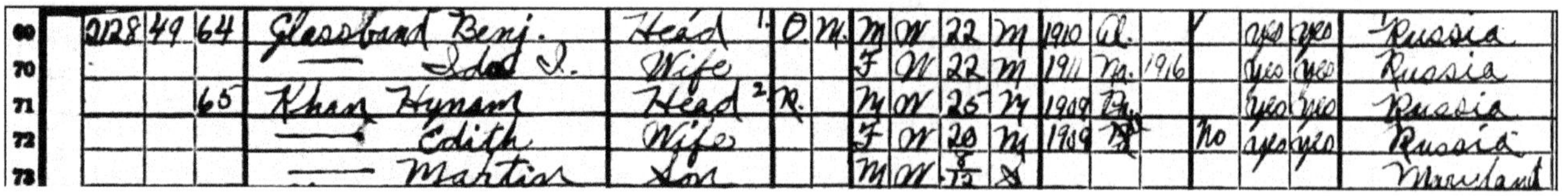

69	2128	49	64	Glassband Benj.	Head	1	O	M	M	W	22	M	1910	Al.			yes	yes	Russia
70				— Ida J.	Wife				F	W	22	M	1911	Na.	1916		yes	yes	Russia
71			65	Khan Hyman	Head	2	R		M	W	25	M	1909	Pa.			yes	yes	Russia
72				— Edith	Wife				F	W	20	M	1909	Pa.		no	yes	yes	Russia
73				— Martin	Son				M	W	8/12	S							Maryland

Figure 128 1920 Census for family of Edith and Hyman Kahn on E. Lombard

Hyman filled out his Petition on January 4, 1924. He called himself "Chaim Kohn aka Hyman Kahn." They were living at 347 E. 27th Street at the time. For this record, he gave his birthdate as Dec. 25, 1894, consistent with his Declaration. He listed his wife Edith's birthplace as Kalarash, Russia and her birthdate as May 15, 1899. This is the earliest record located that lists a birthdate for Edith.

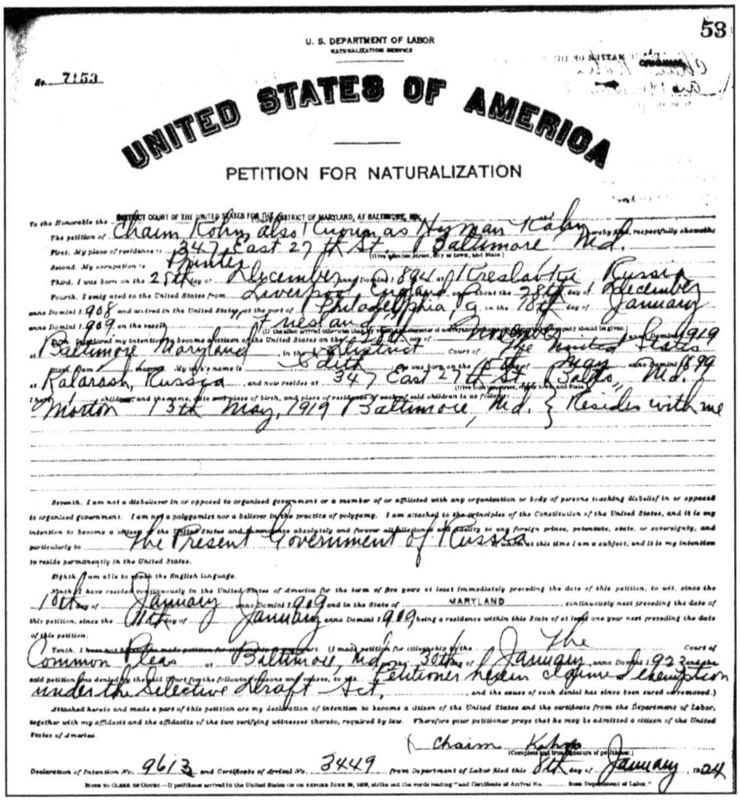

53

U. S. DEPARTMENT OF LABOR
NATURALIZATION SERVICE

No. 7153

UNITED STATES OF AMERICA

PETITION FOR NATURALIZATION

To the Honorable the DISTRICT COURT OF THE UNITED STATES FOR THE DISTRICT OF MARYLAND, AT BALTIMORE, MD.
The petition of Chaim Kohn, also known as Hyman Kahn, hereby filed, respectfully showeth:
First. My place of residence is 347 East 27th St. Baltimore Md.
Second. My occupation is Printer
Third. I was born on the 25th day of December anno Domini 1894 at Kreslablte Russia
Fourth. I emigrated to the United States from Liverpool, England on or about the 28th day of December anno Domini 1908 and arrived in the United States, at the port of Philadelphia, Pa on the 18th day of January anno Domini 1909 on the vessel Friesland
Fifth. I declared my intention to become a citizen of the United States on the 5th day of November anno Domini 1919 at Baltimore Maryland in the District Court of The United States
Sixth. I am married. My wife's name is Edith she was born on the 15th day of Aug anno Domini 1899 at Kalarash, Russia and now resides at 347 East 27th St. Balto. Md.
I have 1 children, and the name, date and place of birth, and place of residence of each of said children is as follows:
Morton 13th May, 1919 Baltimore, Md. Resides with me

Seventh. I am not a disbeliever in or opposed to organized government or a member of or affiliated with any organization or body of persons teaching disbelief in or opposed to organized government. I am not a polygamist nor a believer in the practice of polygamy. I am attached to the principles of the Constitution of the United States, and it is my intention to become a citizen of the United States and to renounce absolutely and forever all allegiance and fidelity to any foreign prince, potentate, state, or sovereignty, and particularly to The Present Government of Russia of whom at this time I am a subject, and it is my intention to reside permanently in the United States.
Eighth. I am able to speak the English language.
Ninth. I have resided continuously in the United States of America for the term of five years at least immediately preceding the date of this petition, to wit, since the 18th day of January, anno Domini 1909 and in the State of MARYLAND, continuously next preceding the date of this petition, since the 18th day of January anno Domini 1909 being a residence within this State of at least one year next preceding the date of this petition.
Tenth. I made petition for citizenship to the The Common Pleas Court of Baltimore, Md. on the 30th day of January, anno Domini 1923 and such petition was denied by the said Court for the following reasons and causes, to wit, Petitioner having claimed exemption under the Selective Draft Act, and the cause of such denial has since been cured or removed.)
Attached hereto and made a part of this petition are my declaration of intention to become a citizen of the United States and the certificate from the Department of Labor, together with my affidavit and the affidavits of the two verifying witnesses thereto, required by law. Wherefore your petitioner prays that he may be admitted a citizen of the United States of America.

Chaim Kahn
(Complete and true signature of petitioner.)

Declaration of Intention No. 9613 and Certificate of Arrival No. 3449 from Department of Labor filed this 8th day of January, 1924

Note to Clerk of Court.—If petitioner arrived in the United States on or before June 29, 1906, strike out the words reading "and Certificate of Arrival No. ...... from Department of Labor."

Figure 129 Hyman Kahn's Petition, Jan. 1924

Hyman and Edith's daughter, Charlotte (married name Green), was born on March 3, 1926. By the 1930 census, they moved to Northeast Baltimore near Pimlico Racetrack at 5010 Queensbury Ave. They own their home which is worth $4500. Hyman is 34, Edith 29, Morton 11 and Charlotte 4. Hyman is described as a "compositor" in a printing office.

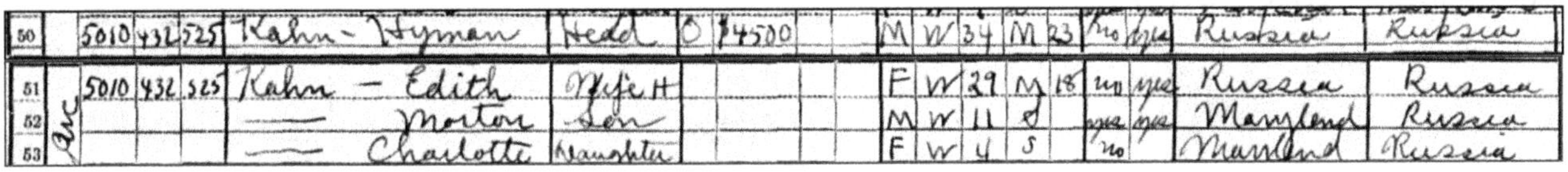

50		5010	432	525	Kahn – Hyman	Head	O	$4500		M	W	34	M	23	no	yes	Russia	Russia
51	Ave	5010	432	525	Kahn – Edith	Wife H				F	W	29	M	18	no	yes	Russia	Russia
52					— Morton	Son				M	W	11	S		yes	yes	Maryland	Russia
53					— Charlotte	Daughter				F	W	4	S		no		Maryland	Russia

Figure 130 1930 Census for the Kahn family

The family is still at the same home in 1940. Their home value is now $5500. Hyman is described as a printer and lithographer. That same year Morton filled out his WWII Draft Registration card. He was 21 and still living at his parents' home on Queensberry Ave. His employer was Blum's Inc. at 305 N. Gay Street in Baltimore. His registration card describes him as 5'10" with brown hair and brown eyes. In 1942, Morton's father, Hyman, filled out his WWII draft registration card. He listed the name of the printing business as Floam Press.

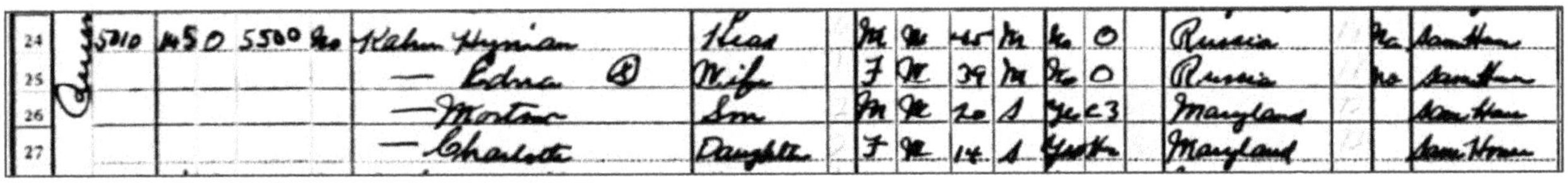

24	Queens	5010	450	5500	No	Kahn Hyman	Head	M	W	45	M	No	0	Russia	No	Same House
25						— Edna ⊗	Wife	F	W	39	M	No	0	Russia	No	Same House
26						— Morton	Son	M	W	20	S	Yes	C3	Maryland		Same House
27						— Charlotte	Daughter	F	W	14	S	Yes		Maryland		Same House

Figure 131 1940 Census for the Kahn family

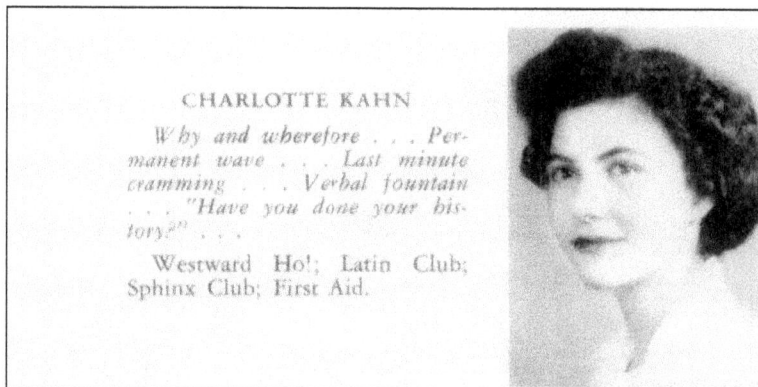

Photo 39 Charlotte Kahn, 1944 High School Photo

The family is still all together in the 1950 census. Hyman is 54, Edith 50, Morton 30 and Charlotte 24. Hyman is still listed as a "printer" in a "Printing Co." Morton in the meantime became a pharmacist in a drug store and Charlotte is listed as a typist in an accounting firm. Neither Charlotte nor Morton have married yet.

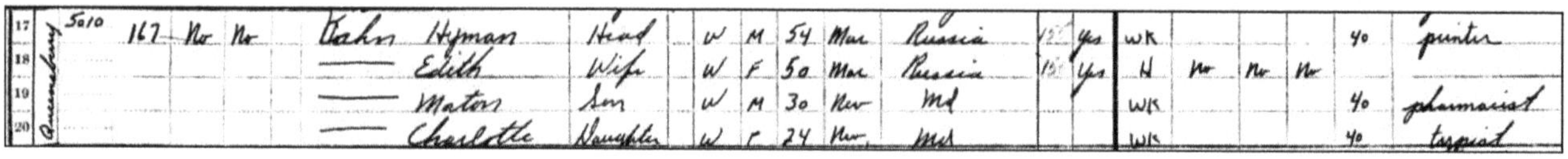

17	5010	167	No	No	Kahn Hyman	Head	W	M	54	Mar	Russia	Yes	WK				40	printer
18					—— Edith	Wife	W	F	50	Mar	Russia	Yes	H	No	No	No		
19					—— Morton	Son	W	M	30	Nev	Md		WK				40	pharmacist
20					—— Charlotte	Daughter	W	F	24	Nev	Md		WK				40	typist

Figure 132 1950 Census for Kahn family

On Dec. 3, 1950, Morton Kahn married Beverley Phyllis Cohen. They subsequently had two daughters, Arlene (married name Sperling) and Debra (married name Goldschmitt). Charlotte Kahn married William ("Bill") Green. They subsequently had two sons, Jeffrey and Howard.

Hyman Kahn passed away in 1970. Edith passed away in 1994.

Bill Green passed away in 2005 and his wife Charlotte passed away in 2006. Morton passed away in 1987, and his wife Beverley in 2016.

***

Records Summary for Sarah (Moskovitch) Goldberg and Family

Nov. 5, 1909 Passenger manifest	Passenger manifest for Max Goldberg and Gertrude (Goldberg) Kauff. SS Chemnitz sailing from Bremen on Oct. 21, 1909 and arriving in Baltimore Nov. 5, 1909. **Mote (Motel/Max) Goldberg**, age 17, clerk and **Gitel Goldberg** (married name **Gertrude Kauff**), age 16, "servant", the word "admitted" is type in the margin. Last residence Kolorasch [Kalarash, now Romania Călăraşi,] and closest relative Abr. Goldberg, Kolorasch GB (Gubernia) Bessarabia, destination Baltimore. [page 2] destination is uncle Sam Moskowitz 316 S. High Street Baltimore, birthplace Russia Kolarasch [Kalarash].
Apr. 29, 1910 US Federal Census, Baltimore	Max G. Goldberg, age 16, nephew [living with his aunt and uncle Anna and Morris Schabb] at 1635 E. Fayette, year of immigration 1909, naturalization status Al[ien]. See the details of the record listed under Anna (Moshkevich) Schabb.
Dec. 26, 1911 Naturalization Declaration	Max Goldberg, nephew, age 18, occupation clerk, 5'5" 130 lbs, born in Kalarasch, Russia, on Aug. 5, 1893, now resides at 1628 [1658?] E. Fayette Street, Baltimore, Maryland, emigrated to US from Bremen, Germany on vessel Chemnitz, last foreign residence was Kalarasch, Russia, arrived at the port of Baltimore on Nov. 4, 1909
July 5, 1913 Passenger Manifest	Record of Abraham Goldberg [husband of Sarah Moskovitch], and two children Edith (later married name Kahn) and Jankel. SS Breslau sailing from Bremen on July 5, 1913 arriving in Baltimore July 26, 1913. Abram Goldberg [husband of Sarah Moskovitch], age 44, trader, Nationality Russia, Race Hebrew, Last permanent residence, Ziwin, Russia, name and address of nearest relative or friend in county whence alien came: uncle Hretz Bilwinsky in Ziwin, Grodno, Russia; **Ides [Edith Kahn]** age 15, occupation maid / [written faintly] "seamstress"; **Jankel** age 6 [page 2] destination Balto Md, passage paid by self, $50 in possession, going to br i l [brother-in-law] S Moszkowicz 1044 N. Franklin str, Balto, birthplace Russia, [City or Town] illegible
1914 Baltimore City Directory	**Edith Goldberg** (later Edith Kahn) and **Gertie Goldberg** (later Gertrude Kauff) are living at 1200 e Baltimore St in Baltimore together.
Jan. 19, 1917 Marriage Record Detroit	Marriage Record for Samuel Kauff and Gertrude Goldberg. **Sam Kauf,** age 24, inspector, born in Russia, parents' names Frank and Gussie, and "**Gurtrude**" Goldberg, age 19, born in Kieschinoff, parents names' Abraham ad Sahria.
Nov. 28, 1919 Declaration of Intention	Hyman Kahn [soon to be husband of Edith Goldberg], age 24, occupation Printer, born in Kreslavki, Russia on Dec. 25, 1894 and resides now at 2128 E. Lombard St. Emigrated to US from Liverpool, England on the SS Friesland; last foreign residence was "Disna" Russia [today Disna, Belarus], arrived at port of Philadelphia on Jan. 10, 1909
Jan. 7, 1920 US Federal Census Detroit	916 Antoine Street, dwelling number 76, **Samuel Kauff**, Head, age 27, immigration year 1900, naturalization status Al[ien], occupation inspector auto [parts?], in auto factory; **Gertrude (Goldberg)**, age 22; immigration year 1910, Frank Kauff age 1 year 4 months

Jan. 3, 1920 US Federal Census Baltimore	2128 Lombard Street, **Hyman Kahn,** Head, 25, Renting, immigrated 1909, PA [naturalization pending], occupation: mechanic, industry: Press, **Edith**, wife, age 20 immigrated 1909, born in Russia, occupation: none, **Martin**, son, 8 months, born in Maryland
Jan. 8, 1924 Naturalization Petition	Petition for Chaim Kohn (aka Hyman Kahn) address 347 East 27th St. Baltimore, occupation Printer, born Dec. 25, 1894 at Kreslavki, Russia, emigrated from Liverpool, England on Dec. 28th 1908 via port of Philadelphia PA on January 18, 1908 on vessel "Friesland"...wife name Edith, she was born on May 15, 1899 at Kalarash Russia, resides same address. 1 child: Morton born May 13, 1919 Baltimore Maryland
Feb. 13, 1926 Divorce Record	Gertrude Kauff and Sam Kauff, married: Detroit Michigan, Jan. 19, 1917, Libellant: wife, Date of decree July 20, 1926, Cause: Extreme Cruelty Frank was 7 at the time.
April 14, 1930 US Federal Census Baltimore	Living at 5010 Queensbury Ave, **Hyman Kahn**, Head, owns home, value $4500, age 34, age at marriage 23, birthplace Russia, occupation Compositor in a Printing Office; **Edith**, wife, age 29, age at marriage 18, birthplace Russia, immigration year 1913; **Morton** son, age 11, birthplace Maryland, **Charlotte** age 4, birthplace Maryland.
July 12, 1941 Declaration of Intention Los Angeles	Declaration of Geetel Kauff aka Gertrude Kauff, address 745 So Normandie LA Calif, occupation dressmaker, 43 years old, born Mar. 27, 1898 in Calaiash Bessaribia [Kalarash, Russia], height 5' 11" weight 115 lbs, race Hebrew, present nationality Bessarabian. Marrital status: "was" married to Sam on Jan. 19, 1917 at Detroit, Michigan, he was born 1893 and entered NY City on unknown. 1 child Frank, born Aug 20, 1918, Detroit Mich. last foreign residence: Colarash Bessarabia, emigrated to US from Bremen Germany, entered at Baltimore MD, under name Gitel Goldberg on Nov. 5, 1909 under name Gitel Goldberg
1953 June 21 Wedding Announcement The Miami News, p. 55	For Frank Kauff: Mr. and Mrs. Allen S. Metzger, 1975 Calais Dr., Miami Beach announce the engagement of their daughter, Miss Anne Claire Metzger to Frank T. Kauff, son of Mrs. Gertrude T. Kauff, Miami Beach.

7.

FAMILY OF MARIESA (MOSHKEVICH) AND MORRIS GOLDFIELD

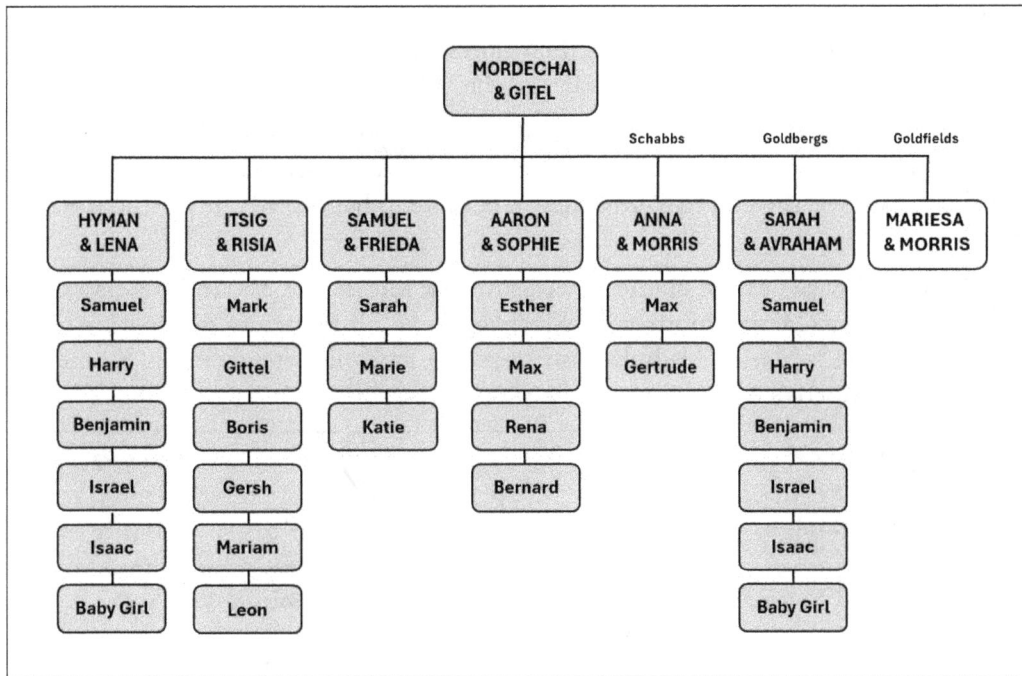

Figure 133 Mariesa (Moshkevich) and Morris Goldfield

According to the family tree, "Mariasha" Moshkovich was the youngest of the "Moskovitch Seven" and was born in 1878 in Ekaterinoslav. In the family tree, her name is spelled "Mariasha." The Yiddish spelling of her name on her tombstone suggests perhaps that her name should be spelled Mariesa (מאריאסע). Her name appears in US records as Marie and Mary. Because she died tragically as a young adult in Baltimore, less information is available about her in the extant records. A great niece, Marie Schabb, born in 1932 was her namesake.

Though Mariesa was the youngest of the "Moskovitch Seven," she was not the last of the siblings to arrive in Baltimore in 1914. Her older brother, Itsig, arrived after WWI. Mariesa's arrival, however, followed that of four older siblings. A decade earlier, her older brother Hyman settled with his family in Canada. About the same time her older brother, Aaron, settled in Baltimore. They were followed in 1906 by her brother Samuel and her sister Anna Schabb who both migrated with their families. The children and husband of her deceased sister, Sarah Goldberg, also arrived in Baltimore by 1913.

***

The Arrival of Marie and Moshe Goldfeld

Mariesa, called Mary and Marie in her records, embarked from Bremen on Jan. 10, 1914, on the SS Neckar with her husband Moshe Goldfeld. They arrived in Baltimore on Jan. 26th. In Baltimore, the surname Goldfeld often appears as Goldfield.

Mosche is described as age 41 and a "taylor." His implied birth year in the manifest is 1872/73. Marie is 38 and a housewife. Her implied birth year is 1875/76 which is a few years earlier than her birth date in the family tree (which has 1878). Other records discussed below suggest she was born in 1880. Though they are 41 and 38 years old, Mosche and Marie have no children on the manifest, and it is not known if there were children who died earlier in Russia. Traveling with them is Marie's nephew, Gersh "Moszkiewicz," the son of her older brother Itsig. Gersh is described as age 17 and a student.

The travelers' last permanent residence is difficult to read in the right-hand columns but looks like "Kisineff" which is confirmed under the name of their closest relative there: Moshe's "br. i. l. [brother-in-law] Itsig Moschevitz," referring to the brother of Marie and the father of Gersh.

Marie was born in Ekaterinoslav according to the oral tradition in the family, like her sister Sarah and brother Aaron. Her siblings who lived in Ekaterinoslav all left for America between 1904 and 1906 before she was married. It is possible she moved to Kishinev to be close to her brother, Itsig, who was still living and raising his family there.

From the second page of their manifest, we learn that Moshe had $50 in his possession and Gersh had $25. They are headed to Marie's brother, "S. Moshkevich 923 E Baltimore St." Marie's brother Samuel was at that address by 1912. Marie's birthplace on page two looks like it might be "Kremenchug" [today Kremenchuk, Ukraine]. Morris's birthplace looks like "Adamivka."

Figure 134 1914 Manifest of SS Neckar for Marie and Mosche Goldfeld and nephew Gersh

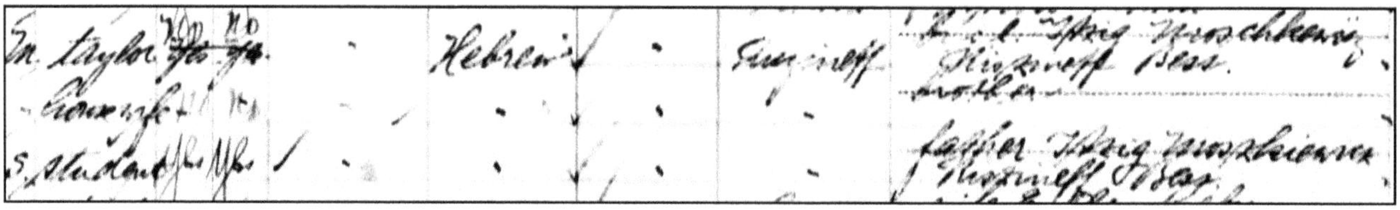

Right-hand columns showing "br. i. l." Itsig Moschevicz as closest relative in Kishinev

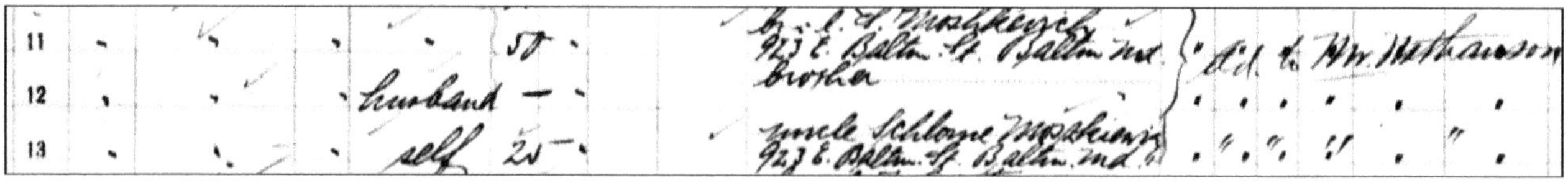

Page 2 of manifest showing their destination is "br. i. l." S Moshkevich 923 E Baltimore St.

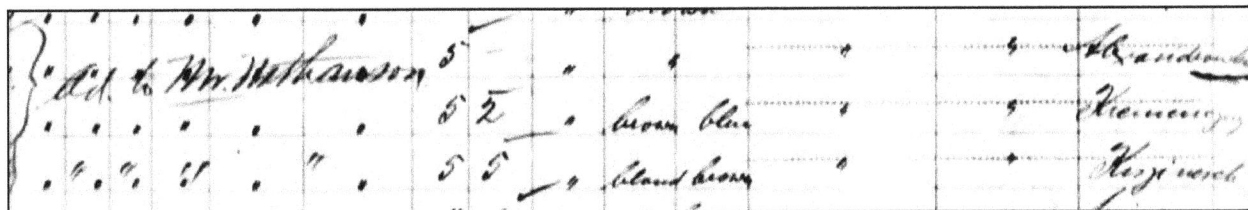

Far-right columns of page 2 showing birthplaces of Morris (Abrandivka?) and Mary (Kremeneguz)

Morris began his naturalization process on April 19, 1916. His Declaration appears next to that of his nephew Gersh (to whom we return later). Morris's record gives his age as 38, his birthdate as Sept. 1, 1877, and his birthplace as Segrinesky Oyezj, Russia. I was not certain where Morris was born until I discovered his brother, Nathan, and his naturalization papers. Nathan spelled his birthplace as "Chigirin," Russia (now Chyhyryn, Ukraine), only 69 km from Kremenchuk, where Marie was born. It seems possible therefore that Morris and Marie met first in Kremenchuk or Ekaterinoslav and subsequently migrated to Kishinev which was their residence before leaving Russia.

In Morris's Declaration he describes himself as a tailor, living at 1046 Aisquith Street in Baltimore with his wife "Mary." Morris was not yet able to write his name in English; his signature is illegible and had to be validated by a witness.

On this document, Morris is younger than he was on his passenger manifest from two years earlier. The US draft for WWI did not start until 1917 so avoiding the draft could *not* have been his motivation for reducing his age. Did he simply forget the age he had given earlier when he migrated?

Figure 135 Morris Goldfield Declaration 1916
with illegible signature

Figure 136 Morris Goldfield Draft Registration Card
Sept. 12, 1918

In the 1916 City Directory, Morris, listed as a tailor, is still at 1046 Aisquith Street. From the City Directory that year, I learned of Morris's brother, Nathan Goldfield, who was living with Morris and Marie at the same address. Records indicate he arrived in the US as "Noah Goldfeld" a few months before Morris and Marie, traveling on the SS Graf Waldersee from Hamburg to New York, and arriving on Oct. 17, 1913. Noah was headed to a friend in New York. He listed "Elisabethgrad" [Ekaterinoslav?] as his last permanent residence which is not far from Kremenchuk.

1916 Baltimore City Directory

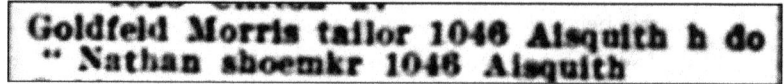

Goldfeld Morris tailor 1046 Aisquith h do
" Nathan shoemkr 1046 Aisquith

In the 1917 City Directory, Morris and Marie were still living at 1046 Aisquith. By the time Morris filled out his WWI Draft Registration in April 1918 (Figure 136 above), he and his wife "Marry" had moved to 2432 Greenmount Ave, just a few houses away from the family of Marie's sister, Anna (Moskevich) Schabb and her husband, who moved there by 1917 to be close to his shoe repair store. Morris signed his Draft Registration card with an "x."

Morris and Marie are still listed at 2432 Greenmount Ave in the 1920 census. They own their home which was "F" (free of mortgage) and a lodger was living with them.

Figure 137 1920 census for Morris and Marie Goldfeld at 3432 Greenmount Ave

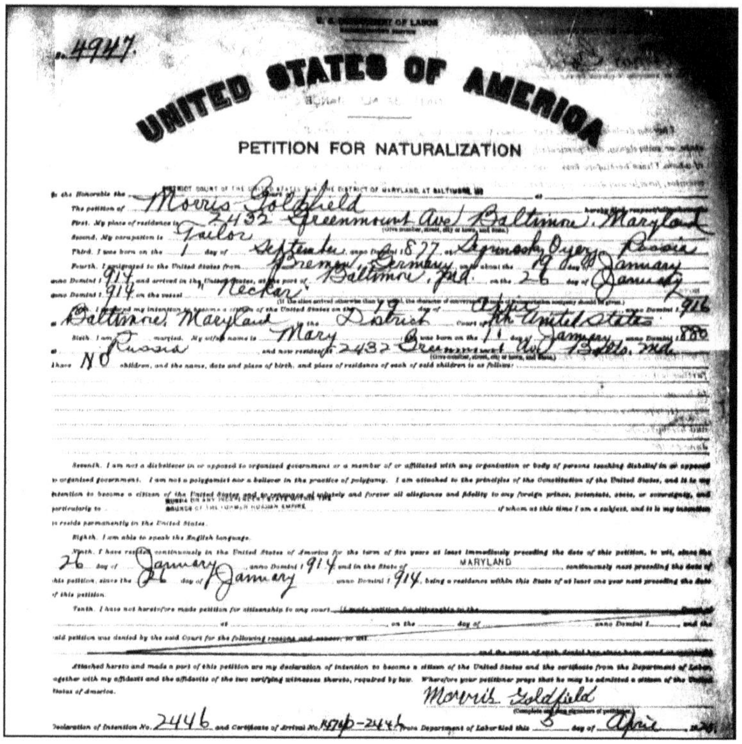

Figure 138 Morris Goldfield's Petition,
April 1920
Witness Signatures of Brothers-in-law,
Aaron Moshkevich and Morris Schabb

On April 5, 1920, Morris filled out his Petition for Naturalization. His personal information is basically identical to that in his earlier Declaration but now reflects their new address at 2432 Greenmount

Ave. This time Morris was able to sign his name. His brothers-in-law, Aaron Moshkevich (Marie's brother) and Morris Schabb (husband of Marie's sister Anna), served as his witnesses.

***

Marie Is Hospitalized

On February 28, 1923, Marie went into the hospital. She died on March 1, 1923. The cause was heart failure—mitral stenosis and a cerebral embolism.

It appears Marie's husband Morris provided the relevant personal information, which thus needs to be taken with a grain of salt. Her birth year is listed as 1880. Her father is listed as "Max Moskewitz" [i.e. Mordechai] and her mother as "Gitel Schwartz." This is the only record I know of that provides a birth surname of Gitel, the matriarch of the family which, therefore, needs more verification.

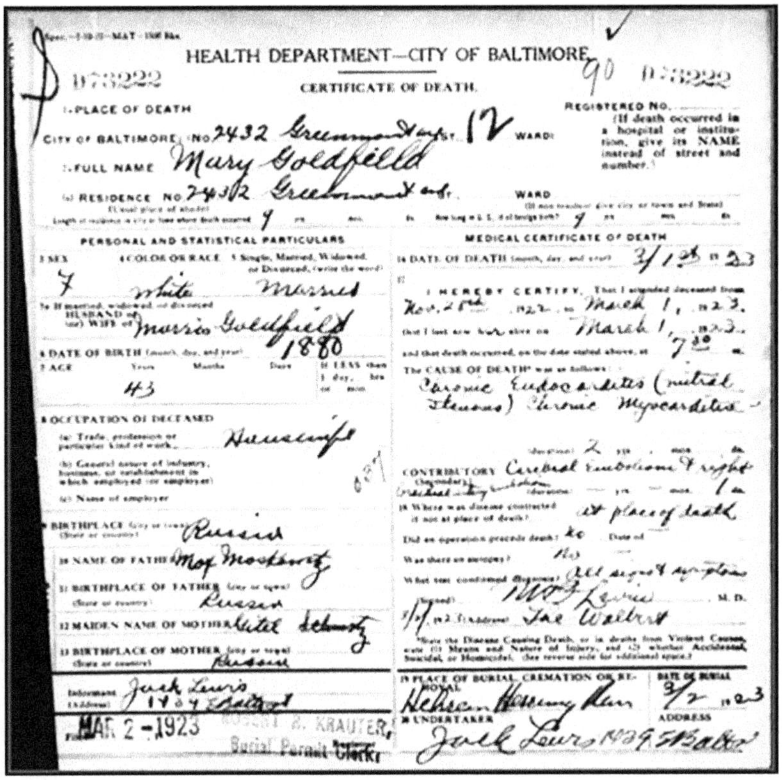

HEALTH DEPARTMENT—CITY OF BALTIMORE

CERTIFICATE OF DEATH.

1. PLACE OF DEATH

CITY OF BALTIMORE, No. 2432 Greenmount Ave. 12 WARD

2. FULL NAME Mary Goldfield

(a) RESIDENCE No. 2432 Greenmount Ave.

PERSONAL AND STATISTICAL PARTICULARS

3. SEX F 4. COLOR OR RACE white 5. Single, Married, Widowed, or Divorced: Married

HUSBAND of (or) WIFE of Morris Goldfield

6. DATE OF BIRTH 1880

7. AGE 43

8. OCCUPATION OF DECEASED Housewife

9. BIRTHPLACE Russia

10. NAME OF FATHER Max Moskewitz

11. BIRTHPLACE OF FATHER Russia

12. MAIDEN NAME OF MOTHER Gitel Schwartz

13. BIRTHPLACE OF MOTHER Russia

Informant Jack Lewis

Filed MAR 2 - 1923

MEDICAL CERTIFICATE OF DEATH

16. DATE OF DEATH 3/1 1923

I HEREBY CERTIFY, That I attended deceased from Nov. 25 1922 to March 1, 1923, that I last saw her alive on March 1, 1923, and that death occurred, on the date stated above, at 7 am.

The CAUSE OF DEATH was as follows: Chronic Endocarditis (mitral stenosis) Chronic Myocarditis

CONTRIBUTORY Cerebral embolism

Where was disease contracted if not at place of death? at place of death

Did an operation precede death? No

Was there an autopsy? No

M.D.

19. PLACE OF BURIAL, CREMATION OR REMOVAL Hebrew ... DATE OF BURIAL 3/2 1923

20. UNDERTAKER Jack Lewis

Figure 139 Death certificate for Marie (Moshkevich) Goldfield

I am not positive what became of Morris Goldfield. I suspect he is the Morris Goldfield who remarried a woman named Lena Berger and settled in Atlantic City. A 1930 census from Atlantic City shows Morris Goldfield, age 49, and Lena, age 39, living with Lena's brother and his family. It is clear this is a second marriage for this Morris. Morris's age at first marriage is listed as 17 (i.e., in 1898) and Lena's is listed as age 37 (i.e., 1928). The record thus makes clear this was a late first marriage for Lena but that Morris had been married previously. Morris and Lena don't have any children listed. Assuming this is the Morris Goldfield who married Mariesa Moshkevich, he apparently passed away childless in 1938.

Here Lies

the woman Mrs. Mariesa

daughter of Mordechai, the Cohen[1]

Passed away the 13th of Adar, 5623

May her soul be bound up in the bond of eternal
life

Mary Goldfield

Died

Mar. 1, 1923

Age 45

---

[1] "The Cohen" indicates Mordechai had priestly lineage and traced his ancestry back to Moses's brother, Aaron.

Records Summary for Mary (Moskevitch) and Morris Goldfield

Jan. 26, 1914 Passenger Manifest	Leaving Bremen Jan. 10, 1914 on the SS Neckar arriving in Baltimore Jan. 26, 1914, **Mosche Goldfeld**, age 41, occupation "taylor," last residence [difficult to read but looks like] Kisineff, closest relative there br. i. l. [brother-in-law] Itsig Moschevitz, Kishineff, Bess. [Bessarabia] with **Marie Goldfeld**, age 38, housewife, last residence same, closest relative there brother traveling with **Gersch Moskewiz** age 17 student last residence same; closest relative there, father Itsiz Moskiewicz, Kishineff, Bess[arabia] destination br. i. l. [brother-in-law] S Moskewich 923 E Baltimore St, also described as uncle Shlome Moskiewitz 923 E. Baltimore, St, MD
Apr. 19, 1916 Naturalization Declaration	**Morris Goldfield**, age 38, Tailor, born in Segrinesky Oyezj, Russia on Sept. 1, 1877, now resides at 1046 Aisquith Street, Baltimore, Maryland, emigrated from Bremen, Germany on vessel "Neckar" last residence was Kessinau [Kishinev], Russia, arrived at Baltimore, on Jan. 26, 1914 [non-English appearing signature)
1916 Baltimore City Directory	**Goldfeld, Morris** tailor 1046 Aisquith h do [=home same address] Goldfeld, Nathan, shoemaker 1046 Aisquith
Sept. 12, 1918 WWI Draft Registration Card	**Morris Goldfield**, 2432 Greemount Ave, Balto MD, age 40, birth Sept. 15, 1878, naturalization: Declarant, occupation: tailor, place of employment same as home address, nearest relative: Marry Goldfield, signed with X
Jan. 16, 1920 US Federal Census Baltimore	**Morris Goldfild**, address 2432 Greenmount Ave, Head, O[wns home] age 46, immigration year 1913, PA [first papers], birthplace Russia, occupation: proprietor of Tailor Shop; **Mary Goldfild**, wife age 46, immigration year 1913, Al [alien], birthplace Russia, occupation none.
Apr. 5, 1920 Naturalization Petition	**Morris Goldfield**, address 2432 Greenmount Ave Baltimore, Tailor, born Sept 1, 1877 at Segrinsoky Oyery, Russia [assumed to be Chyhyryn, Ukraine], emigrated to US from Bremen, Germany on Jan. 19, 1914 and arrived in Baltimore Jan. 26, 1914 on the SS Neckar; wife **Mary** born Jan. 10, 1880 in Russia, same address, no children. witnesses [brother-in-law] Aaron Moshkevich, grocer and [husband of sister-in-law] Morris Schabb
Mar. 1, 1923 Death Certificate Baltimore	**Mary Goldfield**, 2432 Greenmount Ave, 9 years in city, date of death Mar. 3, 1923, Husband: Morris Goldfield, [her] date of birth 1880, age 43, birthplace Russia, name of father Max Moskewitz, birthplace of father, Russia, Maiden name of mother Gitel Schwartz, birthplace of mother, Russia. Cause: Chronic Eudocarditis (mistral stenosis) chronic myocarditis, contributory Cerebral Embolism & right brochial artery embolism.

8.

THE FAMILY OF ITSIG MOSKOVITCH AND RISIA (DOVIDA)

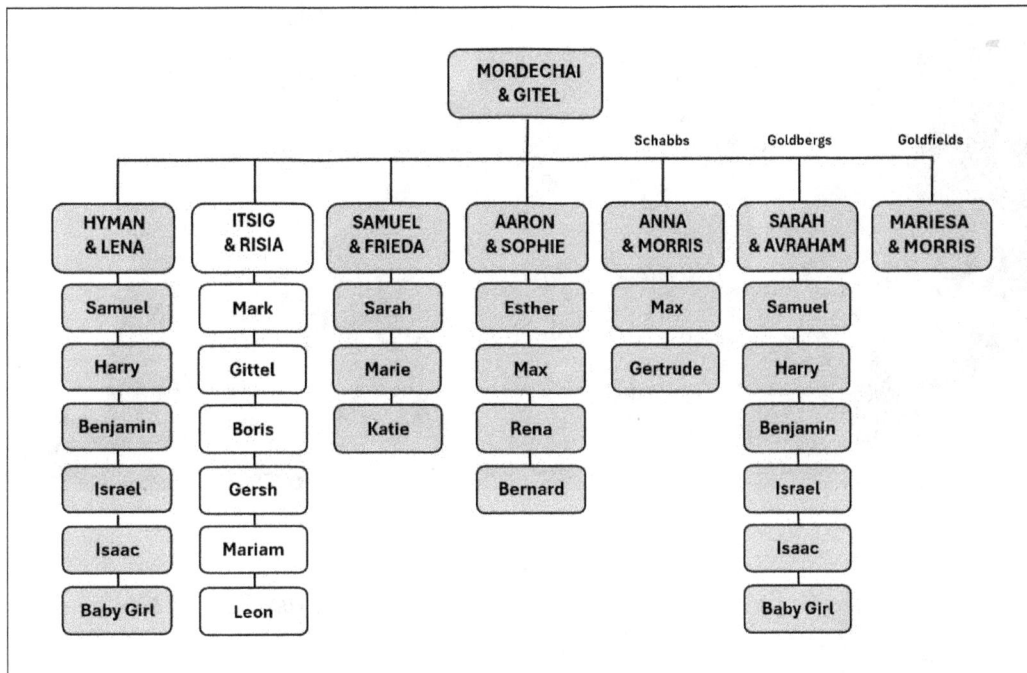

Figure 140 Family Tree of Itsig and Risia

My great-grandfather, Itsig (also called Isko) Moskovitch, was the last of the "Moskevitch Seven" to leave for Baltimore. He probably intended to leave Kishinev earlier and follow his son Gersh and his sister Marie Goldfield to Baltimore when they left in January 1914. But WWI intervened and Itsig was not able to migrate until 1920. When he finally made it to Baltimore, he apparently did not stay long. He returned to his wife Risia and daughter Gitel who never came to the US.

As discussed earlier, Itsig was the second eldest of the "Moskovitch Seven" according to the family tree, though records suggest he may have been the eldest. According to the tree, he was born in Kremenchuk in 1862. We don't know much about Itsig and his wife Risia, since Risia never came to the US and Itsig stayed for only a short time. However, all their children except their daughter Gittel came to the US and we know quite a bit about them. Some of them I remember growing up in Baltimore.

We know Itsig married his wife Risia (Dovida) before 1891 when their oldest son Mordechai (Mark) Moshkevitch was born. It seems likely he was the namesake for Itsig's father, Mordechai, who probably passed away shortly before the birth. Itsig and Risia had six children in total: Mordechai (Mark) (1891-1979), Gittel (1893-1980), Boris (1896-1979), Gersh (Isaac) (1897-1991), my grandmother Mania (Mariam) (1900-1995), and the youngest, Leib (Leon) (1901-1991).

Photo 40 Family of Itsig Moskovitch and Risia (Dovida) in Kishinev, circa 1911

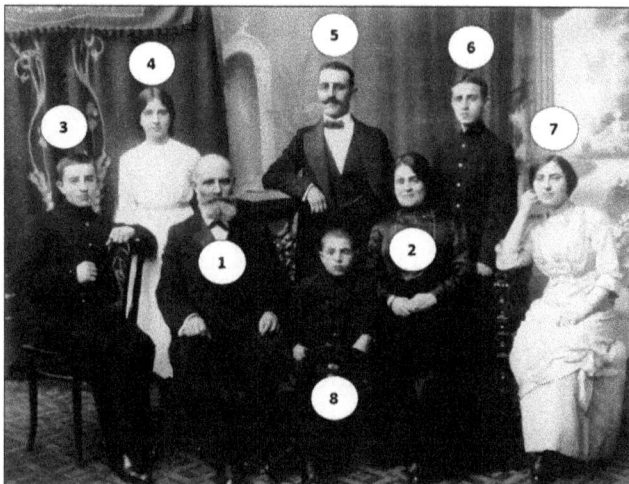

1. Itsig (Isko, Isaac) Moskovitch
2. Itsig's wife, Risia Dovida
3. Boris
4. Mania*
5. Mark
6. Gersh
7. Gittel*
8. Leon

***

---

* The photo, circulating in the family, lists #4 as Gittel and #7 as Mania. However, Mania was younger than Gittel and not much older than Leon #8. I concluded that #4 is Mania, my grandmother, who also looks more like she does in later photos.

Records indicate that the six children who came to the US were born in Kishinev (now Chişinău, Moldava). They apparently lived through and survived the Kishinev pogrom of 1904, which as noted before, was a shocking and terrifying event that undermined Jewish hope for civic equality in Russia. My grandmother Mariam was only 4 at the time. I don't remember her ever once mentioning the event or her life in Kishinev, though, of course, I never asked about it. The family apparently stayed in Kishinev up until WWI and most of the children were still there when Kishinev became part of Romania in 1918. For this reason, those who came to the US after 1918 sometimes have Romania listed as birthplace on their records.

The first of the children to leave was Gersh who, as noted earlier, traveled with his aunt Mariesa to Baltimore in 1914, arriving before WWI broke out in August that year. Gersh was the third in birth order of Itsig and Risia's children. Gersh's father, Itsig, and his brother, Boruch (Boris), followed together in August 1920. Itsig's youngest son Leib (Leon) arrived in December later that same year. Itsig and Risia's younger daughter, Mania (Mariam), headed to Paris in the mid-1920s with her new husband and they made their way to Baltimore only in 1937. Itsig and Risia's eldest son, Mordechai (Mark), ended up in China by 1919 where he met and married his wife, Elizabeth, and where they had two daughters. They finally migrated to Baltimore in 1940. Risia and Gittel never migrated to the US. The detail of these Moshkevich migrations and their lives in Baltimore now follows.

***

The Arrival of Gersh Isaac Moshkevich

The first of Itsig and Risia's children to leave Kishinev was their son Gersh. As noted in the previous part of the story, Gersh accompanied his aunt [Itsig's sister] Mariesa and her husband Morris Goldfield to Baltimore in January 1914.

On the manifest, Gersh is listed below his uncle and aunt on the manifest. The record indicates he was 17 and a student when he arrived in Baltimore. The second page of the manifest describes him as 5'5" and blond. Like several of Gersh's other aunts and uncles, the traveling party made their way across Russia to the port of Bremen.

They embarked from Bremen on the SS Neckar on Jan. 10, 1914, and arrived in Baltimore on the 26th of January. Their destination was the home of Gersh's uncle, Samuel Moshkevich, who was living then at 923 E. Baltimore St. Their last permanent residence is listed as "Kisineff" and Gersh's closest relative there is his "father Itsig Moshkiewicz." Gersh's birthplace is difficult to read on page two but appears to be "Kisjinuerch" and probably was referring to Kishinev.

Figure 141 Manifest of Gersch Moskewicz traveling with his aunt Marie Goldfeld

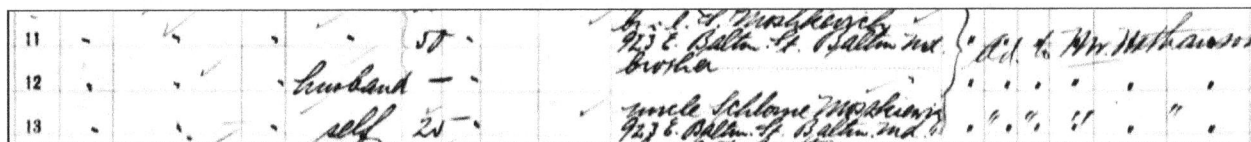

Page 2 of Manifest showing destination uncle Schlome Moschiewiz 923 E. Baltimor. St.

Gersh continued to live with his aunt Marie and uncle Morris Goldfield when he arrived. He is still at their address at 2432 Greenmount Avenue when he filled out his WWI Draft Registration card on June 5, 1918, four years later. That registration was for all males who became 21 years of old following the first registration on June 5, 1917. Gersh listed his uncle Morris Goldfield as the relative who would always know where to reach him.

In the same record, Gersh indicated his birthdate was Jan. 15, 1897, making him 21 years of age. His record confirms that his father, "Itsig," was born in Kremenchuk. At the time he filled out the form, Gersh was working for the Bethlehem Steel Company at Sparrows Point in the Baltimore harbor. The second page describes his eyes as brown and his hair light brown.

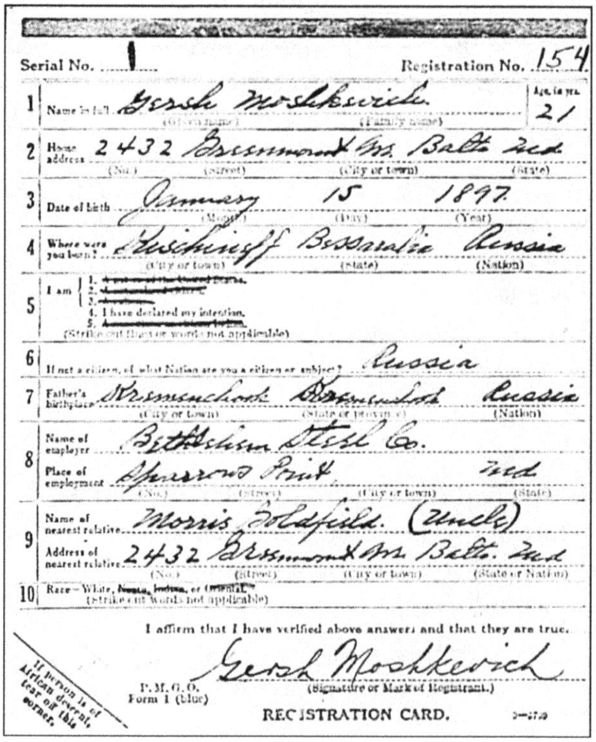
Serial No. 1 Registration No. 154

1 Name in full Gersh Moshkevich (Given name) (Family name) Age in yrs. 21

2 Home address 2432 Bressmont Av. Balto Md (No.) (Street) (City or town) (State)

3 Date of birth January 15 1897 (Month) (Day) (Year)

4 Where were you born? Kischineff Bessarabia Russia (City or town) (State) (Nation)

5 I am 1. ~~a natural-born citizen of the United States~~, 2. ~~a naturalized citizen~~, 3. ~~an alien~~, 4. I have declared my intention, 5. ~~a non-declarant alien~~. (Strike out lines or words not applicable)

6 If not a citizen, of what Nation are you a citizen or subject? Russia

7 Father's birthplace Kremenchuk Kremenchuk Russia (City or town) (State or province) (Nation)

8 Name of employer Bethlehem Steel Co. Place of employment Sparrows Point Md (No.) (Street) (City or town) (State)

9 Name of nearest relative Morris Goldfield. (Uncle) Address of nearest relative 2432 Bressmont Av. Balto. Md (No.) (Street) (City or town) (State or Nation)

10 Race—White, ~~Negro, Indian, or Oriental~~. (Strike out words not applicable)

I affirm that I have verified above answers and that they are true.

Gersh Moshkevich (Signature or Mark of Registrant.)

P. M. G. O. Form 1 (blue)

If person is of African descent, tear off this corner.

REGISTRATION CARD.

Figure 142 Draft Registration Card for Gersh Moshkevich June 5, 1918

Later that year, a letter to the editor in *The Evening Sun* apparently incensed Gersh and prompted him to respond. The letter, published on December 5, 1918 (p. 16), was written by Adam S. Gregorius who believed the recent reports—that the Polish people were persecuting Jews—were exaggerated.

Gregorius argued that further proof was needed. He noted, correctly, that Poland had historically been good to the Jews. And he called for an impartial commission to look at the charges. He also thought the press had blown up the situation and ignored the real tragedy of those who died defending the ancient Polish capital. Gregorius ended his letter with what was an obnoxious and arguably antisemitic anecdote to make his point that Jews were overexaggerating the situation and were ultimately to blame. He wrote:

> The chances are that this "howl in Rome" is resultant from the same attitude as that of a Jew who applied to a Polish magistrate in a provincial town his clothes bespattered with mud, a scratch across his cheek.
> "They're murdering us, gevalt! Send the police!" he appealed.
> "Murdering who?"
> "Us, the Jews!"
> "How have they murdered?"
> "Me, look at me!"
> "What have you done?"
> "I went to collect ten rubles. The chlop [chap?] didn't have it and I took his cow."

"What had you lent him?"

"Five Rubles."

The Evening Sun, Dec. 5, 1918, page 16

A response signed by G. Moshkevich on December 10, 1918 (p. 14) appears to belong to Itsig's son Gersh. If so, the letter provides an interesting window into the mindset and capability of this still relatively new Moshkevich immigrant to Baltimore.

You can tell Gersh was incensed, writing a strong letter of condemnation in what was impressive English for an immigrant who was in the US only four years. He noted that the writer Gregorius began somewhat rationally asking for more proof, but Gersh objected quite vehemently to the anecdote with which Gregorius ended his letter. One can see in this letter the budding mind of a law student who would graduate in 1924.

He writes in conclusion, "Your example, however, Mr. Gregorius, (I don't know who you are) is both out of place and only the result of a desire to appeal to the lowest instincts of your illiterate race....Surely the gentleman who claims that the articles of the massacres are only 'propaganda of an insidious kind' will attempt to prove that his malicious example is not of that kind."

The "Refuge" Offered The Jews Was "Turned Into Hell."

To the Editor of The Evening Sun:

Sir—My attention was called to the letter of Mr. Adam S. Gregorius which was published in yesterday's Evening Sun.

Mr. Gregorius is trying to present the Polish people as an example of innocence. It is true that the whole world knows that Poland had offered a refuge for persecuted Jews, but it seems as if the offered "refuge" was turned into hell.

The Polish representatives in the United States are trying their best to put a curtain upon the inhuman acts which were and are going on in Poland and Galicia. We know how some ignorant elements of the Polish people were treating the Jews in the reign of the Czar of Russia and it is no wonder that they are acting like wild beasts after they were let loose by the newly formed Polish Government.

Something happened in Warsaw, Poland, that unveiled the truthful situation there. In the City Hall of Warsaw a question was raised about the outrages upon the Jews. The leader of the militia answered that the persecutions were not conducted specially against the Jews and, therefore, he does not see any reason why such questions should be raised. But it was shown afterward, notwithstanding the answer of the head of the militia, that sufferers from these brutalities were Jews only.

Massacres were going on in Rosvodoo, Kelz, Bjesko, Chmalnick, Grassov, Lassi, Pschem'shle and in several other towns where thousands upon thousands were killed, burned alive, pillaged and deprived of shelter—entire city blocks torn down—such were the deeds of the innocent lambs of the Polish masses. If in the olden times only knives and clubs were used in slaughtering the Jewish masses, now the modern machine guns and other war instruments are used for their destruction.

It is quite necessary to impress upon your mind Mr Gregorius that such massacres against a race, no matter how small and unprotected it is, will not be accepted by the world as a mere unfortunate happening, and immediate steps will be taken for its protection.

Your first half of the letter up until your unfortunate and unfair example seems to possess a semblance of justice. You wish to rest the case until the report of the combined committee is known—even though you do intimate that the evening papers are obtaining their news from New York Zionist Bureau. Your example, however, Mr. Gregorius (I don't know who you are) is both out of place and only the result of a desire to appeal to the lowest instincts of your illiterate race.

Is it an example of the characteristics or is it supposed to be merely your inverted sense of humor? Surely the gentleman who claims that the articles of the massacres are only "propaganda of an insidious kind" will attempt to prove that his malicious example is not of that kind.   G. Moshkevich.

Baltimore, Dec. 6.

Figure 143 Letter to Editor, signed G. Moshkevich

Five months after this letter appeared, on April 1, 1919, Gersh filled out his Petition for Naturalization. All his personal information is identical to that on his earlier Declaration, except now he is calling himself "Gersh Isaac Moshkevich," adding his middle name and clearly using the Baltimore spelling of his surname.

Gersh does not appear in the 1920 census with his aunt Marie Goldfield or in census records with any of his other aunts or uncles. Nor does he appear in the Baltimore City Directory in 1918 or from 1920-1924. (The year 1919 is missing from the City Directory). I suspect he disappears from these sources because he has gone off to law school, from which he graduated in 1924. He may even have been part of the 1920 entering class which was the first in the University of Maryland School of Law to admit women.

Photo 41 Gersh I. Moshkevich

***

Becoming Gersh I. Moss

In 1923, Gersh appears in the Baltimore City Directory. This is the first record found in which Gersh appears under what became his professional, anglicized name: "Gersh I. Moss." He is living at 2432 Greenmount Avenue with his Aunt Marie and Uncle and Morris Goldfield. Aunt Marie passed away March 1st that year and by 1924 Gersh appears at a new address down the street.

1923 City Directory

> **MOSS**
> " Frank C (Cath) slsmn h2748 Tivoly av
> " Geo (Eva) lab h2455 Buchanan
> " Geo A student 1109 n Bway
> " Gersh I clk 2432 Greenmt av

In 1924, Gersh graduated from law school and his photo shows a handsome seemingly self-assured young man. The yearbook puts a spin on his middle initial, emphasizing that the "I" does not indicate that Gersh was egoistic in his attitude towards other people, but quite the contrary, "his innate modesty does not prevent Gersh from being well-known and having a large circle of friends."

Gersh's name appears among the list of those who passed the bar, published in *The Baltimore Sun* on Sept. 20, 1924, and those that the State Board recommended be admitted to the bar on Oct. 29, 1924. In the latter case, he appears as "Gersh I. Moss," and his address is listed as 2419 Westwood Avenue, apparently having moved out of the home of his deceased aunt. The City Directory that year finds him as a "clerk" at the same address.

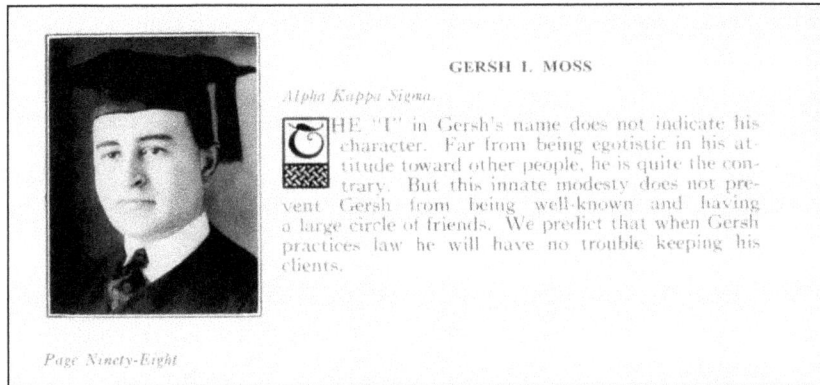

Photo 42 1924 Gersh I. Moss, Law School, University of Maryland

By 1926 and 1927, Gersh is back on Greenmount Avenue, this time at 2468, the home of his other Aunt Anna (Moskevich) Schabb, though he clearly has begun to practice law downtown.

1927 City Directory	" Gersh I lawyer 111 n Charles h2468 Greenmt
1928 City Directory	" Gersh I (Helen E) lawyer 110 e Lexington R310 r1917 Wheeler av
1930 City Directory	" Gersh I (Helen E) lawyer 110 e Lexington R310 r1905 Wheeler av

Having started to establish himself professionally, he must have felt ready to get married. It appears, he married Helen Hornstein in 1927, though a record of their marriage has not yet been located. By 1928, he is living with Helen at the address of her family and their first son, Irwin, was born on March 1, 1928. That same month Gersh's name appears in the *The Baltimore Sun* as "attorney" representing a client against United Railways and Standard Oil Company of New Jersey.

Nora Allen vs. United Railways and Standard Oil Company of New Jersey, $5,000. Plaintiff alleges that she was injured January 3 in a collision between a street car in which she was a passenger and an auto truck at First avenue and First street. Gersh I. Moss, attorney.

Figure 144 Gersh I. Moss attorney listed in one of his early cases
The Baltimore Sun, March 29, 1928, p. 17

Gersh must have been an impressive young man to woo Helen E. Hornstein, who was a second generation American. Helen was born in Maryland in August 1902. Both her parents were also born in Maryland, in 1881. In the 1900 Baltimore census, Helen's father Simon Chia Hornstein was 20 and a bar tender probably working in his father's salon. By 1910, Simon and his wife Fannie had three children, including Helen. In the 1920 census, Simon was a manager in the Regent Theatre. In that same record, Helen was listed as age 17 and was working as a stenographer at Crown, Cork & Seal (today called Crown Holdings, Inc) an American company founded in 1892 in Yardley, Pennsylvania.

The company , Crown, Cork & Seal, where Helen worked, was founded by William Painter, an Irish-born American, who in 1891 invented the crown cap for bottled carbonated beverages and obtained patents for it in 1892. He founded his own manufacturing business, the Crown Cork and Seal Company, in Baltimore and set out on a campaign to convince bottlers that his cap was the right one to use on their products. By 1898, he had created a foot-powered crowner device to sell to bottlers and retailers so that they could seal the bottles with his caps quickly and easily. This helped gain acceptance of his bottle caps. By 1906, Crown had opened manufacturing plants in Brazil, France, Germany, Japan, and the United Kingdom.[2]

The 1930 City Directory lists Gersh and Helen's address at 1905 Wheeler Avenue just down the street from Helen's parents (though the 1930 census shows another couple still living there at the time of the census). Gersh and Helen's second son, Stuart, was born in 1933.

In the 1940 City directory, Gersh and Helen are at 3313 Powhattan. They are in the upper unit above Helen's parents, Simon and Fannie Hornstein. Gersh and Helen are 42 and 39 respectively. Irwin is 12 and Stuart 5. Gersh is listed in private practice.

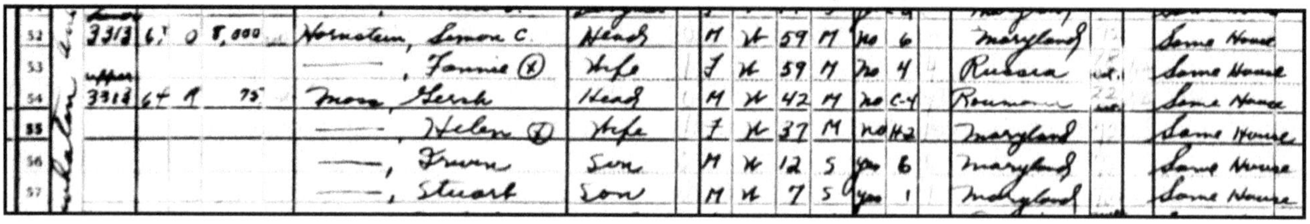

Figure 145 1940 Census of Gersh, Helen, Irwin and Stuart

By the 1950 census, Gersh and Helen have moved to 3610 Copley Road. They are 53 and 47 years old respectively. Gersh is listed as an attorney in private practice. Stuart is still in the household and is now 17 and listed as a delivery boy in a grocery store. Irwin has already left his parents' home and has married Janet Schwartz.

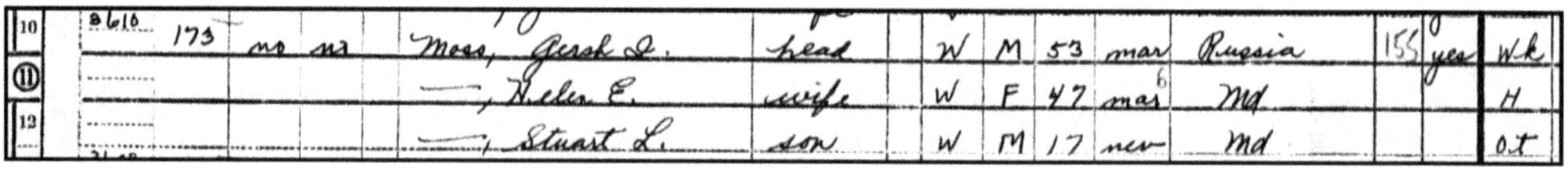

Figure 146 1950 Census for Gersh, Helen and Stuart

Irwin and Janet appear in the 1950 census living at 4000 D Fordleigh Road, a couple of miles from his parents. Irwin is 22 and Janet 20. The census describes Irwin as a "physical science aide" in the area of "Federal chemist writer." Janet is a laboratory technician in a private hospital. Irwin and Janet eventually had three boys: Gary S., Richard S., and Mark D. At some point, Irwin and Janet divorced and Irwin subsequently remarried and had another son, David. Irwin passed away in 1989, pre-deceasing his parents. Gersh passed away in Feb. 1991 and Helen passed away in Dec. 1991.

Stuart became engaged to Marcia Jane Steel in 1953 and they married soon thereafter. They subsequently had one son, Steve. After Marcia and Stuart subsequently divorced, Stuart had a daughter with the woman he was seeing named Sandra Evering. The daughter was named Gabrielle (married name Manske). Gabrielle didn't know who her father was when growing up. A few years ago, she found a second cousin match to me on Ancestry and approached me to see if I could help her identify her father. She had the name "Stewart Moss," on a birth certificate and was seeking information about him. I remembered Stuart from my childhood and with permission from his son (and my second cousin) Steve, I introduced him to his half-sister, Gabrielle. I checked in with Gabrielle while I was writing this narrative, and she gave me an update.

> My information has been updated a bit since then, so let me provide you with my new information! I now know that Stuart and my mom Sandy (full name Sandra) met shortly after Stuart and Marcia divorced. My mother wanted a child but not a marriage, which

---

[2] See "Crown Holdings" in *Wikipedia*. Accessed March 25, 2024. https://en.wikipedia.org/wiki/Crown_Holdings

was a radical idea back then! She subsequently never married. She and Stuart dated for a short bit, less than a year. They had talked about her desire for a child but neither of them was interested in a commitment together. He agreed to help her. He stayed with her for a short while and made sure she had maternity care. Apparently, it was very difficult to get medical treatment as a single woman; without his help, she doesn't think she would have had medical support through her pregnancy. They parted ways before I was born, and I don't think there was any future contact. Stuart met his 2nd wife Pam shortly afterwards. Interestingly, he had told Pam that he had another child, who he believed was a girl. The two of them wondered if they would ever hear from her.

Unfortunately, Gabrielle never got to meet Stuart, but she and Pam have become quite close now and Gabrielle and Steve (her half-brother) have connected and given me permission to include this story.

***

Arrival of Itsig, Boris and Leon

At the end of WWI and shortly before Gersh entered law school, Gersh's father, Itsig (also called Isko and Isaac), and Gersh's brother, Boris, arrived in Baltimore. In the intervening years since they had seen Gersh, WWI had been fought, the Tsar's regime was overthrown followed later that same year by the Bolshevik Revolution. Following the World War, the Russian Civil War (1917–1923) broke out and the Polish-Soviet War (late 1918–1921).

These events likely explain why Itsig and Boris did not leave for America from the northern German port of Bremen, as Gersh did. Instead, father and son headed East, perhaps taking the Trans-Siberian Railroad across Russia into China. Itsig's eldest son, Mordechai (Mark) was already living in Harbin, China, as discussed in detail below, and perhaps they visited him on their way. Perhaps this was the first time Itsig met his son's wife and his first granddaughter Gitel Rachel (called Elia by the family) who was born in Harbin in 1919.

What do we know from several records is that Itsig and Boris somehow got to Yokahama, Japan where they embarked for Canada on Aug. 7, 1920. They arrived in Victoria, British Columbia on Aug. 16th. They then entered the US in Seattle.

On the manifest, Itsig was initially listed as "Otsko Moshkevich," but Otsko was scratched out and "Isko" was written instead. The record describes Itsig as a 58-year-old merchant. His son "Boruch" (Boris) is listed as age 24, also a merchant. Significantly, they were already using "Moshkevich," the Baltimore style spelling of their surname. Correspondence had obviously reached them in Russia from Baltimore, and they knew the adopted Baltimore spelling of their surname.

Their last permanent residence on the record is "Chishinen" [Kishinev, today Chişinău, Moldova] and their closest relative there is listed as Itsig's wife, Mrs. Risia Moshkevich, living at 21 Ekatezindenskia Chisninen. This street has so far not been located in modern or old maps of Kishinev. On page two, Boris's birthplace is also listed as Chisinen, but Itsig's birthplace is Kremenchu[k].

Father and son were headed to Itsig's son (Boris's brother) "Mr. G. [Gersh] Moshkevich" at 2432 Greenmount Avenue. As discussed earlier, this was the home of Itsig's sister, Marie (Moshkevich) Goldfield.

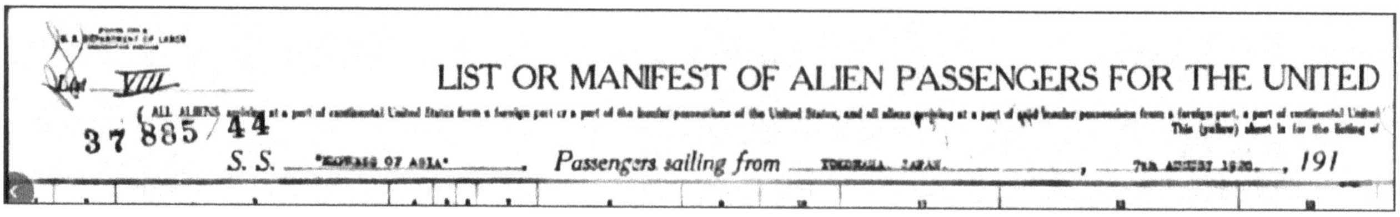

Figure 147 1920 Passenger Manifest of Isko and Boruch on SS Empress of Asia

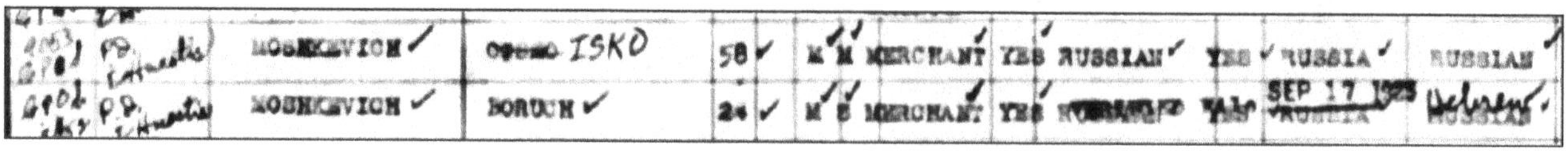

Isko, 58, and Boruch, 24, on passenger manifest

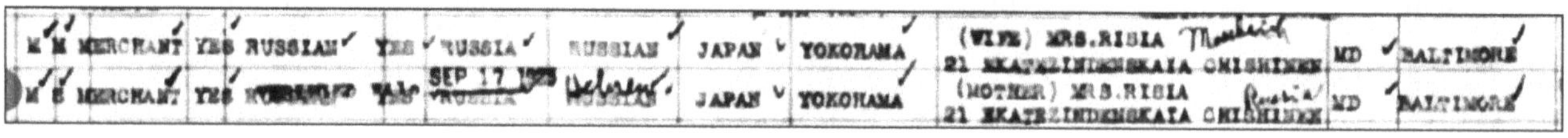

Right-hand columns showing residence Chishinen and wife Risia Moshkevich at 21 Ekatezindensaia

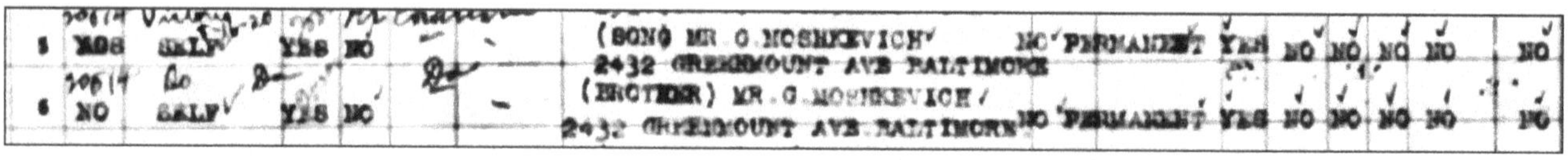

Page 2–Itsko and Boruch headed to son/brother G. Moshkevich 2432 Greenmount Ave, Baltimore

In December 1920, four months after Itsig and Boris landed in the US, Itsig's youngest son, Leib (Leon) began his migration. According to what David Chapin heard from the family, Leon and his future wife, Betty, were socialist agitators while in school. Following the War, they were in danger and had to go underground.

Leon did not need to make the trek eastward via Japan like his father and brother. He was able to make his way from Russia across Europe to the port of Rotterdam. "Leib Moskowitch" sailed on the SS Nieuw Amsterdam leaving Rotterdam on Dec. 10, 1920, and arriving in NY on Dec. 20th. He is described as 19 years old, speaks German, and of "Rumenian" nationality (Kishinev became part of Romania in 1918). Leib's last residence, like his father and brother's, was "Kichineff" in [the country of] "Rumenian." The custom official who wrote down the name of the country did not yet distinguish Romania from Rumenian. Language and nation were still confused linguistically.

Leib's closest relative back in Kishinev was [his mother] Risia Moscokwitch and his destination in Baltimore was his brother "G. I. Moskewitsch" at 2432 Greenmount Avenue. He apparently had not yet learned the Baltimore spelling of his family surname. The document also notes that Leib had a cataract in his left eye—growing up I remember he had a droopy eye—and describes him as 5'6" with black hair and brown eyes. His birthplace is listed as "Kichineff, Rumenian."

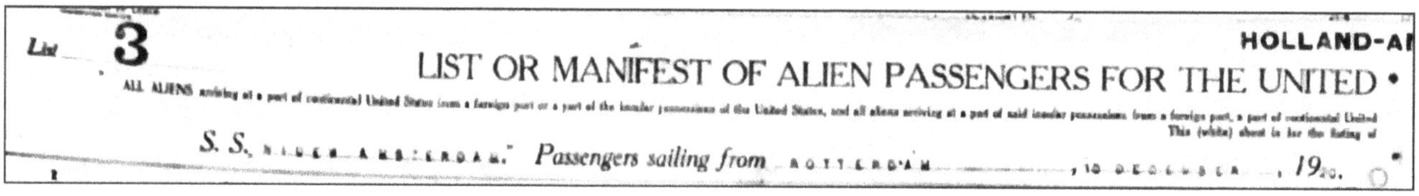

Figure 148 Manifest of Leib Moskowitch (Leon Moss) December 1920

Leib Moskowitch (Leon Moss) traveling to America on SS Niuew Amsterdam

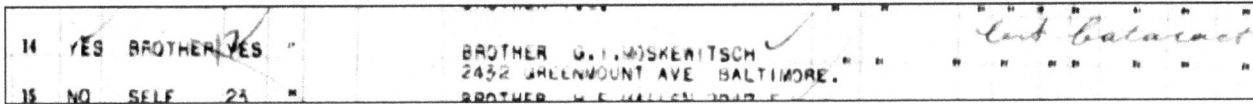

Leib's destination was his brother G. I. Moskewitsch

Leib, now calling himself "Leon Moshkevich," declared his intention to naturalize on June 20, 1922. He used an anglicized version of his first name and the Baltimore spelling of his surname. Leon's birthday is given as Aug. 22, 1901, and his address at the time was 126 W. Lee Street, just west of the Baltimore harbor, apparently moving out of his aunt's home.

A few months after Leon declared his intention, his brother Boris did as well. Boris's Declaration on April 15, 1922, shows he was still living at 2432 Greenmount Avenue at the home of his aunt Marie Goldfield. "Boris" Moshkevich, now using his anglicized name, is described as a shoe salesman, age 25, 5'5" with blond hair and blue eyes. I suspect Boris got involved in shoe sales via the husband of his aunt Anna Schabb, who had a shoe repair business on Greenmount Avenue, as discussed earlier. Boris's birthplace like Leon's is listed as Kishinev, Russia.

Figure 149 Declaration of Leon Moshkevich
June 20th, 1922

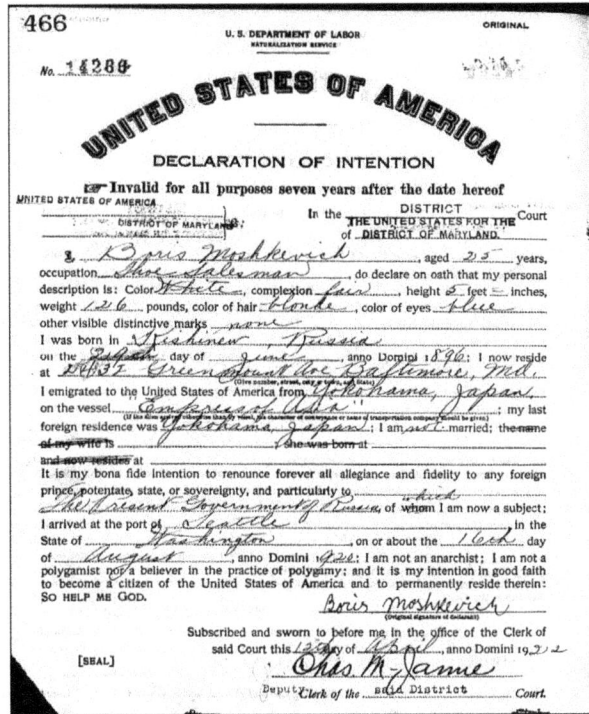

Figure 150 Declaration of Boris Moshkevich
April 12, 1922

In the meantime, Leon was busy planning to bring his future wife from Kishinev to the States. According to Leon's daughter, Reva, now in her 90s, Leon and Betty Pascar were childhood sweethearts from grade school growing up in Kishinev. Leon arranged for Betty to arrive in the US in 1923. Her Naturalization Petition indicates she left Hamburg on June 18, 1923. The ship made a stop in Southampton, and she appears on a manifest from there to New York.

"Basia Paskar" left Southampton England on June 27, 1923, on the SS Homeric and arrived in New York on July 5th. She appears to have traveled alone—an extraordinary feat for a young 22-year-old woman—who also made her way by herself from Romania to the port of Hamburg. Their grandson, David Greenspan, tells me he heard that she managed on her solo voyage by wearing a wedding band given to her by her mother "to discourage the men."

The manifest describes her as single, a tailoress, and a Hebrew of Russian nationality. Her last permanent residence was "Chisinan Bessarabia" and her closest relative there was David Paskar, her father.

U. S. DEPARTMENT OF LABOR

List 14

LIST OR MANIFEST OF ALIEN PASSENGERS FOR THE UNITED

ALL ALIENS arriving at a port of continental United States from a foreign port or a port of the insular possessions of the United States, and all aliens arriving at a port of said insular possessions from a foreign port, a port of continental United

This (yellow) sheet is for the listing of

S. S. "HOMERIC" Passengers sailing from SOUTHAMPTON, JUNE 27th, 19 23.

Figure 151 1923 Manifest of Betty (Pascar) Moss

9	Paskar	Bassia	22	F	S	Tailoress	yes	Russian	yes	Russia	Hebrew

"Bassia Paskar" age 22 tailoress

Russian	yes	Russia	Hebrew	Bessarabia	Chisinan	David Paskar, C hisinan, Bessarabia.	Md	Baltimore

Right-hand columns showing last residence and closest relative David Paskar

9	yes	Uncle	$10	no	-	-	Uncle; Morris Goldfield, 2432 Greenmount Ave, Baltimore, Md	no	Perm

Page 2 destination "Uncle Morris Goldfield"

Betty's destination was her "uncle" Morris Goldfield at 2432 Greenmount Avenue, the address we know where Leon's brother, Gersh, was still living that year according to the Baltimore City Directory. There is no evidence that Morris Goldfield was in fact Betty's uncle, and it seems probable she described him as a relative because he was the uncle of Leon, her "intended." Asserting the relationship eased her way into US and removed doubts that she would be a "likely public charge."

The year Betty arrived, Leon's brothers, Gersh and Boris, were both living with the Goldfield family. It seems likely that Leon was living elsewhere since his 1922 Declaration shows him living on Lee Street and he was apparently already in the University of Maryland School of Commerce (business school) at this time. Perhaps propriety required that Leon live elsewhere after Betty's arrival, which was several months after Morris's wife, Aunt Marie (Moshkevich) passed away (discussed earlier, p. 139 above).

1923 Baltimore City Directory

" Bessie sec 2207 Bryant av
" Boris slsmn 2432 Greenmt av
" Chas (City Illuminating Co) h705 Morelan

1923 Baltimore City Directory

MOSS
" Frank C (Cath) slsmn h2748 Tivoly av
" Geo (Eva) lab h2455 Buchanan
" Geo A student 1109 n Bway
" Gersh I clk 2432 Greenmt av

Betty and Leon were married on Aug. 16, 1925, while Leon was still a junior in the School of Commerce. He graduated in 1926 and was naturalized on July 10, 1926.

Figure 152 School of Commerce [i.e. Business School] 1926

Leon and Betty appear on Park Heights Avenue in 1926, and by 1928 they are renting ("r") at 2904 Oakley Avenue and Leon is listed as a bookkeeper. They are still there in the 1930 census living with a Solomon family. Leon is listed in that census as a purchasing agent for a clothing manufacturer. He eventually became an executive at Schoenemann Inc., a men's clothing company.

1926 Baltimore City
Directory

1928 Baltimore City
Directory

Figure 153 1930 Census for Leon and Betty Moss renting from a Solomon family

While the three brothers (Gersh, Boris, and Leon) were settling into Baltimore, it appears that their father, Itsig Moskevitch, passed away in 1925, according to the family tree. No other records have been identified for him thus far in Baltimore. As noted earlier, Leon's daughter, Reva, recalls hearing that her grandfather, Itsig, went back to Russia, so he may have passed away in Kishinev after going back.

Perhaps Itsig's death was one of the reasons that Boris went back to Europe in 1931, to visit with his mother and sister Gittel who were still back in Russia. It also seems likely he saw his younger sister Mariam who was then living in Paris, since his manifest shows he passed through France. Boris appears on a manifest among a list of US citizens returning from his trip. He departed Cherbourg on Sept. 16, 1931, on the SS Bremen, and he arrived in NY on Sept. 21st.

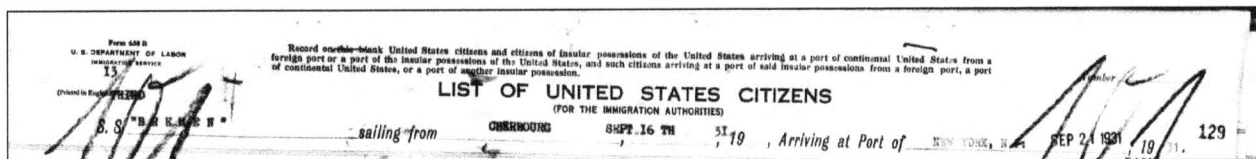

Figure 154 Boris Moss's manifest on SS Bremen from 1931

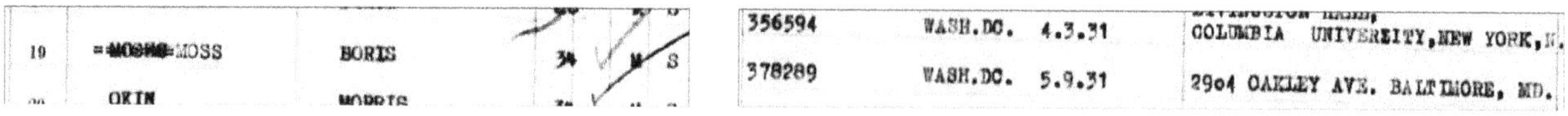

19	MOSS	BORIS	34	S	356594	WASH.DC.	4.3.31	COLUMBIA UNIVERSITY, NEW YORK, N.
					378289	WASH.DC.	5.9.31	2904 OAKLEY AVE. BALTIMORE, MD.

Boris Moss, age 34, living at 2904 Oakley Ave

Boris's 1931 manifest shows he was living with his brother Leon at 2904 Oakley Avenue. Leon and Betty's daughter, Reva, was born in May 1933.

Photo 43 Reva (Moss) Greenspan 1955
University of Pennsylvania Yearbook
(Occupation Therapy)

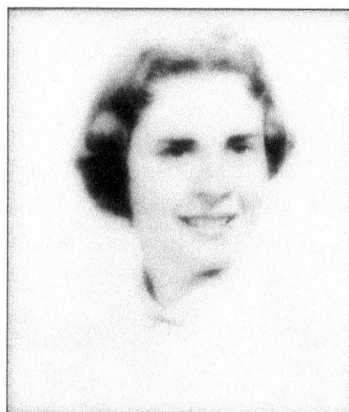

In the 1940 census, Leon, Betty and Reva, are living at 4101 Barrington Road. Leon is 38, Betty 39, Reva 6. A companion, Faye Clifton, is listed living in the household. When I asked Reva who this was, she explained that her mother, Betty, was ill and they had a helper, Faye Clifton, living in the household with them. The census describes Leon as a buyer in a wholesale men's clothing business. In the 1950 census, the family is living at 3613 Cedardale Road. Leon is 48, Betty 49, Reva is 16.

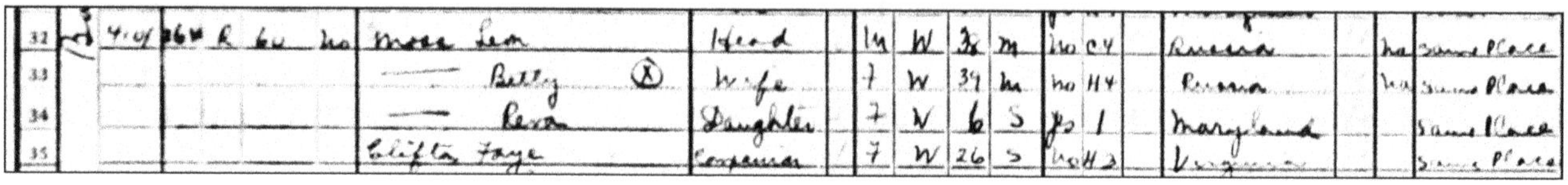

32	Moss Leon	Head	W	38	M	Russia	Same Place
33	— Betty	Wife	W	39	M	Russia	Same Place
34	— Reva	Daughter	W	6	S	Maryland	Same Place
35	Clifton Faye	Companion	W	26	S	Virginia	Same Place

Figure 155 1940 Census for Leon, Betty and Reva

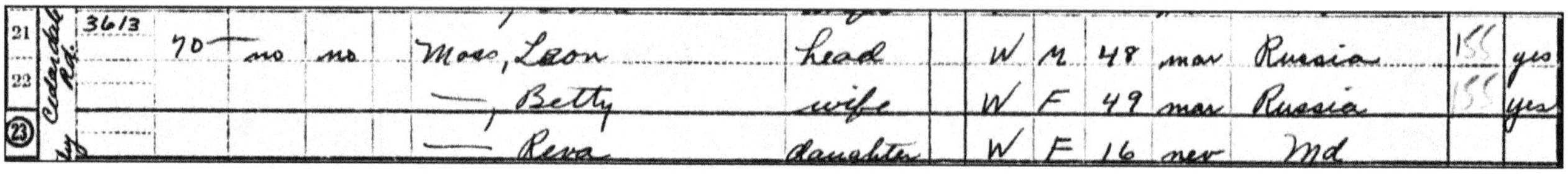

21	3613	Moss, Leon	head	W	M	48	mar	Russia	yes
22		— , Betty	wife	W	F	49	mar	Russia	yes
23		— Reva	daughter	W	F	16	nev	Md	

Figure 156 1950 Census for Leon, Betty, and Reva

As discussed below, Leon became active in the Bessarabian Society in the late 1940s, a social group and philanthropic organization that initially helped orphans from Bessarabia after WWII and that continued to fund worthwhile causes in the US and later Israel.

In the 1950s, Reva married Jack Greenspan and they had three children, David, Jay, and Karen. Reva and Jack subsequently divorced. Leon passed away in 1991. Betty passed away in 1994. Reva is still alive in her 90s while this is being written.

***

Mania Marries and Heads to Paris

While three of Itsko's sons (Gersh, Boris and Leon) were settling into Baltimore, his youngest daughter (my grandmother), Mania Moskovitch, was still back in Kishinev with her mother Risia and her older sister Gittel. There are no family memories recorded about life in Kishinev from the period starting in 1904 when the family began to migrate until the mid-1920s when Mania finally left. How the family survived the pogroms of 1903 and 1905 or dealt with the Russian Revolution and WWI is not known.

Mania (called Mariam in US records) was born in Kishinev like her siblings. A Russian record from Bessarabia which is translated online lists 1900 as her birth year and transliterates her name as "Mar'yem Moshkevich." Her later US Naturalization Petition lists her birthdate as Jan. 13, 1900.

Sometime in the early 1920s, she met and married a debonair man named Solomon Schinker who was born in Odessa on Oct. 26, 1900. Odessa, Russia (now Odesa, Ukraine) was a cosmopolitan port city with many ethnic groups and languages, located on the north shore of the Black Sea. On contemporary maps today, it is 194 km (120 m) from Chişinău to Odessa. The city became the home of a large Jewish community during the 19th century, and by 1897 Jews were estimated to comprise some 37% of the population. Jews were drawn to Odessa for economic reasons and because its location at the edge of the Pale of Settlement gave the community greater freedoms than it enjoyed elsewhere in Russia. This Jewish community tended to be less traditional than others at the time, attracting a great many Jewish intellectuals and over time becoming a prominent center of Zionism.[3]

Photo 44 Solomon Schinker and Mariam (Moskevitch) circa 1925

Almost nothing is known about Solomon Schinker (also spelled "Chinker" on immigration documents) before he married Mariam, and it is not known how they met. These early memories were erased from family memory when their marriage fell apart. I imagine she was taken by this swarthy, young man from Odessa who appeared cultured and educated.

They were married on June 15, 1926, in Chişinău, Romania. A grainy family photo in my mother's collection appears to show Mariam (seated left) with her mother Risia (center) and her husband, Solomon

---

[3] See Steve Zipperstein, *The Jews of Odessa: A Cultural History, 1794–1881.*

(on floor). It is not known if this photo was taken in Paris where they were living after 1929 or in the Moskovitch home back in Chișinău. I suspect the young girl in the photo is their daughter Joan, and that the photo was taken in Paris after 1932.

Photo 45 Mania (left) with her mother Risia (center)
and husband Solomon (on floor)
Date of photo unknown

Not long after they married, Mania and Solomon appear in France. A student ID from 1927–1928 indicates "Mousieur Schenker" was a student in the Ecole Nationale D'Agriculture, and in 1928–1928, he has an identity card for the Institut Agricole D'Algerie and perhaps lived in Algiers for a year.

Figure 157 ID cards of Solomon Schinker in France and Algeria

Photo 46 Risia with her daughter Mariam, about 1931 possibly in Paris

On March 3, 1932, Mania and Solomon's daughter, (my mother) Jeanne, was born in Paris. I suspect the photo of Mariam with her mother Risa was taken during the nine months before the birth—Mariam covering her tummy signifies that she was pregnant with my mother at the time. Perhaps Risia came to France to see her daughter or Mariam went back to Chişinău to see her mother. Maybe this is the same time that Mariam's brother Boris came from Baltimore to Europe and passed through France.

Photo 47 Mariam watching her mother Risia playing Ring Around the Rosie

At some point, the Schinker family settled in Boulogne-sur-Seine, which is only 10 km east of Paris and was annexed as part of Paris in 1929. In the 1930s, Boulogne was one of the most dynamic cities in France. It was here, on the outskirts of the capital, that well-known filmmakers and architects had chosen to live and work.[4] Photos from my mother's family in the period 1932–1937 show them living there before

---

[4] See https://www.visitparisregion.com/en/museum-of-the-1930s. Accessed Jan. 19, 2024.

leaving for the States. Their passenger manifest from 1937 indicates their last address was 251 Gallaeni Street, a main thoroughfare, close to the Seine which runs through the area.

Another photo in my mother's collection shows Mariam watching her mother Risia who is playing Ring around the Rosie with children. The photo probably was taken in Boulogne-sur-Seine. I suspect my mother, who was born in 1932, was among the children circling Risia who came to France for a visit.

***

Mania Goes to Baltimore

In 1937, three years before the Nazi invasion of France, Mania, her husband Solomon Schinker, and 5-year-old daughter Jeanne (Joan) left Paris for Baltimore. Three of Mariam's brothers (Gersh, Boris and Leon) were already well settled there. Mariam also had two uncles (Aaron and Samuel) and an aunt (Anna Schabb) who had been in Baltimore since 1906. Her aunt Mariesa died in Baltimore in 1923 before Mariam arrived. Though a late comer to Baltimore, Mariam was not the last of her siblings to arrive. Her eldest brother, Mordechai (Mark), migrated with his family to the US in March 1940 after WWII began; we'll return to his story below.

The Schinker family departed France from Le Havre on Sept. 29, 1937, on the SS Ile De France. They landed in New York on Oct. 5th. "Salomon" is described as 36 years old and an electrician. Mariam is 37. (Mariam and Solomon were both born in 1900 but Mariam's birthday was earlier in the year). "Jeanne" (Joan) was 5. Solomon and Mariam were able to speak German, Russian and French according to the record. In the nationality column, they are listed "without" [a nationality] signified by the double quotes meaning "ditto" and referring back to what was written above. For Race/People they were identified as "Russian." They may have been hiding or downplaying the fact that they were Jewish or simply didn't see themselves that way.

The right-hand columns show that "Salomon" was born in Odessa and "Mariam" in "Tichinoff" Bessarabia. Paris, France is listed as Joan's birthplace. Their visa was issued on Sept. 20, 1937, and their last permanent residence was Boulogne sur La Seine.

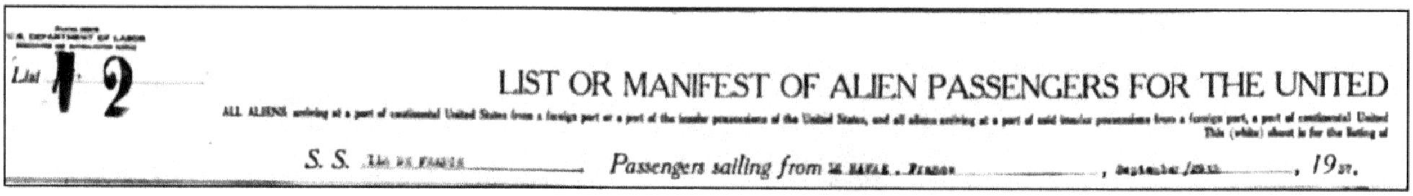

Figure 158 Manifest of the Schinker family

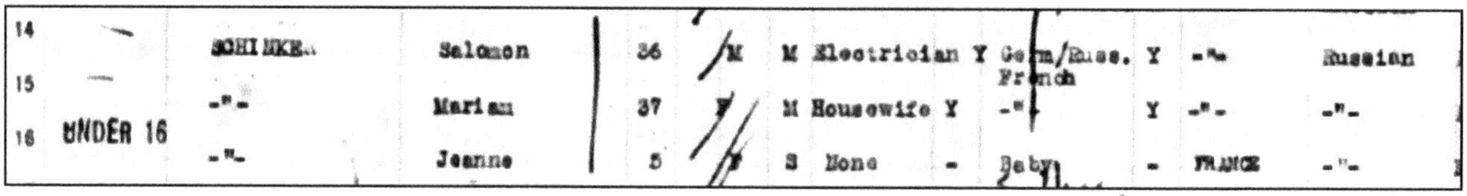

Salomon, Mariam and Jeanne on SS Ile De France

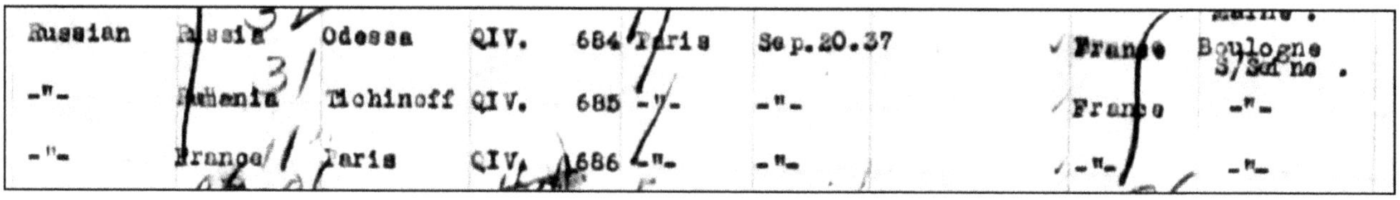

Right-hand columns showing birthplaces, visa date and last residence

14	Home: 25I Rue Gallieni,			----	Md.	Balto.,	Y	self		N	----------------	-----	20,
15	Boulogne sur Seine, France												
15	Home: -"-	"-"-	-"-	----Md.	-"-		Y	Husband		N	----------------		
16	-"-	-"-	-"-	-"-	---- Md.	-"-		Y	Father	/	N	----------------	

Page 2 of manifest showing last address– 251 Rue Gallieni, Boulogne sur Seine

20,	Brother in law: Mr Moss	No Perm	Yes	No	No	No	No		No	No	No	Good	No		5,	9	-"-	Brw. Brw. None
	6I4 - 6I4 Munsey Building, Baltimore			No	Md	No	No		No	No	No	Good	No		5,	6	-"-	Brw. Brw. None
	Brother: -"-	No Perm	Yes															
	33/3 Powhaton Ave.																
	Uncle: -"-	-"-	No Perm	Yes	No	No	No	No		No	No	No	Good	No		-,	-	-"-	Brw. Brw. None

Destination is "Mr [Gersh] Moss

When Mania and Solomon arrived in Baltimore, they were headed to Mariam's brother, Gersh Moss, and gave the address of his law practice which, in the City Directory listing that year, appears as 614 Munsey Building. Gersh and Helen's home address that same year was 3313 Powhaton Avenue. According to a story David Chapin heard from his father, the family thought it was charming that Mania and Solomon's daughter, Joan (my mother) spoke only French when she arrived.

*Photo 48 Mariam, Solomon, and Joan
circa 1936, Boulogne-sur-Seine*

"Salomon Schinker" declared his intention on July 28, 1938, a little more than a year after they arrived. Mariam followed suit on September 13, 1939. Two weeks earlier Germany invaded Poland and WWII began. Russia invaded the other half of Poland four days after Mariam filled out her Declaration.

There was no sign in the records that the Schinker family was on the verge of falling apart. In Solomon's Declaration, they are living at 3639 Reisterstown Rd and Solomon is an electrician. He is described as 5'7" and 170 lbs. with brown hair and brown eyes. Mariam is listed as his wife, born in 1900. Her Declaration shows that while Germany was rolling across Poland, the family had moved to 3318 Auchentoroly Terrace, just across the street from Druid Hill Park. She is 39 and listed as an operator in a millinery business.

She is described as 5'4" and 150 lbs. Her birthday is listed as Jan. 13, 1900. She is described as 5'4" and 150 lbs.

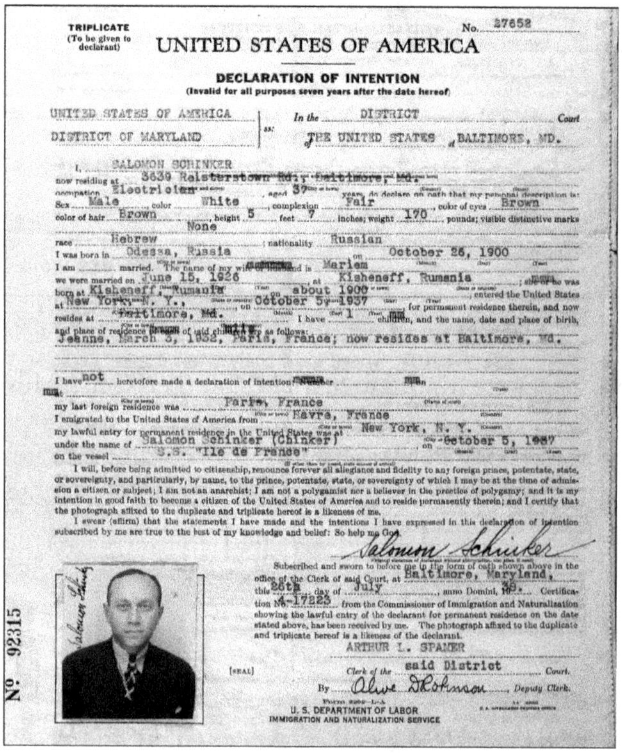

Figure 159 Naturalization Petitions of Salomon and Mariam Schinker

By the April 1940 census, Solomon and Mariam were separated. Mariam and Joan are living with Mariam's brother, Boris, who was still single and living at 4032 Boarman Avenue, a block and a half away from Forest Park Senior High School.

It is not clear what went wrong in Mariam and Solomon's marriage. My mother, Joan, who had a difficult relationship with her father, thought that her mother's brothers did not approve of her father because he did not have a substantive career and was a "ne'er-do-well." There are memories that he may have been an art dealer which perhaps explains their presence in Paris before migrating to Baltimore. (I have vague memories of seeing some art around his apartment in Dupont circle when we visited him when I was a teen). From Mariam and Solomon's earlier photos in Paris, there is no sign of strain or evidence that Solomon could not provide for the family. They look reasonably happy and well-dressed and appear in many photos with friends. Whatever the causes, the marriage fell apart in Baltimore and Mariam and Soloman went their separate ways, though divorce was not so common in those days.

Leon's daughter, Reva, who is in her 90s now, remembers Joan and Mariam coming to live with her family for a time at some point in the 1940s. Joan (my mother) remembered growing up embarrassed that she had parents with foreign accents and that she was the only child she knew who had divorced parents.

In the 1940 census, Mariam's brother Boris is 43 and listed as a salesman in an oil business. That position must have been short lived because by 1942 he is working again for a shoe company. In the same census, Mania is 40, still listed as "m[arried]," and working as a hatmaker in a millinery business. "Jona" is 7.

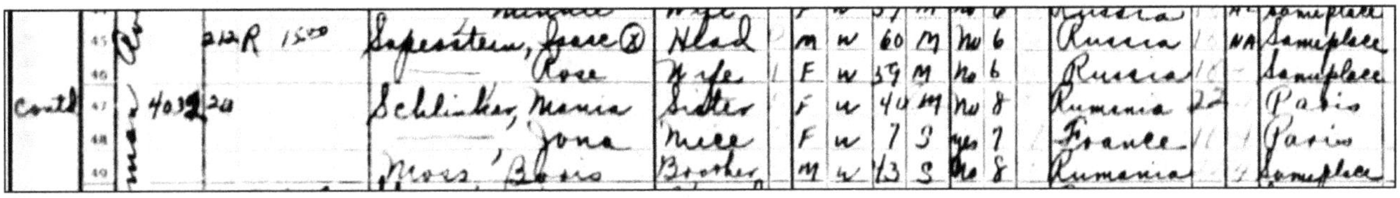

Figure 160 Mania and Joan living with Boris Moss in 1940

Mania, Joan and Boris are all described as relatives (sister, niece and brother) of someone in the household. These attributions confused me at first and I wondered whether they were fudging their relationship with the man named Isaac Saperstein who is listed above them. I spent some time trying to figure out who Isaac Saperstein was.

Only later, I realized that the head of household was their brother Mordechai (Mark) who arrived earlier that year and who appeared on a different page of the census. Mordechai was living at the same address and the census taker recorded his family information a few weeks earlier, as evident from the dates on the top of the two separate pages of their census. Apparently, Boris, Mania and Joan were not home during the census taker's first visit. The census taker came back for follow up a few weeks later and recorded the info about Boris, Mania and Joan, on a subsequent page of the census. Hence, the abbreviation "cont" [continued] written in the far-left column of this record by Mania's name! Mark was the head of household and Mania, Joan and Boris were sister, niece and brother.

Boris's 1942 Draft Registration Card shows he moved to 4006 Bonner Road by that year. He lists his employer as Lion Shoe Co. at 131 Duane St. New York City. His closest relative is listed as his sister-in-law "Mrs. Mark Moss," the wife of his oldest brother, Mark. Mariam and Joan were living there too as evident in a naturalization record index showing Mariam's address when she became a citizen on April 9, 1945.

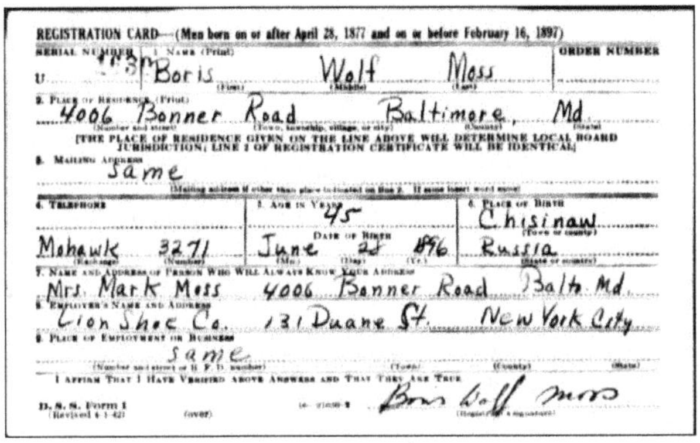

In the meantime, Mariam's husband, Solomon Schinker, had settled at 729 W. North Ave, 3.5 miles away from where Mariam and Joan were living. A notice in *The Baltimore Sun* shows that Mariam started divorce proceedings by Sept. 5, 1941 (p. 27).

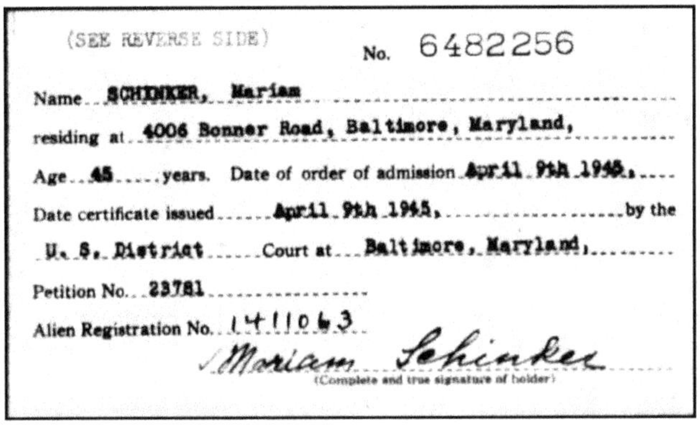

Solomon's Petition from 1942 shows he quickly married again that year. According to the record, he married a woman named Dolly Haney who was born in Profitt, Virginia on May 1, 1914. She was 14 years younger than him and apparently not Jewish. The marriage must have been shocking to the family and to my Mom, who was likely still struggling with the divorce of her parents and her acclimation to America, within five years of their arrival.

Whether Dolly had anything to do with the breakup of Solomon's marriage or was simply a rebound is not known. Nor is it known how they met. In fact, my mother never told me about this marriage, which apparently did not last long. By 1952, Dolly remarried a man named John Edward Taylor. Solomon, as far as I know, did not marry again.

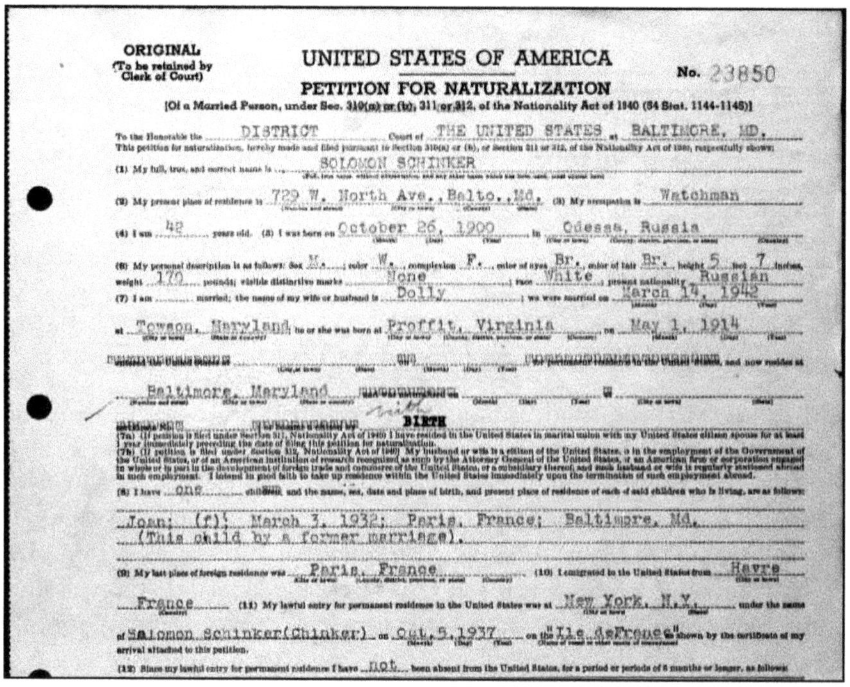
ORIGINAL (To be retained by Clerk of Court)

UNITED STATES OF AMERICA

No. 23850

PETITION FOR NATURALIZATION

To the Honorable the DISTRICT Court of THE UNITED STATES at BALTIMORE, MD.

(1) My full, true, and correct name is SOLOMON SCHINKER

(2) My present place of residence is 729 W. North Ave., Balto., Md. (3) My occupation is Watchman

(4) I am 42 years old. (5) I was born on October 26, 1900 in Odessa, Russia

(6) My personal description is as follows: Sex M., color W., complexion F., color of eyes Br., color of hair Br., height 5 feet 7 inches, weight 170 pounds; visible distinctive marks None; race White; present nationality Russian

(7) I am married; the name of my wife or husband is Dolly; we were married on March 14, 1942 at Towson, Maryland; he or she was born at Proffit, Virginia on May 1, 1914

Baltimore, Maryland

BIRTH

(8) I have one child; and the name, sex, date and place of birth, and present place of residence of each of said children who is living, are as follows:

Joan; (f); March 3, 1932; Paris, France; Baltimore, Md. (This child by a former marriage).

(9) My last place of foreign residence was Paris, France (10) I emigrated to the United States from Havre, France (11) My lawful entry for permanent residence to the United States was at New York, N.Y. under the name of Salomon Schinker(Chinker) on Oct. 5, 1937 on the "Ile de France" as shown by the certificate of my arrival attached to this petition.

(12) Since my lawful entry for permanent residence I have not been absent from the United States, for a period or periods of 6 months or longer, as follows:

Figure 161 Naturalization record of Soloman Schinker

In 1944, Boris married Sarah Schachman who grew up in Newark, New Jersey. Their daughter Judi (married name Robinovitz) whom I spoke to, does not know how they met for reasons that become clear in a moment. I suspect that Boris's role in sales for a New York shoe company may have brought them into each other's orbit. Judi was born in 1946 and has a few childhood memories of going with her father Boris to a warehouse, riding up a freight elevator that closed with rope, and entering a darkened second floor. When the lights were turned on, she remembers seeing thousands of boxes of shoes.

In the 1950 census, Boris, "Sally" and Judith are listed at 4008 Glen Ave, a half block off Reisterstown Road and not far from the location of today's Jewish Community Center. Boris is described as a wholesale shoe salesman. The census shows he was quite a bit older than his wife Sally. He was 53 and she was 39. Judi was 4.

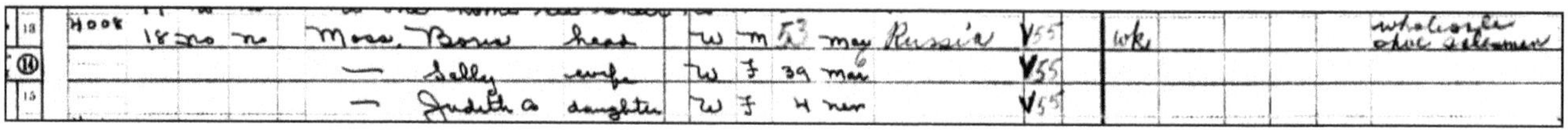

Figure 162 1950 Census of Boris Moss and Family

Tragically, Boris had a stroke when Judi was about six. He was hospitalized, disabled, and never left the hospital. Rehabilitation then was not what it is today. Judi's mother sold their home and moved to New Jersey and prevented her daughter from seeing her father growing up. In about 1970, Boris's brother, Leon, brought Boris and Judi (with her husband Alan Robinovitz) together at his home. It was an emotional few hours for Judi. It was also the last time she saw her father. Judi and her husband Alan have two children: a daughter Karen and a son Jason.

Sometime in the mid-to-late 1940s, after her divorce from Sam Schinker, Mariam met and married Abraham Drezner (also spelled Drazner) from New York. Perhaps Mariam's brother Boris made the connection for them or perhaps the informal Kishinev or Bessarabian network brought this widower, who was also born in Kishinev, together with Mariam. Mariam must have felt financial pressure to remarry. She and her daughter Joan were living with her brother Mark's family and she was working in Baltimore to make ends meet.

Mariam's second husband, Abe, was born in Kishinev in 1897. He first married in 1919 and he and his wife Elsie, who was also from Kishinev, arrived in the US in 1923. Here they had three sons, Nathan, Murray and Harry. Professionally, Abe was a paper hanger in New York. He was widowed in 1943, not long after Mariam and Samuel divorced in Baltimore.

It is not clear when exactly Abe and Mariam met and married, but at some point, Mariam left my mother Joan in Baltimore with her cousins and moved to New York to live with Abe. I have been unable to find a record of Abe and Mariam's marriage or their 1950 census together. Mariam's niece Reva (Leon's daughter) tells me she recalls that she was about 15 years old when Mania remarried, which would have been in 1939, though that seems a few years too early. I'm guessing that Mariam left for New York in the mid to late 1940s. In any case, Joan, alienated from her father Solomon and left in Baltimore with cousins by her mother Mariam, always felt resentful towards her mother's new family and felt that her mother had married beneath her station. That trauma stayed with my mother for the rest of her life. Photos of Mariam with Abe show she found a loving husband and family and was appreciated for stepping in and filling the role of the boys' deceased mother.

Photo 49 Mariam (Moskovitch) (seated) with blended family, second husband Abe Dezner (center), daughter Joan and three stepsons

Joan met Leon Schwartz, her future husband, in Forest Park High school. Leon was a heartthrob and track star at Forest Park. After a year of college at the University of Maryland, Joan dropped out for financial reasons. She was resentful for the rest of her life that her mother's brothers did not offer to help pay her way through college. Joan and Leon married in 1953. They had two sons, Howard (me) born in 1956, and Richard born in 1959. Leon worked in finance in various government agencies (NASA, HEW, NIH). In the mid-1970s, Joan and Leon moved to Newport Beach, California when Leon became Vice-Chancellor of University of California at Irvine.

Mariam and her husband Abe eventually moved to Florida. Abe passed away in 1988. Mariam passed away in 1995 in California near the home of her daughter Joan. Leon passed away in 2003. Joan passed away in 2013.

***

The Amazing Journey of Mark Moss and Family

The last of Itsig's children to arrive in America was Mordechai (Mark Moss). Mordechai was the eldest of Itsig and Risia's children, but the last to arrive. A Bessarabian record that has been translated indicates he was born in Kishinev on June 27, 1891. Since his name was "Mordechai," the same name as his grandfather, we can guess that the patriarch died not long before his namesake was born. A mohel wrote a comment on the birth record of the newborn Mordechai indicating his father [Itsig] was born in Kremenchuk and that his mother's father's name was David. Perhaps this is where Risia's surname "Dovida" originates.

The manifest of the SS Empress of Russia shows that the last permanent residence of "Morduhai" and Elizabeth Moshkevich was Shanghai, China and their closest relative there was Mordechai's brother-in-law, V. Kousher, who, presumably, was related to Mordechai's wife Elizabeth. They received their visa on Nov. 24, 1939. WWII had already begun, and Poland was already split in two between Germany and Russia.

The family sailed from Shanghai to Manila, Philippines, and then on to Victoria and Vancouver, British Columbia. Their manifest indicates they left Manila on Feb. 9, 1940, though the record was officially corrected later and amended to show they left Shanghai on Mar. 1, 1940, and arrived in Victoria and Vancouver on Mar. 16th. Mark's later Petition for Naturalization indicates they traveled from Vancouver on the CPRR (Canadian Pacific Railway) to Portal, North Dakota, where they entered the US on March 18. They made it to Baltimore two days later, on March 20th.

The family's manifest indicates Morduhai was age 48, Elizabeth (known in America as "Liza") 41, Gitel Rachel (called Elia by family and pronounced "Eel-ya") age 20, and Bella, age 10. All four of them were born in different locations, providing an overview of the family's history in the intervening years.

The manifest indicates Mordechai was born in "Chisinau, Rumania" (Kishinev, Russia when he was born). Elizabeth was born quite a distance away in Lutsk, Russia (now Lutsk, Ukaine). Gitel Rachel (Elia) was born in Harbin, China, and Bella in Tientsin (now Tianjin, China). The family had been in China for some time before leaving. What brought Mark and Elizabeth to Harbin, China initially is not known. They may have been part of the influx of Jewish refugees during WWI or in the wake of the Russian Revolution and Civil Wars. The Jewish community of Harbin started in the late 19th century.[5] The Tsars wanted to build an economic foothold in in Manchuria and offered incentives to Jews who settled there. Pogroms in Russia also provided Harbin with a steady supply of fleeing Jewish residents. Demobilized Jewish soldiers also settled in Harbin at the end of the Russo-Japanese War in 1905.

Whatever their motivations for heading to China, it seems likely that Mark and Elizabeth didn't know each other before meeting in Harbin since Mark was from Kishinev, and Elizabeth was from Lutsk. Mark's naturalization record indicates that he and Elizabeth (Guferman) got married Jan. 18, 1918, in Harbin China, just months after the Bolsheviks seized power in Russia. Their daughter Elia (Gitel Rachel) was born in Harbin the following year on May 2, 1919.

---

[5] https://www.jewishvirtuallibrary.org/harbin and https://kehilalinks.jewishgen.org/harbin/Brief_History.htm. See also https://kehilalinks.jewishgen.org/harbin/Jewish_Footprints_in_Harbin.pdf

LIST OR MANIFEST OF ALIEN PASSENGERS FOR THE UNITED

List 3

U.S. DEPARTMENT OF LABOR

ALL ALIENS arriving at a port of continental United States from a foreign port or a port of the insular possession of the United States, and all aliens arriving at a port of said insular possessions from a foreign port, a port of continental United This (white) sheet is for the listing of

S. S. "EMPRESS OF RUSSIA"   Passengers sailing from   MANILA,P.I.   , 9th. February , 19 40.

PASSENGERS EMBARKED AT SHANGHAI,CHINA, 1st. MARCH, 1940.

No. on List	HEAD-TAX STATUS	NAME IN FULL Family name	Given name	Age Yrs. Mos.	Sex	Married or single	Calling or occupation	Able to— Read what language	Able to— Write	Nationality (Country of which citizen or subject)	Race or people	Place of birth Country	City or town, State, Province or District	Immigration Visa, Passport Visa, or Reentry Permit number	Issued Place	Date	Date recording verification of landings, etc.	Last permanent residence Country	City or town, State, Province or District	
1	NON-IMMIGRANT	Moshkevich	Morduhai	48	M	M	Merchant	Yes	English	YesRussian Former	Russian	Rumania	Chisinau	Quota No.171	Shanghai,Nov.24th. China	1939		China	Shanghai	HEAD
	NON-IMMIGRANT	Moshkevich	Elizabeth	41	F	M	Housewife	Yes	English	YesRussian Former	Russian	Russia	Lusk	Quota No.172	Shanghai,Nov.24th. China	1939		China	Shanghai	HEAD
	NON-IMMIGRANT	Moshkevich	Gita Rachel	20	F	S	Secretary	Yes	English	YesRussian Former	Russian	China	Harbin	Quota No.173	Shanghai,Nov.24th. China	1939		China	Shanghai	HEAD
6	NON-IMMIGRANT	Moshkevich	Bella	10	F	S	Student	Yes	English	YesRussian	Russian	China	Tientsin	Quota No.174	Shanghai,Nov.24th. China	1939		China	Shanghai	HEAD

Figure 163 Manifest of Mark Moss and Family

STATES IMMIGRANT INSPECTOR AT PORT OF ARRIVAL

List 3

The entries on this sheet must be typewritten or printed.

States, or a port of another insular possession, in whatsoever class they travel, MUST be fully listed and the master or commanding officer of each vessel carrying such passengers must upon arrival deliver lists thereof to the immigrant inspector
THIRD-CLASS PASSENGERS ONLY

Arriving at Port of   Victoria,B.C. & Vancouver,B.C.   , 19th. March , 19 40.

No. on List	The name and complete address of nearest relative or friend in country whence alien came, or if none there, then in country of which a citizen or subject.	Final destination State	Final destination City or town	Whether having a ticket to such final destination	By whom passage paid?	Whether in possession of $50	Whether ever before in the United States, and if so, when and where? If Yes Year or When? Date	Whether going to join a relative or friend; state name and complete address and if relative, exact relationship	Purpose of coming to United States 25	26	27	28	Whether a polygamist 29	Whether an anarchist 30	31	32	Condition of health mental and physical	Deformed or crippled. Nature, length of time, and cause	Height Feet Inches	Color of— Complexion	Hair	Eyes	Marks of identification
2	Brother-in-law;Mr.V.Kousher, 931 Ave.Joffre,Shanghai, China.	Mary.	Balti-more	Yes	Self	400⁰⁰ Yes No		Brother:Leon Moss,4001 Barrington Road.Baltimore,B.NoPerm. U.S.A.	E.No	Yes	No	No	No	No	No	No	NoGood	No	5 6	FairGrey	GreyLeft Check Dark		Mole on
3	Brother:Mr.V.Kousher, 931 Ave.Joffre,Shanghai, China.	Mary.	Balti-more	Yes	Husband	Yes No		Brother-in-law;Leon Moss, Barrington Road 40.4001 Baltimore,Maryland,U.S.A.E.No	E.No	Yes	No	No	No	No	No	No	Good	No	5 4	FairBrown	Grey Nil.		
4	Uncle:Mr.V.Kousher, 931 Ave.Joffre,Shanghai, China.	Mary.	Balti-more	Yes	Father	Yes No		Uncle:Leon Moss,4001 Barrington Road Baltimore,Maryland,U.S.A. E.No	E.No	Yes	No	No	No	No	No	No	Good	No	5 6	Dark FairBrown	Grey Nil.		
5	Uncle:Mr.V.Kousher, 931 Ave.Joffre,Shanghai, China.	Mary.	Balti-more	Yes	Father	Yes No		Uncle:Leon Moss,4001 Barrington Road Baltimore,Maryland,U.S.A.E.No	E.No	Yes	No	No	No	No	No	No	Good	No	5 -	DarkBrown	Brown Nil.		

Page 2 of Manifest showing destination

Jews in Harbin prospered while Russia was focused on internal problems elsewhere. From 1918-1930, about 20 Jewish newspapers and periodicals were established. There were also a number of Zionist youth clubs. In 1928, when Russia handed the Chinese Eastern Railway over to the Chinese, an economic crisis broke out and many Jews left Harbin, some to the Soviet Union, others to Shanghai, Tientsin, and elsewhere.[6] It seems possible that Mark and Elizabeth headed to Tientsin about this time, since their daughter Bella was born there in 1928.

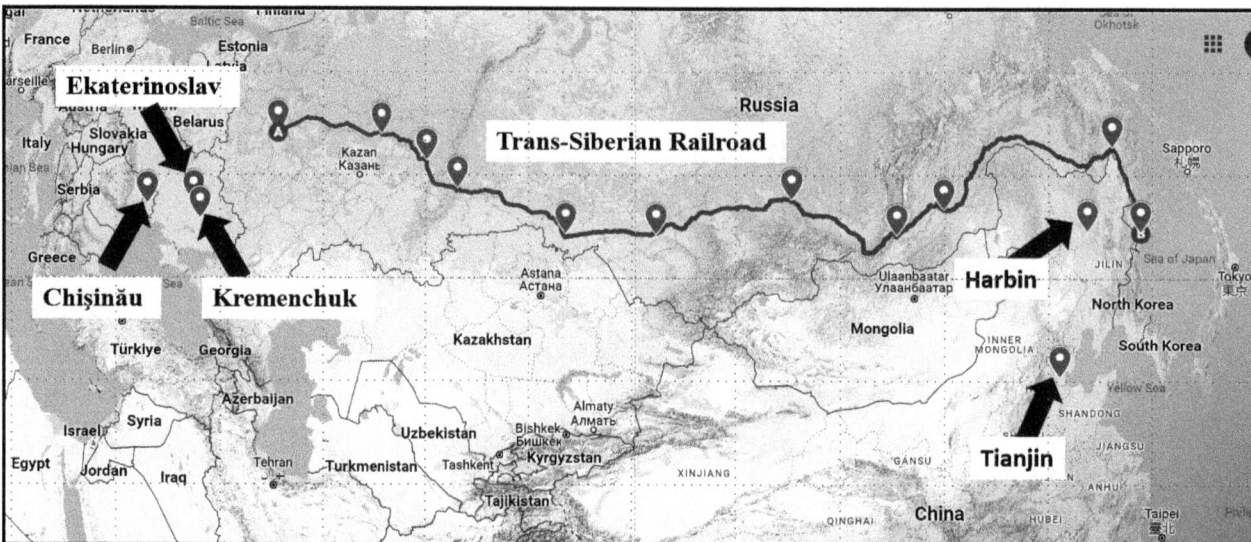

Figure 164 Contemporary map showing the relative distance of Chisinau, Harbin and Tianjin

Tientsin had 500-600 families following the Russian Revolution. "Those who could afford it went to the United States and Europe via Shanghai."[7] The Tientsin Jewish School was established in 1925. It provided free education in Hebrew and English to those children needing it. By 1936 the school had 110 students and 15 teachers. Most of the students, even then, received free education. Statistics from 1934 show 75% of time was spent on general subjects and 25% on Jewish themes. There were 95 students in 1935 of which 79 were Jewish and 16 were of other religions.

***

The arrival of Mark and Liza's family in Baltimore was heralded before it happened. My father and David Chapin's father told each of us similar stories. They heard about a new family arriving from China, and for David's father they were described as cousins. Both were completely shocked when they met them in school, and they didn't look Chinese.

By April 1940, "Moduchai" (Mark) and Elizabeth appear in the US Census in Baltimore. They are living at 4032 Boarman Avenue with their daughter Bella. It is not known where their older daughter, Elia, was living that year; perhaps, she was away in school. It is also not clear who was the son called "Richard Moss" who appears on the census. Mark and Liza had no son named Richard (despite this record) as evident from their naturalization declarations that list their children a few months later. Perhaps the illegible comment in the left column is intended to clarify who he was. I suspect that this Richard was not a Moss and was related in some other way or not at all.

---

[6] See https://www.jewishvirtuallibrary.org/harbin. Accessed 1/20/2024.
[7] https://www.jewsofchina.org/chronology-1904-1940

Mordechai and Elizabeth were living at the same address in the 1940 census where Mark's sister Mariam, her daughter Joan, and his brother Boris were living. As discussed earlier, Mark and his family are listed on a different page of the census. Mark's family is listed as the 213th family visited by the census taker. The previous family visited on their page was number #210. Where were the #211 and #212 families? Apparently, those families weren't home that day, so the census taker came back and recorded their information later, on April 27th. During that subsequent visit the census taker also listed other members of Mark and Elizabeth's household who were present, namely his brother Boris, his sister Mariam and her daughter Joan (see above on page 163).

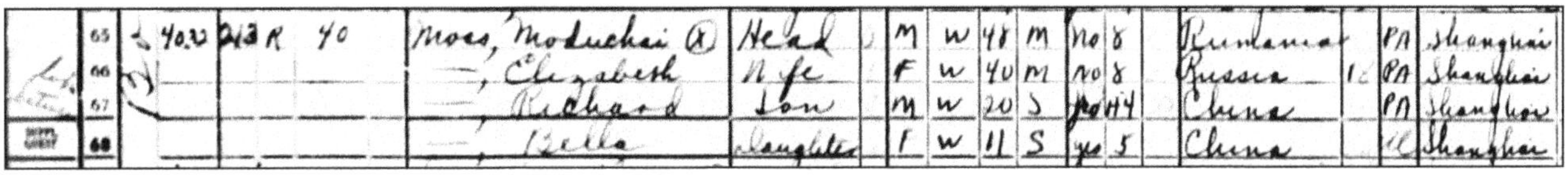

65	40.32	213 R	40	Moss, Mordechai (X)	Head	M	W	48	M	No	8	Rumania	PA	Shanghai
66				—, Elizabeth	Wife	F	W	40	M	No	8	Russia	PA	Shanghai
67				—, Richard	Son	M	W	20	S	No	H4	China	PA	Shanghai
68				—, Bella	Daughter	F	W	11	S	Yes	5	China	"	Shanghai

Figure 165 1940 census of Mordechai and Elizabeth Moss

Within a few months of the census, Mordechai is starting to call himself "Mark Moss." The anglicized version of his name appears as an alternative on his Declaration of Intention from June 5, 1942. Elizabeth's Declaration is signed one day later, on June 6, 1942. The information on both Declarations is consistent. They are the source of Mark and Elizabeth's places of birth and birthdates, their marriage date in Harbin as well as the birthdates and birthplaces of their two children, Gita (Elia) and Bella. They list no son named Richard. A photo of Elia with a tennis racket from the 1940s was in my mother's collection from the time when she and her mother were living with Elia's family in Baltimore.

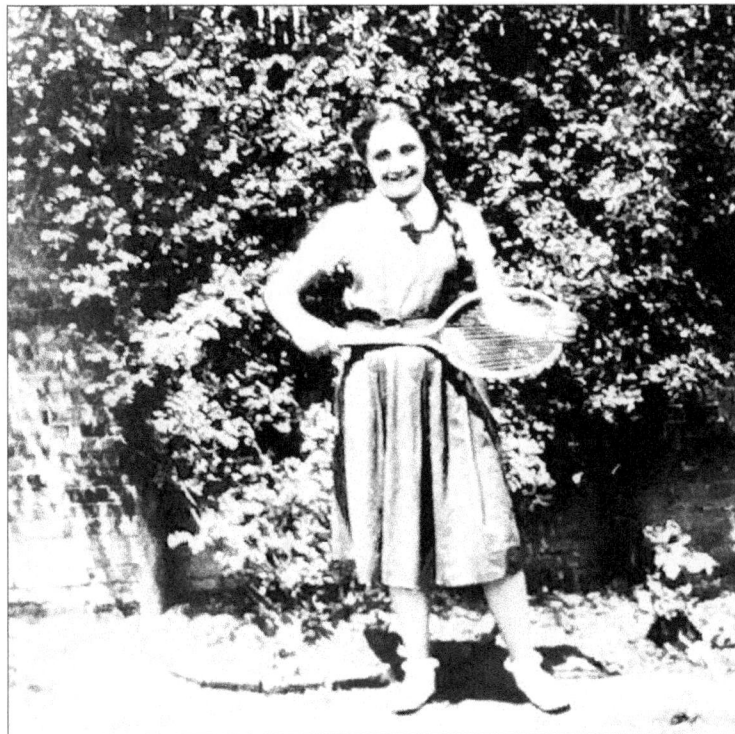

Figure 166 Elia Moss circa 1940, probably in Baltimore

Elia met a musician named Ralph H. Schaeffer and they married in Baltimore on Dec. 12, 1943. By 1946 or earlier they moved to California where "Elia Rachel Schaeffer" signed her own naturalization Petition on May 16, 1946. Her address at that time was 6506 Bella Vista Way, Los Angeles.

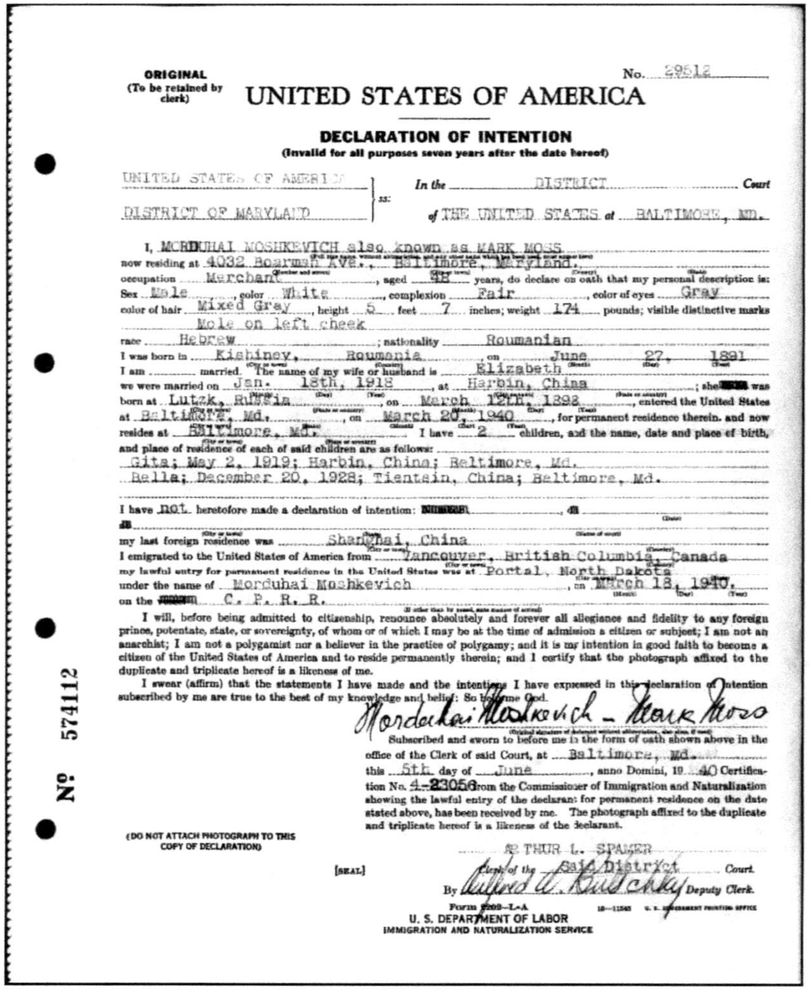

ORIGINAL
(To be retained by clerk)

No. 29518

UNITED STATES OF AMERICA

DECLARATION OF INTENTION

(Invalid for all purposes seven years after the date hereof)

UNITED STATES OF AMERICA, In the .... DISTRICT
DISTRICT OF MARYLAND, of THE UNITED STATES of BALTIMORE, MD.

I, ELIZABETH MOSKEVICH, also known as ELIZABETH MOSS
now residing at 4032 Boarman Ave., Baltimore, Md.
occupation Housewife, aged 42 years, do declare on oath that my personal description is:
Sex Female, color White, complexion Fair, color of eyes Gray
color of hair Dark Brown, height 5 feet 4 inches; weight 148 pounds; visible distinctive marks
None
race Hebrew; nationality Russian.
I was born in Lutzk, Russia, on March 12, 1898.
I am married. The name of my husband is Morduhai Moskevich (Moss).
we were married on Jan. 18, 1918, at Harbin, China
born at Kishinew, Rumania, on June 27, 1891, entered the United States
resides at Baltimore, Md., on March 18, 1940, for permanent residence therein, and now
and place of residence of each of said children are as follows:
Gita; May 2, 1919; Harbin, China; Baltimore, Md.
Bella; Dec. 20, 1928; Tsientsin, China.

I have not heretofore made a declaration of intention: ....
my last foreign residence was Shanghai, China.
I emigrated to the United States of America from VANGOUVER, B. C., Canada
my lawful entry for permanent residence in the United States was at Portal, N. Dakota
under the name of Elizabeth Moshkevich, on March 18, 1940.

I will, before being admitted to citizenship, renounce absolutely and forever all allegiance and fidelity to any foreign prince, potentate, state, or sovereignty, and particularly ...

I swear (affirm) that the statements I have made and the intentions I have expressed in this declaration of intention subscribed by me are true to the best of my knowledge and belief: So help me God.

Elizabeth Moskevich, Elizabeth Moss

Subscribed and sworn to before me in the form of oath shown above in the
office of the Clerk of said Court, at Baltimore, Md.
this 5th day of June, anno Domini, 19 40. Certification No. 4-23055 from the Commissioner of Immigration and Naturalization showing the lawful entry of the declarant for permanent residence on the date stated above, has been received by me. The photograph affixed to the duplicate and triplicate hereof is a likeness of the declarant.

ARTHUR L. SPAMER
Clerk of the said District Court.
[SEAL] By Roland H. Ruttschky Deputy Clerk.

(DO NOT ATTACH PHOTOGRAPH TO THIS COPY OF DECLARATION)

U. S. DEPARTMENT OF LABOR
IMMIGRATION AND NATURALIZATION SERVICE

Nº 574117

ORIGINAL
(To be retained by clerk)

No. 29512

UNITED STATES OF AMERICA

DECLARATION OF INTENTION

(Invalid for all purposes seven years after the date hereof)

UNITED STATES OF AMERICA, In the .... DISTRICT
DISTRICT OF MARYLAND, of THE UNITED STATES of BALTIMORE, MD.

I, MORDUHAI MOSKEVICH, also known as MARK MOSS
now residing at 4032 Boarman Ave., Baltimore, Maryland
occupation Merchant, aged 49 years, do declare on oath that my personal description is:
Sex Male, color White, complexion Fair, color of eyes Gray
color of hair Mixed Gray, height 5 feet 7 inches; weight 174 pounds; visible distinctive marks
Mole on left cheek
race Hebrew; nationality Roumanian.
I was born in Kishinev, Roumania, on June 27, 1891.
I am married. The name of my wife or husband is Elizabeth.
we were married on Jan. 18th, 1918, at Harbin, China
born at Lutzk, Russia, on March 12th, 1898, entered the United States
resides at Baltimore, Md., on March 18, 1940, for permanent residence therein, and now
and place of residence of each of said children are as follows:
Gita; May 2, 1919; Harbin, China; Baltimore, Md.
Bella; December 20, 1928; Tientsin, China; Baltimore, Md.

I have not heretofore made a declaration of intention: ....
my last foreign residence was Shanghai, China.
I emigrated to the United States of America from Vancouver, British Columbia, Canada
my lawful entry for permanent residence in the United States was at Portal, North Dakota
under the name of Morduhai Moshkevich, on March 18, 1940.
on the C. P. R. R.

I swear (affirm) that the statements I have made and the intentions I have expressed in this declaration of intention subscribed by me are true to the best of my knowledge and belief: So help me God.

Morduhai Moskevich – Mark Moss

Subscribed and sworn to before me in the form of oath shown above in the
office of the Clerk of said Court, at Baltimore, Md.
this 5th day of June, anno Domini, 19 40. Certification No. 4-23058 from the Commissioner of Immigration and Naturalization showing the lawful entry of the declarant for permanent residence on the date stated above, has been received by me. The photograph affixed to the duplicate and triplicate hereof is a likeness of the declarant.

ARTHUR L. SPAMER
Clerk of the said District Court.
[SEAL] By Roland H. Ruttschky Deputy Clerk.

(DO NOT ATTACH PHOTOGRAPH TO THIS COPY OF DECLARATION)

U. S. DEPARTMENT OF LABOR
IMMIGRATION AND NATURALIZATION SERVICE

Nº 574112

Figure 167 Mark and Elizabeth's Declarations of Intention, June 1940

```
                                                                    134
ORIGINAL                UNITED STATES OF AMERICA           128884
(To be retained by                                   No.
Clerk of Court)          PETITION FOR NATURALIZATION
            [Of a Married Person, under Sec. XXXXXXXXX 311 XXXX of the Nationality Act of 1940 (54 Stat. 1144-1145)]

To the Honorable the ..... DISTRICT ............ Court of THE UNITED STATES .... at LOS ANGELES, CALIF.
This petition for naturalization, hereby made and filed pursuant to Section XXXXXXXX or Section 311 XXXX of the Nationality Act of 1940, respectively shows:

(1) My full, true, and correct name is  ELIA RACHEL SCHAEFFER (nee Moshkevich) (aka Moss)
                                       (Full, true name, without abbreviation, and any other name which has been used, must appear here)
(2) My present place of residence is 6506 Bella Vista Way  LA 28, Calif. (3) My occupation is  Secretary-Steno
                                    (Number and street)   (City or town) (County)  (State)
(4) I am  27  years old. (5) I was born on  May 15 1919  in  Harbin  China  China
                                          (Month) (Day) (Year)  (City or town) (County, district, province, or state)  (Country)
(6) My personal description is as follows: Sex Fe  color wh  complexion fair, color of eyes gry, color of hair br, height 5 feet 8 inches,
weight 138  pounds; visible distinctive marks  none  ; race white present nationality Russia
(7) I am  married; the name of my wife or husband is Ralph Schaeffer; we were married on  Dec 12 1943
                                                                                          (Month) (Day) (Year)
at Baltimore Maryland  he or she was born at Philadelphia Pa.  on Nov 27 1915
  (City or town) (State or country)         (City or town) (County, district, province, or state) (Country)  (Month) (Day) (Year)

entered the United States at ................ on .......... for permanent residence in the United States, and now resides at
                            (City or town) (State)  (Month) (Day) (Year)
....... with me .......  and was naturalized on ........... at ...........
(Number and street) (City or town) (State or country)       (Month) (Day) (Year)      (City or town)  (State)

certificate No. ...........; or became a citizen by
(7a) (If petition is filed under Section 311, Nationality Act of 1940) I have resided in the United States in marital union with my United States citizen spouse for at least
1 year immediately preceding the date of filing this petition for naturalization.
(7b) (If petition is filed under Section 312, Nationality Act of 1940) My husband or wife is a citizen of the United States, is in the employment of the Government of
the United States, or of an American institution of research recognized as such by the Attorney General of the United States, or an American firm or corporation engaged
in whole or in part in the development of foreign trade and commerce of the United States, or a subsidiary thereof; and such husband or wife is regularly stationed abroad
in such employment. I intend in good faith to take up residence within the United States immediately upon the termination of such employment abroad.
(8) I have  no  children; and the name, sex, date and place of birth, and present place of residence of each of said children who is living, are as follows:

---------------------------------------------------------------------------------
---------------------------------------------------------------------------------
---------------------------------------------------------------------------------
---------------------------------------------------------------------------------

(9) My last place of foreign residence was  Shanghai  China  China  (10) I emigrated to the United States from Shanghai
                                           (City or town) (County, district, province, or state) (Country)                        (City or town)
 China  (11) My lawful entry for permanent residence in the United States was at Portal N. Dak.  under the name
(Country)                                                                      (City or town)   (State)
of Gita-Rachel Moshkevich  on  March 18 1940  on the C.P.R.R.  as shown by the certificate of my
                              (Month) (Day) (Year)   (Name of vessel or other means of conveyance)
arrival attached to this petition.
```

***

Ralph H Schaeffer

Elia's husband, Ralph Schaeffer, was apparently a musical prodigy from a very young age and had quite an interesting career. In a biographical essay about him, his son Jeffrey Schaeffer tells the following story.[8]

> When my dad was about age 4, a fire truck went by their house with the siren on, and my dad could tell what pitch (or note) the siren was in. They verified this by having my dad find the correct key on the little piano that they had. Thereafter my dad could always tell the correct pitch and note of every musical and other tones that he had heard, which was his perfect pitch, rare even among most accomplished musicians.[9] ...

> When my dad was four years old, his dad first got him a little violin and some violin lessons, and they quickly learned that he was very gifted. We have a picture of my dad sitting on the lap of the Mayor of Philadelphia playing a solo piece. He never went to public school, but rather was part home-schooled and attended several local music academies. By the time he was sixteen, his mother took him to New York where he was accepted to study with a very famous violin teacher with the last name of Persinger. He studied with him for a couple of years in New York and then returned to Philadelphia. Not long thereafter, he was admitted to the most famous music college in the country, the Curtis Institute of Music in Philadelphia.

---

[8] Posted on Ancestry, "My Dad's Historical Summary: Ralph Harrison Schaeffer" by Jeff Schaeffer.

Jeffrey also tells the story of how Elia met Ralph:

> It was while he was at Fort Meade that he also played violin solo performances at the USO service organization on the base for other soldiers. My mother, who was living in Baltimore with her family by then having come there from China, also was a very talented pianist, having learned to play piano in Shanghai, China, and she had won a couple of medals for her performances on the local radio station there as well. She would also play piano on occasion at the USO for the Army troops too. It was there that my parents met, and began to perform on stage together as a duet for a few months. Then my dad was discharged from the Army and they started to date.
>
> They married in Philadelphia about a year later. Soon after, my dad wanted to move to Hollywood where he had heard that film studios were now organizing their own orchestras for their film soundtracks and beginning to hire musicians. He could not work for the studios for the first year because of local musician's union residency requirements (Musician's Union No. 47 which he belonged to for his entire life... and for a time my dad worked in night clubs on the Sunset Strip). He and my mom lived in a two room apartment in Hollywood back then and had a big red Irish Setter dog named "Mars." They had "Marsy" as they called him for several years, until they moved into their first home that they built in West Los Angeles near Pico Boulevard and Westgate Avenue (where I was born in 1950), and their dog Marsy became very wild and unmanageable, so they gave him away.

Ralph worked in the Paramount Studio Orchestra as the second chair for about nine years. By 1960 television serial shows had started up that used musical soundtracks. Ralph's son indicates that his father was in the first group of musicians to play on the Lawrence Welk Show on TV, and also to play on such shows as "77 Sunset Strip" "Route 66," "Bonanza," "Gun Smoke" and a variety of other TV shows. It was also during this time that he began to record for a variety of artists such as Frank Sinatra, Dean Martin, Tony Bennett, Robert Goulet, Roger Wagner Chorale, and made occasional appearances on the Tonight Show first with Jack Paar and later with Johnny Carson and the Doc Severinson Orchestra of Johnny Carson's Show from the late 1950s through about 1970.

At a later point, Ralph worked with the Beatles, did one song with the Rolling Stones at RCA records "*As Tears Go By*." He also worked many times with the Beach Boys and was featured on the album "Pet Sounds" which included the song "Good Vibrations."

***

In the 1950 census back in Baltimore, Mark is 59 and Elizabeth is 50 and they are residing at 4006 Bonner Road where they had been since at least 1942. Mark, now 59, is described as a notion salesman in wholesale dry goods. Their daughter, Bella, age 21, is still living with them. She is married to Irv Dubick who is now part of the household. Irv is described as a proprietor in a war surplus store.

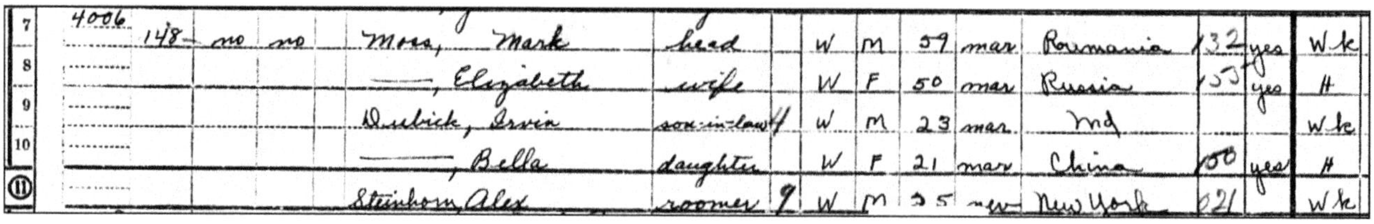

7	4006	148	no	no	Moss, Mark	head		W	M	59	mar	Roumania	132	yes	Wk
8					——, Elizabeth	wife		W	F	50	mar	Russia	153	yes	H
9					Dubick, Irvin	son-in-law		W	M	23	mar	Md			Wk
10					——, Bella	daughter		W	F	21	mar	China	100	yes	H
11					Steinhorn, Alex	roomer	9	W	M	35	nev	New York	621		Wk

Figure 168 1950 Census of Mark Moss and Family

David Chapin told me that his father Jerry made the introduction of Irv Dubick to his cousin Bella. As discussed earlier, Jerry got to know Irv when they served in the US occupation forces in Japan (see photo of them in Japan, p. 71 above). When they both got discharged from the army, they ended up back in Baltimore. Jerry fixed Irv up with his cousin Bella, a recent émigré, and the rest is history. Jerry was Irv's best man at the wedding. In the 1950s, Bella and Irv had two children, Michael and Sherri.

Mark's niece, Reva, tells me that Mark and Elizabeth eventually followed their daughter Elia to California. Elia's sister, Bella, and her husband Irv Dubick followed too. Mark ("Morduchai") Moss passed away in 1979 and Liza ("Elizabeth") passed away in 1991. Bella passed away in 2000, and Elia passed away in 2003. Bella and Irv's son, Michael, passed away in 2020.

Figure 169 Mark and Liza (Elizabeth) at Moss Gathering circa 1960
Behind the Schwartz home (my home) on Boxford Road

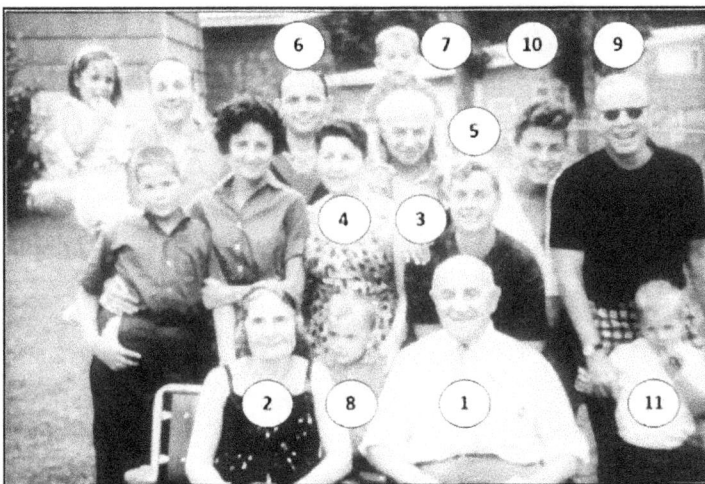

1. Mark Moss
2. Mark's wife, Liza (Elizabeth)
3. Leon Moss
4. Leon's wife Betty
5. Reva Greenspan, daughter of Leon and Betty
6. Jack Greenspan, Reva's husband
7. Reva's son, Jay Greenspan
8. Reva's son, David Greenspan
9. Leon Schwartz, husband of
10. Joan Schinker (Mariam's daughter)
11. Howard (me), son of Joan

Photo 50 40ᵗʰ Wedding Anniversary of Leon and Betty Moss, 1965

1. Leon Moss
2. Wife Betty (Pascar)
3. Daughter Reva Greenspan
4. Reva's former husband Jack
5. Reva's sons Jay
6. Reva's son, David
7. Gersh Moss
8. Gersh's wife Helen
9. Mariam (Mania Moshkevich) Drezner
10. Mark Moss
11. Leon Schwartz, husband of Joan
12. Bernie Moss
13. Mariam's husband Abe Drezner
14. Mariam's daughter, Joan (Schinker) Schwartz
15. Gersh's son, Stuart, his wife Marcia in front of him
16. Gersh's son, Irwin, his wife Janet (Schwartz) in front of him

Figure 170 Moss Siblings Visit Mark and Liza (Elizabeth) in CA, 1965

Middle row (l to r): Mark Moss, Liza (Elizabeth), Mariam (Moss) with husband Abe Drezner
Back row (l to r): Leon Moss, Bella (Moss), her husband Irv Dubick, daughter Sherri, Elia (Moss) and her husband Ralph Schaeffer.
Front row: sons of Bella and Elia, Betty Moss-wife of Leon

***

Visit to Risia and Gittel in Fergana, Usbekistan

After the migration of Mark's family from China to Baltimore, only Itsig's wife, Risia, and their eldest daughter Gittel remained behind. Leon Moss apparently went back to visit them in 1968. A photo in my grandmother's collection from 1968 shows Leon in Fergana, Uzbekistan with his aged mother, Risia, his sister Gittel and her husband Israel Levitt. Leon dated the back of the photo and sent it to his sister Mania who was living in New York.

According to Leon's daughter, Reva, Leon's mother Risia, his sister Gittel and her husband, Israel, fled to the interior of Russia during WWII where they survived.

In 1973, Leon took his grandson, David Greenspan, back to Fergana. David shared his memories with me of that trip.

> It is true that Leon and I went back to Fergana in 1973 where I met Gittel and Abe. They spoke no English so my entire engagement with them was via [my grandfather] Leon translating. A couple of other relatives flew in, one from Georgia, and one from Moscow. I have no recollection of their names.... I recall thinking, often, about how 'backwards' the Soviet Union was compared to Europe and the US. I recall hearing from my grandfather that his sister had recently been moved to an upgraded apartment in anticipation of our visit as it had electricity and running water inside.

We were there for two nights, a terrible disappointment to [my grandfather] Leon who had negotiated as best he could to extend our stay. The original travel plan had just one [day]. The evening of the second night was a great feast at a nearby home. I have no clue who these people were, but I believe just friends. I also recall being told over and over again to eat and sample the many dishes and desserts to the point of being bloated like I had never eaten before!

We spent about 2 weeks in the Soviet Union and visited Moscow, Leningrad, Tashkent and Samarkand. All of this was great for me, all a distraction from the true intention of going for Leon, to see his sister. Even to the last minute he was using blue jeans as bribes to get things done. It gained us an extra half day allowing us on an earlier flight into Fergana and a later flight out.

Photo 51 1968 Leon Moss with mother, Risia and sister, Gittel Levitt, in Fergnana, Uzbekistan

Leon's note to his sister Mania on back of the photo.
"Mania & Abe from mother, Guita [Gitel] [her husband] Israel & me, March 29, 1968 at Fergana

Risia died on March 1, 1971, and her children placed a notice in *The Evening Sun.* According to Reva, Risia lived to the ripe old age of 101. Gittel passed away Dec. 1, 1980.

Figure 171 Obituary of Risia Moshkevitz
The Evening Sun, March 17, 1971, p. 2.

MOSHKEVITZ—(MOSS)   18
The Bessarabian Society of Baltimore regrets to announce the
passing on March 1, 1971, in Fergana, Russia, of RISA MOSHKE-
VITZ, beloved mother of our
president, Leon Moss and members Manya Drezner and Gersh
Moss, of Florida, and Mark Moss,
of California. Members and friends
please attend house of mourning,
5 Slade avenue, Apartment 303.
      LILLIAN L. MORRIS,
      Chairman of the Board.
      MAE DICKOFF,
      First Vice President.

Photo 52 David Greenspan with his Great Aunt, Gittel
and her husband, Israel, 1973
Courtesy David Greenspan

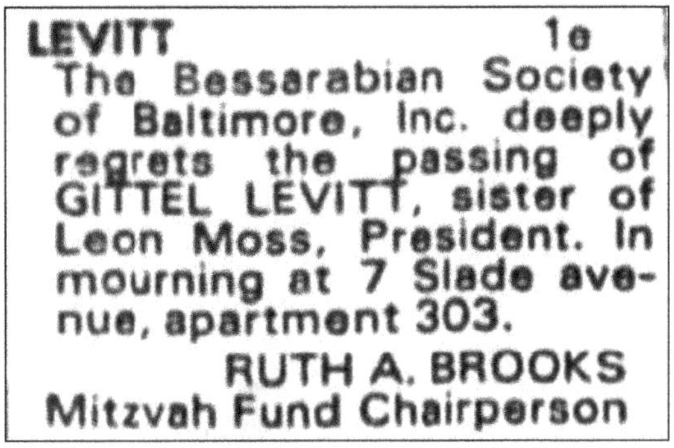

Figure 172 Obituary of Gittel (Moskovitch) Levitt
The Evening Sun, Dec. 1, 1980, p. 43.

LEVITT   1e
The Bessarabian Society
of Baltimore, Inc. deeply
regrets the passing of
GITTEL LEVITT, sister of
Leon Moss, President. In
mourning at 7 Slade ave-
nue, apartment 303.
      RUTH A. BROOKS
Mitzvah Fund Chairperson

***

Leon Moss and the Bessarabian Society

Following WWII as the enormity of the Holocaust and dislocation of European Jews reached the awareness of the American Jewish Community, Baltimore's Bessarabian Jews began to organize a "landsmanschaftn," a philanthropic and social club of individuals who came from Bessarabia. The earliest mention of the society in the English Baltimore papers appears to have been May 24, 1948, ten days after the State of Israel was proclaimed.

That article announced the election on May 16th of Leon Moss to be the new president. Though no mention of the society appears before that date, the society was formed in Baltimore in 1945 by 40 Jews—its purpose to aid orphans from their homeland in the War.[10] In 1958, Leon was unanimously drafted for the 12th straight year as president of the society. The Baltimore Bessarabian Society was considered one of three very active Bessarabian societies in the country. It raised money to support orphans from Bessarabia, for xray machines needed in clinics in Israel, and to support the world headquarters of the Bessarabia society in Tel Aviv.

Leon was elected president at least two more times. *The Evening Sun* covered his election on Jan. 10, 1962 (p. 10). Officers included his brother Gersh Moss. Leon was again installed on Jan. 18, 1965 (p. 13). Leon's name as president appears under obituaries published for members from 1970–1982 after which the society's name disappears from the Baltimore papers.

Figure 173, 1958, Leon Moss, Bessarabian Society
The Evening Sun, Jan. 1, 1958, page 7

Bessarabians Draft Moss

Leon Moss was unanimously drafted to serve for the twelfth straight year as president of the Bessarabian Society of Baltimore.

Other officers are: Dr. William Grossman, first vice president; Israel Koman, second vice president; Gersh Moss, third vice president; Samuel Seiver, treasurer; Mrs. Ida Summer, financial secretary; Mrs. Louise Owrutsky, corresponding secretary, and Miss Esther Shalowitz, recording secretary.

The new officers will be installed Sunday evening, February 2, in the Jewish War Veterans Hall.

---

[10] The origin of the society is mentioned in John Schulion, "Two Bessarabian Projects are Nearing Completion," *The Evening Sun*, Oct. 5, 1970, p. 21.

Photo 53 Moss Cousins 1985

1. Leon Moss, 2) Edith Kahn with grandson Michael Sperling, 3) Dee Schabb (Marie's mother) 4) Edith Kahn's granddaughter, Arlene (Kahn) Sperling, 5) Debra's husband, Norman Goldschmitt with their son, Ryan 6) Ronni (Chapin) Udoff with son Jonathan and 7) Brian Udoff (Ronni's son) 8) Julie (Chapin) Janofsky, 9) Pauline (Zimmerman) Chapin, mother of Julie and Ronni, 10) Jeffrey Janofsky husband of Julie, 11) Marie (Schabb) Schwartz and husband 12) Seymour Schwartz, 13) Bill Green (husband of Charlotte), 14) Eric Udoff (husband of Ronni) 15) Charlotte (Kahn) Green (Edith's daughter), 16) Morton Kahn (Edith's son), 17) Beverley (Cohen) Kahn (Morton's wife), 18) Debra (Kahn) Goldschmitt (Morton's daughter), 19) Howard Green (Charlotte's son)

Records Summary for Itsig Moshkevich and Family

Jan. 26, 1914 Passenger Manifest	Gersh [son of Itsig] is traveling with his aunt Mariasha (Moshkevich) Goldfeld and her husband Mosche Goldfeld. Leaving Jan. 10, 1914 from Bremen on the SS Neckar arriving Baltimore Jan. 26, 1914. **Gersch Moskewiz** age 17, student, last residence Kisineff; closest relative there, father Itsig Moskiewicz, Kishineff, Bess[arabia] destination uncle Shlome [Samuel] Moskiewitz 923 E. Baltimore St, birthplace Kisjinuerch [Kishinev probably]
June 5, 1918 WWI Draft Registration Card	**Gersh Moshkevich**, 2432 Greenmount Ave, Balto Md, date of birth Jan 15, 1897 in Kischineff Bessarabia, Russia, has [already] Declared intention, Father's birthplace Kremenchook, Bessarabia, Russia, employer: Bethlehem Steel Co, place of employment: Sparrows Point [in the Baltimore Harbor] Nearest relative: Morris Goldfield, 2432 Greemount Ave Balto.
Feb. 27, 1919, Declaration	**Gersch Moskiewicz**, student, height 5' 6", 142 lbs, brown hair, brown eyes, distinctive marks: birth mark on left side of face, born in Kishineff, Russia, on Jan 15, 1897, now resides at 1046 Aisquith, emigrated from Bremen, Germany, on vessel "Neckar" last foreign residence was Kishineff, Russia, arrived at port of Baltimore on Jan 26, 1914
Apr. 1, 1919 Naturalization Petition	**Gersh Isaac Moshkevich**, 2432 Greenmount Ave, Baltimore Maryland student, born on Jan. 15, 1897 in Kishineff, Russia, emigrated from Bremen Germany on Jan 9, 1914 on vessel "Neckar" , declared intention on April 19th 1916 [below it says April 1, 1919], not married, signed by [his uncle] Morris Schabb, shoemaker, 2468 Greenmount Ave, and [his uncle] Aaron Moshkevich, merchant 1206 Poplar Grove St.
Aug. [not listed] 1920 Canadian Incoming Passengers in transit to US	**Otsko [Isko] Moshkevich**, age 58, country of birth Russia, race Russian, destination Baltimore MD, occupation merchant, duration: In transit, religion Hebrew. **Boruch Moshkevich**, 24, occupation merchant.
Aug. 7, 1920 Passenger Manifest entering the US State of Washington	For **Isko (Isaac)** and [his son] **Boris Moshkevich** [typed] Departing Yokohama, Japan on SS Empress of Asia Aug 7th, 1920 arriving at port of Victoria / Vancouver Aug. 16, 1920. **Isko Moshkevich** [Ossko scratched out correcting the Canadian record], 58 [implied birth year 1862], Merchant, nationality Russian, race Hebrew, last residence Yokohama, Japan, closest relative there: (wife) Mrs. Risia Moschewitz 21 Ekatezindenskaia Chishinene, destination Baltimore; traveling with [son] **Boruch Moshkevich**, age 24, merchant, nationality Russia [types over this is text that appears to be "Verified Sep 17, 1925], race Hebrew [typed over Russian], last residence Yokohama, Japan, closest relative (Mother) Mrs. Risia 21 Ekatezindenskaia Chishinene, [handwritten is word Russia] destination Baltimore; [page 2] handwritten: Victoria 5-16-20, paid passage by self, $200 in possession, destination (son) [and] (brother) Mr. G. Moshkevich 2432 Greenmount Ave, Baltimore, [duration] permanent, birthplace Russia, Kremenchu [Kremenchuk] and for Boris the birthplace is Chishinew [Kishinev]
Dec. 27, 1920 Passenger Manifest	[Arrival of **Leib Moskowitch (Leon Moss)**] S. S. Niuew Amsterdam sailing from Rotterdam on December 10, 1920 arriving New York Dec. 20. **Leib Moskowitch**, age 19, male, single, occupation none, able to read German, nationality Rumenian,

	Race/People Hebrew, last residence Kichineff Rumenian, closest relative Risia Moskowitch in Kichineff, destination Baltimore, [page 2] passage paid by brother, destination Brother G. I. Moskewitsch 2432 Greenmount Ave, Baltimore, cataract left eye, 5' 6", black hair, brown eyes, birthplace Rumenian, Kichineff.
Jan. 20, 1922 Declaration of Intention	**Leon Moshkevich [Leon Moss]**, age 20, occupation Receiving Clerk, 5' 5" 135 lbs, black hair, brown eyes, born in Kishineff, Russia, on Aug. 22, 1901, now resides at 126 W. Lee Street, Baltimore, Maryland, emigrated to US from Rotterdam, Holland on vessel "New Amsterdam", not married, arrived at port of New York on Dec. 30, 1920.
Jan. 13, 1927 Petition	For **Betty Moss**, Dressmaker, 2304 Oakley Ave, Baltimore, MD, born Feb. 2, 1901 at Kishineff, Roumania, emigrated from Hamburg, Germany about June 18th, 1923 and arrived New York about July 5, 1923 on SS "Homeric". Husband: Leon, born on Aug. 22nd, 1901, at Kishineff Roumania, naturalized July 10, 1926. no children. I was married Aug. 16, 1925. Witnesses: Max Moshevich, attorney, 423 Norman Ave. Leon Moss, Accountant, 2304 Oakley Ave.
Apr. 15, 1930 US Census Baltimore	For **Leon and Betty Moss**, living at 2904 Oakley Ave., sharing a house with Solomon family, Leon Moss, Head, Renting, $24, age 28, born in Russia, purchasing agent for a clothing manufacturer; Betty, wife, age 29, born in Russia,
Oct. 5, 1937 Passenger manifest	Arrival of **Mariam (Moshkevich) Schinker** [daughter of Itsig] and her husband **Samuel Schinker** and daughter, **Joan**. Sailed on the SS Ile De France from Le Havre, France on September 29, 1937 and arrived in New York, Oct 5, 1937. Salomon Schinker, age 36, electrician, reads German/Russian/French, "without" nationality, People/Race Russian, place of birth Odessa Russia, visa issued in Paris, Sep. 20, 1937, last permanent residence Boulogne S/Seine France, Mariam, age 37, housewife, speaks same languages, reads German/Russian/French, "without" nationality, People/Race Russian, place of birth Tichinoff Rumenia, other information same as husband, Jeanne [Joan Schwartz] age 5, French nationality, birthplace Paris France. [page 2] Home address, 251 Rue Gallieni, Boulogne sure Seine, France. Destination: Brother n law, Mr Moss 6I4 Munser Building, [Mariam is headed to brother 3313 Pol? ave
Jun. 13, 1938 Passenger Manifest	[Leon Moss returning from Europe]: **Leon Moss**, age 37, sailed from Le Havre, France on the SS Normandie, arrived in New York, June 13, 1938, address 3812 Copley Rd. Baltimore.
Mar. 16, 1940 Passenger Manifest	Family of "**Morduhai Moshkevich**" [son of Itsig], age 48, merchant, sailing from Manila, F. I. on the SS Empress of Russia, Passengers embarked at Shanghai, China, March 1, 1940, arriving [it appears] at port of Victoria/Vancouver Canada, place of birth Rumania, Chisinau, Nationality Former Russian, Race or People Russian, Quota No. 171, issued Shanghai, Nov 24th 1939, last permanent residence China Shanghai. Elizabeth, age 41, Housewife; place of birth Lusk Russia, Quota No. 172, Gita Rachel, age 20, secretary, place of birth Harbin China, Quota No. 1975, issued Nov. 24th 1939, Bella age 10, student, place of birth Tientsin, China.
Apr. 4, 1940 US Census Baltimore	For **Gersh and Helen Moss**, living at 3313 Powhatan Ave next to inlaws Simon Hornstein and Fannie, Renting, value $75, **Gersh Moss**, Head, age 42, birthplace Roumania, same house in 1935, working as lawyer in private practice; **Helen**, age 37, born in Maryland; **Irwin**, son, age 12, born in Maryland, **Stuart**, son, age 7

Apr. 22, 1940 US Census Baltimore	For **Leon and Betty Moss**, living at 4101 Barrington Rd, **Leon Moss**, Head, age 38, born in Russia, same address in 1935, buyer in wholesale Men's clothing, **Betty**, wife, age 39, born in Russia, **Reva**, Daughter, age 6, born in Maryland, **Faye Clifton**, companion, age 26, born in Virginia, occupation: Companion, Private Family
Apr. 13, 1940 US Census Baltimore	For Family of **Mark and Elizabeth Moss** living at 4032 Boarman Ave. Renting, Value $40, **Moduchai Moss**, Head, age 48, born in Rumania, naturalization PA [first papers submitted] living in Shanghai, China in 1935 with family, merchant in a Retail Grocery; **Elizabeth**, wife, age 40, born in Russia, PA [first papers submitted], **Richard**, son [sic-not their son, unidentified] age 44, born in China, PA [first papers submitted], living in Shanghai in 1935, **Bella**, daughter, age 11, born in China, living in Shanghai in 1935. [Note they were living with Boris, Mania and Joan but their census appears on a different page and was taken on April. 27th (see next)
Apr. 27, 1940 US Census Baltimore	For **Boris Moss, Mania (Moshkevich) Schinker, Joan Schinker**. Note: they were living with brother Mark Moshkevich but appear on a different page of the census and different date. Mania, "sister," age 40, born in Rumania, living in Paris in 1935, occupation hat-maker in a Millenery, Jona [Joan] niece, age 7 born in France, living in Paris in 1935, Boris, borther, 43, born in Rumania, living in same house in 1935, Salesman in an Oil Business.
Jun. 5, 1940 Naturalization Declaration	**(Of Mark Moss) Morduchai Moshkevich** also known as **Mark Moss**, residing at 4032 Boarman Ave., Baltimore, merchant, age 48, gray eyes, mixed gray hair, 5' 7" 174 lbs, mole on left cheek, race Hebrew, nationality Roumanian, wife is **Elizabeth**, married on Jan. 18, 1918 at Harbin China, she was born at Lutzk, Russia on March 12, 1898, entered the US at Baltimore Md, on Mar. 20, 1940, 2 children, **Gita**; [born] May 2, 1919; [at] Harbin, China; [resides now] Baltimore, MD, **Bella**; [born] Dec. 20, 1928; [at] Tientsin, China; [resides now] Baltimore, MD, my last residence Shanghai, China, emigrated to US from Vancouver, British Columbia, Canada, my lawful entry was at Portal, North Dakota, under the name Morduchai Moshkevich, on March 18, 1940 on the C. P. R. R. [Canadian Pacific Rail Road].
Jun. 6, 1940 Naturalization Declaration	**Elizabeth Moshkevich** also known as **Elizabeth Moss**, residing at 4032 Boarman Ave., Baltimore, Housewife, age 42, gray eyes, dark brown hair, 5' 4" 148 lbs, race Hebrew, nationality Russian, born in Lytzk [Lutzk] Russia on March 12, 1898, husband is Morduchai Moskevich (Moss) , married on Jan. 18, 1918 at Harbin China, he was born at Kishinew, Rumania, Russia on June 27, 1891, entered the US at Baltimore Mrd, on Mar. 18, 1940, 2 children, Gita; [born] May 2, 1919; [at] Harbin, China; [resides now] Baltimore, MD, **Bella**; [born] Dec. 20, 1928; [at] Tientsin, China; [resides now] "do" [ibid], my last residence Shanghai, China, emigrated to US from Vancouver, B. C., Canada, my lawful entry was at Portal, N. Dakota, under the name Morduchai Moshkevich, on March 18, 1940 on the C. P. R. R. [Canadian Pacific Rail Road].
Apr. 25, 1942 WWII Draft Card	**Gersh Isaac Moss**, 3610 Copley Road, Baltimore, mailing address 616 Munsey Bldg. date of birth Jan. 15, 1897 in Kishinev, Bessarabia-Russia, closest relative: Helen E. Moss, 3610 Copley Road. Employers name: Self.
Feb. 15, 1942 WWII Draft Card	**Leon Moss**, 3613 Cedardale Road, Baltimore, age 40, place of birth: Kishineff, Bessarabia, Russia, closest contact: **Betty Moss**-same address, Employer: Shoeneman, Inc, 412 West Redwood St. Baltimore.

Apr. 14, 1950 US Census, Baltimore	For **Gersh and Helen Moss**: living at 3610 Copley Rd, **Gersh I. Moss**, head, age 53, born in Russia, attorney in law office; **Helen E.**, wife, age 47, born in Maryland, **Stuart L.**, son, age 17 born in Maryland, delivery boy in a grocery store.
Apr. 13, 1950 US Census, Baltimore	For **Leon and Betty Moss**, living at 3613 Cedardale Road, **Leon Moss**, head, age 48, born in Russia, clothing buyer for a clothing factory, **Betty**, wife, 49, born in Russia; **Reva**, daughter, 16, born in Maryland.
April 17, 1950 US Census, Los Angeles	For **Elia and husband Ralph Schaeffer**, living at 2542 Coolidge, **Ralph H. Schaeffer**, age 34, birthplace Pennsylvania, violinist, Movie Studio, **Elia R**, wife, age 30, birthplace China, **Jeffrey A.**, son, age Mar? [just born?], birthplace California
April 22, 1950 US Census, Baltimore	Family of **Mark and Elizabeth Moss**, living at 4006 Bonner Road **Mark Moss** head, , age 59, birthplace Roumania, notion salesman, **Elizabeth**, wife, age 50, birthplace Russia, **Irvin Dubick**, son-in-law, age 23, born in Maryland, proprietor war surplus store, **Bella**, daughter, age 21, born in China, Alex Steinhorn, roomer, age 25, born in New York, title searcher title guarantee and trust
Apr. 26, 1950 US Census, Baltimore	For **Boris and Sally Moss**, living at 4008 Glen Ave. **Boris Moss**, head, age 53, born in Russia, wholesale shoe salesman, shoe concern, **Sally**, wife, age 39; **Judith**, daughter, age 4.